JFK

The CIA, Vietnam, and the Plot to Assassinate John F. Kennedy

L. Fletcher Prouty

Foreword by Jesse Ventura
Introduction by Oliver Stone

Skyhorse Publishing

Skyhorse Publishing books may be purchased in bulk at special discounts for sales promotion, corporate gifts, fund-raising, or educational purposes. Special editions can also be created to specifications. For details, contact the Special Sales Department, Skyhorse Publishing, 307 West 36th Street, 11th Floor, New York, NY 10018 or info@skyhorsepublishing.com.

Skyhorse® and Skyhorse Publishing ® are registered trademarks of Skyhorse Publishing, Inc.®, a Delaware corporation.

www.skyhorsepublishing.com

10 9 8 7 6 5 4 3 2 1

2013 edition printed for Barnes & Noble, Inc.
ISBN: 978-1-4351-4609-9

Paperback ISBN: 978-1-61608-291-8

Library of Congress Cataloging-in-Publication Data

  JFK : the CIA, Vietnam, and the plot to assassinate John F. Kennedy / L.
Fletcher Prouty ; with an introduction by Oliver Stone.
     p. cm.
  Originally published: New York : Carol Pub. Group, c1996.
  Includes bibliographical references and index.
  ISBN 978-1-60239-731-6 (alk. paper)
  1. Kennedy, John F. (John Fitzgerald), 1917-1963--Assassination. 2. Conspiracies-
-United States--History--20th century. 3. United States. Central Intelligence
Agency--History--20th century. 4. Intelligence service--United States--History--20th
century. 5. Vietnam War, 1961-1975--Secret service--United States. I. Title. II. Title:
J.F.K.
  E842.9.P76 2009
  973.922092--dc22
                                2009024566

Printed in the United States of America

CONTENTS

iv CONTENTS

FOREWORD

By Jesse Ventura

Although the connections between Vietnam and the assassination of John F. Kennedy are just starting to become recognized, Colonel Fletcher Prouty began writing about the links in the 1970s. This book, published after Oliver Stone's 1991 film of the same name, gives details to the notion that an extremely powerful group wanted to remove JFK from the presidency in order to control policy and the direction of the government for the next eight, ten, twelve years, and more

JFK's National Security Action Memorandum (NSAM) 263 called for the total withdrawal of not only U.S. troops, but all U.S. personnel, from Vietnam by 1965. What Col. Prouty has written gives a behind the scenes look at what was really going on and at JFK's understanding that Vietnam would be a disaster. With Iraq and Afghanistan, we see history is repeating itself.

To appreciate the big money involvement that was in place to keep a war economy going, Prouty provides an understanding of the connection between the Military-Industrial Complex and banking.

Col. Prouty describes the pervasive groupthink belief that small winless wars were all that was possible to conduct in the nuclear weapons age. He explains this in terms of the military's realization that large, full-scale war—total war—could no longer be fought after the advent of the hydrogen bomb. He also provides insight to the relatively recent idea of so-called Stateless Terrorism—in lieu of a real adversary an imagined enemy will always need to be invented.

In Vietnam, there was no objective and no real city to conquer in order to declare the war over. Prouty underscores that if Hanoi was ever captured, this would have prompted China to directly enter the conflict. Given this constraint, the city was denied to American Generals making war plans. If you can't take the enemy's capital how do you know when you've won? To understand the military mindset and the idea of a self-made role of the military you need to read this book.

The idea of false flag operations is new to most people, but not to the military. A case in point is Operation Northwoods, which discussed the use of covert actions—including attacks on American cities, ships, and people—to create a pretext to launch an assault on Cuba. Such proposals confront one with the reality of a corrupting influence unimaginable to most: that the Joint Chiefs of Staff would create plans to attack their own people to justify their existence.

Col. Prouty's contribution comes from his work in the Pentagon and his common sense view that someone needed to level the playing field—to let the public know that military spending and goals are completely unrealistic

Few, if any, explain how over one million Tonkinese refugees of the north were moved to the south by the Dulles brothers to set the stage for a civil war that the United States would be called to help resolve. Some of the worst fighting was in the Mekong delta. The problem was that no one knew where Vietnam even was, let alone its history or its area.

It's as if they said Canada was invading the United States but the worst fighting broke out in Florida. The whole thing was a set-up job. Another war with nowhere to go to win. Think about it—how could the Vietminh prevail over the U.S. Air Force, the 7th Fleet, U2 spy planes, B52 bombing campaigns, five thousand helicopters, and, at one time, five hundred and fifty thousand troops? These beggars in black pajamas raised their flag over Saigon. Something is really wrong with the picture, unless you understand there never was a "Grand Strategy."

We have to learn from the past and Col. Prouty is one of the few who explain the uncomfortable truth. This uncomfortable feeling goes on today. How do we know when we've won in Iraq or Afghanistan? Will this repeat in Iran and North Korea? What is the next military action that will be another unwinnable war designed to keep the Defense Department in business despite the astronomical costs as it bankrupts the nation?

To underscore Vietnam's significance to the removal of JFK, the first document LBJ signed was NSAM 273 in which he reversed policy and now instructed his Generals to help the South Vietnamese "to win" their conflict with the north. President Kennedy had been urged many times by his military commanders to commit the United States to victory in Vietnam by including such words in U.S. policy papers and official pronouncements. Kennedy had adamantly refused to tie the United States into such a straitjacket.

Prouty's explanation of the Saigon Military Mission—that it was not military and not a mission—is worth the price of the book alone. It was a CIA operation. The whole war was a CIA invention and this has to be understood first to keep it from happening again. Or again, we will find ourselves at war with another country with weapons of mass destruction that never can be found . . .

It's time that everyone examine what Col. Fletcher Prouty wrote as a warning of what was really going on as opposed to what was reported regarding the Vietnam war and the removal of John F. Kennedy.

INTRODUCTION

The Secret History of the United States (1943–1990)

by Oliver Stone

FLETCHER PROUTY is a man whose name will go down in history. Not as a respected Establishment figure, no. He will be erased from the present history books, his version of history suppressed, his credibility denied, his integrity scorned.

Yet in time he will endure. Young students in the twenty-first century (given the planet's capacity to reform and revive itself before then) will come back to his writings in the alternative written press (small publishing houses, low-circulation magazines) and discover through Colonel Prouty no less than the "Secret History" of the United States, circa 1944 to the present. With this single volume, Colonel Prouty blows the lid right off our "Official History" and unforgivably, sadly, inexorably, for anyone who dares enter this cave of dread and shame, shines his torch forever onto the ugliest nest of vipers the civilized world has probably seen since the dreaded Mongol raiders of the tenth and eleventh centuries.

This is scary stuff. The MK Ultra of espionage books, *JFK* will anger you and make you sad. You will never view the world again in the same light. Behind everything you read or see from this point on will flicker forever your most paranoid and darkest fears of the subconscious motives beneath the killer ape that became man.

Was Stanley Kubrick right in his revelation of the warrior ape in *2001*, throwing the bones of the slain into the air, becoming the spaceship baby of tomorrow? Will we transmute our killer instincts to peace and the search for light? Or will we tread the path of war, not only between tribes, but between us and our environment?

My mother was French, my father American. I had the opportunity young in life to spend summers in France in the 1950s and never once heard anyone young or old ever allude to the massive French collaboration with the Nazis in World War II. In every aspect—even my mother's tale—the truth was denied, ignored, and mostly forgotten. Of such is "history" made—until, of course, contrary events like the Klaus Barbie trial in Lyons, France, surface and tear and remind. Like my film *JFK*.

Such was my experience in writing *Platoon*—out of a feeling that Vietnam was an Orwellian memory hole, to be forgotten, realities distorted by newsmen and official "historians," official body counts, and the official lies that devastated the American character.

I experienced it again in the mid-1980s in Central America, talking to fresh-faced American troops in green uniforms with no memories of Vietnam, save for embarrassed stares, once again lining up to shoot Nicaraguans in the invasion of 1986 that never was. And again in Russia, in the early 1980s, on another screenplay, talking to youngsters with no knowledge whatever of Stalin's crimes, and old people who denied their past out of fear.

Such is the memory of man—at best a tricky one, per Orwell. "Who controls the past controls the future." There is about us a wall, alone, beyond which our conscious mind will not let our unconscious go. That margin, however, fades with the quotient and fashion of time because as time changes so do our mind-sets. The loss of fear allows the mind to drop its censors and think the unthinkable. Such a golden moment. We all know it. The exciting liberation of our own thought process. It is that access point to history which every filmmaker, poet, artist, seeks entry to. To collide with the forces of history—to merge with the backbeat of its onward push. Jack London, John Reed, Upton Sinclair, clashing with the stormy forces of early-twentieth-century history. Glorious cavaliers.

The key question of our time, as posed in Colonel Prouty's book, comes from the fabled *Report From Iron Mountain on the Possibility and Desirability of Peace* by Leonard Lewin (based on a study commissioned by Defense Secretary Robert McNamara in August 1963 to justify the big, planned changes in defense spending contemplated by Kennedy):

> The organizing principle of any society is for war. The basic authority of a modern state over its people resides in its war powers. . . . War readiness accounts for approximately a tenth of the output of the world's total economy.

In illustrating this proposition, Colonel Prouty traces the divergent paths of early 1950s Vietnam—the Saigon Military Mission, Ed Lansdale, Lucien Conein, Tom Dooley, Wesley Fishel, and Archbishop Spellman. How Mao with his guerrilla-war ideology deeply influenced our "civic action" paramilitary concepts in Vietnam and Central America. How the helicopter and its econo-military needs drove us to Vietnam. How the TFX fighter battle between Boeing and General Dynamics split the Kennedy administration. He explains clearly for the first time the vast errors of South Vietnam–appointed President Ngo Dinh Diem—his failure with the Buddhists and his own army; the disastrous "hamlet" program that ruined the South Vietnamese peasant economy; the expelling of the Chinese mercantile society; the influence of Lansdale; the arrogance of America's racist Third World attitudes that blinded us to the true vacuum we created by dividing and marginalizing a wholly artificial client state called South Vietnam in conflict with Vietnam's post–World War II right to determine its own independence.

Colonel Prouty heartrendingly details the destruction of rural peasant life where age-old communal law was based not on authority but on harmony and law was deemed less important than virtue. This tribal society ultimately presents a nonconsumerist code of life that does not depend on "the omnipresent paternalism of the international banker" or the chemical agricultural revolution or modern politics, and this presents a dangerous alternative and loss of market to capitalism.

In a parallel to our own national sense of betrayal over Vietnam starting with the My Lai incident, the Pentagon Papers, the secret bombing of Laos and Cambodia, Colonel Prouty, in a fascinating aside, traces the roots of the key 1950s decisions on Vietnam by the Dulles brothers and goes into the staged Tonkin Gulf incident and the official cover-up that sent us to the war.

Colonel Prouty also explores the true meaning of the Pentagon Papers and the shocking and fraudulent omissions in them, which will blow away the self-congratulatory complacency of our "liberal" media, which,

Colonel Prouty shows us, never really understood the malignant forces that were operative behind the scenes of the Pentagon Papers—and once again robbed us of our history. Tantalizingly, Colonel Prouty points the finger of treason at McGeorge Bundy, then assistant to President Kennedy, who signed the key first draft of NSAM (National Security Action Memorandum) #273 on November 21, 1963, which was in contradiction to all previous Kennedy policy. How, Colonel Prouty speculates, could this happen unless such a person *knew* Kennedy would not be around the next day and "the new president" would? Also there is Bundy's bizarre role in the Bay of Pigs fiasco, reexamined here in a shocking new light.

Having myself spoken with Lucien Conein, our chief CIA operative in Vietnam under Lansdale, I can verify that Mr. Conein totally conformed to Colonel Prouty's version of events at the Diem killing in South Vietnam.

Prouty in effect totally reexamines the Pentagon Papers and the credibility of what a "leaked document" really is and how the media misunderstood; why the cabinet quorum was out of the country when Kennedy was killed *and*, more importantly, misunderstood the almost total reversal of our Vietnam policy in a matter of days after Kennedy's death. Prouty rightly lambastes the media as "a growing profession that fully controls what people will be told and helps prepare us for war in places like Afghanistan, Africa, and the Caribbean, most recently Granada and Panama, the Middle East and other "LDCs"—a banker's euphemism for "less developed countries."

Colonel Prouty pushes on to the true inner meaning of Watergate and leaves you dangling with the clues, making us fully realize we have only heard some forty hours of four hundred hours of one of the most mysterious affairs of American politics, involving possibly Nixon's own most secret revelations on the Kennedy murder. We must ask ourselves, What finally does Richard Nixon know of Dallas?

In another fascinating subtheme, Colonel Prouty shows how the roots of the 1950s decisions on Vietnam essentially emanated from the historically omitted presence of Chiang Kai-shek at the Tehran Conference of 1944—where, like colossi dividing the world, Churchill, Stalin, Roosevelt, and Chaing Kai-shek set forever the fuse of World War III. The enemy for the United States was no longer the Nazi movement but the more pernicious, property-stealing Soviet Communist world-around tribe. And of course, in seeking to destroy this new enemy at *all* costs, Colonel Prouty points once again to the infusion of

Nazi personnel, methods, and ultimately a Nazi frame of mind into the American system—a course which, once seeded, changed forever the way we operated in the world—and led irrevocably, tragically for our Constitution and our history, to the paramilitary domestic coup d'état in Dallas, November 1963.

Colonel Prouty sets the stage for this horrible nightmare with his own personally documented dealings with the Pentagon—a fascinating side glimpse at his involvement in a small coup in Bolivia. He illustrates how Third World politics is more often a game between commercial "In" and "Out" power groups that compete for the lion's share of the money by controlling their marketplaces with the U.S.A.'s help—the government of such a country is a business monopoly over its people and its territory and is motivated as much by pragmatic ideology as by the pragmatic control of the import-export business... by granting exclusive franchises to its friends, relatives, in all things from Coca-Cola to F-14 fighter planes... the supremely powerful international bankers keep the books for each side—how these Ins and Outs acquire bogeyman characteristics like "Communist," "Drug dealer," per the needs of our government and its attendant propaganda arm, our Fourth Estate; how Paz Estenssoro in Bolivia and Noriega in Panama and Hussein in Iraq have changed their identities several times from our "most-wanted" list to our favored-"commercial-ally" list. Prouty further illustrates that in 1975, our government spent $137 billion on military operations in Third World country LDCs and how that money is essentially funneled through American subsidiaries from our military-industrial complex. Money, Colonel Prouty *never* lets us forget, is at the root of power.

Colonel Prouty thus sets the stage for Dallas in all its horror. He explains the true inner myth of our most staged public execution, the "Reichstag Fire" of our era, behind whose proscenium, blinded by the light of surface-event television, the power of the throne was stolen and exchanged by bloody hands. He shows us that Kennedy was removed, fundamentally, because he threatened the "System" far too dangerously. Colonel Prouty shows us the Oswald cover story and how it has successfully to this day, my movie notwithstanding, blinded the American public to the truth of its own history—which requires, I suppose, a degree of outrage at our government and media and an urgency to replace it for the abuse of our rights as outlined in the Constitution and in the Declaration of Independence ("that whenever any Form of Government becomes destructive of... [Life, Liberty and the pursuit of happiness], it is the Right of the People to alter or to abolish it, and to institute new Government...it is their Right, it is their Duty, to throw off such Government and to provide new Guards for their future Security") but which too few of us have the energy for (except maybe the young, whom ultimately Colonel Prouty is addressing).

It is Colonel Prouty—with his background both as military officer and international banker—who shows us concisely that Kennedy was removed not only for his skittish policy on Vietnam and Cuba but because he fundamentally was affecting the economic might of this nation-planet, U.S.A., Inc., and its New World Order. Kennedy undermined, as Prouty fascinatingly outlines, not only the Federal Reserve Board but the CIA and its thousand-headed Medusa of an economic system (CIA: "Capitalism's Invisible Army"), but most dangerously and most expensively (ultimately some $6 trillion in Cold War money) the world-around economic lines of the "High Cabal" and its military-industrial complex so ominously forecast by Eisenhower in his farewell address. In bringing back the ghost of Buckminster Fuller and his great book, *The Critical Path*, Colonel Prouty shows us what we must understand of world history—he probes beneath the Egyptian mast of events and scenery and thousands of Cecil B. De Mille extras—to the very core of history—the Phoenician sail lines, the industrial complex, the distribution of minerals and oil, the exploitation of the planet and *why*, and *who benefits*. These are the key questions of our times—controlling the way you think, the way the media tells you to think, and the way you must think if we are to resist the ultimate desecration of the planet at the hands of U.S.A., Inc., and its New World Order. Environment must be reversed. U.S.A., Inc., must—and can—be reversed with new leadership. Read as companion pieces to Colonel Prouty the unofficial "histories" of Buckminster Fuller in *The Critical Path* and Howard Zinn's *People's History of the United States*, to fully understand the scope of the "octopus" we are in mortal combat with. Churchill, many years ago, called it overtly "The High Cabal." I am not sure, after all these years, that Mr. Churchill was being too dramatic.

Ultimately we must ask who owns America? Who owns reality? This book reads like Gibbon's *Decline and Fall*; we see inside the wheel of our history how our various "emperors" come and go and their relationship to the military machine. Who owns our "history?" He who makes it up so that most everyone believes it. That person wins—as George Orwell so lucidly pointed out in *1984*. If Mr. Hitler had won the Second World War, the version of events now given to us (invasions of

Third World lower slave races for mineral-resource conquest and world-round economic-military power) would not be too far off the mark. But instead of Nazi jackboots, we have men in gray suits and ties with attaché cases—"Lawyer Capitalism," Buckminster Fuller labeled it. Whatever its name, or uniform—*beware*.

I thank Colonel Prouty, who is old now, in his seventies—on the verge of going to the other side. Yet he has paused ("How dull it is to pause, to make an end, to rust unburnished, not to shine in use!" as Tennyson once said) and mustered his final energy and a lifetime's lucidity, and knowing full well the onslaught against his ideas and person that will come from the usual suspects, has once more ventured into the arena with the lions who kill and maim at the very least—and given us his truth at far greater personal expense than the reader of his volume will ever know. I salute you, Colonel Prouty—both as friend and warrier. "Fare thee well, Roman soldier."

May 1992

Stone Discusses His Film *JFK* and Introduces the Real "Man X"

On the Friday before Christmas, in 1991, Oliver Stone's epic film JFK *opened in Washington. Shown in a theater on Capitol Hill for all members of Congress, their families and staffs, and for other invited guests, this movie with its stark portrayal of the death of President John F. Kennedy in Dallas, Texas, on November 22, 1963, has shocked the moviegoing public around the world. As the president of the National Press Club said a month later, when introducing Oliver Stone:* "JFK *may go down as the most talked about movie of the decade."*

That movie was built upon the symbiotic relationship between the courtroom strategy of the Garrison "conspiracy" trial in New Orleans, the classic "anti–Warren Commission" lore of Jim Marrs's "Crossfire" narrative based upon the Dallas scene, and the electric shock treatment of the "Man X" question "Why?" and its stark analysis of the "power elite" of Washington's military-industrial arena.

The movie speaks to all people, and its tragic "Crime of the Century" story has had a global impact, and the dust has yet to settle. Its message lives. The response to that stark "Why?" is "President Kennedy was assassinated as a result of a decision made . . . from within the military-industrial complex of power . . . at a level above the U.S. government to preserve the benefits (to them) of the war in Vietnam by denying his reelection in 1964." That answer was derived from the facts and content of this book.

As Stone has said so frequently, "Had President Kennedy lived, Americans would not have become deeply involved in the Vietnam War." Because of the enormous dollar potential of the war to the great military-industrial complex of the United States and because of other threats to the power elite, it had become absolutely necessary, for them, to bring about this coup d'état on the streets of Dallas. This book in its original form provided vital parts of the movie's theme. In the final analysis, both the movie and book prove beyond all doubt that the government's Warren Commission Report on the Assassination of President Kennedy was contrived and is false; and that the government used the Warren Commission to cover up the facts of the crime with a diversionary story.

As a result of the opening of this movie and amid the uproar that was sweeping across the country, the National Press Club in Washington, D.C., invited Oliver Stone to speak before its members and a nation-wide audience on C-Span television. Stone appeared on January 15, 1992, before a packed auditorium. Katherine Kahler, president of the National Press Club, asked Oliver Stone to clarify a major and frequently asked question: "Does the Deep Throat–Man X character played by Donald Sutherland really exist?"

Stone responded: "I'm very glad this is asked, because so many people have asked me, when they came out of the movie, 'Who is Man X?' Let me just say that Man X exists. He's here today on the podium. He is Fletcher Prouty. He served in the military since before World War II. From 1955 to 1964 he was in the Pentagon working as chief of special operations and in that capacity was with the Joint Chiefs of Staff during the Kennedy years. He was responsible for providing the military support of the clandestine operations of the CIA...that is, 'Black Operations.'"

Oliver Stone had visited Fletcher Prouty in Washington in July 1990 and asked about his work in the Pentagon, especially during the Kennedy years, 1961–63. Stone added, "I understood his own shock and disbelief at what happened to the President and what happened in the years that followed...here and in Vietnam.

"Col. Prouty had never met with Jim Garrison, but over the years he had written many letters to him and had worked on Jim's manuscript before its publication. They were well acquainted, by letters. I took the liberty of having a meeting take place between Mr. Garrison and Colonel Prouty because Jim Garrison had brought Prouty's work to my *attention. Some people have misunderstood and claimed that Man X never existed and that I made him up. I never did. That information in the movie came from Fletcher."*

In summary, Oliver Stone added: "I think Fletcher has served his country well and retired as a full colonel. He's written a book called The Secret Team. *He has been critical of the CIA's illegitimate activities in the fifties and sixties. He knows a lot about it—he briefed people like Allen Dulles, knew them, knew General Charles Cabell, knew the atmosphere in the Pentagon and the CIA at the time, knew General Lansdale. He retired in 1964 from the Pentagon and became a banker."*

Because "Man X" is Fletcher Prouty, the author of this book, the reader will find much more to support what caught the eye of Oliver Stone, among others. As an introductory comment on both his movie JFK *and this book, Oliver Stone delivered the following speech before the Press Club:*

I have been accused by a number of people, some of them journalists, of a distortion of history. If there is any common thread of attack running through those claims of those critics of *JFK*, it is a notion that somehow there is an accepted, settled, respected, carefully thought out and researched body of history about the assassination of John F. Kennedy. All of which I have set out deliberately to subvert, using as my weapon the motion picture medium and taking as my target the impressionable young, who will believe anything as long as it is visual. This distortion of history has come at me from all quarters, although almost entirely, it must be said, from people old enough to know better. And it ignores, deliberately and carefully, the fact that there is no accepted history of these events; and that these terrible times remain the most undocumented, unresearched, unagreed-upon nonhistorical period of our history.

One can read in history books the standard two paragraphs that John F. Kennedy was shot by a lone gunman, who in turn was killed by another earnest vigilante and lone gunman. End of story. But that theory, put forward in twenty-six unindexed volumes by the Warren Commission, from the day it was issued was never even believed by a majority of Americans. The number of people who disbelieve it increases each year. Are we really to believe:

1. That settled, agreed, sanctified history includes, that Lee Harvey Oswald wrote away, under an easy-to-trade alias, for an inaccurate mail-order Italian rifle, called by the Italian army the humanitarian rifle,

because it never killed anyone when deliberately aimed...when he could have anonymously bought an accurate weapon at any street corner in Dallas?

2. Is it sacred history that this semiliterate high school dropout from Ft. Worth, Texas, professing Marxism, was taken to a secret, highly trained marine unit at an air base where the U-2 spy plane flights originated in Japan; given courses in the Russian language; and then permitted to leave the Marine Corps on three days' notice on a trumped-up claim of illness of his mother, who days after his death was the first to make the claim her son was working for American Intelligence?

3. Is it settled history that he then defected to the Soviet Union with a request for travel that included a reference to an obscure Ph.D.'s only graduate institute in Switzerland?

4. Are we to believe it is now history, not to be disturbed except by people like me, that he then went to the United States embassy in Moscow, announced his intention to defect and to turn over U.S. secrets to the Russians, and was permitted to go his way?

5. Is is part of our history which cannot be touched that he then returned eighteen months later to the same U.S. embassy announcing his intention to resume American citizenship and was handed his passport and some funds to enable him to return home?

6. Must one be a disturber of the peace to question the history that says he was met by a CIA front representative when he returned to the United States and that he was never debriefed by an intelligence organization, although 25,000 tourists, that year, were so debriefed?

7. Must one be a distorter of history to question why he then merged into the fiercely anti-Communist, White Russian community of Dallas, although he kept up the absurd front of Marxism; or the equally rabid anti-Communist circle of Guy Bannister in New Orleans?

8. Or how did Oswald just come to have the job a few weeks before, at the Book Depository, overlooking the precise point in the motorcade where Kennedy's car took that unusual eleven-mile-an-hour curve?

9. Or how Oswald came to be spotted by patrolman Marion Baker only ninety seconds after the sixth-floor shooting, on the second floor having a Coca-Cola and showing no signs of being out of breath?

10. Or the too-neat stashing of the rifle without hand prints?

11. And the three cartridges laid out side by side at the window?

12. Or Oswald's cool and calm behavior that weekend, or his claim, the statement, that he was a patsy?

Am I a disturber of history to question why Allen Dulles, who had been fired by JFK from the CIA, which JFK had said he would splinter into a thousand pieces, was appointed to the Warren Commission to investigate Mr. Kennedy's murder? And so on, and so on, and so on.

To accept this settled version of history, which must not be disturbed, was to then call down the venom of leading journalists from around the country. One must also believe the truly absurd, single-bullet theory of the Warren Commission, which holds that one bullet caused seven wounds in Kennedy and Governor Connally, breaking two dense bones and coming out clean, no metal missing, no blood tissue or anything on it. Its path, as you know, utterly ludicrous, entering Kennedy's back on a downward trajectory, changing direction, exiting up through his throat, pausing for 1.6 seconds before deciding to attack Connally, then turning right, then left, then right again, hitting Connally at the back of his right armpit, heading downward through his chest, taking a right turn at Connally's wrist, shattering the radius bone, exiting his wrist; the bullet launches one last assault, taking a dramatic U-turn and burying itself in Connally's left thigh. Later, that bullet turns up five miles from the scene of the crime on a stretcher, in a corridor at Parkland Hospital in pristine condition.

No, ladies and gentlemen, this is not history! This is myth! It is myth that a scant number of Americans have ever believed. It is a myth that an esteemed generation of journalists and historians have refused to examine, have refused to question, and above all, have closed ranks to criticize and vilify those who do. So long as the attackers of that comforting "lone gunman" theory could be dismissed as "kooks" and "cranks" and the writers of obscure books that would not be published by "reputable publishing houses," not much defense was needed. But now all that is under attack by a well-financed and, I hope, a well-made motion picture with all the vivid imagery and new energy the screen can convey. Now, either enormous amounts of evidence have to be marshaled in support of that myth or else those in question must be attacked. Those that question it must be attacked. There is no evidence; so, therefore, the attack is on.

Some journalists of the sixties are self-appointed keepers of the flame. They talk about "our history" and fight savagely those who would question it. But, confronted with the crime of the century, with no motive and hardly any alleged perpetrators, they stand here. Where, in the last twenty years, have we seen serious research from Tom Wicker, Dan Rather, Anthony Lewis, George Lardner, Ken Auchincloss, into

Lee Harvy Oswald's movements in the months and years before 22 November 1963? Where have we seen any analysis of why Oswald, who, many say, adored Kennedy, alone among assassins in history would not only deny his guilt but would claim he was a "patsy"? Can one imagine John Wilkes Booth leaping tothe stage at Ford's Theater, turning to the audience and shouting, "I didn't kill anyone—I'm just a patsy"?

One might ask of the journalists who have suddenly emerged as the defenders of history, What is their sense of history? How much work has the "Sage of Bethesda," George Will, done in the twenty years he has been a columnist to try to uncover the answers to those dark secrets in Dallas 1963? Will Tom Wicker and Dan Rather spend their retirement years examining, closer, the possibility of a second or third gunman; or will they content themselves with savaging those who do? Why is no one questioning Richard Helms, who lied to the Warren Commission, when we know, now, that there was, as of 1960, an increasingly thick "201" file on LHO? Why is no one questioning Mr. Hoover—Hoover's memo of 1961—outlining the fact that someone was using Oswald's name, while Oswald was in Russia, to buy trucks for the Guy Bannister apparatus in New Orleans? Why are none of the reporters questioning Colonel Fletcher Prouty, in depth, or Marina Oswald Porter, who says her husband was working for something bigger; or questioning the alleged hit man, Charles Harrelson, who is in maximum security? Let them deny what they will, but at least ask them!

There is more truth seeking going on now in Russia than there is in our country. What *JFK* has brought out is that those who talk most of history have no commitment to it. An essential, historical question raised by *JFK* has to do not with the "tramps" in Dealy Plaza, not with who might have been firing from the grassy knoll, not with what coalition of Cuban exiles, mobsters, rogue intelligence officers the conspiracy might have been concocted by; but the darker stain on the American ground in the sixties and seventies... Vietnam.

It is Vietnam which has become the bloody shirt of American politics, replacing slavery of one hundred years before. Just as we did not resolve, if we ever did, the great battle of slavery until a hundred years after the Civil War, when we passed the Voting Rights Act of 1965, so it becomes clear that the Vietnam War remains the watershed of our time. And the divisions in our country, among our people, opened up by it seem to get wider and wider with each passing year.

JFK [the movie and the book] suggests that it was Vietnam that led to the assassination of John F. Kennedy, that he became too dangerous, too strong an advocate of changing the course of the Cold War; too clear a proponent of troop withdrawal for those who supported the idea of a war in Vietnam and later came to support the war itself. Was President Kennedy withdrawing from Vietnam? Had he indicated strongly his intention to do so? Had he committed himself firmly against all hawkish advice to the contrary to oppose the entry of U.S. combat troops? The answer to these questions is unequivocally "Yes!"

With this emphasis on the Vietnam policy of President John F. Kennedy, Oliver Stone is relying heavily on his adviser, the author of this book, for these little known facts. Colonel Prouty was one of the writers of Kennedy's NSAM #263, which publicly announced his plan to have one thousand military men home by Christmas and all U.S. personnel out of Vietnam by the end of 1965. This book explains those JFK "Vietnam policies" authoritatively and in considerable detail.

As Arthur Schlesinger, Jr., has attested, President Kennedy signaled his intention to withdraw from Vietnam in a variety of ways and put it firmly on the record with his National Security Action Memorandum (NSAM) #263 of October 11, 1963. Those who try to say it was no more than a call for a rotation of troops or a gimmick and that the Johnson NSAM #273, issued within a week of the assassination, merely confirmed the policy, ignore the obvious question. If LBJ was merely continuing Kennedy's policies, why was it necessary to reverse Kennedy's October NSAM #263?

So the protectors of Vietnam, the new "Wavers" of the bloody shirt, leaped to attack the central premise of *JFK*. "Oliver Stone is distorting history again," again they say, even suggesting that John Kennedy was positioning us for a withdrawal from Vietnam, by even suggesting that... that I am distorting history.

But these defenders of history had very little to say five years ago when it was suggested in the motion picture that Mozart had not died peacefully; but had been murdered by a rival and second-rate composer. Where were all of our cultural watchdogs when Peter Shaffer was distorting history with *Amadeus?*" The answer, of course, is that it wasn't worth the effort. Eighteenth-century Vienna, after all, is not twentieth century Vietnam. If Mozart was murdered, it would not change one note of that most precious music; but if John Kennedy were killed because he was determined to withdraw from Vietnam and never send combat troops to a Vietnam War, then we must fix the blame for the only lost war in our history, for 56,000 Americans dead, and for an as yet unhealed split in our country and among our people.

I've been ridiculed and worse for suggesting the existence of a conspiracy as though only kooks and cranks and extremists suggest the existence of such a thing. But this is the wrong city in which to ridicule people who believe in conspiracies. Is it inconceivable that the President of the United States could sit at the heart of a criminal conspiracy designed to cover up a crime? We know that happened. We would have impeached him for it had he not resigned, just one step ahead. Is it so farfetched to believe in a high-level conspiracy involving the White House, the Joint Chiefs of Staff, the air force, and the CIA to bomb a neutral country and then lie about it in military reports to the rest of the country? But it happened, perhaps more than once. Is it inconceivable that the National Security Council leadership, with or without the knowledge of the President of the United States and with the collaboration of the director of Central Intelligence... not just a few rogues... could be engaged in a massive conspiracy to ship arms to our sworn enemy with the casual hope that a few hostages might be released as a result? But it happened. Does it offend our sense of propriety to suggest that an assistant secretary of state for Latin America might have regularly lied to Congress about raising money abroad to perform things that Congress had forbidden us to do? But that happened! Is it inconceivable that a campaign manager, later to become the director of Central Intelligence, negotiated with a foreign country to keep American hostages imprisoned until after a presidential election, in order to ensure the election of his candidate? We shall see?

But I think, no one thinks it is out of the question anymore. So when JFK suggests that a conspiracy involving elements of a government, people in the CIA, people in the FBI, perhaps people associated with the Joint Chiefs of Staff, all in the service of the military-industrial complex that President Eisenhower warned us about, might have conspired to kill JFK because he was going sharply to change the direction of American foreign policy, is it not appropriate at least to look there for evidence? What was Allen Dulles really up to in those months? Or Charles Cabell, also fired by JFK; or his brother, Earle Cabell, the mayor of Dallas in November 1963?

Thomas Jefferson urged on us the notion that when truth can compete in a free marketplace of ideas, it will prevail. There is, as yet, no marketplace of history for the years before the Kennedy assassination and immediately afterward. Let us begin to create one. What I've tried to do with this movie is to open a stall in that marketplace of ideas and offer a version of what might have happened as against the competing versions of what we know did not happen and some other possible versions as well.

I'm happy to say, thanks not only to the nine million people who have already seen the movie but to the attitude toward the facts they take with them away from the movie, that our new stall in that marketplace of ideas is doing a very brisk business. And we expect by the time this film is played out in video cassettes, etc., that another fifty million Americans will have a little more information on their history.

I am very proud that *JFK* has been a part of the momentum to open previously closed files in the matter of the assassination. Congressman Louis Stokes of Ohio, the chairman of the House Select Committee on Assassinations, has announced his willingness to consider the opening of the files, closed until, you know, the year 2029. And I am hopeful his consideration will ripen into approval. In addition, Judge William Webster, formerly the director of the FBI and of the CIA, has indicated his strong opinion that all of the files—all of the files—House Committee, CIA, and FBI among them, be made public...a proposal, I was extremely pleased last weekend to see, endorsed by Senator Edward Kennedy. In the meantime, we are grateful to Congressman Stokes, Congressman Lee Hamilton, Judge Webster, Senator Kennedy, and others who have indicated a willingness to consider opening these files. Now if the army and navy intelligence services will join suit, it is my hope the American people will have the full truth of this assassination.

PREFACE

THE COLD WAR, along with its various politically managed "battle-grounds" has ended, but the mystery lives on. What was going on? Increasingly we have all begun to realize that the legislative creation of the CIA, the Korean War, the Vietnam War, the Bay of Pigs, the Cuban Missile Crisis, the development of rockets and missiles along with the space program and the moon landings, as well as with the assassination of John F. Kennedy, were craftily orchestrated events designed to fill the gap between what mankind has known as conventional warfare and the incalculable impact of all-out nuclear warfare. In terms of the military-industrial interests there had to be a demand for their products and there had to be attrition of that materiel. Thus preparation for warfare and some form of warfare had to continue. All this was done while carefully avoiding a nuclear exchange.

On top of this, we have now begun to realize that one of the greatest casualties of the Cold War has been the truth. At no time in the history of mankind has the general public been so misled and so betrayed as it has been by the work of the propaganda merchants of this century and their "historians." It was Ralph Waldo Emerson who said, "There is properly no history; only biography," and this may have been said in jest. We have learned, with some frequency, that the biographer himself may have toyed with the truth. Perhaps "autobiography" is a better word for a factually correct history.

This book is a firsthand account of the years since World War II. It carefully documents a major sector of the Cold War from 1943 to 1975 by recognizing the strategically elegant "Saigon Solution" as the long-range plan that was designed and employed by the international power elite to bridge, profitably, that first thirty years, from the end of World War II, on September 2, 1945, to the fall of Saigon, on April 30, 1975. After that they took advantage of the so-called energy crisis of the seventies and the equally contrived financial crisis of the eighties to make unbelievable sums of money from those valuable sources that must include the global trade in drugs.

There are some readers who are unaccustomed to this age-old concept of the *power elite*. One of the better characterizations of this idea was written by R. Buckminster Fuller in his important book *Critical Path*. It reads:

> In our comprehensive reviewing of published, academically accepted history we continually explore for the invisible power structure behind the visible kings, prime ministers, czars, emperors, presidents, and other official head men, as well as for the underlying, hidden causes of individual wars and the long, drawn-out campaigns not disclosed by the widely published and popularly accepted causes of these wars.

It goes without saying that few, if any, credible historians are going to be able to name the individuals who comprise such an elite. One point must be clarified. They are not the Bilderburgers, the Trilateralists, or members of the Council for Foreign Relations. Much more is said on this subject in the chapters that follow, and even then we must realize that one of the greatest strengths of this power elite is that they have learned to live anonymously.

There is, in Lord Denning's book, *The Family Story*, a most pertinent reference to the words of Winston Churchill during a heavy bomber attack on Rotterdam during World War II. Denning reports that Churchill, during a conversation among friends, made reference to a "High Cabal" that has made us what we are. In that sense, Churchill's High Cabal equates with Fuller's "invisible power structure." For a man in Churchill's position, and at the war-time peak of his public career, to make reference to a high, or higher, cabal defines the subject. We live under the influence of such a cabal today, whether we realize it or not. This book opens up the subject for a broad and most practical review.

In general, this historical account follows a chronological format, and in so doing it recognizes the enormous significance of the November 22, 1963, assassination of President John F. Kennedy and of the coup d'état that replaced that administration as a result.

Portions of this book appeared during 1985–1987 in the magazine *Freedom*. Oliver Stone became familiar with its "Kennedy assassination"–related material and used some if it in his film *JFK*. The author worked with Stone as a technical adviser and was portrayed as "Man X," played by Donald Sutherland. However, the principal theme of the book documents the long-range, strategic planning of the Cold War, begun as early as the Cairo and Teheran "Big Four" Conferences of late November 1943, and how that planning led directly, without a single day's interval, from the end of World War II, September 2, 1945, to the United States' involvement in what became the Indochinese war, which began on that same date. These Conference plans also included the Korean war that began five years later, in June 1950.

These facts were confirmed in a speech made by John Foster Dulles before the American Legion Convention in St. Louis, quite coincidently on September 2, 1953, when he confirmed the United States' involvement in this "desperate struggle's first eight years in Indochina." Before that "no win" warfare had ended, not less than $570 billion had been channeled into the coffers of this war-making High Cabal at a cost of 58,000 American lives.

This type of limited warfare was not designed solely for the purpose of making war to make money, as has been the case throughout history for most countries; but it was necessitated by the knowledge, as early as 1943, that the atom bomb would be ready before the end of World War II. As many have recognized, the war did not end until the first of each of the original types of atomic bomb, Implosion and Gun-type, had been given its initial bloodbath public demonstration over Hiroshima and Nagasaki. Then, and only then, did these world-class planners realize that they had made a terrible mistake in funding those nuclear physicists and their industrial backers to produce an atom bomb. From the time of the first use of nuclear weapons until the present, and even more certainly for the future, the atomic bomb demonstrated that effective warfare, as it was known since the dawn of mankind, has ended. The almost timeless era of conventional warfare is over. There will be no more "victorious" wars. There will be moneymaking, meaningless wars. The next real, all-out, and unlimited war will lead to Armageddon on Earth. It will be the last.

Bernard O'Keefe armed the Nagasaki bomb, detonated the 15-megaton BRAVO hydrogen test device in the Pacific, and, before his death, became the chairman of the board of E. G. & G. Inc., one of the nation's leading high-technology nuclear-support companies. O'Keefe wrote:

The fission-fusion-fission bomb permits unlimited destruction in a small convenient package. The radius of destruction (of such a bomb) is measured not in miles but in hundreds of miles, rendering any civil defense by evacuation useless.

(NOTE: He said "radius.")

Furthermore, the series of so-called wars since 1945 were never fought to achieve victory. They were waged for dollars, without a true military objective, under the control of civilian leaders, with the generals in a supernumerary role. In fact, the first twenty years of our "desperate struggle" in Indochina were fought under the operational control of agents of either the Office of Strategic Services (OSS) or the Central Intelligence Agency (CIA) first assisting Ho Chi Minh to establish the independence of Vietnam, and later, when U.S. policy swung around in alignment with the Cold War, to support the French. The few bona fide U.S. Armed Forces generals who were in Vietnam were limited to managing supporting activities, and none of them, at any time, ever served in direct command of combat operations in Indochina. There was always an ambassador, and frequently a CIA agent—under the cover of a general—or both in superior positions. Such is the nature of these new, limited, "make money" wars.

Because of the strategy that continued the moneymaking aspect of warfare and the dilemma created by the advent of the nuclear weapon, no single event of that thirty-year period has been a more serious indictment of the condition of our present government, of our media, and of those of the lawyer-capitalist system, who are in control of both, than the enormity of the "cover story" fabrication about the assassination of President John F. Kennedy. This situation has prevailed for the past three decades... plus. The reason why it has been possible to maintain this enormous "cover story" for decades is that the greater crime committed on November 22, 1963 was that of the coup d'état of the government of the United States. The conspirators took control.

Paramount among the many other reasons for this deplorable condition has been the One World growth of a power elite of international bankers and industrial giants who totally disregard the sovereignty of nations and the individual rights of man. As a result, the history of the Cold War period that began before the end of World War II has been replete with fantasies. A number of those whom we call "historians" are no more than paid hacks with little or no practical experience, and a fixed agenda. Even the official "History of United States Involvement in

Vietnam from World War II to the Present (1968)," popularly known as the Pentagon Papers, contains such amazing propaganda in the chronological record of that period as:

22 Nov 1963   Lodge confers with the President.
              Having flown to Washington the day after the
              conference, Lodge meets with the President and
              presumably continues the kind of report given in
              Honolulu. (see, Vol. II, page 223)

That is the Pentagon Papers' official account of that otherwise momentous day. What possible explanation can there be for the fabrication of that totally untrue bit of official record of the very day that President John F. Kennedy was assassinated as a result of a contract murder? This becomes all the more significant when we realize that this official history was directed by Secretary of Defense Robert S. McNamara and was compiled and written by members of his staff in the International Security Affairs section, under the task force leadership and direction of Leslie H. Gelb, later editor of the *New York Times* and now the president of the Council for Foreign Relations.

This massive study, containing countless other fabrications and significant omissions, was officially presented to the newly appointed Secretary of Defense, Clark M. Clifford, on January 15, 1969. Since that time, as later researchers, writers, and college professors have attempted to describe the thirty years of Vietnam War history, they have been misled by this work and by others that are equally false and contrived.

In contrast, my book has been written utilizing a pattern of chronology and autobiography. I was ordered to active military duty in July 1941, and as an Air Transport Command V.I.P. pilot, I was on duty in Cairo and Teheran during those important, highest level conferences of late November 1943. I participated in one of the initial, pivotal moves of the Cold War in the Balkans during September 1944 while the Soviet Union was still publicly considered to be one of our wartime allies. I was on Okinawa at the end of World War II and had made air transport flights into Japan before the official surrender on September 2, 1945; and returned again to the Far East as commander of a Military Air Transport Service squadron based in Tokyo from 1952 through 1954. During those years, I made many flights into Indochina and what became the nation of South Vietnam in 1954.

In 1955 I was designated by the chief of staff of the U.S. Air Force to establish an office of special operations within that headquarters in compliance with National Security Council (NSC) Directive #5412 of March 15, 1954. This NSC Directive for the first time in the history of the United States defined covert operations and assigned that role to the Central Intelligence Agency to perform such missions, provided they had been directed to do so by the NSC, and further ordered active-duty Armed Forces personnel to avoid such operations. At the same time, the Armed Forces were directed to "provide the military support of the clandestine operations of the CIA" as an official function.

I established that office and created its global clandestine support system. For the next nine years, 1955–1964, I served five of those years with the Air Force, two with the Office of the Secretary of Defense, and two more with the Office of the Joint Chiefs of Staff in that unique function of "supporting the CIA's secret clandestine operations." This book documents the "Saigon Solution"—that complex and powerful element of the Cold war master plan that, according to R. Buckminster Fuller, generated no less than six trillion dollars for its beneficiaries, who were in most cases many of the same members of the military-industrial complex so aptly defined by President Dwight D. Eisenhower in his Farewell Address, on January 17, 1961.

How can that cabal of conspirators who now control this One World be so powerful that it is possible for them to control the minds of our presidents, our media, and our entire educational system? This book is a personal account of the characteristics of that power elite and of its activities on an international scale during the Cold War. There is an overpowering reason why this is important.

The greatest war in the history of mankind came to a sudden and spectacular close with the detonation of the Hiroshima and Nagasaki atomic bombs. Those pivotal events not only brought the Japanese to the surrender table on the battleship *Missouri* in Tokyo Bay on September 2, 1945, but they also caused the ubiquitous highest cabal of this world to realize that they made an irreparable mistake when they permitted, yes, encouraged, nuclear scientists to create the nuclear weapon. They can never put the genie back in the bottle. From now on warfare must be limited, or all-out warfare will obliterate life on Earth.

World War II was over and conventional warfare died with it. In the ancient days, "war began with plunder, and the weapons at hand." Carl von Clauswitz added in 1833 in his book *Vom Kriege* that "war is not merely a political act but a political instrument." That was better; but, it was Alexis de Tocqueville, in his insightful book, *Democracy in America*, of 1835, who began to define "war" in its modern dress: "The secret connection between the military character and that of the democracies was the profit motive." With that precise statement de Tocqueville modernized the true concept of warfare: It is driven by the profit motive; it must be profitable. Another way to put it is that the profiteers make war as a necessity.

How many of us realize that back in November 1943, when Winston Churchill and Franklin D. Roosevelt met in Cairo with Chiang Kai-shek, they were not only making plans for victory over the Axis powers in Europe, they were laying the groundwork for a follow-on period of warfare in eastern Asia, in Indochina (1945), Korea (1950), and Indonesia (1958) following the defeat of Japan? Few historians seem to recall that also in Cairo was Chiang Kai-shek's wife Mei-Ling, the American-educated sister of T. V. Soong, then the wealthiest man in the world, and she actually took part in the work of the conference along with activities of T. V. Soong's Chinese delegates, who were Chiang's advisors.

During October 1943, I had been directed to fly a Geological Survey Team, under the leadership of Gen. C. R. Smith, founder and president of American Airlines and an "oil wise" Texan, to Saudi Arabia. Roosevelt had sent that select team into Saudi Arabia to meet with representatives of the California Standard Oil Company at their remote quarters on Ras Tanura. Following that visit they had been directed to join the President in Cairo. Their glowing report of the "limitless" quantity of petroleum under the sands of Arabia caused Roosevelt to order the expedited construction of a 50,000-barrel-per-day refinery on that site. It was in operation before the end of 1945. Thus began the modern petroleum era in the midst of war.

Even more importantly, after these delegates of Chiang Kai-shek and T. V. Soong had actively participated in Cairo in the planning for the post–World War II activities in the Far East, they flew on to Teheran, for that historic conference with Stalin. The fact that immediately following the Cairo Conference the Chinese delegation was in Teheran for that meeting with Josef Stalin has not been recorded in the history books of this era. This is a most important omission. I was pilot of the plane that flew them there from Cairo. During the sometimes heated exchanges between Roosevelt and Churchill on the subject of "the end of colonialism in Southeast Asia," plans were made by all four conferees for a period of continuing warfare in Indochina, Korea, and Indonesia under the guise of that Cold War "cover story."

In fact, Ho Chi Minh, with an American OSS man and U.S. Army general standing on each side of him, declared the Independence of

Indochina on the same date—September 2, 1945—of the Japanese surrender. That date marks the beginning of the three decades of the Vietnam War, as it was called. But the Cold War actually began even earlier while World War II was still being fought against the Axis powers.

In September 1944, while I was stationed in Cairo, I was asked by the commanding general of the Middle East Command, Benjamin Giles, and by my own Cairo base commander, Gen. Robert J. Smith, to fly them to Aleppo, Syria. There we met with British Intelligence officers who had been informed by their Secret Intelligence Service and by our own OSS that a freight train loaded with about 750 U.S. Air crewmen POWs was secretly en route to Syria from Romania via the Balkans and Turkey. The American POWs had been shot down in the Balkans during air raids on the Ploesti oil fields. The train traveled from Bucharest, Romania, via the Balkans and Turkey to the vicinity of Aleppo.

That night, after returning from Aleppo, I arranged for about thirty transport aircraft to fly on the following day, to that same landing ground north of Aleppo and close to the Turkish border where the railroad track enters Syria. We flew to Syria, met the freight train from Bucharest, loaded the POWs onto our aircraft, and began the flight back to Cairo. Among the 750 American POWs there were perhaps a hundred Nazi intelligence agents, along with scores of Nazi-sympathetic Balkan agents. They had been hidden in this shipment by the OSS to get them out of the way of the Soviet army that had marched into Romania on September 1.

This September 1944 operation was the first major pro-German, anti-Soviet activity of its kind of the Cold War. With OSS assistance, many followed in quick succession, including the escape and carefully planned flight of General Reinhart Gehlen, the German army's chief intelligence officer, to Washington on September 20, 1945.

The war against the Germans ended on May 8, 1945, and an increasing allied force escalated the war against Japan. Around the world, most believed, with the surrender of Japan four month later, that war-making had ended, despite the enormous shadow of nuclear weapons that loomed over the horizon. They were wrong.

Meanwhile, a new, limited, clandestine paramilitary type of warfare emerged in some of the hot spots of the world. The Korean War began in May 1950 and, almost immediately, U.S. Armed Forces accompanied by their new CIA associates became involved. By the time the North Korean forces surrendered, the somewhat dormant warfare in Indochina had flared up, on schedule. Here American participation, as noted earlier, was under the clandestine operational control of CIA agents, most of whom had valuable World War II military experience. By 1954 the United States government for the first time found it necessary to define *covert operations*.

As mentioned previously, the National Security Council Directive 5412 of March 15, 1954, became the U.S. government's basic directive on covert activities. Further it stated emphatically that "such operations shall not include armed conflict by recognized military forces." (Note: it is this stipulation that prohibited the utilization of military "air cover" during the Bay of Pigs operation in 1961.) The CIA became a member of the NSC 5412 Special Group, and responsibility for those covert operations that had been directed by the NSC was assigned to the CIA, with the full support of the military departments, as requested, and with full reimbursement for all "out-of-pocket" expenses.

During a meeting of the President's Special Committee on Indochina, January 20, 1954, the CIA was authorized to include an "unconventional warfare officer, specifically Colonel Lansdale," in a group of five others being sent to Vietnam to create the Saigon Military Mission. This unit was in place by July 1954 in time to support the new president, Ngo Dinh Diem, of the new country South Vietnam. In May 1954, Ho Chi Minh's army defeated the French forces at Dien Bien Phu. A Geneva Conference was convened to arrange an agreement between the new countries of North Vietnam and South Vietnam. One proviso of that agreement authorized any resident of the north who chose to move to the south to do so, and the same applied to those in the south.

On March 8, 1955, in a speech delivered nationwide, Secretary of State John Foster Dulles reported, "So far, about six hundred thousand persons have fled from northern Vietnam, and before the exodus is over the number will probably approach one million. They are destitute and penniless persons with only such possessions as they can carry on their backs." Under the control of the CIA's Saigon Military Mission, they had been transported by U.S. Navy transport ships and by the CIA's Civil Air Transport airline from the north to the Saigon region in the south.

In an effort to account for the success of its work with these "refugees" the SMM declared its tactics to include "psychological warfare." Today, we would more accurately call it terrorism." Is it any wonder that the program labeled "Communist-inspired insurgency" that emerged in the south arose because this horde of displaced people was forced to fight for food, shelter, and the necessities of life? This is the way that the CIA and its sponsors made war in Vietnam. By late 1960 our own forces had created the concept of "counterinsurgency."

All of this was well known to the then-Senator John F. Kennedy. During the years since the end of World War II, he had been a member of the House of Representatives and a U.S. Senator and served on the Senate Foreign Relations Committee. He had met Ngo Dinh Diem during 1953 and had met the Cuban exile political leaders as early as August 1960. They were working with the CIA at that time. He knew as much, or more, about the training of Cuban exiles under the CIA and of their plans for removal of Castro as Nixon did...perhaps more. It was during the final television debate of the presidential campaign with Nixon that Kennedy outmaneuvered Nixon, especially regarding anti-Castro policies, and many believe that this made it possible for him to be elected president in November 1960. It was during this same month, after the election, that the CIA quietly upgraded the Eisenhower administration's March 1960 approval of a modest Cuban-exile support program from small air-drop and over-the-beach operations to a 3,000-man invasion brigade—a plan that Kennedy inherited.

In brief, this Preface is an outline of the national and world affairs of the U.S. government as Kennedy inherited them from the eight-year Republican administration under Eisenhower. At that time, January 1961, I had been in the Pentagon for six years and was working in the Office of Special Operations, a direct function of the Office of the Secretary of Defense, Thomas Gates. This office was, among other things, responsible for the CIA relationship and special operations as well as for reviewing the development and execution of plans and programs of the National Security Agency.

The most noticeable characteristic of that "lame duck" period, which became evident as the Kennedy newcomers began to replace the departing Eisenhower old-timers, was the frequently mentioned and vehemently expressed dislike by the old-timers in the halls of the Pentagon for the new President. This developed as a result of his defeat of Nixon and the end of the Republican administration's policies. It was further exacerbated by the representatives of the military-industrial complex who had been working so successfully with the tenants of the Pentagon since World War II—particularly on the procurement plans for the high-cost "hardware" support of the warfare-to-come in Vietnam. Kennedy was hated from the start. They knew his reputation. He was certain to be a threat to their future expectations.

All of a sudden the die was cast with the sabotage of the Bay of Pigs operation in April 1961. Quite unbelievably, Director of Central Intelligence Allen Dulles, the man in charge of that operation, was out of the country on the day of the landings. Equally troublesome was the fact that the essential, pre-dawn air strike on D-Day by Cuban Exile Brigade bombers from Nicaragua to destroy Castro's last three combat jets that Kennedy, himself, had directed, had been cancelled the night before D-Day by Special Assistant for National Security Affairs McGeorge Bundy. That telephone call by Bundy was made just four hours before the Exile Brigade's B-26s were to take off from Nicaragua on that Kennedy-ordered strike.

Everyone connected with the planning of the Bay of Pigs invasion knew that the policy dictated by NSC 5412, March 1954, positively prohibited the utilization of active-duty military personnel in covert operations. At no time was an "air cover" provision written into the official invasion plan developed by an experienced and highly competent U.S. Marine Colonel and approved, with that stipulation, by the Joint Chiefs of Staff and the President. The "air cover" story that has been created since the failure of the Brigade is incorrect.

President Kennedy reacted quickly and deftly, as soon as the Brigade was forced to surrender. He formed a Cuban Study Group one day after the Brigade's defeat and charged it with the responsibility of determining the cause for the failure of that operation he had inherited from the previous administration. That prestigious and diverse study group consisting of Allen Dulles, Gen. Maxwell Taylor, Adm. Arleigh Burke, and Robert Kennedy, reported that Bundy's telephone call to General Cabell that cancelled the President's air strike order was the primary reason for the failure on the beach and the surrender of the Cuban Exile Brigade.

The language of the report, as written by General Taylor and unanimously agreed to by the group, was used almost verbatim by the president when he issued National Security Action Memorandum, #55, June 28, 1961, which began the process of changing the responsibility "for the defense of the nation in the Cold War similar to that which they have in conventional hostilities" from the CIA to the Joint Chiefs of Staff. When fully implemented, as Kennedy had planned, after his reelection in 1964, it would have taken the CIA out of the covert operations business. This proved to be one of the first nails in John F. Kennedy's coffin.

By mid-1963 Kennedy had arrived at the brink of a decision to keep all American troops out of Vietnam and to withdraw "all U.S. personnel"— military, CIA, and others—"from Vietnam by the end of 1965." Anyone interested in the exact coverage of the steps in this policy making should read the *Foreign Relations of the United States, 1961–1963,* vol. IV, "Vietnam: August–December 1963" by the Department of State and published by the U.S. Government Printing Office, 1991. This official record documents twenty-six highest level meetings in the White House with President Kennedy during the period August 28, 1963, to November 13, 1963. At the same time, my immediate superior officer, Maj. Gen. Victor H. Krulak attended twenty-three of those meetings in addition to making a quick visit to South Vietnam. Such a full schedule, in the White House and with the President among other high officials, in such a concentrated period is most unusual. It shows clearly how closely Kennedy made an analysis of the Vietnam situation his own problem, and it relates precisely the ideas he brought to the attention of his key staff on the subject.

It is significant to note that as General Krulak came and went from the White House during that busy period, including his quick trip to and from Vietnam, he would call several of us on his staff into his office each day, discuss the notes he had made, and give us instructions concerning what he wanted done for the next day's meeting with Kennedy. Quite naturally, I was intimately aware of this planning process, its policies, and precisely what the President intended as Vietnam policy for 1964 and 1965.

The president considered it imperative for Secretary McNamara and General Taylor to visit Vietnam during that troubled time one month before the Diems were to be removed from Saigon to Europe in accordance with his approved plan. At the same, General Krulak was made responsible for producing the final document for President Kennedy that would be known as the McNamara–Taylor Trip Report, October 2, 1963.

It was carefully written by several of us in the Pentagon under General Krulak's guidance, utilizing the notes and personal comments of the President. Charts and photos were added, as necessary, and it was bound in leather. It was not something produced by the two principals during their busy travels. When completed and approved, Krulak arranged for a jet fighter aircraft to rush it to Hawaii where it was given to the travelers in order that they might become completely familiar with it before their plane landed at Andrews Air Force Base in Maryland. As soon as they landed, they boarded a helicopter for the White House, where they ceremoniously gave the report to the president.

The report of October 2, 1963, became NSAM #263 after acceptance and approval of the President and his National Security Council. That

NSAM #263 is dated October 11, 1963. It is the basis for a policy decision confirming that "presently prepared plans to withdraw 1,000 military personnel by the end of 1963" and to "train Vietnamese so that essential functions now performed by U.S. military can be carried out by the Vietnamese by the end of 1965. It should be possible to withdraw the bulk of U.S. personnel by that time."

The Armed Forces newspaper *Stars and Stripes* carried the banner headline U.S. TROOPS SEEN OUT OF VIET BY '65. (Note: Any researcher who looks for NSAM #263 in the Pentagon Papers will find that it was craftily entered as its cover sheet of only three sentences on one page, and about thirty or forty pages earlier the McNamara–Taylor Trip Report of October 2, 1963, is quite craftily entered without reference to the fact that it is the true body of NSAM #263.)

This was the official and carefully drawn policy of the Kennedy administration, as written under the eye of the President. It was no casual or overnight scheme devised for limited purposes. This policy was developed in the face of the fact that at the same time the Buddhist uprising in the country was alarming. It was the positive and well-planned policy of the President. As such, it all but telegraphed the death of John F. Kennedy before his reelection.

In boardrooms, gentleman's clubs, and other secluded rendezvous locales, intimate groups of High Cabal principals quietly discussed this new policy and what it would do to their carefully planned, twenty-year objective: the "Saigon Solution." With NSAM #263 and related policy actions, such as changes in military procurement methods, it was clear that President Kennedy stood between them and their own goals.

It was also clear that this latest "all out by '65" policy was going to assure JFK's reelection. He had to go. With that foremost in their minds, a gradual, firm, and positive consensual decision was reached. The present government must be overthrown. They wanted no more of Kennedy; and they could not abide the thought of a Kennedy dynasty.

With that, a highly professional movement was initiated: Part 1 was a professional hit job by skilled and faceless killers, and Part 2 was an intricate and most comprehensive cover story that gave us such indelible bits of lore as Oswald, Ruby, magic bullet, Warren Commission, and all the rest.

By November 22, 1963, despite the Pentagon Papers' contrived omission of that fact of history, Kennedy was dead. By November 26, 1963, President Johnson had signed NSAM #273 to begin the change of the Kennedy policy announced in NSAM #263 and in March 1964, LBJ signed NSAM #288 that marked the full escalation of the Vietnam War that involved 2,600,000 Americans directly, with 8,744,000 serving with the U.S. Armed Forces during that period.

That was the "Saigon Solution." That is the historical and factually biographical material of this book. As you read this insider's account, it should be noted that it was the former Secretary of Defense Robert S. McNamara, who wrote, in the *New York Times*, February 2, 1983:

I do not believe we can avoid serious and unacceptable risk of nuclear war until we recognize, and base all our military plans, defense budgets, weapons deployments and arms negotiations on the recognition that nuclear weapons serve no military purpose whatsoever. They are totally useless—except only to deter one's opponent from their use.

Amen.

If this nation is to be wise as well as strong, if we are to achieve our destiny, then we need more new ideas for more wise men reading good books in more public libraries. These libraries should be open to all—except the censor. We must know all the facts and hear all the alternatives and listen to all the criticisms. Let us welcome controversial books and controversial authors. For the Bill of Rights is the guardian of our security, as well as our liberty.

John F. Kennedy
October 29, 1960

ONE

The Role of the Intelligence Services in the Cold War: 1945–65, The Vietnam Era

---

"THE DEEPEST COVER STORY of the CIA is that it is an intelligence organization." So said the *Bulletin of the Federation of American Scientists* some years ago. It was a true statement then, and it is even more accurate today. At no time was this more evident than during the Vietnam War years.

Have you ever wondered why the CIA was created, when such an organization had not existed before in this country, and have you ever tried to discover what specifically are the "duties" and "responsibilities" that are assigned to this agency by law? Or why it is that this "quiet intelligence arm of the President," as President Harry S. Truman has called it, and its Soviet counterpart, the KGB, were the lead brigades on the worldwide frontier of what was the Cold War?

In the real world—where more than six trillion dollars have been spent on military manpower, military equipment, and facilities since WWII ended in 1945—we discovered that the major battles of that Cold War were fought every day by Third World countries and terrorists. At the same time, the enormous military might of both world powers proved to be relatively ineffectual, because those multimegaton hydro-

1

gen bomb weapons are too monstrous, and too uncontrollably life threatening, to have any reasonable strategic value.

The existence of these multimegaton hydrogen bombs has so drastically changed the Grand Strategy of world powers that, today and for the future, that strategy is being carried out by the invisible forces of the CIA, what remains of the KGB, and their lesser counterparts around the world.

Men in positions of great power have been forced to realize that their aspirations and responsibilities have exceeded the horizons of their own experience, knowledge, and capability. Yet, because they are in charge of this high-technology society, they are compelled to do something. This overpowering necessity to do something—although our leaders do not know precisely what to do or how to do it—creates in the power elite an overbearing fear of the people. It is the fear not of you and me as individuals but of the smoldering threat of vast populations and of potential uprisings of the masses.

This power elite is not easy to define; but the fact that it exists makes itself known from time to time. Concerning the power elite, R. Buckminster Fuller wrote of the "vastly ambitious individuals who [have] become so effectively powerful because of their ability to remain invisible while operating behind the national scenery." Fuller noted also, "Always their victories [are] in the name of some powerful sovereign-ruled country. The real power structures [are] always the invisible ones behind the visible sovereign powers."

The power elite is not a group from one nation or even of one alliance of nations. It operates throughout the world and no doubt has done so for many, many centuries.

These leaders are influenced by the persuasion of a quartet of the greatest propaganda schemes ever put forth by man:

1. The concept of "real property," a function of "colonialism" that began with the circumnavigation of Earth by Magellan's ships in 1520. A "doctrine of discovery and rights of conquest" was described by John Locke in his philosophy of natural law.

2. The population theory of Malthus.

3. Darwin's theory of evolution, as enhanced by the concept of the survival of the fittest.

4. Heisenberg's theory of indeterminacy, that is, that God throws the dice, and similar barriers to the real advancement of science and technology today.

The first of these schemes derives from the fact that the generally accepted "flat earth" was, all of a sudden, proved to be a sphere by the voyage of Magellan's ships around the world. It is not so much that certain educated men had not already theorized that Earth was round, but that with the return of the first ship *Victoria* the expedition's wealthy financial backers had visual evidence that ships could circumnavigate the world and that because they could, Earth had to be a sphere. Being a sphere, it therefore had to be a finite object, with a finite—that is, limited—surface area. With this awakening the ideas of world trade and related colonial proprietary rights were born.

It may be postulated that this single bit of physical awareness brought about the greatest change in the mind of man since the dawn of creation. Before Magellan's time, mankind had simply accepted as self-evident the fact that there was always more property "out there" over the horizon and that it was not essential that anyone think seriously about the ownership of land, particularly open land. This general idea ended with the return of the good ship *Victoria*.

From that date on (circa A.D. 1520), the powerful rulers of the seafaring countries assumed the ownership of all real property in those discovered lands, and the natural resources on that property became one of the driving forces of mankind. One of the most important occupations of man during later years was that of surveyor. George Washington was a surveyor, outlining vast unknown tracts of land deeded by the King to his favorites, as though the King, and no one else—least of all those who inhabited these tracts—owned them. This paternalistic view of the right to the natives' real property totally disregarded the fact that most of the new land discovered "out there" was, and had been, already populated by others for millennia. The power centers of that period were taking over the real property of the world—no matter who was on it or who had been living there—using little more than the surveyor's chain, the missionary's cross, and the explorers' gun.

By 1600, Queen Elizabeth had founded the East India Company, which was given charter rights to create proprietary colonies anywhere on Earth. During those long years when the British fleet maintained the global British Empire, the East India Company was the structural mechanism of the most powerful men on Earth.

The East India Company founded Haileybury College in England to train its young employees in business, the military arts, and the special skills of religious missionaries. By 1800 it became necessary to initiate the task of making an Earth inventory, that is, to find out what was out there in the way of natural resources, population, land, and other tangible assets. The first man assigned the official responsibility for this enormously vital job was the head of the Department of Economics of Haileybury College.

This man was Thomas Malthus, who, in 1805, postulated the idea that humanity is multiplying its numbers at a geometric rate while increasing its life-support capability at only an arithmetic rate. As a result, it has been universally concluded by the power elite that only a relatively few humans are destined to survive successfully in generations to come. The Malthusian theory thus provides a rationalization for the necessity of somehow getting rid of large numbers of people, any people, in any way—even genocide. With the Malthusian theory as the power elite's philosophical guide, this becomes an acceptable objective, because, they believe, Earth will never be able to support the progeny of so many anyhow. From this point of view, genocide—then as now—is accepted as all but inevitable. Who cares and why be concerned?

The third theory fortifies this approach further. Darwin persuades them to believe that because they survive, at no matter what cost to others and to Earth, they must therefore be—by definition—the fittest; and conversely, because they know they are the chosen, that is, the fittest, they are Earth's assured survivors, fulfilling the prophecy of Armageddon.

The fourth, Heisenberg's nuclear age theory, provides an excuse for their errors and confusion. Certainly, if physical science is found to be indeterminate, economics can be, and so can everything else. Let God throw the dice, and we'll take it from there. The one caution, the power elite later reasoned, was that new scientific discoveries and new technology must never be permitted to overwhelm the status quo as precipitously as the hydrogen bomb had done.

Each of these concepts has been conveniently contrived to fit the occasion; each became the type of theory that is useful at certain times and in certain cases, but can never be proved and in most cases can easily be superseded by a more modern technology, a development of the science involved, or an awareness of the human rights that have been abrogated by the application of these rules of the powerful.

From this point of view, warfare, and the preparation for war, is an absolute necessity for the welfare of the state and for control of population masses, as has been so ably documented in that remarkable novel by Leonard Lewin[1] *Report From Iron Mountain on the Possibility and Desirability of Peace* and attributed by Lewin to "the Special Study Group in 1966," an organization whose existence was so highly classified that there is no record, to this day, of who the men in the group were or with what sectors of the government or private life they were connected.

This report, as presented in the novel, avers that war is necessary to sustain society, the nation, and national sovereignty, a view that has existed for millennia. Through the ages, totally uncontrolled warfare—the only kind of "real" war—got bigger and "better" as time and technology churned on, finally culminating in World War II with the introduction of atomic bombs.

Not long after that great war, the world leaders were faced suddenly with the reality of a great dilemma. At the root of this dilemma was the new fission-fusion-fission H-bomb. Is it some uncontrollable Manichean device, or is it truly a weapon of war?

These leaders have realized now that use of the thermonuclear, fission-fusion-fission type of megaton-plus bomb will destroy mankind, nature, and Earth. Therefore, they have asked, must they abandon the historic madness of all-out uncontrolled warfare, or, in its stead, can they discover and create some alternative to war that will perpetuate nationalism and maintain national sovereignty?

Since the dawn of that first realization, after the atomic devastation of Hiroshima and Nagasaki in World War II, the H-bomb has emerged from the laboratories and has been used to atomize whole islands in the Pacific and whole chunks of the landmass of arctic peninsulas. It can be placed in the nose cone of a rocket-powered intercontinental ballistic missile and delivered, in minutes, to any place on Earth. Or, perhaps even more dangerously, it can be fitted into the trunk of an automobile and parked in an underground garage in any city in the world. A simple telephone beeper rigged to the bomb's initiator will activate that nuclear explosive and pulverize any city of any size and any location.

Such knowledge is sufficient. The dilemma is now fact. There can no longer be a classic or traditional war, at least not the all-out, go-for-broke-type warfare there has been down through the ages, a war that leads to a meaningful victory for one side and abject defeat for the other. Witness what has been called warfare in Korea, and Vietnam, and the later, more limited experiment with new weaponry called the Gulf War in Iraq.

In his remarkable book *Counsel to the President*, Clark Clifford, former secretary of defense under President Lyndon Johnson, very frankly stated the problem that handicapped the military forces in Vietnam: "What was our objective in Vietnam?"

Earlier, in a quandary about what President Johnson himself had meant in his speech of March 31, 1968, Secretary Clifford asked in the book: "What had he intended? Had he deliberately sacrificed his political career in order to seek an end to the war, or had he put forward a series of half measures designed to shore up domestic support, at a lower cost, without changing our objective in Vietnam? Did he know what his objective was?"

These are absolutely alarming questions, coming as they do from a man who had been an adviser to presidents from Truman to Johnson during the most challenging years of the Cold War. He knew that we had been in a war in Vietnam since 1945; yet at the very time that he was the secretary of defense, in 1968, and when American forces in Vietnam had been increased to 550,000 men, he writes that neither he, the President, nor any member of the administration knew what the objective of this country or its military forces was in Vietnam. No army can win any war without a valid and tangible objective.

Then, during a meeting in the White House on May 21, 1968, of the President; Secretary of State Dean Rusk; the military adviser to the President, Walt Rostow; the chairman of the Joint Chiefs of Staff, Earle Wheeler; and himself, Clark Clifford made this amazing statement: "With the limitations now placed on our military—no invasion of the north, no mining of the harbors, no invasion of the sanctuaries—we have no real plans or chance to win the war."

There are, in the academic terms of a Clausewitz or other scholars of the evolution of warfare, nine principles of warfare; and paramount among these is that of the "objective." What possible chance is there for victory when generals have not been given a clear description of the national objective for which they and their men must fight and die and in its place are given a list of incredible limitations?

Because of this failure of leadership at the top, America sacrificed 58,000 men and spent no less than $220 billion. No wonder Clark Clifford and his associates were confounded by what they had inherited, from prior administrations, in the name of a "war" in faraway Indochina. This is one reason why it is so important to clarify that what was called a "war" during the first twenty years (1945–65) of this conflict was actually a massive series of paramilitary activities under the operational control of the CIA.

This is what the hydrogen bomb and the clandestine services have done to the art of war. Under these circumstances, no commander today can be given an objective such that if he begins to achieve it, and therefore appears to be on the road to victory, he will force his enemy to resort to that weapon of last resort, the hydrogen bomb.

Our six presidents of the Vietnam War era, 1945–75, were faced with this dilemma. None of them, or any member of their staffs, have expressed it better than Clark Clifford in his book, or Gen. Victor H. Krulak in *First to Fight*, his most important military book.

Today the power elite can see no assured survival for themselves and their class if hydrogen bombs are utilized in warfare. Up until the end of WWII, this power elite on both sides of the fray, who exist above the war, have always been assured of survival. In any war in the future in which there is an exchange of H-bombs, there can be no assured Armageddon-type survival for the chosen, for mankind, for all of nature, or for Earth itself.

Under such circumstances, since survival is the strongest drive in man, what form can war take, given that it is viewed as a necessity and that the men of this power elite have that final choice to make? This question has given rise to a concept of a controlled or limited type of warfare and has been widely discussed within such groups as Prince Bernhard's "Bilderbergers" in Europe and by their NATO friends in SHAPE Headquarters (Supreme Headquarters Allied Powers Europe). As the hydrogen bomb has increased in power and been given a world-around capability by rocket-powered ICBMs, or worse still, been put in the hands of terrorists, even this contrived "limited war" concept has been dropped. As a result, the present strategy is based upon what has been known as the Cold War.

Faced with this dilemma and with their continuing belief in the contrived theories of Malthus, Darwin, and Heisenberg, world leaders turned—to some degree, even before the end of WWII—to an alternative, all-new type of invisible war to be waged under the cloak of propaganda, black budgets, and secrecy. They called it the Cold War. Before that contrivance ended with the collapse of the Soviet Union, it had already cost more than six trillion dollars and millions of lives. Perhaps, as Mao Tse-tung has said, "It is man's last war, because it will never end or ever result in victory for anyone." It will only assure the attrition of manpower and matériel, and it will dangerously pollute Earth, to a point that will be beyond the control of mankind and nature to reverse and control.

On the other hand, it was a very real killing war. Its battles loomed everywhere, and its dead were counted in the millions. More of the casualities were noncombatants than uniformed soldiers. It was the Secret War, the Invisible War. From the point of view of those in power, it was a welcome substitute. It consumed the population and the product of the munitions makers and was reasonably controllable on the side of the offense.

But the Cold War as an alternative to the real thing was a failure from a military point of view. For one thing, there were no clear-cut victories; nor could there have been any. We have witnessed the deterioration of the concept of national sovereignty because of it and for such other reasons as the existence of global communications, satellite networks, international finance, and the enormous power of transnational business enterprises. We have seen the rise of the strange, nonmilitary power of the small nations of the Third World. The whole scheme of warfare is being turned upside down by bands of terrorists who defy the great powers. They cannot be controlled with H-bombs and modern armies. Terrorism makes a mockery of "Star Wars." If the tactics of terrorism were to be employed in strength, it would create a situation that no one could handle. The greater the potential victory, the closer the war would move to the nuclear threshold.

This is why the American military leaders in Korea, Vietnam, and the Gulf were not permitted to win. They were told only to "kill" and to run up the "body count," but not to fight a real war, because the closer they got to an assured victory in Vietnam, the closer they would have been to the nuclear threshold. Our military leaders were never permitted to approach that barrier.[2]

Gen. Douglas MacArthur had to accept that strategic fact on the south bank of the Yalu River in Korea. Gen. Creighton Abrams learned it when he proposed to President Johnson that he be authorized to capture Hanoi instead of maintaining a perimeter around the Cercle Sportif club in Saigon. And now the terrorists have learned it and use the knowledge to defy everyone, the big powers and their lesser neighbors alike.

This is why, even before the end of World War II, the newly structured bipolar confrontation between the world of Communism and the West resulted in the employment of enormous intelligence agencies that had the power, invisibly, to wage underground warfare, economic and well as military, anywhere—including methods of warfare never before imagined. These conflicts had to be tactically designed to remain short of the utilization of the H-bomb by either side. There can never be victories in such wars, but tremendous loss of life could occur, and there is the much-desired consumption and attrition of trillions of dollars', and rubles', worth of war equipment.

One objective of this book is to discuss these new forces. It will present an insider's view of the CIA story and provide comparisons with the intelligence organizations—those invisible forces—of other countries. To be more realistic with the priorities of these agencies themselves, more will be said about operational matters than about actual intelligence gathering as a profession.

This subject cannot be explored fully without a discussion of assassination. Since WWII, there has been an epidemic of murders at the highest level in many countries. Without question the most dynamic of these assassinations was the murder of President John F. Kennedy, but JFK was just one of many in a long list that includes bankers, corporate leaders, newsmen, rising political spokesmen, and religious leaders. The ever-present threat of assassination seriously limits the number of men who would normally attempt to strive for positions of leadership, if for no other reason than that they could be singled out for murder at any time. This is not a new tactic, but it is one that has become increasingly utilized in pressure spots around the world.

It is essential to note that there are two principal categories of intelligence organizations and that their functions are determined generally by the characteristics of the type of government they serve— not by the citizens of the government, but by its leaders.

Under totalitarian or highly centralized nondemocratic regimes, the intelligence organization is a political, secret service with police powers. It is designed primarily to provide personal security to those who control the authority of the state against all political opponents, foreign and domestic. These leaders are forced to depend upon these secret elite forces to remain alive and in power. Such an organization operates in deep secrecy and has the responsibility for carrying out espionage, counterespionage, and pseudoterrorism. This methodology is as true of Israel, Chile, or Jordan as it has been of the Soviet Union.

The second category of intelligence organization is one whose agents are limited to the gathering and reporting of intelligence and who have no police functions or the power to arrest at home or abroad. This type of organization is what the CIA was created to be; however, it does not exist. Over the decades since the CIA was created, it has acquired more sinister functions. All intelligence agencies, in time, tend to develop

along similar lines. The CIA today is a far cry from the agency that was
created in 1947 by the National Security Act. As President Harry S.
Truman confided to close friends, the greatest mistake of his administration took place when he signed that National Security Act of 1947 into
law. It was that act which, among other things it did, created the Central
Intelligence Agency.[3]

During WWII the four Great Powers—the United States, Great
Britain, China, and the Soviet Union—opposed the Axis powers:
Germany, Italy, and Japan. Enormous military and economic forces, on
each side, were locked together in the greatest armed conflict in history.
The Russians alone suffered more than 20 million casualties. In June
1944, I flew an air force transport aircraft from Tehran to the vicinity of
Kiev in the Ukraine. I never saw such widespread destruction of cities
and towns. The great city of Rostov was absolutely leveled. One would
think that as a result of the enormity of this combined struggle, such a
union of forces, welded in the heat of World War II, would remain
joined forever.

However, even before the surrender of Germany and Japan, we began
to hear the first rumblings of the Cold War. The Office of Strategic
Services, and particularly its agents Frank Wisner in Bucharest and
Allen W. Dulles in Zurich, nurtured the idea that the time had come to
rejoin selected Nazi power centers in order to split the Western alliance
from the Soviet Union. "Rejoin" is the proper word in this case. It was
the Dulles-affiliated New York law firm of Sullivan & Cromwell that had
refused to close its offices in Nazi Germany after the start of WWII in
1939, even while Great Britain and France were locked in a losing
struggle with Hitler's invading forces. Therefore, the Dulles OSS
"intelligence contacts" in Nazi Germany during the war were for the
most part German business associates with whom he was acquainted.

On August 23, 1944, the Romanians accepted Soviet surrender terms,
and in Bucharest the OSS rounded up Nazi intelligence experts and
their voluminous Eastern European intelligence files and concealed
them among a trainload of 750 American POWs who were being quickly
evacuated from the Balkans via Turkey. Once in "neutral" Turkey, the
train continued to a planned destination at a site on the Syrian border,
where it was stopped to permit the transfer of Nazis and POWs to a fleet
of U.S. Air Force transport planes for a flight to Cairo.

I was the chief pilot of that flight of some thirty aircraft and was
stunned by the discovery of two things I would never have suspected: (1)
A number of the Americans had had one or both legs amputated at the

knee by their Balkan captors, solely for the purpose of keeping them immobile (the plane I flew had airline seats rather than canvas "bucket" seats, and the men on my plane had lost one or two legs in that barbaric manner), and (2) concealed among these POWs were a number of Balkan Nazi intelligence specialists who were being taken out of the Balkans ahead of the Soviet armies by the OSS.

As far as I know, this was one of the first visible clues to the emergence of the "East-West" Cold War structure, even while we and the Russians were still allies and remained partners in the great struggle against the Germans.

It was this covert faction within the OSS, coordinated with a similar British intelligence faction, and its policies that encouraged chosen Nazis to conceive of the divisive "Iron Curtain" concept to drive a wedge in the alliance with the Soviet Union as early as 1944—to save their own necks, to salvage certain power centers and their wealth, and to stir up resentment against the Russians, even at the time of their greatest military triumph.

I was only a pilot on that flight, and in no way involved in the diplomatic intricacies of that era, but I have always wondered whose decision it had been, back in mid-1944, a year before the end of World War II, to override the present alliances and to initiate a split between the West and our wartime partner the Soviet Union while we were still firm allies.

This first fissure in the wartime structure was evidence of a long-range view of Grand Strategy from a level above that of the leaders we knew in public. The power elite had already set plans in motion for the post–World War II period that we have known as the Cold War. This is one of the best examples I have found revealing the work of the power elite, as distinct from that of the men who are the visible national leaders. As World War II came to a close, the long-range Cold War plan was already in existence, filling the vacuum created by the end of that conflict.

That long-range decision had to have originated from a center of power above the Roosevelt-Churchill-Stalin level, because it ignored the World War II alliance represented by those three wartime leaders and went its own independent way.

As a result of a masterful propaganda campaign begun by a select group of Nazis, most of us have been led to believe that it was the British who first recognized the Communist threat in Eastern Europe, that it was Winston Churchill who coined the phrase "Iron Curtain" in referring to actions of the Communist-bloc countries of Eastern Europe, and that he did this after the end of World War II. The facts prove otherwise.

Churchill did not coin the memorable phrase; he merely embellished it and exploited it. The true story follows.

Just before the close of WWII in Europe, when the Russian army and the combined American and British armies were rushing to meet each other over the bodies of a defeated German army in a devastated country, the German foreign minister, Count Lutz Schwerin von Krosigk made a speech in Berlin, reported in the London *Times* on May 3, 1945, in which he used the Nazi-coined propaganda phrase "Iron Curtain" in precisely the same context repeated later by Churchill in Missouri. Then, on May 12, just three days after the German surrender had taken place, Churchill wrote a letter to Truman, who had become President one month earlier after the sudden death of Franklin D. Roosevelt, to express his concern about the future of Europe and to say that an "Iron Curtain" had come down to conceal everything that was going on within the Russian sphere of Eastern Europe.[4]

This was a clever thrust by the old master, along the road to widening the tensions and splitting the alliance between the Soviet Union and the Western powers. This deft move by Churchill planted the seed of a potent idea in the mind of the new president, early and at a most opportune time.

Nearly one year later, on March 4 and 5, 1946, Truman and Churchill traveled on the President's special train from Washington to Missouri, where, at Westminster College in Fulton, Churchill delivered those historic lines: "From Stettin in the Baltic to Trieste in the Adriatic, an Iron Curtain has descended across the continent."

Most historical publications and media sources would have us believe it was this memorable occasion that marked the end of the wartime alliance with the USSR and the beginning of the Cold War. But, as we have seen, this was not so. The Grand Strategy decision to create a new bipolar world had already been made in 1944–45,[5] and the partners in this new global power structure were to be the United States, Great Britain, France, Germany, and Japan, three of the WWII victors and two of the vanquished.

The great array of forces of WWII were rapidly disbanded by President Truman in 1945. He disbanded the OSS on October 1, 1945, and shortly thereafter, on January 22, 1946, he issued a directive creating a new Central Intelligence Group (CIG) to be jointly staffed and funded by the Departments of State, War, and Navy. During these postwar years, a massive new propaganda line trumpeted across the land that the United States represents the world of free enterprise and that it would destroy socialism.

For this purpose, this new type of warfare was born, and its continuing battles were to be waged in Third World countries by a secret and invisible army. The OSS, the CIG, and later the CIA constituted the advance guard of that secret army in the United States.

Although the alliance between the West and the Soviet Union during WWII had been welded in the heat of battle, it had never been on too firm a footing. This was especially true of its structure in the Far East. The Chinese leader, Chiang Kai-shek, was as much a dictator as either Hitler or Mussolini. He was our ally, and his greatest wartime threat came from the Communist faction under Mao Tse-tung, who was allied ideologically with Stalin. As the fortunes of war began to shift from Europe to the Far East during the latter part of 1943, it became essential that there be a "Grand Strategy" meeting among the great Allied powers. They had never met together.

In this climate, President Roosevelt maneuvered to have Chiang Kai-shek join him in Cairo for a November 22–26, 1943, meeting with Churchill. Roosevelt wanted to create the atmosphere of a "Big Four" by placing Chiang on the world stage. Chiang appeared in Cairo, along with his attractive and powerful wife, Madame Chiang Kai-shek—née May Ling Soong, daughter of Charlie Jones Soong and sister of T. V. Soong, at that time the wealthiest man in the world. Few pictures produced during WWII have been more striking than those of Chiang and Roosevelt "apparently" joking with each other on one side and an "apparently" convivial Churchill and Madame Chiang smiling together on the other.

As a result of this conference, the public learned that Chiang had promised to increase Chinese support of British and American plans to sweep through Burma to open a new, and more practical, road via Burma to China and that the United States would base units of its new giant B-29 bombers at the front in the China-Burma-India theater for direct attacks upon the Japanese, via bases on the mainland of China.

With the close of the Cairo Conference, the Churchill and Roosevelt delegations flew to Tehran for their own first meeting with Marshal Stalin. This much was released to the public. A fact that was not released, and that even to this day has rarely been made known, is that Chiang and the Chinese delegation were also present at the Tehran Conference of November 28–December 1, 1943.

As noted, the Big Four alliance was "jerry-rigged" at best. There were

many strategic matters that had to be resolved. With the agreement by
the West to invade France a matter of priority, these other matters
involved plans for the defeat of Japan. First of all, Stalin agreed to join
the war against Japan once Germany surrendered. In return, he agreed
to help Chiang by speaking to his friend Mao Tse-tung about relaxing
military pressures against Chiang's Nationalist Army from that front in
China. In fact, only one week after the Allies had invaded Normandy,
Mao Tse-tung made a rare public pronouncement that he would aid
Chiang in his fight against Japan. In other words, Roosevelt and
Churchill had lived up to their promises made in Tehran, and Joe Stalin
had lived up to his.

These agreements have become public, but others that have had an
enormous impact upon Far East developments since WWII have not.
First of all, most historians doubt that Chiang and his wife actually
attended the conference in Tehran. I can confirm that they did, because
I was the pilot of the plane that flew Chiang's delegation to Tehran.
(Chiang and his wife traveled either with Roosevelt or in another U.S.
military aircraft.)

During these important meetings, plans for the future of Southeast
Asia were discussed, and many of the developments that we have
witnessed from 1945 to 1965 undoubtedly had their origins in Cairo and
Tehran. They were not simply social gatherings because Madame
Chiang was there; more likely, because she was there, much more
important business was discussed than might have occurred otherwise.
Again we witness the ways of the power elite—and not necessarily those
of the nominal leaders, who so often are no more than their puppets.

Of interest to our story about Vietnam, it will be noted:

At the Tehran Conference in 1943, Stalin and Chiang Kai-shek
both approved Roosevelt's proposal for a trusteeship for Indochina,
but Churchill was vehemently against the idea. Roosevelt said he
told Churchill that Chiang Kai-shek did not want either to assume
control over Indochina or to be given responsibility for administering a trusteeship in Indochina.

Churchill replied, "Nonsense," to which Roosevelt retorted,
"Winston, this is something which you are just not able to
understand. You have four hundred years of acquisitive instinct in
your blood and you just do not understand how a country might
not want to acquire land somewhere if they can get it. A new
period has opened in the world's history, and you will have to
adjust to it."[6]

Sometime during the next year, 1944, Roosevelt added, on this subject: "The British would take land anywhere in the world even if it were only a rock or sandbar."[7]

The reader should note the special significance of this exchange in Tehran as it pertains to the "real property" propaganda scheme mentioned above. As Roosevelt confirmed, this has been a paramount driving force of British foreign policy since the days of Queen Elizabeth and the founding of the East India Company during the century following Magellan's voyage and the return of the ship *Victoria* with the proof that Earth was, in fact, a sphere with a finite surface and fixed distribution of the wealth of its real property and natural resources.

This is an unusually important bit of history. The Roosevelt family, and especially the Delanos, have owed their wealth to the old "China trade." They were well aware of the work of the British East India Company in the Far East since A.D 1600. President Roosevelt was right when he said to Churchill, "You have four hundred years of acquisitive instinct in your blood."

Once the world leaders and great financiers of that earlier period realized that the surface of Earth was finite, and therefore limited in area, and that the natural resources of Earth were limited, too, they began immediately to "stake out their claims" on all the land they could grab, regardless of whether or not it was already inhabited. As the years progressed, they came to believe that "they had the right." Evidence of the belief in this "right" exists to this day—witness Vietnam and the continuing Kurdish problem in the Middle East, where recently created borders have left the ancient Kurds with no homeland of their own.

Roosevelt, who understood this concept well as a result of his own family's China Trade connections, emphasized a point that he knew to be true: the centuries of belief on the part of British leadership, among others, that the territories they "discovered" (despite the fact that the indigenous population may have been there for thousands of years) belonged to them. Churchill gave evidence that this same East India belief in the proprietary colony was still alive when he and the other leaders discussed postwar plans for Southeast Asia. He felt perfectly comfortable making such colonialist decisions about these countries, with or without their consent.

This driving force continues. When oil is found in the Middle East, it is controlled by the petroleum companies. When gold is found in South Africa, it is controlled by corporate mining interests. And, if such things of value cannot be controlled by direct colonization, they are controlled by an equally powerful and oppressive economic force called the World Bank or International Monetary Fund. In the process, genocide is practiced regularly to limit "excesses" and to preserve Earth for the "fittest." More than anyone else, Franklin D. Roosevelt understood this characteristically "British instinct," and when confronted with the grave issue of "postwar colonialism" at the meeting of the "Big Four" in Tehran, he spoke boldly to Churchill—in front of the Chinese, who had suffered so much from the East India Company mentality, and before the Russians, who had suffered so much from British economic power after World War I.

That was truly a momentous discussion in an unequaled setting, as reported in one of this government's own publications. Why hasn't more been written about this story, and why hasn't the simple fact that Chiang and his influential wife, May Ling Soong, were there in Tehran to witness this drama between Winston Churchill and Franklin D. Roosevelt been included in history books of the time?

Churchill never forgot, and never forgave, Roosevelt for this exchange. During the Yalta Conference in early February 1945, the subject of "trusteeships" for various British, French, and Dutch colonies came up again. When the heads of state (Churchill, Stalin, and Roosevelt) met during that session, Churchill was reported to have "exploded," declaring: "I absolutely disagree. I will not have one scrap of British territory flung into that arena...as long as every bit of land over which the British flag flies is to be brought back into the dock, I shall object as long as I live."[8]

Before departing from this subject, I should add a brief personal account that ties together these two most unusual stories. As I was flying the Chinese delegation from Cairo to Tehran in a VIP Lockheed Lodestar, I had to land at the airport in Habbaniya, Iraq, for fuel. While we were on the ground, an air force B-25 arrived. The pilot, Capt. Leon Gray, was a friend of mine, and with him as copilot was Lt. Col. Elliott Roosevelt. They were both from an aerial reconnaissance unit in Algiers.

During this refueling interlude, I introduced the Chinese to Elliott and his pilot. Elliott told us that his father had invited him to attend the conference because he wanted him to meet Marshal Joseph Stalin. This meeting in Tehran between Elliott and Stalin became part of a most unusual incident that took place only a few years later.

As reported in *Parade* magazine on February 9, 1986, Elliott Roosevelt wrote that he had visited Stalin in 1946 for an interview. This had reminded him of something quite extraordinary that had occurred at the time of President Roosevelt's sudden death less than two months after the Yalta Conference.

At that time, 1945, Soviet ambassador Andrei Gromyko had been directed by Stalin to view the remains of the dead President, but Mrs. Roosevelt had denied that request several times.

While Elliott was with Stalin in 1946, this subject arose again. According to Elliott Roosevelt, this is what Stalin said:

> "When your father died, I sent my ambassador with a request that he be allowed to view the remains and report to me what he saw. Your mother refused. I have never forgiven her."
>
> "But why?" Elliott asked.
>
> "They poisoned your father, of course, just as they have tried repeatedly to poison me. Your mother would not allow my representative to see evidence of that. But I know. They poisoned him!"
>
> "'They'? Who are 'they'?" Elliott asked.
>
> "The Churchill gang!" Stalin roared. "They poisoned your father, and they continue to try to poison me. The Churchill gang!"

One of the best-kept and least-discussed secrets of early Cold War planning took place sometime before the surrender of Japan. It had a great impact upon the selection of Korea and Indochina as the locations of the early "Cold War" hostilities between the "Communists" and the "anti-Communists."

Despite the terrific damage done to mainland Japan by aerial bombardment, even before the use of atomic bombs, the invasion of Japan had been considered to be an essential prelude to victory and to "unconditional" surrender. Planning for this invasion had been under way for years. As soon as the island of Okinawa became available as the launching site for this operation, supplies and equipment for an invasion force of at least half a million men began to be stacked up, fifteen to twenty feet high, all over the island.

Then, with the early surrender of Japan, this massive invasion did not occur, and the use of this enormous stockpile of military equipment was not necessary. Almost immediately, U.S. Navy transport vessels began to show up in Naha Harbor, Okinawa. This vast load of war matériel was reloaded onto those ships. I was on Okinawa at that time, and during some business in the harbor area I asked the harbormaster if all that new matériel was being returned to the States.

His response was direct and surprising: "Hell, no! They ain't never goin' to see it again. One-half of this stuff, enough to equip and support at least a hundred and fifty thousand men, is going to Korea, and the other half is going to Indochina."

In 1945, none of us had any idea that the first battles of the Cold War were going to be fought by U.S. military units in those two regions beginning in 1950 and 1965—yet that is precisely what had been planned, and it is precisely what happened. Who made that decision back in 1943–45? Who selected Syngman Rhee and Ho Chi Minh to be our new allies as early as mid-1945?

This is another one of those windows that permits us to see that some decision had to have been made in some detail by the power elite; yet there is absolutely no record of who made the decisions and for what purpose. Such action is rarely, if ever, proved by positive testimony. In such instances, circumstances bear more compelling witness than proof gained from other sources. As the years have passed, we have witnessed the proof. The U.S. involvement in what later became known as the Vietnam War began on the very day of the Japanese surrender, September 2, 1945. We have seen the remainder of the scenario unfold over the years.

In 1945, OSS units working with Syngman Rhee in Korea and with Ho Chi Minh in Vietnam had set up and coordinated these enormous shipments of equipment into those two Japanese-devastated countries. Those shipments forecast that in these two locales would be fought the two greatest conflicts of the Cold War to date and that both would be fought "Cold War style," without a military objective and to no victorious conclusion. If, and when, other such conflicts occur, they will necessarily follow the same pattern and will reach similar conclusions, as we have seen more recently in the "Gulf War."

By the end of WWII the great financial powers of the Western world, aided by their omnipotent Wall Street lawyers, had decided it was time to create a new world power center of transnational corporations and, in the process, to destroy the Soviet Union and socialism. To achieve this enormous objective they chose as their principle driving force the covert power and might of the CIA and its invisible allies.

They began this move cautiously. During 1947, the Congress worked on legislative language that would establish a new National Security Council (NSC), a new Department of Defense (DOD) with a Joint Chiefs of Staff (JCS) structure, and separate departments of the army, navy, and air force. Almost as an afterthought, the National Security Act of 1947 provided for the creation of a Central Intelligence Agency.

There was much opposition to this concept. The United States had never before had, in peacetime, a full-fledged intelligence agency operating in the international arena. Traditionally, there were intelligence organizations in the army, navy, FBI, and Treasury and State departments; but these were all specialist staffs designed to perform the work required for the functional support of their various masters. Furthermore, the work of these traditional organizations was almost always limited to pure intelligence and did not intrude into the area of "fun and games," or clandestine operations.

Therefore, when the language of the National Security Act of 1947 was drafted—primarily as written by that most gifted lawyer-statesman Clark Clifford—it was designed to calm the waters. It was the intent of the sponsors of this legislation to have the CIA created, no matter what the language of the law contained, in order to get over the threshold. They knew that no matter what was written into the law, the CIA, under a cloak of secrecy, could be manipulated to do everything that was requested of it later.

The law that was passed by Congress and signed by President Truman created this Central Intelligence Agency and placed it under the direction of the National Security Council. The agency's statutory authority is contained in Title 50 U.S.C. Section 403(d). To facilitate the creation of the agency, its expressed legal duties were limited to "coordinating the intelligence activities of the several departments and agencies in the interest of national security." This modest language was chosen specifically to overcome objections expressed by such members of Congress as Rep. Clarence Brown (R-Ohio), who said:

> I am very much interested in seeing the United States have as fine a foreign military and naval intelligence as they can possibly have, but I am not interested in setting up here in the United States any particular central police agency under any President, and I do not care what his name may be, and just allow him to have a Gestapo of his own if he wants to have it. . . .
>
> Every now and then you get a man that comes up in power and that has an imperialist idea.

T W O

The CIA in the World of the H-Bomb

WHEN HE IS UP AGAINST a team of determined financiers, transnational industrialists, and their crack Wall Street lawyers, even the President of the United States can be frustrated, misled, and confused. Harry S. Truman became President on April 13, 1945, after the death of Franklin Delano Roosevelt, while the country was deeply involved in the greatest armed conflict of history—the world war against the Axis powers of Germany, Japan, and Italy (which by that time had surrendered). Truman had been vice president under Roosevelt, but at the time he became President he had never heard of the secret work on the atom bomb or of its creator, the Manhattan Project. He was also not aware that "the Office of Strategic Services had issued a policy paper in April 1945 (before the surrender of Germany) stating that the Russians seemed to be seeking to dominate the world, and recommending that the U.S. take steps to block Russian expansionism."[1]

Furthermore, he had not been told that an element of the underground OSS, along with its British counterparts, had been working covertly with the Nazis and with Nazi sympathizers in Europe as early as September 1944 and that plans had been made to alienate the United States's wartime ally, the Soviet Union, and to create a hostile, bipolar world. Harry Truman was not aware of, nor acquainted with, the reality of that invisible superpower elite that Winston Churchill called the High Cabal. He was told the details of the Manhattan Project on April

20

25, 1945, and learned about these other facts of public life through harsh experience.

Germany surrendered on May 9, 1945. The war against Japan had been accelerated, culminating in the costly battle of Okinawa. On July 19, 1945, Truman arrived in Potsdam, a suburb of Berlin, for his first meeting with the Soviet leader, Joseph Stalin, and the wartime leader of Great Britain, Winston Churchill. He had to deal with them as equal allies despite the widening rift being created clandestinely between them.

On July 25, 1945, exactly three months after he had first learned of the atomic bomb, Truman took the opportunity to tell Stalin privately that the United States had successfully developed a major new weapon. He did not tell Stalin that this new weapon was based on a harnessing of the atom for explosive purposes. In response, Stalin showed no interest whatsoever and gave no substantive reply. Truman was perplexed. Did Stalin already know about the success in New Mexico of the first atomic explosion, on July 16, 1945? Had he somehow known about things that Truman himself did not know, long before Truman knew them? We may never know; but this is the way of the clandestine world.

More importantly, was Stalin aware of the fact that the Cold War had already begun and that the Soviet Union would no longer be a full partner in the Western alliance? Stalin did not reveal his hand, but as we have later discovered, he ordered his own experts, under Igor Kurchatov, to accelerate the Russian nuclear program.

Truman's low-key announcement about this new weapon to Stalin at Potsdam was, without a doubt, the starting point of the greatest and most futile arms race in history. The world had moved into the awesome era of nuclear power and clandestine operations.

For Truman, these Potsdam sessions were a rare education, if nothing else. On the one hand, he learned to deal with Stalin, and on the other hand, he saw his strongest and closest ally, Winston Churchill, depart abruptly when his party failed to win in the concurrent British elections. This placed another burden on Truman. He had first to meet and then to become acquainted with the new prime minister, Clement Attlee, and his newly assembled staff of British advisers during the course of a momentous series of meetings.

Of course, Truman was not alone. The President was surrounded by his military and diplomatic staff, a coterie of longtime political cronies, and one other man who went generally unnoticed.

This other man was Edwin Pauley, a prominent oilman from California, a bank director, and a construction company executive. His official position was head of the American delegation to the Allied Reparations Commission in Moscow. Pauley was the quiet representative of the world of finance, industry, and power. His job was to see that the new President adhered to the course already planned for the "Cold War" world.

"The first impression that one gets of a ruler and of his brains," Machiavelli wrote, "is from seeing the men that he has about him."

We may be sure this very point was not lost on that shrewd veteran of the Kremlin, Stalin, as he looked around the room at Truman and his staff. The Truman team was formidable, belying the Truman "country boy" image. The post–World War II era, it was clear, would be managed and guided by the demands and specifications of those financiers, industrialists, and Wall Street lawyers who were so well represented at Potsdam.

While in Potsdam in July, Truman received the news of the successful test-firing of an atomic device at Alamogordo, New Mexico. During the next week, there were countless discussions among the American staff and with the British concerning whether or not to use the atomic bomb in Japan. Truman had two principal options: He could modify the "unconditional surrender" terms of the Roosevelt policy toward Japan, which would permit the Japanese to retain their emperor, or he could refuse to modify the terms and give Japan no alternative but to continue to fight until the United States had used the atom bomb.

The consensus that guided Truman's decision was that the bombs should be used, as much to impress the Soviets and the rest of the world with their overwhelming power as to further crush the hapless Japanese. The rationale was that the use of the bombs to bring about the abject surrender of the Japanese would save millions of lives—American and Japanese—by precluding a costly invasion of a kamikaze-indoctrinated country.

The first bomb was dropped on an already war weary Japanese population at Hiroshima on August 5 and a second over Nagasaki on August 9. The Japanese surrendered on August 14. During the final stages of the war, the Japanese had been unable to send aircraft up to attack American bombers, because they lacked essential parts and, quite frequently, fuel.

As a gesture of hospitality, the Japanese had opened the American prisoner-of-war camps in Japan weeks before the bombs were dropped, and hundreds of Americans wandered freely throughout Japan, waiting for the day when the first American transport aircraft would arrive to carry them away. I was a pilot of one of the first heavy transport aircraft to land at the only Japanese air base that had not been destroyed by bombs, near Atsugi, not far from Yokohama, during late August 1945.

As we flew down through the heavy cloud layers that were remnants of a major hurricane that had swept over the islands of Japan, we broke out into a rainy overcast over Tokyo Bay and saw the ships of the U.S. Navy at anchor, with the battleship *Missouri* in their midst. The air base at Atsugi was covered with new Japanese aircraft that had never seen combat. We saw some military trucks. They were operating on methane and were made entirely of wood, except for the most vital parts, which had to be made of steel.

Everywhere we looked, we found overwhelming evidence that the Japanese dream of empire had been shattered. It was clear that the long-planned invasion of Japan would have been unnecessary, even without the use of the two atomic bombs.

We took off from the Atsugi airfield after leaving a contingent of U.S. Marines there to serve with General MacArthur's bodyguard and flew low over Yokohama and Tokyo. Although I had seen war-devastated cities in Russia, in Europe, and in the Philippines, I had never experienced anything to equal the "firebomb" destruction of Tokyo. It was total. More than fifteen thousand people had died by asphyxiation in a single city block where I rented a house during 1952–54, in the Shibuya-Ku district. Tokyo, that enormous city, had been so flattened that, from our low-flying aircraft, we had an unobstructed view of trolley cars operating from one side of the downtown area to the other. Almost every building had been destroyed, and the streets were a mass of rubble.

We flew quite low down the east coast of the main island, Honshū. In one of the most memorable and stark manifestations of utter surrender that can be imagined, the Japanese people had tied broad strips of white cloth to the ends of long bamboo poles. They had then bound these poles to the top branches of the ever-present pine trees. The whole country appeared to be flying the white emblem of surrender.

In the school playgrounds, the children stopped their games and stood frozen, with heads lowered, as our big aircraft flew over them. Fortunately for all of us, we were not on a bombing mission. Then we came to the ruins of what had once been the city of Hiroshima. As I have said, I have seen the destruction of warfare. I had always put the shell of the Russian city of Rostov at the head of my list of the most devastated cities. During the ebb and flow of the great battles in Russia, Rostov had been destroyed four times, twice by the attacking Germans and twice by the returning Russians. But here was Hiroshima just five hundred feet below us. On the coast, at the end of a small valley, what remained of that beautiful city looked like the ashes of a bonfire that, all of a sudden, had been blown out by a massive gust of wind. Nothing moved. Only the pattern of the streets and bridges preserved the identity of a once-proud city.

When President Truman returned to Washington following his meetings in Potsdam, he announced the results of the conference. At the same time, it was announced that a second atomic bomb had been dropped on Nagasaki. Japan surrendered, and the necessary documents were signed on September 2, 1945, by all parties on the deck of the *Missouri*. World War II was over. A historic era had ended—with implications that no one in the world fully grasped at that time. Never again would it be possible—or desirable—for those with the power over a nation or an alliance of nations to wage an all-out, unfettered, classic war on another group of nations with an expectation of victory that would include an assurance of their own survival. Nuclear weapons had changed all that.

That span of history, from man's first use of clubs and spears to the mass destruction of World War I and World War II—with machine guns, tanks, artillery, ships, and aircraft—had ended with the advent of the atom bomb. If anyone in power was not convinced of this fact by 1945, he had only to wait for the results of the hydrogen bomb tests in the fall of 1952. That single blast, the Mike Shot on Eniwetok Atoll, blew a hole deeper than the height of the Empire State Building. Or he could have waited a bit longer, for the Bravo test shot of the lithium-deuteride "fission-fusion-fission" H-bomb of 1954, when fallout created lethal dosages of radioactivity for 140 miles downwind in a belt 20 miles wide, in addition to massive destruction far greater than that of the earlier test at Eniwetok.

During the postwar years, a number of important events took place as mankind was herded from the old era to the new. The Cold War, based upon a structured East-West confrontation, provided the basis for a new type of very lethal, global conflict that would depend upon large, invisible armies concealed under the benign cover of intelligence organizations. Almost immediately after the end of hostilities, the great armed forces that had fought World War II were dismantled and disbanded. Nearly all of their arms, ammunition, and other matériel were salvaged, sold, or given away to make way for new procurement.

The early creation of the Central Intelligence Agency and of the Office of Policy Coordination (OPC) was an inevitable progression after World War II. With the decision already made to turn the Soviet Union, almost overnight, from a wartime ally to a "peacetime" adversary, it became necessary to create an organization that could, in time of "peace," continue the eternal conflict using the networks of agents and spies in Eastern Europe that had been established by the Allies and by the Nazis during the war. The utilization of the World War II Nazi agent networks in Eastern Europe and the Soviet Union became a major characteristic of the new Cold War strategy. The CIA was joined by "Allies" foreign and domestic, governmental and civilian.

In fact, "peacetime operations" became the new Orwellian euphemism for military-type covert operations, often on a mammoth scale. These "peacetime operations" were carried out whether or not they were secret and whether or not they could be disclaimed plausibly, without benefit of a declaration of a state of war among the adversaries. This was an important shift. Any country—whether it was the United States or the Soviet Union, or even a smaller country, such as Greece or Israel—that employed its undercover forces in peacetime, within the borders of another country with whom it was not officially at war, ignored and degraded the age-old concepts of the independence of nations and of national sovereignty.

On October 1, 1945, Truman directed the termination of the OSS. While the legislation for the new defense establishment and the CIA was being written and debated, the President established the Central Intelligence Group as an interim measure. The existence of the CIG made it possible to maintain the covert-agent assets of the wartime OSS wherever they existed and to provide organizational cover for former Nazi general Reinhard Gehlen and his intelligence staff, along with their voluminous files of former Nazi, anti-Communist agents and spies that were concealed in the undercover networks of Eastern Europe and in the USSR.

Allen Dulles had been instrumental in arranging, with Gehlen, for this most unusual conversion of one of Hitler's most sinister generals into an officer in the U.S. Army, but the details of Gehlen's personal surrender and subsequent flight to the United States—in General Eisenhower's own VIP aircraft—were arranged by U.S. Army officers. The senior officer of this plan was Eisenhower's chief of staff, Gen. Walter Bedell Smith, who served immediately after World War II as the U.S. ambassador to Moscow, and, upon his return from Moscow in October 1950, as the director of central intelligence. Also involved in this plan was Col. William Quinn, later Lieutenant General Quinn and head of the Defense Intelligence Agency (DIA).[2]

It is important to note the active role of these U.S. Army officials in this unprecedented move of Hitler's own intelligence chief, Gehlen, directly into the U.S. Army as an officer by a special act of the Congress. This was not a casual incident. The move, planned before the end of the war with Germany and directed from the top, was a classic example of the work of the power elite.

Shortly after the passage of the National Security Act of 1947, the National Security Council met, on December 19 of that year, for the first time. The council had hardly waited for the ink to dry on the new law before it ignored its stricture—that the CIA limit itself to the "coordination" of intelligence—and rushed the fledgling agency into covert action. National Security Council Directive #4 directed the newly appointed director of central intelligence, Adm. Roscoe Hillenkoetter, "to carry out covert psychological warfare," much against his own professional desires. To this end, a "special procedures group" was set up immediately, and, among other things, it became involved in the covert "buying" of the nationwide election in Italy.

This early covert operation was considered successful, and in 1948 the National Security Council issued a new directive to cover "clandestine paramilitary operations, as well as political and economic warfare." This new directive gave birth to a new covert action unit that replaced the "special procedures group." In deference to the language of the law, if not the intent, this new unit—the most covert of all sections—was named the Office of Policy Coordination.

As quoted earlier, "The deepest cover story of the CIA is that it is an intelligence organization." The OPC was headed by Frank Wisner, formerly the OSS station chief in Romania. Frank Wisner and Allen Dulles, then with the OSS in Switzerland, were among the first U.S. officials to begin contact in 1944 with selected Nazis and Nazi sympathizers—with a "Blowback" ("exfiltration" of former Nazis with desired technological skills) operation known as the "Deep Water" (code name only) project—for their eventual evacuation to the United States.

Of course, the ostensible reason given in most instances for this unusual action was that these Nazis were scientists and technical experts whose skills would be useful in the United States and that it was necessary to keep them out of the hands of the Soviets. As we know today, this was hardly the truth. It was Wisner who had arranged a transfer of a large number of prisoners of war from the Balkans via

Turkey and Cairo in the fall of 1944. Among this large group—mostly American flight crew members who had been shot down during heavy bombing attacks over the Ploesti oil fields of Romania—were a number of pro-Nazi intelligence specialists who were fleeing the Balkans, scattering before the approach of the Russian army.

In his new position with the OPC, Wisner was able to control a large group of Eastern European agents in a massive network of spies. At the same time, he could protect them and their U.S. contacts against hostile, anti-Nazi, and Soviet capture—possibly even assassination. The OPC was a little-known, most unusual organization, especially within the U.S. government, where such deeply covert activity had never taken place before.

As initially created, the OPC was totally separate from the CIA's intelligence collection (another function not specifically authorized by law) and analysis sections. The OPC's chief had been nominated by the secretary of state and approved by the secretary of defense. The funds for this office were concealed, as were much of the CIA funds, in the larger budget of the Department of Defense. Policy guidance and specific operational instructions for the OPC bypassed the director of central intelligence completely and came directly from State and Defense. In other words, the OPC was all but autonomous.

It is in this example of the OPC that we discover most clearly how the new invisible army was brought into the government and created in secrecy. There was no law that authorized such an organization or the wide range of covert functions it was created to perform. When it began, the director of central intelligence, if asked, could have denied that he had anything to do with it, and no one would have thought—or dared—to ask the secretaries of state or defense if they had become involved in covert operations or to ask them about an organization they could claim they did not know even existed. As we see, this most covert office was buried as deep within the bureaucracy as possible, and its many lines to agents and secret operations were untraceable.

Despite all this secrecy, however, the OPC grew from about three hundred personnel in 1949 to nearly six thousand contract employees by 1952. A large part of this sudden growth was due to the additional demands for covert action and other special operations that grew out of the Korean War and related activities. One of the first things Gen. Walter B. Smith did, when he returned from Moscow and became director of central intelligence, was to take over OPC completely and sever its connections with State and Defense—except for the concealment of funds in Defense and for the rather considerable support that was always provided by military units for these clandestine activities around the world.

This brings up another important characteristic of the invisible army. While the CIA administered the operations of this fast-growing organization, with its six thousand employees, it could always rely upon the military for additional personnel, transport, overseas bases, weapons, aircraft, ships, and all the other things the Department of Defense had in abundance. One of the most important items provided regularly by Defense was "military cover." OPC and other CIA personnel were concealed in military units and provided with military cover whenever possible, especially within the far-flung bases of the military around the world—even in Antarctica.

The covert or invisible operational methods developed by the CIA and the military during the 1950s are still being used today despite the apparent demise of the Cold War, in such covert activities as those going on in Central America and Africa, and even in such highly specialized activities as the preparation of "assassination manuals" of the type that was written by the CIA and discovered in Nicaragua in 1984. That manual was only a later version of one developed by the CIA in the 1950s. Today all of this clandestine activity amounts to big business, and the distinction between the CIA and the military is hard to discern, since they always work together.[3]

THREE

The Invisible Third World War

THE WORLDWIDE INVISIBLE WAR waged by the Soviet KGB and the
American Central Intelligence Agency over the past fifty years, and
under the cover that these war-making organizations were in fact
intelligence organizations, was being fought with novel tactics. Not only
was this type of underground warfare secret, but so were its methods.
Discerning readers were not surprised, then, to discover on an inside
page of the *New York Times* on July 25, 1985, a tiny two-inch article,
datelined Zaragoza, Spain, describing one of these Cold War battles,
being fought with these secret tactics.

TWO SPANISH OFFICERS SENTENCED
FOR ROLES IN FAKE EXECUTIONS

ZARAGOZA, Spain, July 24 (UPI)—Two army officers who herded
villagers into a public square for mock executions were sentenced
today to prison terms of four and five months, military authorities
said.

A military tribunal ruled Tuesday that officers, Capt. Carlos
Aleman and Lieut. Jaime Iniguez, had been overzealous in
carrying out orders.

"They were ordered to stage a mock invasion of a town and to
make it as realistic as possible, but they went too far," said a
Defense Ministry spokesman, Lieut. Jesus del Monte.

This bizarre incident occurred in Spain. Similar events, using the same tactics, take place somewhere in the world almost daily, despite the apparent demise of the Cold War. They have one unique characteristic, seldom if ever seen in regular warfare, that sets them apart. Incidents such as this one, reported by the *Times*, serve to incite warfare rather than to bring it to an end. To give the age-old concept new meaning, "They make war...out of practically nothing."

The methods used in Spain are almost precisely those used by the CIA in, among other cases, the Philippines in the early 1950s and Indochina from 1945 to 1965. These will be discussed in later chapters. It is important to note that tens of thousands of foreign "paramilitary" and Special Forces troops have been trained at various U.S. military bases under CIA supervision and sponsorship. Some of this training is highly specialized, using advanced weapons and war-related matériel. Some of it takes place at American universities and even in manufacturing plants, where advanced equipment for this type of warfare is being made.

Then there are the paramilitary forces of other nations that have been trained in the Soviet Union. Today these graduates, by the tens of thousands, are the leaders of the "elite" forces of many countries and the professionals used to breed a world of international terrorists. For the most part, they are not individuals or members of some small group, but participants in a most sophisticated, worldwide complex of organizations. The Spanish example is a perfect case study in describing the methods and tactics of such units. (For illustrative purposes, examples of operations in other countries will be merged with the Spanish example to portray more comprehensively the potential of these tactics.)

The Spanish army's Special Forces troops had been ordered to "stage a mock invasion of a town and to make it [look and feel] as realistic as possible." The army was ordered to create a battle that would appear to support evidence of insurgency. This is one of the secret methods of the secret war. These special armed forces are used as agitators. It is as though the fire department were being used to start fires, the police department employed to steal and kill, and doctors ordered to make people sick, to destroy their brains, to poison them. Such clandestine operations are designed to make war—even when they have to play both sides at the same time.

First of all, as stated so accurately in Leonard Lewin's *Report From Iron Mountain*,[1] "allegiance [to the State] requires a cause; a cause requires an enemy," and "...the presumed power of the enemy sufficient to warrant an individual sense of allegiance to a society must be proportionate to the size and complexity of the society."

Therefore, on a global scale, the Cold War required the USSR and the United States to have been enemies by need and by definition. Ever since the Bravo detonation of the hydrogen bomb, the world's political, economic, and military system has had to be bipolar. Those without massive weapons and the means to deliver them could not possibly take part effectively in such global warfare.

It has been politically necessary for each major power to have an enemy, even though both major powers knew that they no longer had any way to benefit from a traditional "all-out" war. Neither one could control its own destiny or its own society without the "threat" of the other. On a lesser scale, as we shall see in the Spanish example, the existence of "insurgents" lent validity to the charge of a "Communist-supported" insurgency, even though the scope of the "conflict"—that is, the "mock invasion of the town"—was purely local.

All leaders of all nations know that, as stated in *Report From Iron Mountain*, "The organization of a society for the possibility of war is its principal political stabilizer. It is ironic that this primary function of warfare has been generally recognized by historians only where it has been expressly acknowledged—in the pirate societies of the great conquerors."

That is the historical perspective. It has been the primary reason for the necessary prosecution of the Cold War—"necessary," that is, in the minds of those who are unable to see, or who choose not to see, that there are other reasons than conflict for the existence of Earth and man.

The Spanish application of this tactic of the secret war is interesting and threatens us all. In this case, the two army officers had been ordered to attack a town, with regular Spanish troops (albeit some of them disguised as natives), and to make it look and feel realistic. As undercover warriors, they were trained to do this. (No doubt, some were trained in the United States, where many of the weapons, activities, and techniques mentioned below are used in training.) Under other conditions at other times, these same trained men might have been told to hijack a civilian aircraft; they might have been told to set up a mock car-bombing; they might have been told to run a mock hostage operation. There is no difference. The only military objective of these battles, and of this type of global conflict, is to create the appearance of war itself.

Now, the Spanish, for reasons of their own, had decided to teach this town a lesson. To initiate this campaign, a psychological-warfare propaganda team arrived in town. They put up posters, made inflammatory speeches in the village square, and showed propaganda films on the walls of buildings at night to stir up the village, warning of the existence and approach of a band of "terrorist-trained insurgents." That night, as the movies were being shown before the assembled villagers, a firefight kit, prearranged to explode in sequence to resemble a true skirmish, was detonated on a nearby hillside. Flares and rockets filled the sky. A helicopter gunship or two joined the mock battle scenario. By the time this Special Forces PsyWar team left that town, the whole region had been alarmed by the presence of these "insurgents." The stage was set for the "mock invasion of the town," as ordered.

A few nights later, these two Spanish army officers (was the CIA involved?) divided their regular force into two groups: (a) the pseudoinsurgents and (b) the loyal regular forces. The "insurgents" took off their uniforms and donned native garb, the uniform of the "Peoples' Insurgents." Then they faded into the darkness and began to attack the town. First there was sporadic gunfire. Then some buildings went up in flames. Several big explosions occurred, and a bridge was blown up. The "insurgents" attacked the town as the villagers fled into the night. There was more gunfire, more burning and explosions. The "terrorists" looted the town and fired into the woods where the townspeople were hiding.

As the sun rose, an army unit in a convoy of trucks raced toward the town, entering it with guns ablaze. Above, a helicopter gunship added to the firepower. The "terrorists" were gunned down, left and right (all staged with blank ammunition). The others were rounded up and thrown into extra trucks under heavy guard. In short order, the victorious regular army captain had liberated the town. A loudspeaker in the helicopter called the villagers to return. All was safe! Fires were extinguished. Things returned to near normal.

Meanwhile, the captain remained with his interrogators, questioning the prisoners. Two "insurgent" leaders were discovered with false "terrorist" papers in their pockets and led back to the village square in chains. Charges were read against them, and the villagers observed them backed against the wall and shot! No sooner had the bodies hit the ground than they were picked up and tossed into the nearest truck. Justice had been done.

All trucks moved down the road. The battle was over. Before leaving, the captain turned to the town's mayor and warned him against further terrorism. The townspeople cheered the heroic captain as he left the town in command of the convoy. The forces of justice had been victorious. They drove on a few more miles, and the whole gang—loyal army and "terrorists"—had breakfast together. The "dead" men joined the feast.

This was the "mock battle." Although I have added technical details to the Spanish scenario, I have been to such training programs at U.S. military bases where identical tactics are taught to Americans as well as foreigners. It is all the same. As we shall see later, these are the same tactics that were exploited by CIA superagent Edward G. Lansdale and his men in the Philippines and Indochina.

This is an example of the intelligence service's "Fun and Games." Actually, it is as old as history; but lately it has been refined, out of necessity, into a major tool of clandestine warfare.

Lest anyone think that this is an isolated case, be assured that it was not. Such "mock battles" and "mock attacks on native villages" were staged countless times in Indochina for the benefit of, or the orientation of, visiting dignitaries, such as John McCone when he first visited Vietnam as the Kennedy-appointed director of central intelligence. Such distinguished visitors usually observed the action from a helicopter, at "a safe distance." A new secretary of defense, such as Robert McNamara, who had never seen combat, especially combat in Southeast Asia, would be given the treatment. It was evident to other, more experienced observers that the tracks through the fields had been made by the "Vietcong" during many rehearsals of the "attack." The war makers of Vietnam vintage left nothing to chance.

During the 1952–54 time period, when I flew into the Philippines, I spent many hours talking with Ed Lansdale, his many Filipino friends, such as Juan C. "Johnny" Orendain, Col. Napoleon D. Valeriano, and members of his CIA "anti-Quirino" team and heard them tell these same stories. They all worked with Ramon Magsaysay in those days and related how he would divide his Special Forces into the "Communist HUKs" and the loyal military and then attack villages in the manner described above. Before long Ramon Magsaysay had been "elected" president of the Philippines, and President Quirino was on his way out. Later, when I worked in the same office with Lansdale in the Pentagon, he would relate how he and his Saigon Military Mission teammates applied similar tactics in Indochina, both North and South.

Not long after the CIA had been created, limited by law "to coordinate intelligence," the National Security Council authorized the supersecret Office of Policy Coordination, under the wartime OSS station chief in Romania, Frank Wisner, to carry out certain covert operations of a similar nature. This is the organization Ed Lansdale was assigned to in November 1949. There he worked under an experienced Far East hand, Col. Richard G. Stilwell, in the Far East/Plans division. The clandestine warfare in Greece and Bulgaria, which occurred at about the same time, is another example of OPC's undercover work.

During the late forties, the CIA organized itself and grew. In these same years the OPC grew faster, and when Gen. Walter Bedell Smith, General Eisenhower's chief of staff during WWII, returned from Moscow, where he had been the U.S. ambassador, to become the director of central intelligence, one of his first official acts was to have the OPC removed from the secretary of state and the secretary of defense and to have it placed directly under his control in the CIA. Although there was no lawful basis for this momentous move, it was done without formal protest. Everyone involved knew that the real reason for the creation of the CIA was to be the lead brigade of U.S. forces during the Cold War period.

Then, with the election of President Eisenhower in 1952, Allen W. Dulles was made the director of central intelligence, General Smith became the deputy secretary of state, and John Foster Dulles was made secretary of state. The high command for the Cold War was in place, and the stage was set for the CIA's dominant role in the invisible war. The Korean War, which had begun in 1950, had served to cover the CIA's rapid expansion into that field.

By 1952 it had been decided that the time had come to replace Quirino as president of the Philippines. Since he was, ostensibly, a good friend of the United States and avowedly an anti-Communist, it would require some delicate diplomacy to bring that about. The reasons for the forced removal of a national leader do not always follow ideological or political lines. It is more likely, as in the case of Quirino, that he had relaxed his business priorities with the United States in favor of other countries, thus reducing American exports to the Philippines. And that could be sufficient grounds for the removal of a leader in the big power game of the nation-states.

While the United States maintained the customary diplomatic relations with the Quirino government and had a strong ambassador in Manila, that ambassador had on his staff a strong CIA station chief, one George Aurell. This cloak of normalcy could not be changed. The ambassador urged Quirino to hold an election. Elections would be good for Quirino and would serve to quell the opposition, said to consist of a Communist-supported HUK rebellion. Other than that, Quirino saw no opposition and no problems with an election. An election was scheduled—for later.

Meanwhile, unbeknownst to the ambassador and Aurell, the CIA slipped into the Philippines an undercover team headed by one of its superagents, Edward G. Lansdale. Although the true reason for his presence in Manila was not divulged to these senior Americans, this agent had access to certain anti-Quirino Filipinos. His ostensible role was to train selected Filipino army troops in PsyWar and other paramilitary tactics; his primary role, in fact, was to oust Quirino and to install Ramon Magsaysay in the office of president. The men selected for duty with Lansdale were put on regular training schedules with the U.S. Army and were trained outside of the Philippines. Then they were slipped back later into the Philippines and into their usual army units.

At the same time, all throughout the islands, the "HUK insurgency" was escalated by secret operations. News began to surface about the growing HUK insurgency. The HUKs were beginning to be found everywhere. There were reports of "HUK detachments" on all the islands. The rise of this notional "Communist" influence gave President Quirino what he thought was a strong platform. The Cold War "make war" tactic was well under way. Then the CIA made its move.

Lansdale had selected a handsome young Philippine congressman, Ramon Magsaysay, to play the role we have seen in the above scenario from Spain. He was to stage "mock attacks" and "mock liberations" on countless villages throughout the islands. Villages were attacked and destroyed by the "HUKs." Captain Magsaysay and his loyal band charged into town after town, killing and capturing the "HUKs" and liberating each village. This CIA agent had been equipped with the equivalent of a bookfull of blank checks that he used to finance the entire campaign. The CIA pumped out a flood of news releases, produced and projected propaganda movies, and held huge rallies—all to build up the reputation of the new "Robin Hood," Ramon Magsaysay. The plot was a success, and soon Magsaysay was made secretary of defense. Then, when the election campaign began, he ran for president against Quirino. Quirino was stunned by the entry of the "HUK Killer" hero into the campaign. But the president had one more ace up his sleeve: He had the traditional power to control the ballot boxes and to count the votes. An honest election was quite impossible in the Philippines.

The election was held. Magsaysay was certainly more popular than Quirino. Just prior to the election, the "HUKs" stirred themselves and rekindled Filipinos' memories of the gallant captain who had liberated their villages with a hot machine gun slung across his arm. The votes for Magsaysay poured in from all the islands. Then, from his office in the army, he sent out a command. He ordered his own loyal army troops to guard every voting site. Army men sealed and loaded the ballot boxes into trucks and drove them to Manila, where all the votes were counted, in public. As they said on the streets, "Under those conditions a monkey could have won against Quirino." Quirino was outmaneuvered by this new tactic. Magsaysay won easily and became president of the Philippines.

In Manila, Quirino was not the only man stunned by these events. So was the American ambassador and, even more so, his CIA station chief, George Aurell. They finally realized that the CIA had kept them in the dark by concealing the true role of one of its most powerful undercover teams. The CIA had quietly pulled off the deal, right under their noses. Another battle in the Cold War had been won over "the forces of communism"—or so they were led to believe.

Magsaysay had become president as a result of the application, many times over, of the same scenario that those two officers in Spain had used in their mock attack. With Magsaysay president, the city was too small for the U.S. ambassador, CIA station chief, and CIA secret agent—the Magsaysay creator, with his Madison Avenue–type warfare and election campaign. Also, quite magically, it seemed that the HUKs had vanished. Cecil B. deMille could not have staged it any better.[2]

These are examples of the new intelligence methods that are actually "make war" tactics. The Spanish incident and the Magsaysay "election campaign" serve to illustrate how they work. The incidents recounted below will serve to broaden the reader's understanding of the CIA's worldwide operations.

During the late forties, there was trouble in Greece, and the fledgling CIA got a foothold there and began to develop a major empire in that region. Greece became a base for overflight reconnaissance aircraft. Secret airfields were used in Greece and in Turkey; and from the time of the murder of Premier Muhammad Mossadegh of Iran, in 1953, the CIA was the most potent force behind the shaky throne of the Shah of Iran.

Foreign nationals from all over the world were trained in the methods of secret operations—that is, the use of high explosives, sabotage, communications, etc.—at military bases in the United States under CIA sponsorship. The CIA developed many of its own facilities around the world, but in most cases the agency concealed its presence on military facilities in one guise or another. Many of the skilled saboteurs and terrorists of today are CIA students of yesterday. Many skilled terrorists in Iran have gone to CIA schools and other training facilities and have become experts with the weapons and tactics of the trade. The first aerial hijackings were publicly solicited by the United States in return for big cash awards, plus sanctuary. Chuck Yeager, that grand old man with "The Right Stuff," was sent to Okinawa in 1953 to fly a MiG fighter plane that had been flown there by a Chinese pilot in return for a large cash reward. It's all part of the undercover game.

In the state of Virginia, CIA saboteur and explosives training at a secret facility, not too far from Colonial Williamsburg, created so much noise that wealthy neighbors complained to their senators. So the CIA had that training site moved to a more remote area in North Carolina, and it was used later for the Bay of Pigs operations.

This is no small business, and by the end of 1953 all signs pointed to Indochina: Vietnam, Laos, and Cambodia, a region of great wealth. It was freeing itself from Japanese occupation and French control and appeared to be "threatened" by Communists, so it was ripe for the application of the tactics of the CIA's invisible war.

The inconclusive Korean War had ground to a halt. The battleground of the Cold War was being moved from one region to another. As we mentioned earlier, more than one-half of all the military matériel once stockpiled on Okinawa for the planned invasion of Japan had been reloaded in September 1945 and transshipped to Haiphong, the port of Hanoi, Vietnam's capital. This stockpile had amounted to what the army called a 145,000 "man-pack" of supplies, that is, enough of everything required during combat to arm and supply that many men for war.

Once in Haiphong Harbor, this enormous shipment of arms was transferred under the direction of Brig. Gen. Philip E. Gallagher, who was supporting the OSS, and his associate, Ho Chi Minh. They had come from China to mop up the remnants of the defeated Japanese army. Ho's military commander Col. Vo Nguyen Giap, quickly moved this equipment into hiding for the day when it would be needed. By 1954, that time had come.

The Vietnamese Independence League (Viet Nam Doc Lap Dong Minh Hoi) or Vietminh, well armed with all this new American-made equipment, were waging a relentless guerrilla-type war against the

French, who had no idea that these rebels were so well armed or where such a vast store of arms had come from. In 1946, the French, thinking they would easily have their way, had reneged on giving the Vietnamese their freedom and independence. The British had withdrawn from India and Burma and the Dutch had left Indonesia, but the French had refused to leave Indochina. By 1954, sporadic guerrilla warfare had escalated and the French forces were in deep trouble. They had gotten themselves trapped in a small valley at Dien Bien Phu and were seeking more direct aid from the United States. The Cold War rumbled on, while the H-bombs remained in storage, gathering dust.

By mid-January 1954, the beleaguered French had 11,000 troops in fifteen battalions at Dien Bien Phu; the opposing Vietminh had 24,000 well-armed men in nineteen battalions. Nevertheless, the National Security Council believed this number of the Vietminh was insufficient to take Dien Bien Phu and defeat the French. However, they ordered a contingency plan to be drawn up by Allen Dulles, director of central intelligence, in the unlikely event of a French defeat.

During this NSC meeting of January 14, 1954, Secretary of State John Foster Dulles proposed that the United States prepare to carry on guerrilla operations against the Vietminh if the French were defeated, to make as much trouble for them as they had made for the French and for us. He believed the costs of such operations would be relatively low and that such a plan would provide an opportunity for the United States in Southeast Asia. The National Security Council agreed that the director of central intelligence should develop this plan for certain contingencies in Indochina.

This is the way these activities are initiated and directed. The warfare in Vietnam grew out of the events of this meeting just as assuredly as the explosion of a stick of dynamite is caused by the ignition of the fuse. It was this same John Foster Dulles in Korea, serving as no more than a "bipartisan consultant" to the Department of State in June 1950, who had said, "No matter what you say about the president of Korea [Syngman Rhee] and the president of Nationalist China [Chiang Kai-shek], those two gentlemen are the equivalent of the founder of the church...they are Christian gentlemen."

Then, while still in Korea, on June 19, 1950, John Foster Dulles made a most unusual speech before the Korean Parliament: "The American people welcome you as an equal partner in the great company of those who make up the free world.... I say to you: You are not alone. You will never be alone so long as you continue to play worthily your part in the great design of human freedom."

The Koreans, taken completely by surprise, wondered what he meant by those words. Less than one week later, when the North Koreans invaded South Korea, they found out. On the very next Sunday, while Dulles was still in Japan, the Korean War broke out with an attack on the south by the North Koreans. For someone of his stature—a senior partner of the largest law firm in New York City, Sullivan & Cromwell, and a man who had found a worldwide platform in the World Council of Churches—these had been most unusual statements on many counts. They were surpassed only by his "prediction" of the outbreak of the Korean War at that time. As for his other statement about "Christian gentlemen," few there are who have held the same opinion of President Rhee and Generalissimo Chiang, particularly the latter.

That was 1950; by January 1954, this same trio of Cold War activists—John Foster Dulles, Walter B. Smith, and Allen W. Dulles—were busy moving the center of operations from Korea to Indochina after an incidental interlude with Quirino in the Philippines.

On January 29, 1954, a meeting of the President's Special Committee on Indochina convened in the office of the deputy secretary of defense, Roger M. Kyes. The ostensible purpose was to discuss what could be done to aid the French, who had made some urgent requests for military assistance. A major item on the agenda of this meeting was the reading of the "Erskine Report" on Indochina. Gen. Graves B. Erskine, USMC (Ret'd), was assistant to the secretary of defense, special operations, 1953–61, and under President Eisenhower was chairman of the Working Group of the President's Special Committee on Indochina.[3] This important report "was premised on U.S. action short of the contribution of U.S. combat forces."

At the end of the meeting Allen Dulles, then the director of central intelligence, suggested that an unconventional-warfare officer, Col. Edward G. Lansdale,[4] be added to the group of American liaison officers that Gen. Henri Navarre, the French commander, had agreed to accept in Indochina. The committee thought this arrangement would prove to be acceptable and authorized Dulles to put his man in the Military Assistance Advisory Group (MAAG), Saigon.

The start of a new phase of the OSS/CIA activity in Indochina, this step marked the beginning of the CIA's intervention into the affairs of the government of Indochina, which at that time was French. It was not long before the reins of government were wrested from the French by the Vietminh, after their victory at Dien Bien Phu under the leadership of our friend of OSS days, Ho Chi Minh.

With this action, the CIA established the Saigon Military Mission

(SMM) in Vietnam. It was not often in Saigon. It was not military. It was CIA. Its mission was to work with the anti-Vietminh Indochinese and not to work with the French. With this background and these stipulations, this new CIA unit was not going to win the war for the French. As we learned the hard way later, it was not going to win the war for South Vietnam, either, or for the United States. Was it supposed to?

This is the way the CIA's undercover armies work, as they have operated in countless countries since the end of WWII. They move unobtrusively with a small team, plenty of money, and a boundless supply of equipment as backup. They make contact with the indigenous group they intend to support, regardless of who runs the government. Then they increase the level of activity until a conflict ensues. Because the CIA is not equipped or sufficiently experienced to handle such an operation when combat intensifies to that level, the military generally is called upon for support. At that time the level of military support has risen to such an extent that this action can no longer be termed either covert or truly deniable. At that point, as in Vietnam, operational control is transferred to the military in the best way possible, and the hostilities continue until both sides weary of the cost in men, money, matériel, and noncombatant lives and property. There can be no clear victory in such warfare, as we have learned in Korea and Indochina. These "pseudowars" serve simply to keep the conflict going. As we have said above, that is the objective of these undercover tactics.

This concept of the necessity of conflict takes much from the philosopher Hegel (1770–1831). He believed that each nation emerges as a self-contained moral personality. Thus, might certifies right, and war is a legitimate expression of the dominant power of the moment. It is more than that. It is a force for the good of the state since it discourages internal dissent and corruption and fosters the spiritual cement of patriotism.

The Center for Defense Information has reported, "During the past forty years there have been 130 wars of varying intensity, including forty-one that are active today, in which no less than 16 million people have died" (report circa 1985).

Of course, these were not true, all-out wars. They were the deadly skirmishes of the undercover armies of the Cold War. This enormous, smoldering cauldron is still boiling (as we have seen with "Desert Storm" in Iraq) and will not stop as long as warfare remains synonymous with nationhood. The elimination of war, in our structured society that is so much dependent upon superstition, implies the inevitable elimination of national sovereignty and the traditional nation-state. As the *Report From Iron Mountain* so aptly finds, "The war system [is] indispensable to the stable internal political structure...war provides the sense of external necessity without which no government can long remain in power....The organization of a society for the possibility of war is its principal political stabilizer....The basic authority of a modern state over its people resides in its war powers." You will have noted during the 1992 election campaign the frequency of the suggestion that the President may resort to "another" war in order to strengthen his popularity before the election.

Because there is no way to wage war with the H-bomb, there is no proper strategic role for today's armed forces. Thus, WWIII must be directed covertly by the so-called intelligence services. It has been a war between the CIA and the KGB, as one might expect; but as we have seen in these examples from Spain and the Philippines, it is sometimes no more than a conflict of the "make war" scenario, with the CIA,[5] or the KGB, creating and supporting both sides. The prevalence of worldwide terrorism shows this to be so.

FOUR

Vietnam: The Opening Wedge

ON SEPTEMBER 2, 1945, the representative of the Emperor of Japan signed the surrender papers laid before him by Gen. Douglas MacArthur on the deck of the battleship *Missouri* in Tokyo Bay. With that ceremony, the great drama of history called World War II came to a close. At that time, the Allied forces of the United States, China, Great Britain, and the Soviet Union declared themselves victors, and the military forces of fascism under Hitler, Mussolini, and Hirohito were declared to be the vanquished.

That is what historians have recorded, but what they failed to note is that this historic ceremony did not so much mark the end of war as it simply ended that chapter, that scenario, with that cast of characters.

Behind the scenes, American and Soviet intelligence services had plotted the next chapter in the book of war. They had already begun to drape an "Iron Curtain" over the borders of Eastern Europe to widen the split in the wartime alliance between the Soviets and the Western powers. It had already been decided by these clandestine services that a new bipolar world would be created, divided on the issue of communism. In the councils of the power elite[1] the issue was, as it has been for centuries, the absolute necessity of controlling society by the threat of war and the essential ceremonies of the perpetual preparation for war— what is now called "defense."

By September 2, 1945, this power elite had learned of its monstrous oversight, the greatest error of its lengthy hegemony over mankind.

Unwittingly, they had encouraged their scientists and engineers to design and produce nuclear weapons. These weapons had been detonated over Hiroshima and Nagasaki, and with the dropping of these two nuclear bombs, a horrifying realization crashed down upon the members of the power elite. War, their most essential and valuable tool—that device which had made it possible for them to control society and to maintain the existence of nations and of national sovereignty—had been taken from them by their own scientists. They no longer had even the fifty-fifty option of the duelist. All that remained to them was a choice between no war—and suicide. A war waged with hydrogen bombs would most certainly annihilate the combatants and end life on Earth. Their role in the war-making game would have to change. Thus, we have had the Cold War and other types of contrived conflict.

So, with the signing of that now-famous document on the deck of the battleship *Missouri*, a new form of war was launched in a world that believed what it read in the newspapers—that "the Last Great War" had ended.

From September 2, 1945, forward and for as long as mankind could be manipulated through a media that fully controlled what people would be told, the great powers would go through all of the motions involved in the preparation for war and in making war. But wars would henceforth be victoryless conflicts in controlled and limited scenarios.

Even the distinction between "us" and "them" and between "friend" and "foe" would have to be created arbitrarily. To lend this new warfare credibility, the power elite would create a bipolar world with two major superpowers, declared to be deadly enemies, armed to the teeth, and violently opposed to each other on every count. Each would be fortified as a defense against the other. This piling on of arms would increase annually, with no end in sight.

By September 2, 1945, this new scenario had been outlined. All that remained was to mold the opinion of the world, changing it from the mind-set of World War II to a new alignment based upon a massive East-West confrontation.

On that same date in the capital city of Hanoi, in Vietnam, a Declaration of Independence was signed by Ho Chi Minh as president of the new nation, the Democratic Republic of Vietnam (DRV). As incredible as it seems today, the declaration began with the famous lines "All men are created equal. They are endowed by their Creator with certain inalienable rights, among them are Life, Liberty, and the Pursuit of Happiness...."

Before the ink was dry on the documents being signed on the battleship *Missouri*, the first major battlefields of this new Cold War, Korea and Vietnam, had been selected and were being stocked with arms. All that remained was to create the political climate for the bipolar world and to line up the combatants, who, at this time, remained unaware of their new roles. Whereas Great Britain, the United States, and the Soviet Union had been allies against Germany, Italy, and Japan, all of this was going to change, even before World War II had ended.

When Ho Chi Minh signed the Declaration of Independence for his new nation on September 2, 1945, he read the following lines from that document: "A people who have courageously opposed French domination for more than eighty years, a people who have fought side by side with the Allies against the Fascists during these last years—such a people must be free and independent."

After his long struggle on the side of the United States and the Chinese against the Japanese, and with concrete evidence of U.S. support in the form of a vast shipment of arms, Ho Chi Minh had good reason to believe that his days of fighting to end French domination of his country were coming to a close.

The Japanese had surrendered and were leaving. The French had been defeated by the Japanese and would not return—or so he thought. Meanwhile, in the streets of Hanoi, agents of the Office of Strategic Services (OSS), continued to work with the Vietminh, who had rapidly taken control of North Vietnam when the Japanese war effort had collapsed.

Vo Nguyen Giap, Ho's brilliant military commander, while serving as minister of the interior of the provisional government, delivered a speech describing the United States as a good friend of the Vietminh. That, too, was in September 1945.

The manipulative strings of the power elite had not yet been pulled. The political roles had not yet been changed. It would take a few years of skillful propaganda to prepare the world for the new scenario. Time would pass before the power elite could create a new enemy—the Soviets and communism; and new friends—the former Fascists, Germany, Italy, and Japan, who were now to be known as friendly "anti-Communists."

On September 2, 1953, exactly eight years after World War II formally ended, President Dwight Eisenhower's new secretary of state, John Foster Dulles, delivered a major address before an American Legion convention in St. Louis. Although most of Dulles's remarks focused upon the final stages of the Korean War, which had ground to a frustrating stalemate, he included a most significant statement with regard to communism and Indochina. Dulles said:

> The armistice in Korea does not end United States concern in the Western Pacific area. A Korean armistice would be a fraud if it merely released Communist forces for attack elsewhere.
>
> In Indochina, a desperate struggle is in its eighth year.... We are already contributing largely in matériel and money to the combined efforts of the French and of Vietnam, Laos, and Cambodia.

In this remarkable statement, the "eight years" that Dulles cited on September 2, 1953, coincides precisely, to the day, with that date of September 2, 1945, when the surrender documents were signed in Tokyo Bay, when the ships sailed from Okinawa bound with an enormous supply of arms for Korea and Vietnam, and when the Declaration of Independence of the new Democratic Republic of Vietnam was signed by Ho Chi Minh in Hanoi, with American officials by his side. That could hardly have been a coincidence. World events are planned.

It was also almost eight years to the day when the first American casualty—Maj. A. Peter Dewey of the OSS—occurred in Vietnam. He was killed in a skirmish on the outskirts of Saigon on September 26, 1945.

John Foster Dulles, Eisenhower's secretary of state, recognized that September 2, 1945, was officially the date of the start of that "desperate struggle" in Indochina—later to become known as the Vietnam War. More importantly, during those eight years, the anti-Communist climate had been tuned to a hysterical pitch, both at home and abroad. South Korea had been invaded by "Communist" forces from the north, and through an intimate new medium known as television, moving pictures of an ongoing war were brought into the homes of millions of Americans for the first time. Families also watched while Sen. Joseph McCarthy detailed the internal threat of communism in government and industry. The public viewed the scenario directly, and as the power elite wanted it to: The Soviet Communists were the "enemy" all over the world. Ho Chi Minh and the Democratic Republic of Vietnam were no longer our friends. They, too, were now part of the "Communist" enemy.

Thus, although Secretary of State Dulles confirmed that the superpowers had been involved in a great invisible war and that it actually had begun on the same day that World War II ended, no one seemed to notice. Today it might be more accurate to say that the world war did not end, but that only the sides changed, and that the majority of the victims of that new type of warfare were the noncombatants of the Third World.

That new invisible war, based on East-West alignments, was, more than ever before, dependent upon the justification provided by a propaganda line that stretched all the way back to the early nineteenth century, to the genocidal theories of Malthus and Darwin.

As stated earlier, the Center for Defense Information had revealed in 1985 that "over the preceding years there had been 130 wars of varying intensity, including forty-one that were still active at that time in which no than 16 million people had died. This is a gross number that could match the casualty figures of almost any other period in history. For those who agree with Malthus, such enormous losses are to be expected; for those who agree with Darwin, those who survive are by definition the fittest.

The chain of events in Indochina from 1945 to 1965 that had led to the intervention of regular U.S. military forces there reveals the methods employed by the invisible services to produce this scale of global warfare and destruction. During the years 1945–53, the eight years alluded to by Secretary of State Dulles, the web was being drawn, and new alliances were being craftily woven. Friends became enemies; former enemies became allies. Whole new governments were formed to provide the political linkages essential to the requirements of the new bipolar structure of the world.

In many cases, the United States or the Soviet Union armed both sides of a conflict at different times. Dulles admitted in his St. Louis speech that the United States had been contributing to both sides of the newest "desperate struggle," that is, "to the combined efforts of the French and of Vietnam"—a rare admission, and true. As major manufac- turers of military supplies and equipment, it mattered not at all to the great industrial combines of the United States who bought their products. War was the best business in town.

Around 1960, the CIA made arrangements to have Soviet tank parts manufactured in the United States and delivered to the Egyptian army, which was equipped with Soviet-built tanks, in an attempt to prove that the United States was a more reliable friend and supplier to the Egyptians than their ally Russia. In this instance, as in many others, the

CIA was living up to the name given to it by R. Buckminster Fuller: "The Capitalist Welfare Department." Of course, this is what perpetual warfare is all about. One of the fundamental purposes of the Cold War has been to escalate arms production and sales on a global basis. This promotion is one of the things that the CIA does best.

(Because the early history of the Cold War and in particular of events in Indochina during the years 1945–65 is so fragmented, unclear, and unconventional, I am beginning here to enter the period of the withdrawal from Vietnam of the Japanese, the British, the Chinese, and the French, the creation and dissolution of Vietnamese governments, unconventional military activities, and a power elite tapestry that is intricate and complicated. During all of these years, it was the American presence and influence that continued. On the next several pages, I introduce several subjects that I know need more elaboration. I am setting the stage and urge you to read on to these answers and explanations as they enter the pages of history in a more lucid form.)

Since the OSS had been active in Indochina since World War II, it did not take long for its successor, the CIA, to begin to influence the flow of military equipment into that part of the world. Ho Chi Minh had been supplied with a tremendous stock of military equipment by the United States, and he expected to be able to administer his new government in Vietnam without further opposition.

But on September 23, 1945, shortly after the Democratic Republic of Vietnam had issued its Declaration of Independence, a group of former French troops, acting with the consent of the British forces that had arrived in Saigon from their sweep through Burma in the last days of World War II and armed with Japanese weapons stolen from surrender stockpiles, staged a local coup d'état and seized control of the administration of Saigon.

They installed the French government there once again. This move returned the Cochin—the southern sector of Vietnam—to French domination, although it had been agreed at the Potsdam Conference[2] that the British army was to have administrative control of the area. Now there were two governments in South Vietnam, with the British army remaining outside the flow of events and Ho Chi Minh's Democratic Republic of Vietnam in the north.

Based on the record of those years, the Vietminh hoped for American assistance or mediation in attaining their independence from the French. French entrenchment in Vietnam was not limited to its military. Vietnam was an old French colony. A number of French families had been born and raised there, as their parents had been. There were major French business interests there, such as the great Michelin rubber industry. The French banks in Indochina were among the most powerful in Asia. It was one thing to remove the French army; it was an entirely different matter to remove French interests. This is what the Vietminh wanted. They got neither.

The American secretary of state, Cordell Hull, in May 21, 1944, said, "It should be the duty of nations having political ties with such people [as the Indochinese]... to help aspiring peoples to prepare themselves for the duties and responsibilities of self-government, and to attain liberty."

On October 25, 1945, a senior Department of State official, John Carter Vincent, stated, "This [the Hull policy] continues to be American policy." His speech confirmed the earlier agreement and gave credence to Vietminh expectations. But this faith in the system proved to be fruitless.

All remaining Japanese forces had been rounded up and had surrendered to the British military command in Saigon by November 30, 1945. By January 1, 1946, the French had assumed all military commitments in Vietnam. Then, on January 28, 1946, command of all French forces in Vietnam passed from the British to Gen. Jean Leclerc of France. Thus began another phase of U.S. military aid in Indochina, this time to the French. Negotiations between the French and the Democratic Republic of Vietnam began early in 1946. Ho Chi Minh traveled to Paris in midyear, but the conference failed due to French intransigence. He continued his own efforts at negotiations until September, without obtaining the agreement he sought.

Fighting broke out between the French and the Vietminh in late November 1946, and by the end of the year guerrilla warfare had spread all over Vietnam. All hope for settlement of this French/Vietminh dispute evaporated in 1947, and by the end of 1949 the war had become a major international issue.

This is the way it was. There can be no clearer picture of events of that time. We do not have precise answers as to why we gave U.S.arms to Ho Chi Minh in 1945 and then a few years later provided Ho's enemy, the French, with $3 billion of our arms. The situation is not supposed to be clear. The plan made before the end of World War II was to make war in Indochina, and this was the way it was done. From 1945 to 1975, there was warfare of one kind or another.

Behind the scenes, the French, with U.S. acquiescence, were

forming an anti-Communist national puppet government under the leadership of the former emperor, Bao Dai. As a result, by the end of 1949, there were three aspiring governments in Vietnam: the French colonial administration, Bao Dai's State of Vietnam, and Ho Chi Minh's Democratic Republic of Vietnam.

As early as 1947, the "anti-Communist" national elements of government included Ngo Dinh Diem, the man whom the United States would make president in 1954. But in 1948, Diem refused to support a French proposal for a "provisional central government." This three-way structure was quite essential to the long-range plan for the invisible war. The French had already decided that they had to get out of Vietnam. They were becoming seriously involved in Algeria, much closer to home, and their own internal political problems were severe.

However, if the French had withdrawn before the United States was ready to enter the contest, the only government in Vietnam would have been the Democratic Republic of Vietnam. No one else could have contested the Ho Chi Minh regime. Therefore, the invisible war game required a new government to offset the Democratic Republic. The reluctant Bao Dai inherited the task. As the Soviets put it, this was a new "puppet government formed by the French with the blessings of the Americans." They were absolutely correct.

By February 1950, both Great Britain and the United States had established diplomatic relations with the new State of Vietnam in the south, even though each relationship was no more than an empty shell. When all these details had been formalized, the situation was ready for development as a war front.

On May 8, 1950, Secretary of State Dean Acheson announced that the United States would give both economic and military aid to France and to the State of Vietnam. The value of this military assistance surpassed $3 billion. One month later, we were at war in Korea, and the war in Vietnam had become another international crisis—in reserve.

These events closed the circle. At no time were things out of control. The same ponderous glacier that had been set in motion on September 2, 1945, when those heavily laden transports left Okinawa for Korea and Vietnam, had never stopped moving. By mid-1950, important military action, short of nuclear force, was under way. What had begun as a realignment of forces and the production of a bipolar world had become a full-fledged "hot war" on the two chosen battlefields, Korea and Vietnam. It is important to note that it was during these two wars that the CIA developed from a fledgling "intelligence" agency into its true form as master of American clandestine services. It had expanded enormously and matured.

Another common misconception is that the CIA acts by and for itself. This is not quite true. It is an "agency." It carries out the orders of others, as their agent. The CIA is the opening probe, the agitator or facilitator. In many respects it operates something like a law firm. It seldom if ever makes plans. It always acts in response to some other initiative. Right behind it comes its strong and ever-present allies, the rest of the government infrastructure, along with the willing support of the entire military-industrial and financial community.

FIVE

The CIA's Saigon Military Mission

IT WAS January 8, 1954. Dwight Eisenhower had been President of the United States for one year and was presiding over a meeting of the National Security Council with twenty-seven top-echelon national security advisers in attendance. When the subject turned to U.S. objectives and courses of action with respect to Southeast Asia, the President—our foremost World War II military commander—said, as recorded at the time, "with vehemence":

> The key to winning this war is to get the Vietnamese to fight. There is just no sense in even talking about United States forces replacing the French in Indochina. If we did so, the Vietnamese could be expected to transfer their hatred of the French to us. I cannot tell you how bitterly opposed I am to such a course of action. This war in Indochina would absorb our troops by divisions![1]

It must be added here that one of the great weaknesses in the approach to South Vietnam taken by the United States in those early days was an oversight that continues to this day. It has been the failure to recognize that the piece of real estate historically known as Cochin China but that we call South Vietnam was not, and never has been, a sovereign nation-state. It has never truly governed itself, despite the fact that Indochina has a history of thousands of years. This significant failure of perception made all attempts at "Vietnamization," while the Democratic Republic of Vietnam to the north was held by Ho Chi Minh, little more than words. A new country was being created and being asked to fight a major war, both at the same time. That was impossible, as we learned too late.

At the time of Eisenhower's comment, the indeterminate region of "South" Vietnam was under French military control, and the French army was at war with Ho Chi Minh and his "Vietminh" government. During that period and under those conditions, there was no way that the Vietnamese of the south, without a government, without leadership, and without an army, could have fought for their independence against the Democratic Government of Vietnam, which we ourselves had armed so well after World War II.

Eisenhower made a powerful and correct statement of policy, but he seriously overlooked these basic facts of Vietnamese history. Eisenhower wanted "to get the Vietnamese to fight" their war for their own country. He wanted to "Vietnamize" the war. President John F. Kennedy made essentially the same statement nine years later when he issued one of the most important documents of his administration—National Security Action Memorandum #263—of October 11, 1963, saying that the Vietnamese should take over "essential functions now performed by U.S. military personnel... by the end of 1965," thereby releasing all U.S. personnel from further duty in Vietnam.

By 1963, the people of South Vietnam had a little more experience with self-government than they did in 1954; but with the death of Ngo Dinh Diem and his brother Nhu on November 2, 1963, even that small beginning suffered a serious setback. South Vietnam had never had the tradition of being a nation. Most of its rural populace had no concept of, or allegiance to, a government in Saigon, other than memories of the one hundred years of French rule, which they loathed.

This serious oversight was not limited to Eisenhower and Kennedy. In an extract from his book *Counsel to the President*, which first appeared as "Annals of Government: The Vietnam Years" in *The New Yorker* magazine in May 1991, former Secretary of Defense Clark Clifford makes many similar remarks. He has written: "... our objectives in Vietnam depended more on the capabilities of our allies in Saigon than on our own efforts." There was no one closer to the policy and thinking of our six "Vietnam era" presidents and their key advisers than Clifford. All of these presidents, three Democrats and three Republicans, made two serious mistakes in their Vietnam policy:

1. They seriously overestimated the ability and character of this either nonexistent or very new Diem government of South Vietnam, and

2. Perhaps the most serious oversight of all was that not one of these six presidents ever stated a positive American military objective of that war. The generals sent to Saigon were told not to let the "Communists" take over Vietnam, period. This does not constitute a military objective.

Clifford asked himself those questions when he wrote: "First, can a military victory be won? And, second, what do we have if we do win?" These are meaningful questions, especially coming from the man who served as secretary of defense under President Lyndon Johnson in 1968.

What Presidents Eisenhower and Kennedy meant in their comments is clear enough under conventional circumstances, but their views made little sense given that the South Vietnamese were not a nation. Even when Ngo Dinh Diem had been established as the president of South Vietnam, in 1954, he had no governmental structure, no armed forces, no police, no tax system, etc. We aided Diem. We aided his subordinates. We armed and fed his troops—whoever they were. We provided billions of dollars in aid, but doing all those things does not make a government that can stand on its own feet in the face of a skilled and dedicated adversary that wanted to create a free Vietnam.

Ngo Dinh Diem was himself part of the problem. Perhaps Lyndon Johnson said it best, in 1961, during an interview in Saigon with Stanley Karnow, author of *Vietnam: A History:* "Shit, Diem's the only boy we got out there." Diem had been born in 1901 in the village of Phu Cam. He was not a native of Cochin China, but was from the vicinity of Hue. He was a Catholic, a staunch nationalist, and an anti-Communist.

In 1933, he had been minister of the interior in the Bao Dai government under French colonialism. After the Japanese had been defeated in 1945 and driven from Indochina, Diem was active against the French. In 1950 he left Vietnam for exile in the United States and lived at the Maryknoll Seminary in New Jersey, where, among other things, he washed dishes.

Then, on May 7, 1953, Francis Cardinal Spellman of New York arranged for a luncheon visit to the U.S. Supreme Court Building and introduced Ngo Dinh Diem to Justice William O. Douglas, Sen. John F. Kennedy, Sen. Mike Mansfield, Mr. Newton of the American Friends Service Committee, Mr. Costello of the Columbia Broadcasting System, and Edmund Gullion and Gene Gregory of the Department of State. There Ngo Dinh Diem discussed Indochina for about an hour and answered questions, chiefly from Douglas and Kennedy. Diem had been introduced to this distinguished group as a "Catholic Vietnamese Nationalist." An account of this important luncheon meeting is to be found in *Foreign Relations of the United States, 1952–1954*, vol. 13.

With reference to President Eisenhower's comment before the National Security Council on January 8, 1954, relative to "[getting] the Vietnamese to fight," it may be noted that during this May 7, 1953, meeting Ngo Dinh Diem himself may have initiated that theme. According to the official account, "He thought that the French military understood the problem better than the French civil government. In any case, the French could not beat the Communists and would have to rely on the Vietnamese to do it. They could not get the Vietnamese to undertake the task, however, unless the Viets had more freedom."

At no time did Diem, or anyone else, suggest what could be done to arrange for "the Viets [to have] more freedom."

Diem left the United States in 1953 and continued his exile from Vietnam in a Benedictine monastery in Belgium. On June 18, 1954, Bao Dai asked Diem to become premier in his government. Diem arrived in Saigon on June 26, 1954, met Lansdale on June 27, and formally assumed that office on July 7, 1954. After an election campaign carefully orchestrated by the CIA and Lansdale, Diem became president of South Vietnam on October 1954.

Another thing we must remember is that we had been aiding the French from 1946 up until their defeat by the Vietminh at Dien Bien Phu in May 1954. In other words, we had been helping the enemy of the South Vietnamese people right up until a few months before we installed Ngo Dinh Diem as the new president of this previously nonexistent country. It seems strange that President Eisenhower would want to "Vietnamize" the war in January 1954, six months before the new government, under Ngo Dinh Diem, had been established and during a period when we were still aiding the French. Such factors had a great impact upon the actions of this emerging country during the period of the Vietnam War.

This oversight, not only on the part of Eisenhower and Kennedy, but also on the part of most Americans, seriously handicapped both countries during the thirty years of American support of the Vietnamese and their warfare in that piece of real estate. Something had to be done to create a viable government and to coalesce the populace before it could act on its own behalf. This is where all of our best intentions failed so badly. Even in America, more than a century and a half elapsed between the landings at Jamestown and Plymouth Rock and the battle with the redcoats in Lexington and Concord. During that time those early settlers evolved into Americans, and were not simply an aggregate of English, German, Irish, and French people.

Despite this critical oversight, that was the commander in chief speaking during that important National Security Council meeting of January 1954 to the secretary of defense, the secretary of state, the chairman of the Joint Chiefs of Staff, and the individual chiefs of each of the military services, among others. That was his policy.

President Eisenhower could not have expressed his views on the subject of a "Vietnam War" more forcefully. He knew that we did not belong there. Yet less than a month later, on January 29, 1954, many of the same officials who had been at that meeting, including the vice president, the secretary of state, the secretary of defense, and the director of central intelligence, ignored the President and made plans to get on with the business of making war in Indochina.

In the words of Dr. Stephen E. Ambrose, Eisenhower Professor of War and Peace at Kansas State University:[2]

> We have dropped more bombs on Indochina than all the [other] targets in the whole of human history put together....
>
> Indochina contains enough bomb craters to occupy an area greater than Connecticut's 5,000 square miles.... We have released more than 100 million pounds of chemical herbicides over more than 4 million acres....
>
> Two American medical doctors estimate that South Vietnam [alone] has suffered 4 million casualties....

In the south, Vietnam was under French control simply because there was nothing else for that area. The French used Bao Dai as their puppet-in-command; but he reigned from the Riviera and was seldom in Vietnam. Finally, in mid-1954, when the United States took the initiative to install Ngo Dinh Diem as president of the newly established country of South Vietnam (i.e., south of the 17th parallel), that piece of real estate began to have a government, at least in name.

Diem had no congress, no army, no police, no tax system—nothing that is essential to the existence of a nation. At the same time he had a strong, skilled, and experienced enemy—Ho Chi Minh's North Vietnamese army. For this reason, many of the requests made upon the

Diem government during the period from 1954 to 1963 were quite unrealistic. But this fact never seemed to occur to the leaders of our own government or to those who tried to carry out liaison with Diem's government, as though it were, and had been, an equal member of the family of nations. We shall see this problem arise throughout the decade that followed.

Lest there are still some among us who believe that the President runs this country, that the Congress participates effectively in determining the course of its destiny, and that the Supreme Court assures compliance with the Constitution and all federal laws, let them witness this action, and the results of this blatant disregard for all elements of government, as we find it on the record.

Among those at the January 8, 1954, meeting of the National Security Council, when the President made his views known so forcefully, was Allen W. Dulles, director of central intelligence and brother of the secretary of state. There was no way that Allen Dulles could have misunderstood those words of President Eisenhower's. There was no way that any of the others at that meeting could have misunderstood or have had any question whatsoever about "how bitterly opposed" the President was to placing U.S. troops in Indochina. But this is not how things work when modern underground warfare is involved. This is not how the CIA and its counterpart, the Soviet KGB, have waged their worldwide invisible wars. Nothing whatsoever has ever deterred them from the essential business of making war.

These are incredible men, these defiers of presidents. One might say that they do not need them. Ambassador George V. Allen, after a state dinner with John Foster Dulles, said, "Dulles spoke as if he had his own line to God and was getting his instructions from a very high source."[3]

Allen Dulles was also a lawyer and a partner with Sullivan & Cromwell. The brothers were in touch with the power elite, and a mere President influenced them not at all. So many qualified people who have worked "close to the seat of power"—men like Winston Churchill, R. Buckminster Fuller, Prof. Joseph Needham and Ambassador Allen— confirm that these so-called leaders get their instructions from a very high source. These "leaders" are all fine actors, and certainly not true rulers, as we witness in the example of this National Security Council meeting of January 1954. This is true not only in the world of politics but is equally true of banking, industry, academia, and religion.

This explains why so many of the visible activists in high places are lawyers. In that profession they are trained to work under the direction of their clients. They have been educated for such service in the higher universities, many of them with courses designed for just such purposes. And they are further trained in the major international law firms that make a business of providing many of their skilled "partners" for top-level government service, for directorships on bank boards, and for major industrial positions.

In the case of Vietnam, the course followed by the U.S. government was established by these two international Wall Street lawyers, John Foster Dulles and Allen Welch Dulles, among other, more invisible powers. A review of the record of the early days of the war in Vietnam will reveal how they did it.

On January 14, 1954, only six days after the President's "vehement" statement against the entry of U.S. armed forces in Indochina, Secretary of State John Foster Dulles said: "Despite everything that we do, there remained a possibility that the French position in Indochina would collapse. If this happened and the French were thrown out, it would, of course, become the responsibility of the victorious Vietminh to set up a government and maintain order in Vietnam."

The secretary added:

[I do] not believe that in this contingency this country [the United States] would simply say, "Too bad; we're licked and that's the end of it."

If we could carry on effective guerrilla operations against this new Vietminh government, we should be able to make as much trouble for this government [the Vietminh-formed Democratic Republic of Vietnam] as they had made for our side and against the legitimate governments of the Associated States[4] in recent years. Moreover, the costs would be relatively low. Accordingly, an opportunity will be open to us in Southeast Asia even if the French are finally defeated by the Communists. We can raise hell and the Communists will find it just as expensive to resist as we are now finding it.

What John Foster Dulles said exposed the method used to circumvent the views of the President about the introduction of U.S. forces: first, by ignoring him completely, and, second, by changing the words from "making war" to "raising hell" with "guerrilla operations." Note also that Dulles assumed, as we all did, that there would be some government in existence in the south that could take care of itself and its people.

This is how American intervention and direct involvement in the

Vietnam War began—in opposition to the words of the President and in compliance with the longer-range Grand Strategy of the power elite. After all, we had been arming all sides in Indochina since 1945. According to a record of the January 14, 1954, National Security Council meeting, it was: "b. Agreed that the Director of Central Intelligence [Allen Dulles], in collaboration with other appropriate departments and agencies should develop plans, as suggested by the Secretary of State [John Foster Dulles], for certain contingencies in Indochina."

Two weeks later, on January 29, the President's Special Committee on Indochina[5] met to discuss these plans developed by the director of central intelligence. During this meeting, it was agreed that he could add "an unconventional-warfare officer, specifically Colonel Lansdale," to the group of five liaison officers that had been accepted by the French commander, General Henri Navarre.

In this manner, the CIA created the Saigon Military Mission and sent it from Manila to Indochina. This "military mission," undoubtedly the most important single "war-making" American organization established in Indochina between 1945 and 1975, was seldom in Saigon. It was not a military mission in the conventional sense, as the secretary of state had said. It was a CIA organization with a clandestine mission designed to "raise hell" with "guerrilla operations" everywhere in Indochina, a skilled terrorist organization capable of carrying out its sinister role in accordance with the Grand Strategy of those Cold War years.

By 1954, the French had created a fragile, basically fictitious government of the State of Vietnam under Emperor Bao Dai. It was said that none of the members of his Chamber of Deputies could have mustered twenty-five votes from their "constituencies." This made the issue quite clear to the Vietnamese, even if it could be concealed from the rest of the world. Through seven years of war, the Vietnamese people's choice was between the French and Ho Chi Minh's Democratic Republic of Vietnam.

The Vietnamese government that Eisenhower believed ought to be fighting the Vietminh on its own behalf did not exist in 1954. Thus, the choice of the predominant number of these Indochinese was overwhelmingly Ho Chi Minh. They felt no loyalty to Bao Dai, who lived in Paris, and they hated the French.

This was the situation when the CIA created the Saigon Military Mission on January 29, 1954. At this meeting, Allen Dulles was accompanied by his deputy, Gen. Charles P. Cabell; George Aurell, formerly chief of station in Manila; and Edward G. Lansdale. Lansdale, who had been in the Philippines since 1950, working as an agent of the CIA with Ramon Magsaysay and others to defeat President Quirino, had been ordered by the CIA to return to Washington for this series of meetings on Vietnam, preparatory to returning to Saigon to head the newly formed Saigon Military Mission. In his own book *In the Midst of Wars*, Lansdale says:

> Dulles turned to me and said that it had been decided that I was to go to Vietnam to help the Vietnamese, much as I had helped the Filipinos. Defense officials added their confirmation of this decision.
>
> I was to assist the Vietnamese in counterguerrilla training and to advise as necessary on governmental measures for resistance to Communist actions.

Lansdale would continue in Vietnam, as he had in the Philippines, to exploit the cover of an air force officer and to be assigned to the Military Assistance Advisory Group (MAAG) for "cover assignment" purposes. He was always an agent of the CIA, and his actual bosses were always with the CIA.

A statement made by Lansdale is quite relevant:

> I had been told that I was to help the Vietnamese help themselves. As far as I knew, this still was almost impossible for an American to do. The French ran Vietnam as a colony, with a minimum of Vietnamese self-rule. Chief of State Bao Dai was in France.
>
> It was true that France had said that Vietnam was independent, but the French issued and controlled Vietnam's currency, ran the national bank, customs, foreign affairs, armed forces, and police, and had a host of French officials placed throughout the administrative system. The French high commissioner for Vietnam was the real authority. Was the shock of Dien Bien Phu and the conference at Geneva causing a change of status? I simply didn't know.

I had met Ed Lansdale and many of his Filipino associates in Manila in 1953–54, and we were both assigned to the Office of Special Operations in the Pentagon during the late fifties and early sixties. I have heard him speak of his serious problems with the French in Saigon, which were so severe that he thought he might be killed by them. He had similar problems with certain Vietnamese. However, his Saigon Military Mission and its tough, experienced team managed to "raise hell," weather the storm, and present the U.S. government with a full-fledged, ready-made war by the spring of 1965.

The Saigon Military Mission entered Vietnam clandestinely to assist the Vietnamese, rather than the French. This was their "official" objective—on paper. Again it might be asked, Who did they mean by the "Vietnamese"? They had the same problem Eisenhower did. What Vietnamese government was there to help? As members of that team understood their orders, they were to wage paramilitary operations against the enemy and to carry out psychological warfare. They might not have known who their friends were, but they knew who their enemy was—the Vietminh. They also knew their job. They did not waste much time on "advisory" work or on PsyWar "Fun and Games." They were in Vietnam for bigger game. They were a band of superterrorists.

It must be kept in mind that the SMM was a CIA activity and that when its members said they were going to promote PsyWar and propaganda they had a different concept of these things than did the military. They saw their role as promoting sabotage, subversion, labor strikes, armed uprisings, and guerrilla warfare.

Their propaganda activity included the use of radio and newspapers, leaflets delivered by the millions from converted USAF B-29 bombers, posters, slogans, exhibits, fairs, motion pictures, educational and cultural exchanges, technical exchanges, specialized advertising, and help for the people in disaster areas. They attempted to do everything possible to exploit the nationalistic feelings of the people in an attempt to unite this new country.

Another characteristic of their work was the use of paramilitary organizations. Such units are no more than a private army whose members accept some measure of discipline, have a military-type organization, and carry light weapons.

The most interesting aspect of the SMM was that its leaders were firm believers in the *Little Red Book* teachings of Mao Tse-tung and spread the word accordingly. That book contained the doctrine of guerrilla warfare as practiced during the Cold War. Years later, after Lansdale had come home from Vietnam, he made many speeches at the various war colleges. Almost without exception he enumerated the "three great disciplinary measures" and the "eight noteworthy points" of Mao Tse-tung's great Chinese Eighth Route Army.

I was the pilot of U.S. Air Force heavy transport aircraft on many flights from Tokyo to Saigon via the Philippines from 1952 to 1954. When Lansdale's team members were on board the plane during some

The CIA's U-2 spy plane. President Eisenhower's hopes for a "Crusade for Peace" were dashed when the CIA—against Ike's specific order—sent a U-2 spy plane on a long-range overflight of the Soviet Union from Pakistan to Norway. On May 1, 1960, it made a forced landing near Sverdlovsk. Despite Soviet claims and news reports, the U-2 was not shot down. Allen Dulles himself testified to that fact before the Senate, and Eisenhower has written the true story in his memoirs. It suffered engine failure that may have been induced by a pre-planned shortage of auxiliary hydrogen fuel.

Captain Francis Gary Powers, pilot of the U-2, landed alive and well and in possession of a number of most remarkable identification items, survival kit materials, and other things spies are never allowed to carry. Did he know he had them in his parachute pack, or did someone who knew the U-2 had been prepared to fail put them there to create his "CIA spy" identity?

President Eisenhower had ordered all overflights to cease during the pre-summit conference period. The author, supporting a major CIA overflight program in Tibet, grounded all aircraft involved. Why was one U-2 ordered on its longest-ever overflight at that time?

Kennedy's totally unexpected election gave him an enormous fund that had been pre-packaged for the expected Nixon administration. The eventual $6.5 billion procurement of the Tactical Fighter Experimental (TFX) was the largest single peacetime procurement contract of its time. A fierce controversy raged over which aircraft manufacturers would get that money. Secretary of Defense Robert S. McNamara (lower left), with the shrewd assistance of JFK's Secretary of Labor Arthur Goldberg (lower right), eventually awarded the contract to General Dynamics and Grumman, the manufacturers whose procurement plans would do the most good for the 1964 presidential campaign.

UPI/Bettmann Newsphotos

William Colby, who later became the Director, Central Intelligence, claimed before a Congressional committee that during the time he supervised the Phoenix program in Indochina, at least 60,000 Vietnamese had been killed "in cold blood" by his agents. Colby is shown holding a shotgun during a January 1969 inspection tour of a "pacified" area in Vietnam.

Helicopters were used to deliver troopers of the First Cavalry Division to the site of a raid on the "Little Iron Triangle" near Bong Son, South Vietnam. A B-52 bombing raid had already killed most of the Viet Cong in the area. Overall, in Vietnam, bomb craters destroyed the land over an area the size of the state of Connecticut.

The author writes, "There is ample evidence to show President Kennedy was killed because he was moving to end the Cold War. The Cold War was basic and essential to the support of the CIA as well as the Pentagon. It was also a necessary part of the conflict required to generate the funds for the continually expanding military-industrial complex of the world."

A large, cleared patch of land on the fork of the river to Saigon was the site of a French Army "Gun Tower" fortification, when this photo was taken by the author in October 1953. This fortification was designed to control river traffic and to protect Saigon from guerrilla assault.

An April 1954 view of the port of Saigon, taken by the author. The shallow, muddy river was often blocked by the hulls of large ships that had been exploded by underwater mines and sunk. Saigon was, at that time, the only port in the southern half of Indochina that could handle ships of ocean-going size.

During the spring of 1954, while the French army was being destroyed by Ho Chi Minh's forces at Dien Bien Phu, this photograph taken by the author over the French military base at Saigon shows huge stockpiles of unused American military equipment in storage.

The French were forced to surrender to the Vietminh on May 8, 1954.

Tonkinese northern Catholic refugees on their way to South Vietnam with their belongings. More than 660,000 were transported in U.S. Navy ships under the supervision of CIA's Saigon Military Mission.

Over one million of these fixed-base, agricultural people were uprooted and moved with their skimpy belongings to South Vietnam, where they were left among the unprepared ancient people of Cochin China. They were penniless, homeless, foodless, and unwanted. Inevitably they became bandits, insurgents, and fodder for the war that came later.

The Dulles brothers and CIA's Saigon Military Mission "raised hell" to such a degree that 1,100,000 Tonkinese left their homes in the north and were transported 1,500 miles or more to a future of uncertainty and hostility in the newly created South Vietnam, 1954–1955. Transport was by Navy ships and the CIA's Civil Air Transport airline.

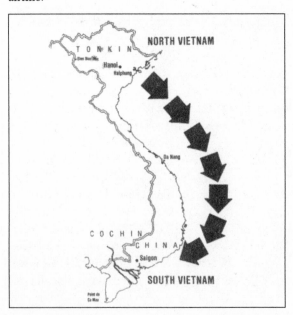

of those five-hour flights between Manila and Saigon, we discussed the Magsaysay campaign being waged by the CIA against Quirino and the plans that were being made for a new government in Vietnam—a new government to be supported by the United States, after the French departure.

It may be noted here that although National Security Council records and Department of State records show that the Saigon Military Mission did not begin until January 1954, there were other CIA activities in Vietnam, Cambodia, and Laos (such as the White Cloud teams) long before 1954, and some members of the SMM had participated in these earlier activities as far back as 1945. All of this was formally endorsed by the agreement to create the SMM in 1954. Although there was no real South Vietnamese government for the SMM to support during the early months of 1954, there was going to be one; the Dulles brothers would see to that.

The Saigon Military Mission was sent to Vietnam to preside over the dissolution of French colonial power and over the bursting of the Bao Dai "State of Vietnam" bubble. The Dulles brothers knew, by January 1954 if not long before that, that they would be creating a new Vietnamese government that would be neither French nor Vietminh and that this new government would then become the base for continuing the decade-old war in Indochina. That was their primary objective.[6]

The Dulles brothers were in a position to make sure that both the French and the Bao Dai interests were defeated. Dien Bien Phu fell on May 8, 1954. The international agreements that were signed in Geneva, Switzerland, on July 21, 1954, with both the United States and South Vietnam abstaining, restricted, on paper, all official American representation in Vietnam to those who were there then, and only for the first 300 days after the agreement was signed.

Thereafter, the introduction of arms, equipment, and personnel was prohibited, except for normal rotation of military personnel and for the replacement of items in kind. The agreement prohibited the establishment of any new military bases. This meant that the SMM had to be in place by mid-May 1955. In some respects the SMM disregarded this agreement. I flew military equipment, such as ground radars made in Italy, into Saigon during this period, when we had to paint out the original addresses and retype the manifests while the plane was in the air. We had to fly through India, and India was a member of the International Inspection Team in Saigon. At the time of the Geneva accords, the United States had delivered aid to Indochina at an original cost of $2.6 billion. (As a military planning factor, "life-of-type" follow-on support generally multiplies the original cost by a factor of ten.)

Edward G. Lansdale, chief of the SMM, arrived in Saigon from Washington via Manila on June 1, 1954, less than one month after the defeat of the French garrison at Dien Bien Phu. All over Vietnam, the Vietminh and other nationalist villagers were quickly consolidated in the north and other areas where they predominated. The defeated French units were disarmed, and their equipment and supplies were taken over by the Vietminh, thus increasing the Vietminh arsenal enormously. What they could not take away they destroyed. Every night, during my flights to Saigon, I could hear explosions in and around Saigon and other stronghold areas.

At times the Saigon River, the only supply channel into South Vietnam, became impassable as a result of enemy attacks and the number of ships that had been sunk in the channel. The airport at Tan Son Nhut was ringed with coils of barbed wire. Despite this precaution, the French World War II aircraft parked there were destroyed by explosions set by Vietminh sappers night after night. The entire country was seething with underground warfare.

This was the climate in which the Saigon Military Mission began operations. The Geneva accords called for a political division of the 1,600-mile-long country at the 17th parallel—roughly an equal half-and-half split, north and south. During the early months of its existence, the Saigon Military Mission reported that its first official task was "to create a refresher course in combat PsyWar...and Vietnamese army personnel were rushed through it." The report was written just as though there were a South Vietnam and a South Vietnamese army—neither of which existed in any form until at least July 21, 1954. But that wasn't exactly what the SMM was doing anyhow.

The Saigon Military Mission began operations on the ground in Indochina on June 1, 1954. Ngo Dinh Diem, the newly appointed president, arrived in Saigon on July 7, 1954. How are a new government, and a new nation, created? How does a man who has lived in exile outside of a country for years (and keep in mind the fact that South Vietnam had never been a country) come back, under the auspices of a totally foreign nation (the United States), and all of a sudden assume the role of president? Where does his government infrastructure and its people come from? Where do his police and army come from? Where does the money come from?

In other words, here was an ancient section of Asia with more than 30 million people divided over millennia into villages, regions, and loosely knit nations. Except for the ten-year-old Democratic Republic of Vietnam, which had never had an opportunity to get itself organized in peace, this entire region had no government. The French, who had provided for the constabulary, had gone. The Chinese, who for centuries had provided for the simple village economy, were frustrated and, under Diem, were being sent away. What remained was near anarchy. The fighting and rioting were actually a form of basic banditry, banditry to obtain the most basic needs of life. It was not even a civil war.

This is where the Saigon Military Mission stepped in and, in a series of adroit political moves, helped Diem gradually extend his authority in the creation of a central government. The SMM's greatest weapon was a blank U.S. government checkbook from the CIA that enabled the mission to do, and to buy, anything.

What was done in those earliest days of 1954 set the stage for the warfare that followed over the next twenty years. During the first two and a half years of that period, no American was closer to the Diem brothers (Ngo Dinh Nhu was the head of South Vietnam's CIA counterpart and the strongman of the new country) than Ed Lansdale. He became concerned that the Public Administration Advisory Program planned by the American embassy was going to be too slow and that something had to be done quickly to fill the void left by the French and the Vietminh, who had returned to the north after the Geneva agreements were signed, and to make Diem's new administration effective without delay. What he recommended and what was done deserve a few words.

Lansdale called this his "Civic Action" program. He describes it as a "cycle including not only political indoctrination, physical toughening, and learning to use tools at the training camp, but a further period of service in a hamlet or village where they would help the inhabitants build schoolhouses, roads, bridges, pit latrines, and similar public works, as well as help establish self-government." This is an interesting development for an organization that had been created to go to Vietnam and "raise hell," to use Foster Dulles's words. Lansdale was taking a page out of his past.

Shortly after the Japanese attack on Pearl Harbor on December 7, 1941, Lansdale had joined the Office of Strategic Services. He said later that he left that organization and joined U.S. Army Intelligence. It has been my experience that few men have actually left an intelligence organization and joined the military. More likely, they have simply arranged things so that they could exploit "military" cover.

Be that as it may, during World War II, after the Italian army had surrendered, we learned that during the Fascist dictatorship the cities and towns of Italy had been so long without effective government that they needed assistance in order to reestablish some sort of local administration. The army set up units for this work, called Civil Affairs and Military Government. These CAMG units proved so successful that they continued on into the north of Europe as the Allied armies rolled into Germany.

In a little-known development, the OSS noted what was being done and quite secretly began to develop a similar capability for Asia. As you may recall, General MacArthur had not permitted the OSS to operate in the Pacific Theater. But the OSS managed to get into the Pacific with its Civil Affairs and Military Government idea via U.S. Navy channels. A special school was opened on the Princeton University campus, followed by language schools at Monterey, California. With the surrender of Japan, this program came to an abrupt end. However, certain observant people—such as Lansdale and his boss, Gen. Richard Stilwell—realized the potential for such an activity during the Cold War. In 1960, Lansdale, Gen. Sam Wilson, and I wrote much of that doctrine into the new Army Special Forces manual.

When Lansdale was sent to the Philippines in 1950, he created a Civil Affairs Office there. He had prevailed upon President Ramon Magsaysay to create a psychological-warfare division as part of his own presidential staff and then had named it the "Civil Affairs Office." Here is no place to develop this relationship further. But it should be noted that this novel military task—if ever it really was military—began with WWII and then moved right into the Cold War under the sponsorship of the CIA.

Inevitably, Lansdale moved this concept of civil affairs to Vietnam with him. Under Gen. John W. O'Daniel, the head of the Military Assistance Advisory Group (MAAG), there were four staff divisions: Army, Navy, Air Force, and Pacification. Lansdale headed Pacification, which ostensibly had a civil affairs–type role. However, the Vietnamese objected violently to the word "pacification." They well knew that it had been a most sinister French colonial practice, devised by Gen. Louis-Hubert-Gonzalve Lyautey in North Africa and used later by the Chinese in Northern Indochina, meaning that a region was "pacified" when all of its people had been killed. Other parts of the civil affairs program became known as the Strategic Hamlet project of later years. And, before the war was over, the CIA had set up the Phoenix program, supposedly along civil affairs lines; actually, it became one of the most brutal and murderous creations of the war. As a result of the Phoenix program alone, tens of thousands of Vietnamese were killed.

It is necessary to understand this side of the Vietnam campaign in order to realize why we were never able to win the minds and hearts of the people and why this type of warfare did not lead to victory. It reminds us again of the days of the British East India Company and its members' lack of concern over genocide because of their inbred training in the theories of Malthus and Darwin. ("These gooks will never be able to feed themselves anyhow, so why does it matter if they die? And, we are the fittest anyhow.") These are strong forces once inbred, and they show themselves in such campaigns as that which occurred in Indochina between 1945 and 1975 and again in the Middle East "Gulf War" of 1991.

Almost from the beginning, Diem was faced with an attempted coup d'état. This threat was ended when the CIA bought off Gen. Nguyen Van Minh and other rivals and packed them off to Paris. But this did not get Diem a needed army and a palace guard for his own protection. There were in the vicinity of Saigon some independently powerful sects. One of them was Cao Dai. By early 1955, the CIA was able to buy off the leader of this sect and place his army under Diem. Then, in June 1955, the army of another sect, the Hoa Hao, was defeated with money—its leader was bought off and his forces joined the government army. A third sect, the Binh Xuyen, better known as the "Binh Xuyen Bandits," had been running the vice racketeering and the casinos in Cho Lon, a suburb of Saigon.

The CIA was able to arrange for its leader, the "Big Bandit," Le Van Vien, to give up his forces and travel to Paris. All of a sudden there were a lot of wealthy ex-generals from Vietnam on the French Riviera. In Asia, as in most of the rest of the world, nothing talks like the American dollar, and the SMM checkbook had begun to create a government army for the almost defenseless, and totally powerless, Ngo Dinh Diem.

I am aware of the fact that most of the history books about the earlier days of warfare in Vietnam present rather elaborate accounts of how the Diem administration acquired these "sect" armies. That had to be the "cover story." I have talked at great length with Lansdale on this subject. I was in Vietnam myself during those days, and I know that the "sect" armies, which were actually nothing more than modest paramilitary forces, had been easily bought up by the American dollar as a price of doing business in Vietnam. It is interesting to read Lansdale's account in his own book, *In the Midst of Wars*, and the account in his biography, *Edward Lansdale*, by Cecil B. Curry. Both of these books are burdened with a very heavy coating of "cover story" over these events and cannot be taken as realistic accounts.

Most Asian armies of that type are no more than groups of men with families that are one day ahead of starvation. They have joined the army for a bowl of soup and some rice, per day, for themselves and their destitute families. It was this kind of army that the Saigon Military Mission said it was rushing through a course in "Combat PsyWar," among other things.

One of the first "classes" of these troopers was flown to the vicinity of Hanoi, put in native garb, and told to run around the city spreading anti-Vietminh rumors. They were ordered to pass out leaflets that had been written by members of the Saigon Military Mission and to perform various acts of sabotage, such as putting sugar in the gas tanks of Ho Chi Minh's trucks and army vehicles. Later, the Saigon Military Mission discovered that these "loyal" troops usually just melted away and lined up for soup with some of Ho Chi Minh's forces.

By midsummer more men had joined the SMM, and its mission was broadened. Its members were now teaching "paramilitary" tactics— today called "terrorism"—and doing all they could to promote the movement of hundreds of thousands of "Catholic" Vietnamese from the north with promises of safety, food, land, and freedom in the south and with threats that they would be massacred by the Communists of North Vietnam and China if they stayed in the north.

This movement of Catholics—or natives whom the SMM called "Catholics"—from the northern provinces of Vietnam to the south, under the provisions of the Geneva Agreement, became the most important activity of the Saigon Military Mission and one of the root causes of the Vietnam War. The terrible burden these 1,100,000 destitute strangers imposed upon the equally poor native residents of the south created a pressure on the country and the Diem administration that proved to be overwhelming.

What Americans fail to realize is that the Southeast Asian natives are not a mobile people. They do not leave their ancestral village homes. They are deeply involved in ancestor worship and village life; both are sacred to them. Nothing could have done them more harm than to frighten them so badly that they thought they had a reason to leave their homes and villages.

These penniless natives, some 660,000 or more, were herded into Haiphong by the Saigon Military Mission and put aboard U.S. Navy transport vessels. About 300,000 traveled on the CIA's Civil Air

Transport aircraft, and others walked out. They were transported, like cattle, to the southernmost part of Vietnam, where, despite promises of money and other basic support, they were turned loose upon the local population. These northerners are Tonkinese, more Chinese than the Cochinese of the south. They have never mixed under normal conditions.

There was no way these two groups of people could be assimilated by a practically nonexistent country. It is easy to understand that within a short time these strangers had become bandits, of necessity, in an attempt to obtain the basics of life. The local uprisings that sprung up wherever these poor people were dumped on the south were given the name "Communist insurgencies," and much of the worst and most pernicious part of the twenty years of warfare that followed was the direct result of this terrible activity that had been incited and carried out by CIA's terroristic Saigon Military Mission.

Moreover, these 1,100,000 Tonkinese Vietnamese were, of course, northerners—that is, the "enemy" in the Vietnamese scenario. However, since the Diems were more closely affiliated with natives of the north than the south, it was not long before a large number of these so-called "refugees" had found their way into key jobs in the Diem governmental infrastructure of South Vietnam.

When one thinks about this enormous man-made problem for a while, he or she begins to realize that much of the Vietnamese "problem" had been ignited by our own people shortly after the Geneva Agreements were concluded. Nothing that occurred during these thirty years of warfare, 1945–75, was more pernicious than this movement of these 1,100,000 "Catholics" from the north to the south at a time when the government of the south scarcely existed. (The figure of 1,100,000 used here is from a John Foster Dulles speech while he was secretary of state.)

Although the men of the Saigon Military Mission had many other duties in Vietnam, their biggest task was to keep Ngo Dinh Diem alive, and they solved this problem in a typical CIA manner for ten years.

If the truth were known, the chief of state of most Third World countries today—under the rules of the superpower world game—owes his job and his life, day by day, to an elite palace guard that he can control and, he hopes, trust.

In many countries around the world, the leaders of the elite guard have been trained by the CIA or the KGB. Originally, Diem had none of these essentials of power, so the Saigon Military Mission turned to the Philippines, where it had just succeeded in ousting President Quirino and putting Magsaysay in the Presidential Palace.

The Saigon Military Mission borrowed one of Ramon Magsaysay's closest friends and aides from his own elite guard: Col. Napoleon Valeriano.

Valeriano had selected and trained Magsaysay's elite guard. This amazing Filipino would later play an important part in the Bay of Pigs operation in 1961. He arrived in Saigon with three junior officers from the same Filipino elite guard to begin the process of selecting Vietnamese who for one reason or another could be expected to be loyal to Ngo Dinh Diem. These candidates were then flown to Manila for training and indoctrination.

One way to guarantee loyalty to the ruler is to employ only those men who have wives and children and then to provide a place for those wives and children to live—as hostages. This hostage environment helps to assure "undying loyalty."

Slowly, Diem was able to act more and more as the head of state, just like his more experienced counterparts in Laos, Cambodia, Thailand, and Burma, all of whom had been beneficiaries of similar CIA elite guard assistance.

During this period, relations between the nominal chief of state, Bao Dai, and the premier, Diem, worsened. In 1955, Ngo Dinh Diem, the CIA's newcomer, called for a popular referendum in this newly delineated piece of real estate called South Vietnam to decide whether Bao Dai should continue as chief of state or whether the country should become a republic under his own leadership as president.

It was quite an experience to prepare for an election in a new country that had never had a real one before, especially when many of its millions of residents did not know the country existed or where its borders were located or who Ngo Dinh Diem was. With its recent experience of a similar nature in the Philippines, however, the CIA felt quite certain that this "free, democratic" election would favor its man. In any case, the leaders of the SMM were going to see that their men counted the ballots.

It was in response to challenges like this that the SMM's special talents revealed themselves. Someone located and then ordered one million tiny "phonograph" toys. They were delivered with a brief political speech recorded by Ngo Dinh Diem. The villagers, who had never seen or heard of anything like this before, were astounded. Such modern "witchcraft" as this "voice in a box" helped guarantee the election of Diem.

Diem received 98 percent of the vote, and on October 26, 1955, he proclaimed the area south of the 17th parallel—actually the legal line of demarcation was the river known as Song Ben Hai, but it was usually referred to as the 17th parallel—the Republic of Vietnam. As a result of this election, Ngo Dinh Diem became its first president.

This brought matters full circle. At the National Security Council meeting of January 29, 1954, the Dulles brothers laid plans for the creation of a new nation that would be backed by the United States, to continue the then "nine-year" war in Indochina.

It had taken them almost two years to witness the defeat of the French, the dissolution of the Bao Dai government, the movement of Ngo Dinh Diem from exile to the position of premier in Saigon, and finally Diem's installation as president and "Father of his Country" in South Vietnam. None of this could have happened without the skillful undercover work of the CIA and its experienced Saigon Military Mission.

SIX

Genocide by Transfer—
in South Vietnam

NINE YEARS of the manipulation of the American war-making machine in Indochina began to pay off for the power elite in a big way in 1954. By that time, American blood had been shed in Indochina, and nearly $3 billion had been spent. A major conflagration was in the offing. By the end of the Indochinese phase of the Cold War, the cost would be estimated at more than $500 billion, 58,000 American lives, and a serious decline of American prestige.

The French, in Indochina since 1787, had been defeated at Dien Bien Phu in May 1954 and were on their way out. The CIA's Saigon Military Mission arrived in June. Secretary of State John Foster Dulles had said, "We could carry on effective guerrilla operations [in Vietnam]...and we can raise hell." This was precisely what the SMM was there to do: to establish an undercover paramilitary campaign and to raise hell. It had been given the power, the support, and the checkbook by the CIA.

Meanwhile, the Geneva Conference that was to work out a cease-fire between the Vietminh, the French, and the State of Vietnam had convened on April 26, even before the French defeat at Dien Bien Phu on May 7. This conference established a demarcation zone at, or near, the 17th parallel, which divided the former French colonial land into two nearly equal sections. The north would be the Democratic Republic of Vietnam, and the south was to become the State of Vietnam and later, on October 26, 1955, the Republic of Vietnam.

Before the conclusion of the Geneva Conference, in the summer of 1954, the CIA's SMM had begun its political, psychological, and terrorist activities against the native population in the northern regions. Using a well-equipped cadre of saboteurs, it performed many terrorist acts in Hanoi and surrounding Tonkin. SMM agents polluted petroleum supplies, bombed the post offices, wrote and distributed millions of anti-Vietminh leaflets, printed and distributed counterfeit money.

As was intended, these clandestine activities played right into the hands of the war makers by creating a growing rift between the Vietminh and the Tonkinese Catholics. No blame was laid upon the SMM until later, when SMM-trained Vietnamese turned themselves in to the Vietminh.

In their own words, as found in documents released by Daniel Ellsberg with the Pentagon Papers,[1] leaders of the SMM wrote that the mission had been sent into North Vietnam to carry out "unconventional warfare," "paramilitary operations," "political-psychological warfare," and rumor campaigns and to set up a Combat PsyWar course for the Vietnamese. The members of the SMM were classic "agents provocateurs."

This activity of the SMM produced one of the most amazing, unusual, and important war-making events of this century—the mass exodus of more than one million Tonkinese natives, presumably Catholics, who were caused to leave their ancestral homeland and pour into the disorganized, strange, and inhospitable southland of Cochin China, as described earlier.

Without a doubt, this mass of Catholic northerners and its unwelcome impact upon the population of the south had more to do with the scope, severity, and duration of the American-made war in Vietnam than anything else. It was an astounding event, for many reasons. First of all, how was such an enormous movement of otherwise immobile people brought about, and how were so many motivated to move that far from their ancient, ancestral homes, land, and villages? Had they been scared to death? And how was everything kept so secret? Most news sources and historical reviews have either avoided or neglected these subjects.

At the time this exodus began in mid-1954, the State of Vietnam as a government was all but nonexistent. Yet it had been placed in charge of all the real estate south of the 17th parallel and of its ancient, settled, and peaceful population, variously estimated at from 10 to 12 million.

There can be no denying the fact that the influx of these hundreds of thousands of strangers on the already war weary (from World War II under the Japanese, from the French battles to retake Cochin China, and from the nine years of war against the Vietminh) southern population pushed them both to the breaking point. They were not the victims of a civil war in the classic sense so much as they found themselves in a situation analogous to that of the American Indians, when hundreds of thousands of Europeans invaded their North American homeland and decided they would take it over for themselves. With the Catholic Ngo Dinh Diem in power, these intruders actually thought they had that right.

As reported in the book *Vietnam Crisis:*[2]

> The confused situation in Vietnam following Geneva was marked by the exodus of refugees from the zone north of the 17th parallel. The refugee movement was encouraged by the State of Vietnam and was carried on with substantial aid from the United States. France had first thought the movement would be limited to a few thousands of people, but it soon took on mammoth proportions. The influx of refugees in the zone south of the 17th parallel contributed to the existing political confusion. The authority of the central government of the State of Vietnam was badly factionalized by years of war and political turmoil, and the army and "sects" (Hoa Hao, Cao Dai, and Binh Xuyen) virtually constituted states within a state.

This quite typical interpretation of events that involved one million people leaves many crucial, as yet unanswered questions. The account says a little about the plight of the refugees and nothing about their reluctant hosts—the people of the south. Vietnam was possibly the most "un-Western" of all Asian countries. The Vietnamese had no way to leave their ancestral villages. They could not pack the family into the old Chevy and head down the road for some unknown destination a thousand or fifteen hundred miles away. They had no superhighways with convenient fast-food stops and welcoming motels. At that time, the one north-south railroad line was inoperative and not an alternative.

Indochina is a very ancient land. Vietnam was old in the days of the early Egyptians, Babylonians, and Persians. It is one of the oldest settlements of mankind. To those settled, village-oriented people, obligations to parents and to the emperor were the cement of the Confucian order. Cochin China, the French colony, had changed somewhat as a result of the French occupation that took place between 1861 and 1867, but Annam and Tonkin had not. Yet it was the "unchanged" Tonkinese who were fleeing, and this was what made it all the more remarkable.

To the Tonkinese, the village was a most important institution. In the village, the clans were strong, and the basis of the clan was the veneration of ancestors, which ensured strong attachment to the village and to the land. Each village had a shrine—the "dinh"—which contained the protective deity of that village. The cohesive force of the village was a sense of being protected by those spirits of the soil. Village affairs were in the hands of a council of elderly notables, but there was a considerable degree of autonomy. It was said, "The power of the emperor stops at the bamboo fence."

The village did pay a tax to the higher authority and did provide young men for military service. In Vietnam, however, law was not based on authority and will but on the recognition of universal harmony. As in all parts of the world, the basic object of rural government was to provide security. As a result, in Vietnam the traditional demand was not for good laws so much as for good men. Law was deemed less important than virtue.[3]

This describes the village and the land-based society of these natives who had become refugees in their own homeland as a result of the psychological terrorism instigated by the SMM and its religious allies. By all accounts, they had to be the least likely people who ever lived to leave their ancestral soil for some unknown and inhospitable alternative. Little has been said about this clandestine provocation that created such deep fear, but it has to be considered one of the primary causes for the Americanization of the Vietnam War. Once we realize this, we begin to have a much deeper appreciation and understanding of the power of the CIA's SMM and its unconventional political and psychological warfare techniques not only in Vietnam but elsewhere.

To use John Foster Dulles's phrase, the SMM knew how to "raise hell," and the fury of its threats caused 1.1 million of this village-based people to leave. The other side of the coin—and perhaps the explanation for the relative silence of the Vietminh during this massive emigration—is the fact that among these hundreds of thousands of fugitives were thousands of fifth-column Vietminh who concealed their movements southward within the greater mass of refugees.

Throughout the long history of the warfare, and in Cochin China especially, it was always difficult to tell friend from foe. During my many trips there at this time, I was often told, "The barber who uses his razor to shave you in the morning will cut your throat with that same razor after dark."

More than anything else, the Vietnam War was marked by internal strife. Some of the most vicious fighting during the early years of that struggle took place in the Camau Peninsula and other remote southern areas that had always been relatively wealthy farmland, peaceful, and, by geography, most removed from the Tonkin strongholds of the Vietminh.

The reason for this was partly due to the impact of the infiltration by the Vietminh fifth column and the troublesome impact of hundreds of thousands of refugees. It was just the sort of situation the CIA and the KGB desired in order to keep the invisible war boiling. After its first year in Indochina, the SMM reported that it had been able to arrange for the transport of these refugees, as though transport were all there was to this enormous exodus. As a result, a contract was let, through U.S. government sources, to Civil Air Transport (CAT) Airlines to provide an airlift to augment navy transport operations.

For those who have not heard of this airline, and the many other airlines like it, CAT Airlines was a CIA proprietary corporation chartered in Delaware and based on Taiwan but available for CIA needs anywhere in the world. SMM arranged for the U.S. Navy to provide a sealift from North Vietnam to the south. The scope of the project was so massive as to be unbelievable. CAT's primary aircraft were the World War II, Curtiss-manufactured U.S. Air Force C-46 type, in civilian dress. It would have taken more than ten thousand flights or more than one thousand U.S. Navy boatloads carrying one thousand refugees each to move one million people one thousand miles.

By sharing the load and by recognizing that many of these fleeing refugees walked to the south, the burden on CAT Airlines and on the U.S. Navy was made somewhat more reasonable. It still remains one of the major mass movements of people in modern times. Why was it done? Why was such an inhumane activity planned and carried out? There can be but one answer. It was to provide the climate, and the fodder, for the war in Vietnam.

But how was it done? How could the SMM and its mentors get away with such an enormous operation?

Ho Chi Minh and all northern Vietnamese, at the time of the Geneva Agreements, believed the nation to be "one." They did not want a division of their country. As the Geneva Agreements had guaranteed, there was to be an election in order that the people might choose the government of a single unified Vietnam. Ho Chi Minh had said this repeatedly in many public addresses. There were many "incidents" as a result of this exodus, such as the one in Ba Lang in January 1955, when Ho's Democratic Republic of Vietnam used force against the "Catholics" who were attempting to flee from north to south.

Most Americans believe that if an agreement is reached by concerned governments at a conference, as happened in Geneva in 1954, that agreement is going to be fulfilled. The agreement did provide for transfer of natives from one zone to another; but the war makers working at the command of the power elite read that small paragraph in a much different way. They had decided to make a big conflagration in Indochina, and this was a certain way to do it. The delegates to the Geneva Conference did not plan this deadly confusion. Their unseen mentors did—and, as circumstances prove, their mentors won the day.

Despite these uprisings in the north, and quite unaccountably, the CIA's CAT aircraft and the U.S. Navy ships operated in and out of northern ports and transported a major share of these people to the south—dumping them there upon the Cochin Chinese near Saigon.

The people themselves were subjected to massive rumor campaigns and other PsyWar batterings by the SMM and by the Catholic hierarchy in the north. The evacuation of these hundreds of thousands of Catholic Tonkinese had begun in southwestern Red River delta areas in Tonkin, under the urging of the Catholic bishoprics of That Dien and Bui Chu. This started one of the most amazing episodes of the entire thirty-year war and provided one of its least-known and least-understood causes. In addition, it was said the French issued similar evacuation orders.

While it was happening, the U.S. Department of State asserted that it had not been informed of this massive and crucial action. This claim, however, could not have been true. On June 29, 1954, a joint American-British note to the French government included a paragraph:[4] "... provides for the peaceful and humane transfer, under international supervision, of those people desiring to be moved from one zone to another in Vietnam."

The Americans, British, and French knew about this mass exodus and kept it very secret. The Geneva Conference on the Cessation of Hostilities in Vietnam concluded its work on July 20 and 21, 1954. As a result, a cease-fire was scheduled to take place in southern Vietnam at 8:00 A.M. on August 11, 1954. The closing article of those Geneva Agreements, Number 14, a scarcely noticed few lines, read: "... any civilians residing in a district controlled by one party, who wish to go and live in the zone assigned to the other party, shall be permitted and helped to do so by the authorities in that district."

The brutal and sinister meaning of this "genocide by transfer" was skillfully concealed under the cloak of gentle words. The American-British note spoke of a "peaceful and humane transfer." The Geneva Agreements speak of those people "who wish to go and live," as though they were being kind and thoughtful by providing a means for these people who had lived all their lives in a settled village environment, as their ancestors had for more than ten thousand years, to get up and move.

The people of the world, most of whom had never even heard of the Tonkinese and had no idea of their ancient village history, were supposed to think that this offer to transfer these poor people a thousand miles or more was a most benevolent gesture. And, what is even worse, the people of the world were never supposed to learn that this movement of one million people was really intended—by the war makers—to provide all the elements for a bitter chapter of the Cold War.

This is how the Americanization of that warfare began. Looking back over the decades, it is incomprehensible to think of one million settled, peaceful, penniless people being uprooted in this manner and moved to southern Vietnam. Consider what it would take to cause a million New Yorkers to leave their homes, their friends, and their jobs and move to Alabama, where they would be heartily disliked as intruders, strangers, and troublemakers. But this is what was done. And it was done by the CIA just after that agency had overthrown the government of Guatemala, the government of the Philippines, and the government of Iran. Vietnam was simply the unlucky place chosen for the next major phase of the Cold War.

The role of these refugees in the creation of the intensity of this warfare was important. Although the French military had been igno-miniously defeated, it was prepared to survive "the painful glory of Dien Bien Phu." As French foreign minister Christian Pineau said to the Council of the Republic, "I am in a good position in this house to say that when the government of Monsieur Diem was formed I declared very clearly that it was not in my opinion the best formula." But, he said, "a commercial agreement links us with the country."

The French military had left, on orders from Diem—but the huge Michelin rubber interests were still there, and the French banking interests and other commercial establishments were still there, so all was well for the French. They were in place to benefit immeasurably from the Americanization of the war. This was true also of the entrenched Chinese mercantile groups, the Australians, and the New Zealanders, who, because of their relative proximity to Indochina, became the greengrocers, merchants, and bankers in Vietnam (particularly for the enormous illicit fortunes made in Vietnam) during the "American episode."

It was one thing for the one million refugees to leave northern Vietnam; it was an entirely different matter for them to arrive in the South to take up homes, land, and key jobs.

As has been stated above, in 1954 and 1955 the south was disorganized. It had never been a true nation-state. Diem, its premier and later its president, was an outsider from Annam who had long been living in exile. All police power had vanished with the departure of the French. The economy had been shattered with the ouster of the Chinese in response to a Diem edict. And the nation had no army to protect its leader or to defend the republic.

Into this mess came the one million, one hundred thousand.

Cochin China, the land of the south, was an ancient, rural land. It was the rice bowl of Asia. Long before the war era, more than 13.5 million acres of land had been planted with rice. As far back as 1931, Cochin China had been growing more than two million tons of rice a year. By the 1950s, this figure had been increased to six million tons. South Vietnam had been a major exporter of rice; under Diem, with the economy in chaos, it was forced to import rice to feed the people. This was one of the most horrible legacies of the war years.

The people of Cochin China were relatively wealthy. They lived comfortable, peaceful lives and their village-type local government had been perfected over thousands of years. They needed little from the outside world, and the outside world scarcely knew they existed.

Then the exodus began. The first Interim Report of the International Commission for Supervision and Control in Vietnam, dated December 25, 1954, said: "The commission took measures to secure freedom of movement in the case of about eight thousand refugees."

The foreign secretary of Great Britain, Anthony Eden, said in the House of Commons on November 8, 1954: "The House should recall that in Vietnam...arrangements [had] to be made to move tens of thousands of the population from the region of Hanoi to the South...."

A September 19, 1954, Franco-American communiqué said: "In this spirit France and the United States are assisting the government of Vietnam in the resettlement of the Vietnamese who have of their own free will moved to free Vietnam and who already number some three hundred thousand."

A message from President Eisenhower to Premier Diem on October 23, 1954, said: "Your recent request for aid to assist on the formidable project of the movement of several hundred thousand loyal Vietnamese citizens away from areas which are passing under a de facto rule and political ideology which they abhor, are being fulfilled. I am glad that the United States is able to assist in this humanitarian effort."

Then, in a speech delivered nationwide over radio and television in the United States on March 8, 1955, Secretary of State John Foster Dulles said: "As always, when international communism moves in, those who love liberty move out, if they can. So far, about six hundred thousand persons have fled from northern Vietnam, and before the exodus is over, the number of refugees will probably approach one million. It is not easy for southern Vietnam to absorb these new peoples. They are destitute and penniless persons with only such possessions as they can carry on their backs."

It is exceedingly strange to look back to that time and discover that the officials closest to the action, the International Commission, thought that eight thousand people were moving. The British thought "tens of thousands" were moving. The French, who were still very much on the scene, estimated the number at three hundred thousand. Then the prime mover himself, John Foster Dulles, told it as it actually was, nearly, predicting that the figure would "approach one million."

As the refugees moved into the south, the U.S.-advised Diem government began to place many of these Catholics in key offices. Typical of the way things developed, Dr. Tran Kim Tuyen, a northern Catholic who had left Tonkin China in 1954, was made chief of the Office of Political and Social Affairs, the secret government apparatus that had been organized by the CIA to keep tabs on dissenters.

In Communist countries, this is called the "block" system. It is an oppressive, omnipresent internal spy organization that uses teachers to gather information from children, wives to tell on husbands, and employers to inform on employees.

Thousands of these northern Catholics were put into such positions of responsibility by the CIA and the Diem government.

It didn't take long before the friction between the southern natives and the Diem-favored northern intruders broke out into fighting and riots. These peaceful southern farmers and villagers rebelled against the intrusion of these refugees on their land, in their villages, and in the new Diem government, which none of them liked anyway.

Before long, the "friends," according to the Diem brothers and their CIA backers in Saigon, were the one million northern Catholics, and the "enemy"—or at least the "problem"—was the native southerners.

The time was right to fan the flames into war and to bring in the Americans. The first wave of Americans to arrive were the "Do Gooders," or, as others have seen them, the "Ugly Americans."

In an attempt to create a new nation, to provide it with the means to defend itself with police and an army, to develop its agriculture and economy, and to create schools and hospitals, all kinds of Americans were brought into Indochina to work with the CIA and its Saigon Military Mission, to work with the growing U.S. Military Assistance Advisory Group, and to increase the manpower of the CIA's many proprietary companies in Southeast Asia and their burgeoning band of mercenaries.

The next stage of the Americanization of Vietnam was being set. The plan was to destroy the ancient villages and to replace them with all the advantages of the Western way of life. Someone had decided it was time for the Vietnamese to have the luxury of fast-food hamburgers and fried chicken, not to mention Cadillacs and TV, served up with the American brand of home-view violence and ideology.

There is, and has been for centuries, in the highest-level power structure, a determination to destroy mankind's traditional way of life, that is, that of the village. Traditional village life is effective, timeless, and impregnable. It is, above all, self-sufficient, something that American urbanization is not. Villagers have solved the problems of the necessities—food, clothing, and shelter—on a modest scale, and they do not need the omnipotent paternalism of the international banker, the chemical revolution, or the politics of the modern jungle. They would not recognize a lawyer if they saw one. They are not dependent upon the next eighteen-wheel, semitrailer truck for today's food, either.

But Indochina was slated to be the next area for Malthusian destruction, and the Americans and the Vietminh knew how to do it. Their mentors in the CIA and KGB saw that they did it according to the planned international scenario. The American plan caused Diem, as its agent, to issue two relatively unnoticed edicts:

(1) the French must leave, and

(2) the Chinese, alleged to be sympathetic to the communism of China, must leave.

These edicts, which appeared to make sense from the Diem perspective, raised the level of internal warfare and assured the destruction of the Vietnamese village-type economy and way of life; that is, no law and order and no food and water. In the process they paved the way for the entry of the U.S. Army, Navy, Air Force, Marines, and Coast Guard to take part in the Vietnam War, under the guidance of the CIA's master planners and the ambassador who remained in Saigon on the job, despite the nondiplomatic formalities of such a war.

SEVEN

Why Vietnam? The Selection and Preparation of the Battlefield

"WHY VIETNAM?" Why was this remote, backward, ancient land chosen, as far back as 1943 or 1944, to be one of the major battlegrounds of the Cold War? A dog-eared copy of a 1931 *National Geographic* likens Vietnam to a Garden of Eden. What was there about this historically serene Asian land that caused it to be chosen to be devastated by this massive war?

I say "chosen" advisedly. Who had directed that one-half of that great stockpile of weapons and other war-making matériel that was delivered to Okinawa for use during the invasion of Japan should, instead, be transshipped to Vietnam? Decisions of such magnitude would have to, one would think, have been made by such men as Roosevelt, Truman, Churchill, Clement Attlee, Stalin, and Chiang Kai-shek; but these men weren't making "Cold War"—that is, "communism vs. anti-communism"—decisions at that time.

Questions like these require that we begin to think of the Cold War and its half century in terms of an awareness of a super power elite that can, and does, make such monumental decisions. Lest it appear that I am making these allegations out of thin air, may I suggest that others, now and at other times, have come to similar conclusions. Winston Churchill, in conversations with intimate friends during World War II, made reference to a "High Cabal." R. Buckminster Fuller wrote

positively and powerfully of a super "power elite." Dr. Joseph
Needham, the great Chinese scholar at Cambridge University, writes of
a Chinese belief in "the Gentry" as a similar "power elite." This is a
serious subject, and one that concerns us all. The "Why Vietnam?"
question causes us to later ask, "Why John F. Kennedy?" We shall see
why.

To probe further, why did the Vietnam War cause the dean of
American military correspondents, Hansen W. Baldwin, to write, in the
foreword to Adm. U.S.G. Sharp's book *Strategy of Defeat*, the following:

> ... for this first defeat in American history—the historical blame
> must be placed squarely where it belongs—not primarily upon our
> military leaders whose continuous and protracted frustrations
> burst forth from these pages—but upon the very top civilian policy
> makers in Washington, specifically the Commander in Chief
> [President Lyndon B. Johnson].

Admiral Sharp, who was the commander in chief of the Pacific
(CINCPAC) and thus the senior American military man in the area,
wrote, "The Vietnam episode was one of the most controversial eras of
U.S. history.... When we accepted defeat... we seemed to be clearly
saying to the world that what we had ultimately lost was our concern for
the responsibilities, indeed the honor, that goes with a leadership role.
If this is true, I fear for the peace of the world." Lt. Gen. Victor H.
Krulak, USMC (Ret'd), formerly the commander of the Fleet Marine
Force Pacific, tells a similar story in his fine book *First to Fight*.

This is what allows me to write from my own knowledge and
experience. My immediate boss for two years was General Krulak.
During those years I also knew Admiral Sharp. Before I worked for
General Krulak, I served in the Office of the Secretary of Defense under
both Thomas Gates and Robert McNamara. I have worked closely with
Allen Dulles and his brother, Foster Dulles. I feel that it is essential to
set forth important elements of this historical period in a way that will be
most useful to the reader. We need to understand the CIA and its allies.
We need to know why we were in Vietnam, or at least what caused us to
be there, so that when we arrive at the year 1963 and the "1,000 Days of
Camelot" we shall be ready to understand the true handwriting on the
wall. These next chapters have the creation of that awareness as their
objective.

Years after the Vietnam War had been brought to a close, Gen. Paul
Harkins, head of the U.S. Military Assistance Command in South

Vietnam from February 1962 to June 1964, said he had never been told what the American military objective was in that war. If that is true—and I have no reason to believe that it is not—then why were we there? What was the real purpose of that massive thirty-year struggle that cost 58,000 American lives, as much as $500 billion, and the lives of millions of noncombatants? What kind of a war can be waged without an objective?

Carl von Clausewitz, the nineteenth-century Prussian general and military writer, declared that of the nine principles of warfare, the most important is that of the "objective." "If you are going to fight a war and you intend to be the victor," he said, "you must have a clearly stated and totally understood military objective." Furthermore, that objective should issue from the highest authority in the land. It is not just permission or authority to "do something." As we shall see here, there was no official U.S. government directive and objective, of a military nature, in Vietnam at any time.

During World War II, when Gen. Creighton W. Abrams led the point brigade of Gen. George S. Patton's victorious Third Army after the invasion of France, he had a military objective that old "Blood and Guts" Patton had put in plain words: "Cross the Rhine; destroy the German army; shake hands with the Russians." That is the kind of job a military man can do, and Abrams did it. That objective led to victory on that front.

More than two decades later, General Abrams, one of the great armored force commanders, was appointed by President Lyndon Johnson to replace Gen. William Westmoreland as commander of U.S. military forces in Vietnam. During a rousing "halftime" speech for the benefit of the general and his staff officers at the White House, Johnson said, "Abe, you are going over there to win. You will have an army of five hundred and fifty thousand men, one of the most powerful air forces ever assembled, and the invincible Seventh Fleet of the U.S. Navy offshore. Now go over there and do it!"

General Abrams, good soldier that he was, remained silent as he reached out to shake the President's hand. In the rear of that room, however, another army general, a member of Abrams's staff, a man who had been with him during WWII, spoke up. "Mr. President," he said, "you have told us to go over there and do 'it.' Would you care to define what 'it' is?"

LBJ remained silent as he ushered the general and his men out of the Oval Office. That, in a nutshell, is the story of the military role in that long, terrible, winless war. We had no "objective," that is, no reason to be there.

For General Westmoreland, the man who served during those hectic years of the Johnson escalation of the war, the objective of the war became the "body count"—the number of dead "enemy" reported in a given period of time. A related objective was "enemy strength estimates"—the number of enemy troops calculated to be in the field. It was assumed that if the body count was going up, the strength of the enemy must be going down. The more "bodies" that could be counted, the closer we were supposed to be getting to victory.

Few men, if any, had more experience with the inner workings of Vietnam policy, at the Washington level, than Lt. Gen. Victor H. Krulak. He served as special assistant for counterinsurgency and special activities on the Joint Chiefs of Staff during the Kennedy years, 1962–63. He was my immediate boss in SACSA for all of that period. The general was a rare and gifted man who might well have been appointed commandant of the Marine Corps had President Kennedy lived.

He left the Pentagon in 1964 to serve as commanding general of the Fleet Marine Force Pacific, with responsibility for all marines in the Pacific Ocean area. That was in itself an oddly structured assignment. His immediate boss in Honolulu was Adm. U.S.G. Sharp, commander in chief Pacific; yet the commanding general over the marines fighting in Vietnam was Gen. William Westmoreland, who had an ambassador and a senior CIA station chief looking over each of his shoulders in Saigon.

Some years later, General Krulak wrote in *First To Fight*: "I saw what was happening [in Vietnam] as wasteful of American lives, promising a series of protracted, strength-sapping battles with small likelihood of a successful outcome."

With this in mind and drawing upon his considerable combat experience in World War II, which included those final heavy battles on Okinawa, Krulak came up with a strategic plan designed to achieve "victory" in Vietnam. With this plan in hand, he flew to Saigon to present it to General Westmoreland. Westmoreland was unable to concur with Krulak's plan. So Krulak returned to Honolulu and presented the plan to Admiral Sharp, who liked it and directed Krulak to take the plan to Washington to present it formally to the U.S. Marine Corps commandant, Gen. Wallace M. Greene.

General Greene approved the plan and made arrangements for Krulak to present it to Robert S. McNamara, secretary of defense. Krulak knew McNamara well from his long service with the Joint Staff in the Pentagon. McNamara agreed with the plan, but then did something that uncovers the real source of power with respect to top-level decisions affecting activities in Southeast Asia during the sixties.

McNamara suggested, "Why don't you talk to Governor Harriman?" Averell Harriman, formerly ambassador to the Soviet Union, was then serving as assistant secretary of state for Far Eastern affairs. I might add that Harriman comes as close to a model for the power elite as I can think of—with one qualifying exception: He lived a most public and ostentatious life. But perhaps that was a role he was chosen to play by his peers.

Harriman graciously invited General Krulak to join him for lunch at his elegant home in Georgetown. Following their luncheon, Governor Harriman invited the general to present his strategic plan for achieving victory in Vietnam. When he got to the climax of the plan, which recommended "destroy the port areas, mine the ports, destroy the rail lines, destroy power, fuel, and heavy industry," Harriman stopped him and demanded, "Do you want a war with the Soviet Union or the Chinese?"

Krulak later wrote, "I winced when I thought about the kind of advice he was giving President Johnson and Secretary of State Dean Rusk."

And, Krulak sums up, "We [the USA] did not have the Washington-level courage to take the war directly to the North Vietnamese ports, where every weapon, every bullet, truck, and gallon of fuel that was prevented from entering the country would ultimately contribute to the success of our arms and the preservation of our lives in South Vietnam."

I know General Krulak to be a dedicated American and a tough, battle-hardened marine. He did not stop with this rebuff in that drawing room of Governor Harriman's home in Georgetown. The commandant of the Marine Corps arranged for Krulak to meet with President Johnson in the White House to discuss the same strategic plan.

About this rare event, Krulak writes: "His first question was 'What is it going to take to win?'"

In response, Krulak listed:

1. Improve the quality of the South Vietnamese government...

2. Accelerate the training of the SVN forces...

3. We have to stop the flow of war materials to the North Vietnamese...before they ever cross the docks in Haiphong....

Then, with his mind on those crucial moments with Governor Harriman, he added, cautiously:

4. "Mine the ports, destroy the Haiphong dock area...."

At that point in the briefing, Krulak writes, "Mr. Johnson got to his feet, put his arm around my shoulder, and propelled me firmly toward the door."

Think carefully of this "Vietnam Scenario." General Krulak summed up this experience by writing:

It was plain to me that the Washington civilian leadership was taking counsel with its fears. They were willing to spend $30 billion a year on the Vietnam enterprise but they were unwilling to accept the timeless philosophy of John Paul Jones: "It seems to be a truth, inflexible and inexorable, that he who will not risk cannot win."

At this point General Krulak, among others, realized that the Washington strategy was, in his exact words, "a losing strategy." I might add that when Krulak's good friend Adm. U.S.G. Sharp wrote his own book about Vietnam in retrospect, he wrote it under the title *Strategy for Defeat*. This is precisely the way those top military men felt about that war.

America had been told by such experienced men as Generals of the Army Omar Bradley and Douglas MacArthur and Gen. Matthew Ridgway that we could never win a Vietnam-style land war in Asia. They understood the problem, too.

They recalled the old story from the days of the Japanese war in China during the 1930s. The Japanese, with their greater firepower and attack aircraft and their more mobile mechanized divisions, wrought terrible destruction on the Chinese. The headlines posted on bulletin boards throughout China gave the figures for battle after battle. It was said that one old man, reading these totals of Chinese and Japanese losses on the ratio of 10 to 1 and 20 to 1 in favor of the Japanese, turned to a friend beside him and said, "Look at those lists, from city after city; just look at those losses. Pretty soon, no more Japanese."

Many of the older, more experienced American generals looked at the hopeless conflicts in Korea and Vietnam and remembered that story. At the rate it was going, the American casualty rate was becoming similar to that of the Japanese—pretty soon, no more Americans.

This is the account of the generals and the admirals. They saw the terrible losses, and they knew there were more to come. Note carefully that it was not the story of the ambassador and of the CIA's chief of station. The CIA had set the tone and other parameters of the warfare. This was how the battles of the Cold War were planned.

On the other hand, that was all Westmoreland had to fight for, that is, the body count. Through the decades of the war, the count mounted into the millions. They continued to count the bodies, and no one asked: "Who are these people who are being killed?" Were they really the "enemy"? Were any of those pajama-clad people really a threat to the United States?

There is something remarkable about that word "enemy." First of all, during wartime, the adversary, by tradition, is supposed to be in uniform. When the Yankee rebels at Lexington and Concord saw the redcoats coming, they had no trouble identifying the "enemy." Things were so different in Vietnam. First of all, the Vietcong had no uniforms. Without an "enemy" in uniform, whom do you shoot?

No one believes in killing in cold blood, but if someone is declared to be an "enemy," then cold-blooded killing of everyone in sight becomes morally permissible, and is even encouraged by an application of the theory of Malthus: "There won't be enough food anyway; so what's wrong with killing them?"

An example of this line of reasoning occurred when, in November 1985, the former director of central intelligence, William Colby, appeared on Larry King's late-night talk show. At one point, King brought up the subject of assassinations by the CIA, while making reference to political assassinations and to the agency's assassination manual, which had been discovered in Nicaragua. Colby came back with a most interesting, and troubling, response. He said that there had been a time when the CIA had set up certain political assassinations, but that as DCI from 1973 to 1976, he was proud of the fact that he had been responsible for ending that practice. Colby then said that he did not approve of killing anyone in cold blood. Without hesitation, he added that this view did not include the "enemy." An enemy, he said, should be killed.

This is the same man who, when he headed the dreaded Phoenix program in Vietnam, took credit for the fact that at least sixty thousand

Vietnamese had been killed "in cold blood" by his American, Korean, Filipino, Taiwanese, and Vietnamese agents.

This raises a fine point with reference to the Vietnam War. In that war, who was the enemy? And who decided who was the enemy? This most basic question, in warfare, causes us to consider with care the account of the "1,100,000 Tonkinese refugees." These people had been moved as the result of a hypothetical humanitarian cause in order the create an enemy scenario.

When these one-million-plus Tonkinese from the north were moved into the Saigon area, as has been discussed, you can imagine the impact these destitute and penniless strangers had upon the totally unprepared and disorganized people of the south? Can you imagine the impact of the sudden movement of one million strangers, we'll say, from the Kansas City area to Los Angeles? This situation by itself created riots, unrest, and general disorder wherever these hordes of people settled. It created enemies, hundreds of thousands of them. This factor alone bred warfare, as the CIA had planned it would.

Then the American advisers to Ngo Dinh Diem tightened the screws a few more turns. They advised Diem to issue two far-reaching national directives, to wit:

1. All French local government officials had to turn over their responsibilities to Vietnamese and leave the country. Among other things, the French had been administering the village constabulary system for decades. This system maintained law and order.

2. All Chinese residing in and doing business in Vietnam had to leave. For the most part the Chinese maintained the local, grass-roots economic system of the rich agricultural country-side.

The ostensible reasons for both of these directives seemed reasonable enough. The French had agreed to leave anyway, and there was no reason why they should delay their departure just because they were involved in local government. But basic law and order, especially in the rural farming regions, had been administered by the French. With their departure this essential government service disintegrated, and it was not adequately replaced by the newly formed Diem government.

Additionally, a rumor campaign was started to explain that the Chinese were, no doubt, spies for the Chinese Communists and the

Vietminh; and that, if they were not spies, they were at least supportive of communism.

Both of these directives were forcefully carried out, and before long, the French and Chinese had departed. Many of them were members of families that had been in Indochina for generations. The results of these directives marked another broadening of the definition of "enemy"; in every village, those who had been friends of the colonial French or the entrepreneurial Chinese were moved closer to the "enemy" category.

One cannot understand too completely the strength of the village way of life for these ancient people. It began with family loyalty, which was regarded as the most respected value in Vietnamese life. The most significant religious ceremonies of these people were the rites regarding family ancestors. After a man's family came his farm. A farm consisted of village property cultivated by that family for centuries. After the family and farm came the village, and for millions of Indochinese the village was the only political structure they knew. For centuries they had been allowed to govern themselves. The senior council of village notables selected a First Notable, called the Tien Chi (in the north) or the Huongca (in the south). Theirs was the last word required for the settlement of significant financial and juridical problems. It was here that the American advice to Diem had been most damaging.

The loosely knit, French-monitored constabulary system provided an adequate framework for most legal matters. It easily provided for law and order. Now law and order collapsed.

On the other hand, the Chinese had, for centuries, been the local entrepreneurs. They kept commerce alive and well in the remote, autonomous regions. Now commerce came to a standstill.

The only outside influence from the source of higher authority was that of the tax collector and the military draft. From 1890 on, the French had introduced the land tax and a head tax. Under French control there was not much difference in the communal organization and administration of these thousands of villages, whether in Tonkin, Annam, or Cochin China.

This fragile and ancient network of basic government broke down. Diem and his American advisers were not even aware of this fact and so did not bother replacing it. The collapse could have been expected even under normal conditions; but in South Vietnam in the late 1950s, with one million Tonkinese Catholics thrust into this once stable and docile society at the same time that law and order vanished, the results were predictable. There was widespread banditry as the Tonkinese flocked together to steal food and other necessities, including farmland. There were riots, and before long many formerly peaceful villages had become a no-man's-land where native owners were the enemy in the eyes of the intruders and their friends in the government of Saigon. The definition of "enemy" was being broadened to include the longtime stable natives.

While these destructive forces were taking place, Ngo Dinh Diem's new government was being urged by its American advisers to organize and pacify the country and to drive out the Communists. Before that could be done, an "enemy" had to be somehow identified. I have heard people on the streets of Saigon say that as Diem's forces raced across the land in American trucks and American helicopters, they decided that "anyone who ran" was the enemy. How could anyone tell? How do you identify the enemy under such conditions? Certainly not by the gratuitous exhibit of redcoats.

In the ancient art and practice of warfare, especially at the most basic local level, there is a brutal system of interrogation and control for the purpose of identifying "friend" and "foe" that has come down through the years. It is sometimes known as the "One Hand" or "Five Fingers" system.

The French were using this system in Algeria, and it was passed through the clandestine services from the French to the American CIA and thence to their Vietnamese "elite guard" that had been trained by the Filipinos. It works, most effectively, like this:

1. An armed group rushes into a village and immediately intimidates its people by burning huts and shooting a few random people, if necessary, and then rounding up everyone else in the center of the village.

2. The invaders know that the elders are the leaders, so they single out the oldest active male and order him to point out the members of his family, then have them stand by him in one group. The invaders may have brought with them some informer or agent who will select this elder for them.

3. This first group becomes the "thumb," or Group 1 on a scale of 5. Then the intruders ask the elder, "Who of the remaining villagers were close to the French or the Chinese? He points out a few families. They are thenceforth declared to be "enemy" and become Group 5.

4. The elder is asked who are his own enemies or persons he does

not trust. These, too, are thrust into Group 5. (There is no point in asking, "Who are the Communists?" The villagers wouldn't know. They don't know the word or its implication as "enemy.")

5. Then the others in the village are asked which group they are closest to, and the elder is asked to verify this. These "indefinite" groups are logically numbered 2 or 4. Group 2 identifies with the leader, his relatives, and his friends. Group 4 identifies with the "enemy," Group 5.

6. Those who belong to none of the above groups become Group 3; this is usually the largest of the five groups.

The invaders tell the chosen elder that he will be responsible for the administration and defense of his village. Then they order the chief to "train" Groups 3 and 4 and to move them closer to his trusted circle, or they will be eliminated.

Before they leave, the invaders either shoot the members of Group 5 or tie them up and take them away for "reorientation" and "pacification." This places the village in the hands of the elder and leaves no "enemies" there. The Group 5 members will never be seen again.[1]

In the Five Fingers system, it can be seen that if the invaders, perhaps with prior knowledge, had selected a Tonkinese "refugee" as the leader of Group 1 in the village, the natives and owners of the village property would automatically be put in Group 5 and either be killed or removed. This would be justified, since they would have been "identified" as the "enemy."

This process made it possible for the newcomers to take over many villages; the system was used all over Vietnam during those terrible early days when there was no true government and after the one million northerners had moved in, before anyone had ever heard the word "Vietcong" and its Communist connotation. The natives became the enemy.

With the departure of the Chinese, an even more fundamental problem was created. The ancient economic system was destroyed and with it the basic food and necessities-of-life economy that had supported millions of otherwise moderately prosperous Cochin Chinese. When the Vietnamese farmer harvested his plentiful crop of rice, he filled baskets woven of rice straw by the women of the families. He loaded those rice-filled baskets into his sampan (flat-bottomed boat) and poled it along one of the ever-present canals to the central village, where his crop was converted by means of a most efficient economic process into a certain amount of the basic necessities of his and his family's life— essentially salt, tools and blades, fabric, and silver.

It had long been the custom for each farm family to go to the village and pile their baskets of rice beside the others. Each farmer, by long custom, had a supply of small black sticks (about the size of Magic Markers) with his name or symbol on each stick, and he would place one in each of his baskets of rice. (None of these comparatively wealthy farmers had a broker or other system of marketing.)

On market day, the Chinese merchant would arrive in his large sampan. All of the rice baskets, removed from the village square, would be loaded onto his boat, at which time the village elder would collect all of the marker-sticks. The Chinese merchant then bought the rice, based upon the going price per basket multiplied by the number of sticks. In turn, the village elder bought from the merchant the salt, tools, fabrics, and other assorted needs from that account. If there was a balance to the credit of the village, the Chinese merchant paid it in silver coinage of intrinsic value. Each farmer benefitted according to the tally of his sticks.

This age-old system created the market for the farmer's produce and provided him with the basic necessities of life in exchange for his labor—until the impact of the Diem edicts that ousted the French and the Chinese. The farmers from these many villages knew nothing about the edict or about the departure of the French and Chinese. Then came the first rice harvest and the first market day after the edict.

Thus, by market day, they had cut the rice, woven the baskets, poled the sampans into town, and placed their sticks in each basket in the village square. They had no telephones. They had no broker. They had no way of knowing that the Chinese merchant was not coming. Their harvests of rice rotted where they lay in baskets in the village.

What would you do with a crop if no marketing system existed to purchase it and there was no means to move it to a national or world market?

One crop cycle could pass, perhaps two or three, but eventually these villagers had to have necessities. In many of the villages, the greatest necessity was potable water. Even though they were knee-deep in brackish rice-paddy water all day, they frequently had to buy their drinking water. They bought it from the same Chinese merchants. After the Chinese left, when the villagers had no water, they had no place to go. When they did not get enough rainwater to fill the huge earthen jars every family owned for their supply of drinking water, they drank brackish water. They became ill. (Throughout history, water contamination has been one of the most effective weapons of war.)

So the stronger men of the village banded together to get water, salt, and the other necessities of life by the oldest means known to man: banditry. This was not political or criminal; it was not ideological. It was a last-resort effort to obtain simple and elementary needs. And one village attacked another in order to get water—to live.

This situation created a deadly, low-level, self-perpetuating turmoil. Diem's fragile new country was falling apart in the most unlikely of places—in the regions that had always had the most prosperous farms and in the zones farthest from Hanoi. Unrest spread through the most fertile, most stable, and most wealthy regions of the new State of Vietnam. Back in Saigon, the Diem government and its American advisers were totally unaware of the true causes of this unrest, but they were ready with their Pavlovian interpretation. It was, they said, the result of "Communist subversion and insurgency." Chronologically, this situation began to be identified and studied by the Americans at just the time that Kennedy became President. The concept of "counterinsurgency" had been heard in the Pentagon before the end of the Eisenhower administration; but it came into full flower with the arrival of the Kennedy administration.

The Americans' only embarrassment, if they considered it at all, was that the most serious rioting was taking place in the southernmost regions of the State of Vietnam, those areas farthest from any appreciable "Communist" infiltration. The Diem government and its American advisers had created the causes of the rioting, but they wanted the rest of the world to believe otherwise. They had much bigger things in mind.

With no system of law and order to replace that used by the French, with no organized means of merchandising to replace that of the Chinese, and with no need for taxes because of the easy access to free-flowing American dollars, the Diem government was not close to the citizenry and had no idea what to do about the rioting, banditry, and boiling unrest. It turned to its American advisers for aid.

Meanwhile, all over South Vietnam, the rioting spread. The rice-producing villagers raced everywhere in a crazed search for essential necessities. They overran other communities—rubber plantations, fishing villages, lumber villages, etc.—in fierce, uncontrollable local battles.

All of this was seriously amplified by a different kind of trouble caused by the influx of the one million strangers from the north. These invaders needed the same things as their hosts: the basic necessities of life. They had left their homeland and found themselves in a new land that was seething with unrest.

To the recently arrived American advisers, such as those in Secretary McNamara's "Combat Development Test Centers," a quick-fix concept designed to correct such problems, the American perception of this conflagration was clear: This rioting and insurgency must be the work of the Communists. The Communists, they reported, had infiltrated the refugees and now were linking up with an underground fifth column of natives to create havoc and to embarrass the new Diem government in Saigon.

"Communist-led subversive insurgency" became the buzzwords, and in the United States "counterinsurgency" became the answer. The CIA's Saigon Military Mission and its undercover terrorism and propaganda campaigns were paying off splendidly for the creators of the Cold War. All of Indochina had been prepared for war by them and their undercover activities, and the American armed forces were coming. By the time the American troops arrived, South Vietnam would be seething with an identifiable "enemy." This had been the objective of those who'd ordered the movement of the 1,100,000 Tonkinese natives in the first place.

During this period, as in the late 1950s and the closing years of the Eisenhower administration, the general perception was that the fighting in Laos was actually much more serious than the rising problems in Vietnam. The CIA and its U.S. Armed Forces "Special Forces" allies were playing a monumental role, behind the scenes, in Laos, Burma, and Thailand. This was kept quite distinct from their activity in Vietnam.

In late 1960, when the departing President, Dwight Eisenhower, met with his successor, John F. Kennedy, he told him that the biggest trouble spot would be in Laos and that with Ngo Dinh Diem in Saigon, he had little to worry about there. U.S. participation in Laos is another story, but one factor of the fighting in Laos did have a most significant impact upon the escalation of the war in South Vietnam: It began the evolution of an entirely new set of tactical characteristics of that warfare.

A full squadron of U.S. Marine Corps helicopters had been secretly transferred, at the request of the CIA, from Okinawa to Udorn, Thailand, just across the river from Laos. The helicopters that saw combat in Laos were based and maintained in Thailand by U.S. Marines. These military men did not leave Thailand; the helicopters were flown to the combat zones of Laos by CIA mercenary pilots of the CAT Airlines organization, under the operational control of the CIA.

In those days, in accordance with the provisions of National Security Council Directive #5412, every effort had been made to keep U.S. military and other covert assistance at a level that could be "plausibly" disclaimed. The theory was that if these operations were compromised in any way, the U.S. government should be able to "disclaim plausibly" its role in the action. In other words, these helicopters had been "sterilized." There were no U.S. Marine Corps insignia on them, there were no marine serial numbers, no marine paperwork, no marine pilots. This was at best a thin veneer; but the veneer was needed to make it possible to use the marine equipment.

Back in Saigon, CIA operators wanted those helicopters transferred to Vietnam. Many of the CIA agents who had been infiltrated into South Vietnam, contrary to the provisions of the Geneva Agreements, had been moved there secretly from Laos. While in Laos they had become accustomed to the use and convenience of this large force of combat helicopters. They wanted them in Vietnam, where they proposed to use them to transport South Vietnamese army troops to fight the fast-growing numbers of "enemy" who were rioting for food and water in the rice-growing areas of the Camau Peninsula. This helicopter movement was planned to be the CIA's first operational combat activity of the Vietnam War. It turned out to also be the first step of a decade of escalation of that war.

At that time, all American military aid to South Vietnam was strictly limited by the "one for one" replacement stipulation of the 1954 Geneva Agreements. The CIA could not move a squadron of military helicopters into South Vietnam, because there were no helicopters there to replace. So movement of those helicopters from Laos would have to be a covert operation. Any covert operation could be initiated and maintained only in accordance with a specific directive from the National Security Council and with the cooperation and direct assistance of the Department of Defense.

The CIA's first attempt to have these helicopters moved for combat purposes came in mid-1960 and was an attempt to beat the system. Gen. Charles P. Cabell, the deputy director of central intelligence, called one of his contacts (who happened to be this author) in the Office of Special Operations (OSO), a division of the Office of the Secretary of Defense

(OSD), to see if these helicopters could be moved to Vietnam quickly and quietly, on an emergency basis, because of the outbreak of rioting all over the country.

In those days, the Office of Special Operations followed the policy set forth by Secretary of Defense Thomas Gates, which closely followed the language of the law, that is, the National Security Act of 1947. The pertinent language of that act states that the CIA operates "under the direction[2] of the NSC."

At the time of General Cabell's call, OSO had received no authorization for such a move, and the request was denied on the ground that such a move would be covert and that the NSC had not directed such an operation into Vietnam. During the Eisenhower and Kennedy administrations, the letter of this law was followed carefully.

In most cases, the CIA did not possess enough assets in facilities, people, and materiel to carry out the operations it wanted to perform. Therefore, the CIA had to come to the military establishment for support of its clandestine operations. The Defense Department would not provide this support without an agreed-upon NSC directive for each operation and usually without a guarantee of financial reimbursement from the CIA for at least "out-of-pocket" costs. This kept the CIA at bay and under reasonable control during these more "normal" years.

There is an interesting anecdote from this period that reveals President Eisenhower's personal concern with clandestine operations. Control of the CIA has never been easy. During the early part of Eisenhower's first term, the NSC approved a directive—NSC 10/2— that governed the policy for the development and operation of clandestine activity. The NSC did not want covert operations to be the responsibility of the military. It said, quite properly, that the military's role was a wartime, not a peacetime, one. Therefore, such operations, when directed, would be assigned to the CIA. At the same time, it had long been realized that the CIA did not have adequate resources to carry out such operations by itself and that it was better that it didn't.

Thus, the NSC ruled that when such operations had been directed, the CIA would turn to the Defense Department, and when necessary, to other departments or agencies of the government, for support.

Sometimes the support provided was considerable. President Eisenhower was quite disturbed by this policy. He saw that it would create, within the organization of the CIA, a surrogate military organization designed to carry out military-type covert operations in peacetime. It would follow, he thought, that the CIA might, over the years, become a very large, uncontrollable military force in itself. He could not condone that, and he acted to curb such a trend.

President Eisenhower had written in the margin of the first page of the NSC 10/2 directive, on the copy that had been sent to the Defense Department: "At no time will the CIA be provided with more equipment, etc., than is absolutely necessary for the support of the operation directed and such support provided will always be limited to the requirements of that single operation."

This stipulation by the President worked rather well as long as the Office of the Secretary of Defense enforced it strictly. Later, certain elements of the military turned this directive around and began to use the CIA as a vehicle for doing things they wanted to do—as with the Special Forces of the U.S. Army—but could not do, because of policy, during peacetime.

This situation was confronted seriously by President Kennedy immediately following the failure of the Bay of Pigs operation in April 1961.[3]

By the early 1950s, former President Harry S. Truman was saying that when he signed the CIA legislation into law, he made the biggest mistake of his presidency. In those same years, President Eisenhower had similar thoughts, and he did everything he could to place reasonable controls on the agency. Both of these men feared the CIA because of its power to operate in secrecy and without proper accountability.

During the Eisenhower administration, the Defense Department was usually scrupulous about this note penned on NSC 10/2 by the President and was careful to limit support to that needed for the current operation. The result was that there was always close cooperation and collaboration between the agency and the Defense Department on most clandestine operations. In other words, the clandestine operations carried out during that period were usually what might be called joint operations, with the CIA being given operational control. This applied to the development of all "military" activities in Vietnam, at least until the marines landed there in March 1965.

This NSC policy applied to that request for helicopters from General Cabell of the CIA and accounts for the fact that his original request was vetoed by the Defense Department. This veto required the CIA to prepare its case more formally and to go first to the NSC with its request for the helicopters. In those days, the NSC had a subcommittee, the "5412/2 Committee," or "Special Group," that handled covert activities. This group consisted of the deputy undersecretary of state, the deputy secretary of defense, the President's special assistant for national security affairs, and the director of central intelligence, the latter serving as the group's "action officer." In 1957, the chairman of the Joint Chiefs of Staff also became a member. Approval for these helicopters was eventually obtained from this Special Group, and the secretary of defense authorized the Office of Special Operations to make all arrangements necessary with the Marine Corps to move the aircraft to Vietnam—secretly—from Udorn, Thailand, to an area south of Saigon near Camau.[4]

Perhaps more than any other single action of that period, this movement of a large combat-ready force in 1960 marked the beginning of the true military escalation of the war in Vietnam. From that time on, each new action under CIA operational control moved America one step closer to intervention with U.S. military units under U.S. military commanders.

By 1960–61, the CIA had become a surrogate U.S. military force, complete with the authority to develop and wage warfare during peacetime.[5]

In the process, the CIA was fleshed out with U.S. military personnel who had been "sheep-dipped"[6] to make it appear that only civilians were involved. This process was to have a detrimental impact upon the implementation of the Vietnam War: It put CIA civilian officials in actual command of all operational forces in the fast-growing conflict, at least until 1965. As an additional factor, the concealment of military personnel in the CIA led to many of the problems that the armed forces would later delegate to the League of Families of Prisoners of War in Southeast Asia.

By the time this policy giving the CIA "operational" control over all American pseudomilitary units in Vietnam was changed, the "strategy" of warfare in Southeast Asia had become so stereotyped that such true military commanders as Generals Westmoreland and Abrams found little room to maneuver. They were required to take over a "no-win," impossible situation without a military objective, except that of the overriding Grand Strategy of the Cold War: that is, to make war wherever possible, to keep it going, to avoid the use of H-bombs, and to remember Malthus's and Darwin's lessons that the fittest will survive.

Therefore, when the NSC directed a move of helicopters to Vietnam, it ordered the Marine Corps unit at Udorn to be returned, with its own helicopters, to Okinawa. New helicopters of the same type were transported from the United States—meaning, of course, that new procurement orders of considerable value were placed with the helicopter-manufacturing industry, a business that was almost bankrupt at the time.

At the same time, the CIA had to put together a large civilian helicopter unit, much larger than the original Marine Corps unit, with maintenance and flight crews who were for the most part former military personnel who had left the service to take a job at higher pay and a guarantee of direct return to their parent service without loss of seniority. This meant that overseas, combat wage scales were paid to everyone in the unit, at a cost many times that of the military unit it replaced.

As soon as the helicopters arrived and were made ready for operational activities, the CIA's "army" began training with elite troops of the new South Vietnamese army. They were being hurried into service against those villages where the most serious "refugee-induced" rioting was under way. This operation opened an entirely new chapter of the thirty years of war in Vietnam.

Now who was the enemy? When CIA helicopters, loaded with heavily armed Vietnamese soldiers, were dispatched against "targets" in South Vietnam, who could they identify as "enemy"? It was during this period that we heard the oft-repeated reply "Anyone who runs away when we come must be the enemy."

With the passage of time and with the incitement of low-level warfare in South Vietnam while this helicopter campaign was being prepared, the "enemy" was more and more the native population of the villages of southern Vietnam. They were indeed fighting; but they had been forced to fight to defend their homes, their food, and their way of life against the starving refugees from the north. The CIA's Saigon Military Mission had proved its "make war" prowess. In that mixing bowl of banditry, everyone was the "insurgent," everyone was the enemy. Additionally, Diem's two edicts driving out the French and the Chinese exacerbated the problem across the land. As things developed, many of Diem's newest and finest troops were members of that one-million-strong invading force of "Catholic" refugees. They had now become the "friends" of Saigon against the local and native "enemy."

As discussed earlier, the CIA's Saigon Military Mission had arrived in Saigon in 1954. It was now 1960. President Eisenhower was winding down his two-term administration, and the young Senator John F. Kennedy was organizing his own group of friends, relatives, and experts to gain the office of the presidency and to set in motion the historic events of those momentous days of Camelot.

We have prepared the way for the main focus of this book with a detailed discussion of the origin and activities of the CIA and with a systematized review of the buildup and early escalation of the warfare in Vietnam. These events present a significant view of the Cold War and what challenges the new President would face. Of course, they are far from the whole story. A brief look at a few other CIA-related activities will serve to broaden the scope of the scene in Washington on the threshold of the sixties.

In May 1960, President Eisenhower had planned to culminate his dream of a "Crusade for Peace" with the ultimate summit conference with Nikita Khrushchev in Paris. On May 1, 1960, a CIA spy plane, a high-flying U-2 with Capt. Francis Gary Powers at the controls, overflew the Soviet Union from Pakistan and made a crash-landing at Sverdlovsk in the heart of Russia and by so doing wrecked the hopes of the summit conference and the dreams of Eisenhower and Khrushchev, two old warriors who understood each other.

As a footnote to that important event, it was Allen W. Dulles himself, giving testimony before a closed-door session of the Senate Foreign Relations Committee, who said positively that, despite Soviet claims, the Powers U-2 had not been shot down but had descended because of engine trouble. This important statement by Dulles has been little noted by the press, and little thought has been given to exactly why that aircraft had "trouble" at such a critical time.[7] Later, Eisenhower confirmed that the spy plane had not been shot down by the Soviets and had indeed lost engine power and crash-landed in Russia. Its unauthorized flight was another part of the Cold War game designed to deny President Eisenhower his Crusade for Peace.

As another chapter of the Cold War, in March 1960, President Eisenhower had approved the beginnings of a clandestine campaign against Fidel Castro in Cuba. Later, during the summer of 1960, while Vice President Richard Nixon was stepping up his campaign to succeed Eisenhower, the VP secretly met with the NSC, urging more action against Castro.

At the same time, Senator Kennedy, with equal secrecy, was meeting with the eventual leaders of the Cuban exile brigade that landed on the beaches at the Bay of Pigs. Manuel Artime Buesa, the beach commander, met with Senator Kennedy at the Kennedy home in Palm Beach, Florida, and in his Senate offices on Capitol Hill[8] along with Manuel Antonio de Varona and José Miro Cordona—both former premiers of Cuba—and other Cuban exile leaders of the time.

Perhaps unknown to both aspiring candidates, Eisenhower had

categorically laid down the law to the CIA and to the Defense Department: There would be no acceleration of anti-Castro activity during the lame-duck period of his administration, so that the new President, whether it was Nixon or Kennedy, would not have to confront a situation that had already been decided upon and set in motion.

During the crucial TV debates between Nixon and Kennedy in late 1960, Nixon, who had been attending all the NSC meetings on the subject of Cuba, felt that he had to play down the anti-Castro rhetoric because of his personal involvement and the requisite bonds of secrecy. On the other hand, JFK, who did not benefit from that official knowledge and was not bound by secrecy but who was well aware of the subject matter because of his closeness to the Cubans, forcefully challenged Nixon and took the initiative on that subject during the debates. The edge gained from that single subject may have provided JFK with the votes that gave him his narrow victory in November 1960.

After the election, some quick moves were made by the CIA to "lock in" its projects before the new administration took over in January 1961. At Fort. Bragg, North Carolina, an all-new U.S. Army Special Forces organization was hastily increased in size, and its secret mission was enlarged to include "peacetime" covert activities.

At the same time, an international school was set up at Fort Bragg to provide training for counterpart troops from many nations throughout-the world. This school, although later called the John F. Kennedy Center, was not initiated by President Kennedy, as many believe, but was opened in late 1960 by the then deputy secretary of defense, James Douglas. The Green Berets of Vietnam fame were born there and shortly thereafter were ready to begin their long march to Saigon.

Similar clandestine camps were rushed into being in Panama, Guatemala, and Nicaragua for the brigade of Cuban exiles, along with other training sites in Miami, at Eglin Air Force Base in Florida, and in the Lake Pontchartrain area near New Orleans. Aircraft of various types were brought in from CIA assets all over the world, as were CAT pilots. The old, reliable Filipino clandestine experts joined the underground teams.

Then, in December 1960, President-elect Kennedy made a surprising announcement. He had decided to keep Allen W. Dulles as his director of central intelligence and J. Edgar Hoover as head of the FBI. With this announcement, the stage was set for the 1960s—the decade in which hundreds of thousands of American fighting men would see action in the escalating war in Vietnam.

EIGHT

The Battlefield and the Tactics, Courtesy CIA

WITH THE ELECTION of John F. Kennedy to the office of the President of the United States of America, there was an influx of new men into the higher appointive echelons of the government. Nowhere was this change more pronounced than in McNamara's Office of the Secretary of Defense and, from there, throughout the Pentagon. It was said that there were more Phi Beta Kappas in that office than ever before. True, but this did not ensure that they were the best military minds.

However, they overcame their lack of military experience and knowledge through study and dedication to their jobs. They learned from their environment, among the older and more stable bureaucrats. Most important, they brought with them new ideas, new perspectives, and new goals. Nowhere was this more evident than in their approach to the unconventional problems of the Cold War and its greatest battlefield at that time, Indochina.

One thing became quite clear before too many months had passed. They, and their young President, had come to stay the course. They laid out long-range plans through the first four years and clearly intended to be there for the second four, when their work would come to fruition. And next there was Bobby, and then Teddy. There was always the possibility of "the Dynasty."

I had been assigned to the Office of the Secretary of Defense in 1960 when Thomas Gates, the Morgan Guaranty Trust banker from New York, was secretary. As a businessman, he ran the Pentagon and the military establishment as a businessman would. He was an excellent secretary of defense.

My military assignment carried over into the McNamara era. He was one of the new world of businessmen. He had been a Harvard professor and had gone directly to a high position with the Ford Motor Company. Much was made of the fact that Kennedy had selected the president of the Ford Motor Company to be the secretary of defense. Few noted at the time that when McNamara came into the Pentagon as the appointee to the job, he had been the president of Ford no more than a month.

I was called to brief Mr. McNamara on a military activity related to CIA operations on the second or third day he was in office. As had been the custom under Mr. Gates, I prepared a briefing paper on the subject that was only two or three pages long. I discussed it with McNamara and left it in his hands. Just as I reached my office, I received a call asking me to return.

When I arrived, his executive officer—an old friend of mine— informed me that Mr. McNamara had read my brief paper, liked it, and wanted me to go back and write up the whole business. Over the course of the rest of the day I composed about twenty-five pages and returned them to the secretary's office. The next morning I found them on my desk with a brief note: "Fine. Just what I wanted" It was signed by McNamara.

I have thought of that small, introductory incident many times, and I recall that I had said to myself, That man is the secretary. He is going to see mountains of paper. If he wants long briefs loaded with statistics, instead of short summaries, he will never make it. He'll be buried in bureaucratic paper.

The Kennedy administration was like that. The men nearest to him were old friends, former associates, family. JFK would rather discuss a serious matter with a roomful of friends than with the National Security Council or any of the other committees that proliferate in official Washington.

This is the way Kennedy came to the White House. After all, he had grown up as the son of the American ambassador to Great Britain. He had served with the U.S. Navy during World War II. Since World War II he had been a member of Congress, first as a representative and then as a senator. As the record shows, he was a voracious reader, and he involved himself in a broad spectrum of interests. He was a young man with a lot of experience and the capacity to learn. He was a searching questioner.

As President, he inherited many interesting programs. Two of them played a major part in his life as President. His decisions concerning those projects created the tensions and pressures that brought about his sudden and untimely death. Had Kennedy lived, America would not have become militarily involved in Vietnam. Had he lived, he would have been elected to a second term, and during that term his plans and his goals would have reached fruition. Only his assassination in Dallas on November 22, 1963, kept him from achieving those goals.

When he took office, he was confronted with the immediacy of the CIA's plan to invade Cuba utilizing a brigade of U.S.-trained Cuban exiles. Concurrently, he listened to two important briefings about the situation in Vietnam. President Eisenhower had told him that the Southeast Asian problem nation would be Laos and that Vietnam was no place to become involved with American troops. The other Vietnam briefing came from Edward G. Lansdale, who had just returned from a long visit with Ngo Dinh Diem. Some of those who were at the briefing believed that Kennedy intended to make Lansdale the next ambassador to Saigon.

January 1961 was memorable for another most important event. In that month, Nikita Khrushchev made his famous speech pledging Soviet support of "wars of national liberation." Almost everyone in the new administration was inclined to believe that unconventional warfare was likely to be vitally important during the decade of the sixties, as we shall see.

Kennedy knew that the conflict in Southeast Asia had been instigated under the covert leadership of the World War II Office of Strategic Services and the CIA on one side and by the Soviet KGB and the Chinese on the other. Khrushchev's challenge was ominous, and Kennedy did not doubt that it focused on Cuba and Vietnam. Even before the JFK inauguration, McNamara and a team of close associates moved into a suite of offices in the Pentagon. McNamara attended the "Pre-Brief"[1] intelligence-report sessions every morning. He began, right away, concentrating on Vietnam.

As we have seen in this account of the CIA and the progression of the Vietnam era, there were four major steps in this development of conflict in Southeast Asia, by the OSS and CIA on one side and the KGB, with Chinese assistance, on the other, all leading to the inevitable American-tion of the war.

Most of the Kennedy team did not realize that the first step along this Cold War trail had begun in September 1945, the month that the Japanese surrendered to end World War II, with that shipment of arms and other war matériel—approximately one-half of that which had been scheduled to have been used by American troops during the invasion of Japan—from the stockpiles on Okinawa to Haiphong Harbor near Hanoi. There an American OSS team turned them over to Ho Chi Minh and his military commander, Col. Vo Nguyen Giap. The other half of that invasion stockpile went to Korea.

None of us were able to discover, during these early McNamara sessions, who had made that decision in 1944 or 1945. It was an enormously important decision at the time and had monumental impact on the development of the Cold War over the next thirty years. During those next decades, the Vietminh would become a truly formidable foe. One thing we should have learned from that costly experience in Vietnam was that the Vietminh defeated a full array of American military power, including an army of as many as 550,000 men, and in the process had destroyed more than five thousand U.S. helicopters.

With no air force or navy to speak of, the Vietminh proved tough enough to outlast both the mighty U.S. Seventh Fleet and a modern air force equipped with everything from fighter-bombers and U-2 reconnaissance aircraft to B-52 strategic bombers. They took all we could muster, short of nuclear weapons, including the horrendous Christmas 1972 bombing of Hanoi, and survived to hoist their own flag over Saigon.

This tragic debacle of American arms brought to mind the words spoken by Sen. Barry Goldwater during an address in 1983 before a group of retired military men in Washington, D.C., that the trouble with the American military forces at that time was that they had no "Grand Strategy." Had Kennedy lived, Goldwater would not have had to make that address.

Step number two was an amazing operation, unnoticed by almost everyone on the new Kennedy team. They did not realize that during the mid-fifties, more than 215,000 half-terrorized Tonkinese natives had been flown to South Vietnam, 660,000 more had been transported there by sea with the U.S. Navy, and hundreds of thousands of others had traveled by foot and by other means. This horde of destitute people flooded the south and began to take over villages, jobs, the police organization, the army, and many of the top jobs in the new Diem government.

Early in this period the Saigon Military Mission planners had come up with a civic action program "to place civil service [read "Tonkinese"] personnel out among the people, in simple dress, where they would work alongside the people, getting their hands dirty." (This is from the official report prepared by Edward G. Lansdale and presented to the new President during a White House meeting in January 1961.)

When a training center, established in Saigon for SMM's civic action program, failed to recruit any native (southern) volunteers, Diem/ Lansdale "selected a group of young university-trained men from among the refugees [read "invaders"] from North Vietnam." Diem ordered the civic action teams and the army commanders to work together on a "pacification" campaign.

As a result, the immediate beneficiaries of this effort were, more often than not, the northern Catholic invaders.

This situation, as was intended, created the matrix of war—and predictably the "enemy," as often as not, turned out to be the southern natives, while the government was augmented by the Catholic invaders. Between 1955 and 1960 this inflammatory situation became worse every year, and it was exacerbated by steps three and four, to follow.

Ngo Dinh Diem published two edicts at the suggestion of his American advisers, many of them from Michigan State University under the leadership of Diem's political mentor, Wesley Fishel.

The third step came when Diem ordered the French to turn over any government positions they held and leave the country. This order destroyed the effective, but fragile, constabulary system, and in a short time there was no law and order in the new country.

The fourth step in the development of this smoldering internal warfare concerned the issuance of a second edict that directed the Chinese to leave, on the assumption, it said, that they were Communists or Communist sympathizers.

This had a destructive impact on the economic system, as mentioned earlier. The Chinese had been the brokers. They purchased the rice, other crops, lumber, etc., and in return provided money and the necessities of life for the village. This simple, basic village-oriented economic system had kept a most effective political system alive for centuries. When the Chinese left, this system collapsed. Diem was so inexperienced and so poorly advised that each time he came out with new orders, the situation worsened. In villages where the council form of government had existed for centuries and was the supreme political authority, Diem abolished all elections in June 1956. He followed this by abolishing all municipal elections. These errors tended to help thrust the northern Catholics into positions above the local people. As we have said earlier, the natives of southern Vietnam were rapidly being made into an enemy, known as the Vietcong.[2]

By 1960, the situation in South Vietnam was beyond control. The troubles that had been created by Diem's edicts played directly into the hands of the Vietminh. If anything, the Vietminh were the greatest beneficiaries of this terrible situation. The country was falling into their hands.

Having been busy setting up this operation from behind its cloak of secrecy since 1945 (as the OSS), the CIA was ready by 1960 to come out into the open in what was known as "the war to save South Vietnam and all of Southeast Asia" from the onrush of communism—precisely the type of "war of national liberation" that Khrushchev had vowed to fight. This Cold War intrigue, abetted by "domino theory"[3] fears, was ready to pay off with its first series of moves, which would eventually put hundreds of billions of dollars into the pockets of the military-industrial complex of the world.

The CIA's first major operational plan to achieve this ambitious goal for its allies involved the movement of a U.S. Marine Corps squadron of twenty H-19 Sikorsky helicopters from Udorn, Thailand, to the vicinity of Saigon. This was a most crucial and pivotal development. It not only introduced a major unit of modern equipment into South Vietnam, but in doing so it ignored the restrictive terms of the 1954 Geneva Agreement. Before long there were four hundred helicopters in South Vietnam, at a time when the only U.S. military personnel in that country were restricted by President Kennedy to the role of "advisers."

In retrospect, it may seem unbelievable that somewhere in Vietnam lie the rusting hulks of five thousand helicopters lost by American forces, by far the majority of them lost after Kennedy's death in 1963. This was a stark tribute to one of the most foolhardy chapters in the long history of warfare. The loss of five thousand helicopters with crews, passengers, and the dollars they represented makes the "Charge of the Light Brigade," with all of its tragic overtones, seem like a rainy day at a Sunday School picnic by comparison.

The massive deployment of helicopters in Vietnam, spawned by a secretary of defense who preached "cost-effectiveness" while his department practiced utter waste, makes the helicopter itself a symbol of that war. It is scarcely conceivable that so little tactical effectiveness, across the board, could have been achieved at so horrendous and staggering a cost. In a war that produced so very little of anything upon which we can look with pride, the helicopter certainly has to stand head and shoulders above all others as the symbol of waste, mindlessness, and extravagance.

At one point during the war, the famous Israeli general Moshe Dayan, who had led his forces in a dash across the Sinai in the 1967 war against the Egyptians, went to Vietnam as an observer and writer. No stranger to Vietnam, General Dayan went out into the battle zones with U.S. troops and studied the combat he found there.

The general made his conclusion clear that his "lightning war" tactics would not work in Vietnam and then added, "Helicopters may be first-class equipment, but the way they are being used in Vietnam, they are wasted."[4] As much as anything we are aware of, this underscores the great significance of that first CIA move of military helicopters from Laos to Vietnam in 1960. That single action opened the doors to the wanton expenditure of hundreds of billions of dollars—for what?

That was one measure of the helicopter fiasco. There is another. Using a very conservative approach, we can estimate that the loss of five thousand helicopters resulted in no fewer than fifteen thousand to twenty thousand American deaths, based on average crew size and taking into account that many helicopters were lost on the ground, and many others were destroyed without the loss of life. Yet a great number were destroyed with a full crew and a load of American troops. Even if the lower figure of fifteen thousand is accepted, it represents a little less than one-third of all American fatalities in Vietnam. Many of these helicopter and human losses were operational, but a surprising proportion of them were nonoperational—the vehicles just crashed by themselves, without enemy action.

Helicopter losses were staggering. "Of the 6,414 total aircraft-related deaths, to April 17, 1971, 1,792 occurred in fixed wing operations, and 4,622 in rotary [helicopters]," according to a U.S. Air Force policy letter of May 1971.

An even more shocking statistic from the same policy letter follows: Of the 4,622 deaths in helicopter crashes, 1,981, or 43 percent, were "casualties not from action by hostile forces." If you had helicopters, you did not need an enemy.

Not only was the helicopter a tragic and costly adjunct to an altogether tragic and costly war, but it is entirely possible that the helicopter—or more specifically, the voracious demand for support that is directly related to and attributable to the helicopter—was instrumental in creating a situation that had much to do with the unfortunate and unnecessary escalation of the war. By all standards, the demand for manpower to support helicopter operations proved massive.

Helicopters sent to Vietnam in 1960 for what had appeared to be a noncombatant role resulted in the broad exposure of Americans to hostile fire. Once American blood had been spilled in Vietnam, no matter what the cause, it became a matter of national pride and interest to avenge those deaths and, as it was commonly expressed, to "drive out Communist-inspired subversive insurgents."

This whole helicopter saga had begun with that brief telephone call from the deputy director of central intelligence to the Office of Special Operations in the Office of the Secretary of Defense in December 1960, when he sought to obtain the transfer of a squadron of U.S. Marine Corps helicopters from Udorn, Thailand—where they were being used in a CIA program in Laos—to Vietnam. This movement of "cover-unit"[5] helicopters caused the displacement of the first few pebbles that became a major avalanche in South Vietnam.

It should be noted that this initial call in 1960 from the deputy director of central intelligence, Gen. C. P. Cabell, came shortly after the First National Bank of Boston had arranged for the Textron Corporation to acquire the Bell Helicopter Company. The CIA had arranged a meeting in the Pentagon in order for a vice president of the Boston bank to discuss Cold War uses of, and demand for, helicopters before it recommended the merger to the officers of Textron. It was the Bell-built "Huey" that became the most-used helicopter in Vietnam.

In earlier days, these old H-19 Sikorsky helicopters had been used to provide transportation for the indigenous security forces of the Saigon government, who would range over the villages of the lush rice-growing country of the southernmost Camau Peninsula. At that time, rioting and banditry had broken out because the Chinese brokerage system had collapsed. This had nothing whatsoever to do with the Vietminh, the Vietcong, or communism. These were simply desperate people deprived of food and water by the removal of the Chinese.

Diem's government misinterpreted this banditry and violence as insurgency and chose to attack and wipe out these "hot spots of communism." Thus, the CIA's helicopters were used in an attempt to suppress a "violent" situation. American advisory personnel flew the helicopters, and American "civilians" maintained them. South Vietnamese police manned the guns.

It is worthwhile to note how fundamentally important an offshoot of this action became. These villages were surrounded by water, but the water was brackish and undrinkable. As a result, huge earthen jars, passed down from generation to generation, were used to store fresh water. During dry periods these jars were replenished by shipments delivered by the same Chinese-owned sampans that came at harvest time to pick up the rice. When these sampans no longer came, water supplies became precarious. Working with the brutal logic of the ignorant, Diem's police machine-gunned these lifesaving earthen jars in the so-called Communist villages. From this time on, these villagers became maddened by the lack of potable water and by the tragedy of their situation.

Tens of thousands of these terrorized and desperate people became homeless migrants, called "Vietcong" and subversives, in their own homeland. Without intent and without choice, they fell upon residents of other villages that still had water and food. They turned into bandits. Thus, the tens of thousands in turmoil became hundreds of thousands labeled "enemy."

What else could Diem's people tell their benevolent American advisers and counselors, who had given them the helicopters and helped them into power in the first place? Of course, it was not all altruism on America's part. The CIA had been working for fifteen years to bring this struggle to the point where American forces would have to become involved, bringing all their expensive military equipment with them. It became tactically expedient to make use of these helicopters as a throttle on the pace of the war. Whenever villages were attacked, "insurgency" flared up among the people. This created an active "enemy" and gave the new Diem Self Defense Force units, and the new army and its Philippines-trained elite units, plenty of action. From this modest and ostensibly innocent beginning, the United States followed up by sending helicopters by the thousands into Vietnam.

As the strife heated up in 1961, Secretary McNamara created Combat Development Test Centers in Vietnam to study firsthand how the war should be waged. The helicopter became more intimately associated with close-in combat. A wild, carefree helicopter sweep was more thrilling than a motorcycle race along the California oceanside, and ten times as hell-raising. American and Vietnamese gunners armed with automatic weapons sprayed indiscriminate barrages into villages and forest havens from one end of the country to the other. When more action was desired, they dropped napalm to set the flimsy huts of the villages on fire. It was at this time that Agent Orange was introduced as a military weapon. It was intended by McNamara's "Whiz Kids" to defoliate the jungles of Vietnam so that the gunners in the helicopters could better seek out their targets, that is, those Vietnamese who ran away as the helicopters approached.

In those earlier days, tactical intelligence was nonexistent. Helicopter crews dashed out on missions, little knowing where they were going or what they would find when they got there. They shot at anyone and anything that moved. Those were the days of deadly ambushes of American helicopters and of blind attacks upon any target. Because of the helicopter's slow speed and vulnerability, the crews soon learned how costly a 55-mph flight at gun-range altitude could be. They abandoned higher-altitude flights and resorted to very low level "nap of the earth" tactics. This put the odds in their favor, because they were able to reduce their exposure time if they remained consistently below treetop level over the rice fields. The tactic generally paid off, except for chance encounters with wily ground teams.

For a while, losses were cut, but then the battle-wise bandits found a way to turn this tactic to their favor. The combat helicopter of that 1960–66 period was overtaxed when it had to fly two hundred miles in a round-trip with any more than ten passengers and their military equipment. The bandits learned that if they struck a target village in order to set up a helicopter counterattack less than sixty or seventy miles from the helicopter base, they would allow the helicopter pilots discretion to fly a deceptive and devious flight path to the target, providing the helicopters with a margin of safety against ambush.

However, when they attacked a target that was eighty to one hundred miles from the helicopter base, the pilots were forced to fly a more nearly straight-line flight path at low-altitude, "nap of the earth" levels to the target and back. In such situations, it was much more feasible for the bandits to set up an ambush. And this is just what they did, repeatedly.

Having learned this tactic, the bandits had won a definite advantage. They knew where the helicopter base was, and they had the option to attack any village they wanted in order to set up a situation that would lure a helicopter response. By observing the preparatory action at the base, they could alert the ambush parties by radio that the helicopters were en route.

Teams of natives equipped with any weapons they could find would lie in the tall grass in fields along the intended flight path of the massed helicopters. Then they would wait for the helicopters to fly overhead.

One of their most effective tactics involved the use of a bow and arrow barrage. These archers had none of the style and color of Robin Hood, but they were just as lethal. They would lay upon their backs in the fields with crude, heavy bows across their feet, upraised to the aerial target. When the helicopters approached, they would load their bows with heavy, clublike projectiles that were fastened to twine, wire, rope, or vines. The air would be filled with this trash, which would catch in the rotor blades, bringing down as many as fifteen helicopters at one time.

As the years passed and escalation of the war took place, more and more airfields were built and covered with helicopters. It was no longer necessary to fly long missions. Refueling stops were more frequent, and thus cargo tonnage increased. The battle helicopter "gunships" were developed, and these aircraft, bristling with machine guns and rockets, gave better than they received. This situation gave rise to the next level of enemy tactical measures to prey upon the ever-lucrative helicopter target.

To these homeless men in the bush, the helicopter was still the best and most worthwhile target. They were densely concentrated on airfields all over Vietnam. This was just the type of target that a small, stealthy band could attack, hit and run, with little fear of loss and great expectation of spectacular results. With great care and stealth, the enemy moved mortars and short-range rockets close to the airfields. Without warning, a wild barrage of weaponry would descend from the sky, and large numbers of sitting-duck helicopters would be lost. These sneak attacks took their toll as total helicopter losses climbed into the thousands.

The primary objective of guerrilla forces in this type of warfare is not to become involved in major battles but to keep hitting the enemy where he is most vulnerable, to make him bleed to death.

To those who have seen the hand of the Kremlin behind all this master strategy, it must be clear by now that if the objective of the Communists in Southeast Asia was to see the United States sacrifice men and money in tremendous quantities while they themselves gave up little money and no men, Vietnam was the ideal situation. It bothered the Kremlin not at all to see Asians die along with Americans. In fact, as long as the war continued, the Soviets won on a relative basis over Asians and Americans at the same time. The war in Indochina was a classic example of how this modern concept of "war by attrition" could prove successful.

The Indochinese were the innocent victims in this struggle, because their homeland had been chosen as the battleground for this impossible contest that earned more than $500 billion for the military-industrial power elite. The helicopter war exemplified the success of this guerrilla strategy, both from the Pentagon's point of view and from that of the detached, chess-playing men in the Kremlin, who understood that you must give up a little to win a lot.

Helicopter operations can be likened to an iceberg. The good and the glory, if any, were seen at the top; the cost and the tragedy were submerged. Sometimes this submerged mass shows itself above the wave. Statistics are not always the best resort, but they serve a useful purpose. The study of statistics was what Secretary McNamara liked best. Those statistics forecast that a helicopter-augmented war machine would churn out big dollars.

For many, many years, all military helicopter operators in the army, air force, and marines had attempted to maintain their ungainly machines at a 50 percent or better "in-commission" rate. This means that, at that time, they expected one out of every two helicopters on hand to be flyable.

The army, for example, for years plugged away at a 49 percent rate and strived for better. Such a rate was affected by many factors and would most likely have been lower than 49 percent had not a great number of helicopters in the field been factory-new, making it nearly certain they would be in commission. A 50 percent rate was considered good. Newer models may have exceeded this rate for brief periods, but then their high support costs created problems of their own. The significance of this 50 percent in-commission rate was felt most when evaluated in terms of operational factors. For example, to move one hundred men one hundred miles in one day at the rate of ten men per helicopter actually took twenty helicopters. This ensured that ten would be ready to perform that job, because 50 percent, or ten helicopters, would not be available at any given time.

Keep in mind also that in the typical Vietnamese tactical situation, it was no more than one hundred miles to the operational site, and then another one hundred miles back, and there was no fuel at that base in the hostile zone. As a result, moving one hundred men two hundred miles in one day for a mission at midpoint took twenty helicopters. At unit price, this doubled the cost of operation.

The next cost showed up in personnel. A twenty-helicopter squadron consisted of some two hundred men. Two or more of these squadrons required supply and maintenance units of an additional two hundred men each and the food, housing, and fuel elements essential to support their operations.

As a result, a continuing demand for operations that required an average of twenty helicopters per day to transport two hundred men one hundred miles actually required a base with forty helicopters and close to one thousand operational, medical, headquarters, and support personnel—not including those who provided housing, food, fuel services, transportation, and the vital function of twenty-four-hour-a-day perimeter defense.

Between 1960 and 1962, when the American military advisory strength in South Vietnam was limited to 16,000 men, Gen. Paul Harkins, then the senior commander in Saigon, complained bitterly that with a ceiling of 16,000 men, he could get only 1,200–1,600 effective combat advisers, because most of the rest were confined to logistical support work. The bulk of that support work and cost was related to the helicopter.

Gen. Earle Wheeler, at that time director of the Joint Staff,[6] ordered an analysis of the Harkins complaint that led to the Okanagan study[7] of helicopter operations in Vietnam. The study revealed that not only was General Harkins's complaint well founded; it was learned that a major segment of the oversized logistics contingent was directly involved in the support of helicopters that General Harkins himself had requested, little realizing the resultant burden of his action.

The surprising thing revealed by this study was that this was true even when most of the helicopters in Vietnam were assigned not to the army but to the CIA[8] and much of the maintenance was being performed by highly paid contract civilians.

The helicopter mushroom grew, and it generated greater demands of its own. Helicopter bases were soft and vulnerable targets. They needed vast supporting perimeter defenses. These defenses created a heavy demand for "noncombatant" U.S. military personnel. Because these perimeter guard elements were sparsely positioned and were immobilized by the nature of their task, they became centers of little wars of their own, thus heating up the intensity of combat throughout the land.

As opposition increased and became more sophisticated, helicopter formations were seeded with gun-carrying helicopters. Because the gunships carried no combat troops at all, the ratio of men carried, per aircraft per mile, dropped. With this, the cost per man transported, related to the number of helicopters per mission, skyrocketed again.

There is much that can be said in support of the tactical employment of the helicopter in warfare. But there are very few missions of such exceedingly high priority that they can best and most profitably be performed at the cost that helicopters incur. And even if certain operations can be justified, do they occur with enough frequency that they require the continuing availability and maintenance of operational helicopter units?

We have noted the loss of five thousand helicopters, the loss of fifteen thousand or more American lives, and the loss of not less than $1 billion in direct cost; yet we have not scratched the surface. The helicopter is one of the most costly vehicles to maintain and operate of any device ever built, and in South Vietnam the cost per hour of civilian maintenance and facilities was without equal. The helicopter is a voracious consumer of engines, rotors, and spare parts—all of which had to be airlifted from the United States, halfway around the world.

Although the helicopter can land in a space roughly equal to its own length, large numbers of helicopters must be gathered onto major airfields in order that supplies, fuel, and other services may be brought to them efficiently. The vast number and expense of helicopter airfields must be added to all the above.

Of course, these are not the only costs and the only burdens. The military services have thousands of pilots and aircraft crewmen. But these men (and now women) cannot be used for helicopter operations; all helicopter crews must be specially trained. All of these helicopter-related requirements cost heavily in men, money, and material things.

In a war in which the true measure of victory and defeat must be measured in terms of the cost and attrition on each side, the helicopter was found to be the biggest contributor to both cost and attrition. In retrospect, we discovered that the Russians, the Chinese, the North Vietnamese, and the Vietcong never had to contend with anything like it on their side. They won because we lost so much.

This paradoxical situation has caused many of us who were close to that action to wonder what might have happened if the war in Vietnam had been a "normal" war, with aerial strike forces on both sides? Imagine the havoc and devastation that could have occurred if a real, first-class enemy had been able to mount effective air attacks against those airfields where the helicopters were massed. The losses would have been catastrophic. We could not have justified having created such targets in the first place in the face of sophisticated opposition.

This helicopter episode has been a tragic lesson. The copters were introduced by the CIA and used by the agency to cause the escalation of the war. Once the pattern had been set, the military commanders who came later, in 1965 and thereafter, were caught in a tactical bind they could not break.

Much has been said and written about the number of Americans in Vietnam during the Kennedy administration, and there are many who attempt to place the blame for the escalation of that conflict on him. The facts prove otherwise.

As I have shown above, there was a ceiling of 16,000 personnel during the 1960–62 years. This is true; and it must be kept in mind that those Americans, except for such limited assignments as the Military Assistance Advisory Group, were there under the operational control of the CIA. When General Harkins complained about the few combat-effective men he had available, he learned that only 1,200 to 1,600 of the 16,000 personnel in Vietnam were in that category. The rest, more than 14,000, were support troops, and most of them for helicopter support. This was a relatively small number of combat troops considering that the overall total rose to 550,000 within the decade.

According to interpretations of these data that attempt to place the blame for the Vietnam War on Kennedy, the *New York Times* publication of "The Pentagon Papers" states, "President Kennedy, who inherited a policy of 'limited-risk gamble,' bequeathed to Johnson a broad commitment to war." This is contrived and incorrect. The *Times* all but ignored President Kennedy's important National Security Action Memorandum #263, October 11, 1963, that, as official policy, ordered 1,000 men home from Vietnam by the end of 1963, and all U.S. personnel out of Vietnam by the end of 1965. That was the carefully planned Kennedy objective announced scarcely one month before his untimely death.

It was not until President Johnson had signed NSAM #273 on November 26, 1963, that the course of the Kennedy plan began to be changed, and this trend became most apparent with the publication of NSAM #288 in March 1964.

The directed escalation of the war began under Johnson, as we shall see. Had Kennedy lived, all the madness that happened in Vietnam after 1964 would not have taken place. President Kennedy had vowed to bring one thousand Americans home from Vietnam by Christmas 1963 and to have all U.S. personnel out of Vietnam by the end of 1965. Kennedy's death brought about a total reversal of that carefully structured White House policy and that sincere promise to the American people.

NINE

The CIA in the Days of Camelot

ONE OF THE BITTEREST electoral battles of the century was fought in 1960, when Sen. John Fitzgerald Kennedy of Massachusetts was elected President over the incumbent vice president, Richard Milhous Nixon. For Nixon and his longtime backers[1] in and out of government, the defeat on November 8 proved staggering and unexpected. They had many concrete plans for the next four years, and their dreams had been deflated by that "half-a-vote-per-precinct" loss.

Years later, Nixon wrote one of the most unusual articles ever published for the millions of readers of *Reader's Digest*. Under the title "Cuba, Castro and John F. Kennedy," the article appeared in the November 1964 issue.

Nixon began with these remarkable sentences: "On April 19, 1959, I met for the first and only time the man who was to be the major foreign policy issue of the 1960 presidential campaign; who was destined to be a hero in the warped mind of Lee Harvey Oswald, President Kennedy's assassin; and who in 1964 is still a major campaign issue. The man, of course, was Fidel Castro."

Nixon had been Dwight Eisenhower's vice president during the 1950s, and before that, going back to 1947, had served in both the House and the Senate. He knew Washington well, and the great industrial, legal, and banking combines that are so closely enmeshed with the government. In the article, he looked back over the hectic earlier years and linked the four factors that were uppermost in his mind:

118

1. the 1960 election
2. Fidel Castro
3. the death of the President, John F. Kennedy
4. the alleged assassin, Lee Harvey Oswald.

He wrote almost nothing about the growing warfare in Southeast Asia, even though he knew very well that it had been under way since 1945, when a vast shipment of American arms was put in the hands of Ho Chi Minh in Vietnam. By 1964, it had run its complex course, a course he had encouraged under the direction of the CIA.

Nixon's article was published just one month after the release of the twenty-six-volume report of the Warren Commission, which made public the incredible finding that Lee Harvey Oswald, acting alone, had been responsible for the death of John F. Kennedy. It is astonishing that, since Nixon's article was actually written before the Warren Commission report was issued, he had arrived at the same finding as that highly confidential report with his identification of Lee Harvey Oswald as "President Kennedy's assassin."

It is worth noting that a member of the Warren Commission also wrote an identical finding before the report was published. Gerald R. Ford's article "Piecing Together the Evidence" appeared in *Life* magazine on October 2, 1964, before the Warren Report came out.

These two men—subsequently Presidents—for some reason found it necessary to put on the record, as soon as they could and before the official publication of the Warren Commission Report, their support of the theory that Lee Harvey Oswald was the lone assassin. This allegation of theirs was not true. Anyone with a few minutes of spare time can prove that Lee Harvey Oswald was not the lone assassin. Why did both of these men feel compelled to say that he was? To whom were these public figures beholden?

It has been established that Nixon was in Dallas on the day, and at the exact time, that JFK was shot—12:30 P.M., Central Standard Time, November 22, 1963.[2] Oddly, he avoided that fact in his *Reader's Digest* article. Nixon wrote:

I boarded a plane [in Dallas on the morning of November 22] to New York. We arrived on schedule at 12:56. I hailed a cab. We were waiting for a light to change when a man ran over from the street corner and said that the President had just been shot in Dallas. This is the way I learned the news." [NOTE: A man told him the news]

In the November 1973 issue of *Esquire* magazine, there's the following imaginative quote by Nixon:

I attended the Pepsi-Cola convention [in Dallas] and left on Friday morning, November 22, from Love Field, Dallas, on a flight back to New York... on arrival in New York we caught a cab and headed for the city... the cabbie missed a turn somewhere and we were off the highway... a woman came out of her house screaming and crying. I rolled down the cab window to ask what the matter was and when she saw my face she turned even paler. She told me that John Kennedy had just been shot in Dallas. [NOTE: This time a woman told him the news]

That is not the end of Nixon's version of that busy day. The Nixon story that appears in Jim Bishop's book *The Day Kennedy Was Shot* is said to be the "official" account:

At Idlewild Airport [now JFK Airport] in New York... reporters and photographers had been waiting for the American Airlines plane... among [the passengers] was Nixon. As he got off the plane, he thought that he would give "the Boys" basically the same interview he had granted in Dallas... Nixon posed for a few pictures... got into a taxi-cab... was barely out of the airport when one of the reporters got the message: The President has been shot in Dallas.

Nixon covered up the important fact that he had been in Dallas at the very time Kennedy was killed with that erroneous recollection which he included in the *Reader's Digest* article. Why did Richard Nixon not want anyone to know that he was actually in Dallas at the time of the assassination? Why did he so categorically pronounce Oswald to be the killer before the specious evidence of the Warren Commission had been made public? Does he have other information that he has been concealing to this day? It is uncanny that he so positively linked Cuba, Castro, Oswald, and Kennedy while at the same time completely omitting other important events. They were his priority; he must have had his reasons.

Nowhere was Nixon's bias more evident than in another passage from the *Reader's Digest* article: "Fidel Castro, therefore, proved to be the most momentous figure in John F. Kennedy's life," wrote Nixon. This was Nixon's version. Would Kennedy have agreed?

As these chapters on the CIA and its role in the warfare in Southeast

Asia arrive at the threshold of the Kennedy era, it is important to realize that JFK's ascendance to power was a much more ominous transition than many have understood. An analysis of Nixon's unusual comments will make this clear.

Castro and the Cuban situation in 1960 were the major foreign policy issues during the Nixon-Kennedy campaign, principally because Nixon had made them so.

On March 17, 1960, President Eisenhower had approved a rather modest CIA proposal for "A Program of Covert Action Against the Castro Regime"[3] developed by the CIA and endorsed by the Special Group[4] consisting of a deputy undersecretary of state, a deputy secretary of defense, the director, of central intelligence, and the special assistant to the President for national security affairs. As an ex officio member, Vice President Nixon was almost always present at these meetings.

This proposal later became known as the Bay of Pigs operation. Nixon not only knew of the President's approval but, as vice president, was one of the prime movers of that top-secret CIA project. As he wrote for *Reader's Digest*: "I was one of only three members of the President's Cabinet who had been briefed on it, and...had been the strongest advocate for setting up and supporting such a program."

During the campaign, this inside awareness of a highly classified CIA operation created a cruel dilemma for Nixon. Both Democratic and Republican headquarters knew, as they approached the fourth television debate of that campaign, that the presidential race was neck and neck. Nixon, with his eyes on Kennedy, wrote:

> I was faced with a heads-he-wins, tails-I-lose proposition. If in the TV debate I were to reveal the existence of the [CIA's Cuban] training program...I would pull the rug out from under Kennedy's position. But, if I did so, the project would be doomed. I had only one choice: to protect the security of the program.

JFK, unrestrained by such top-secret security considerations, advocated "that the United States openly aid anti-Castro forces inside and outside Cuba." The Kennedy attack had been released in time to appear in the afternoon papers, before the television debate went on the air. In this release the headlines said: "Kennedy Advocates U.S. Intervention in Cuba; Calls for Aid to Rebel Forces in Cuba."

Each candidate was battling with all guns blazing; as in love and war, there are no limits in a political contest. Nixon's assessment of

Kennedy's wiles fell short. Again, in the *Reader's Digest* article, he wrote: "In a speech before the American Legion convention... I had gained the initiative on the issue...."

It is hard to believe the shrewd Nixon still believed, in 1964, that "[he] had gained the initiative on this issue." He should have known that after that very same American Legion convention, he had easily been outfoxed by Jack Kennedy. Kennedy proved his wide knowledge of this CIA project by his comments during the 1960 TV debates and during the progression of events that followed.

Immediately after the American Legion convention, the top-ranking ringleaders of the Cuban exile community, some of whom had been on the platform with Nixon at the convention, flew directly to Washington for a strategy meeting. Where did that meeting take place? Right in the private confines of Senator Kennedy's Capitol Hill office. Kennedy had stolen a march on Nixon. He made himself totally aware of all that was going on in that top-secret CIA program, and when the time came to fire the big guns, during the fourth television debate, he did. He had all the facts.

His handling of this major issue was so effective that he won the television debate handily and then won the closest presidential election in history over the outgunned Nixon. At that time, Nixon may have taken a page from the Kennedy clan motto: "Don't get mad, get even." A bold counterattack began. Nixon and his cronies determined to get even. Most old-line bureaucrats know that the time to make huge gains is during that "lame duck" period between the election in November and the inauguration of the new President in January. At no time is this gambit more opportune than at the end of an eight-year presidential cycle.

The CIA and its bureaucratic allies in key government positions made some telling moves that, in retrospect, show how astutely they had read the presidential tea leaves. When Eisenhower had approved the CIA "Cuban exile" proposal, he had one thing in mind. Since the Castro takeover on January 1, 1959, tens of thousands of Cubans had fled the island. In Ike's view, the best way to provide for these refugees, at least those of military age, was to put them in the army or in an army-type environment, where they would get food, clothing, and shelter while they became oriented to the American way of life. After that they could go it on their own. Thus, he approved a plan to put thousands of them into an "army" training program—and no more than this.

The CIA, however, saw this as an opportunity to go a bit further. The

CIA's presentation, made by Allen Dulles on March 17, 1960, to the National Security Council,[5] was divided into four parts, one of which was "the development of a paramilitary force outside of Cuba for future guerrilla action."

This was later expanded by the CIA to read:

> Preparations have already been made for the development of an adequate paramilitary force outside of Cuba, together with mechanisms for the necessary support of covert military operations on the island. Initially a cadre of leaders will be recruited after careful screening and trained as paramilitary instructors. In a second phase a number of paramilitary cadres will be trained at secure locations outside of the United States so as to be available for immediate deployment into Cuba to organize, train, and lead resistance forces recruited there both before and after the establishment of one or more active centers of resistance. The creation of this capability will require a minimum of six months and probably closer to eight. In the meantime, a limited air capability to resupply and for infiltration and exfiltration already exists under CIA control and can be rather easily expanded if and when the situation requires. Within two months it is hoped to parallel this with a small air supply capability under deep cover as a commercial operation in another country.

This is precisely how the CIA presented its proposal, and this is the way such clandestine operations generally begin. At the time of approval, the President believed the concept of paramilitary action, as described, was to be limited to the recruitment of Cuban exile leaders and to the training of a number of paramilitary cadres of exiles for subsequent use as guerrillas in Cuba. Let no one be misled into believing President Eisenhower approved an invasion by a handful of Cuban refugees—not the man who had led the massive and successful Normandy invasion on June 6, 1944.

When this Cuban exile program was initiated, the CIA and its allies in the military had prepared a curriculum[6] to provide the students in training with background information on Cold War techniques. A portion of this training described what is meant when the CIA uses the term "paramilitary":

> Paramilitary Organizations: We Americans are not very well acquainted with this type of organization because we have not experienced it in our own country. It resembles nothing so much

as a private army. The members accept at least some measure of discipline, and have military organization, and may carry light weapons. In Germany in the 1920s and early 1930s the parties of the right and the Communists had such organizations with membership in the hundreds of thousands. It is readily apparent what a force this can be in the political life of a country, particularly if the paramilitary forces are armed, when the supremacy of the army itself may be threatened.

Following formal authorization from the White House Special Group, which included Nixon, the CIA set out to recruit three hundred Cuban exiles for covert training outside the United States. As with most such programs, the CIA began in accordance with NSC directives to come to the military for support. An inactive U.S. military base in Panama, Fort Gulick, was selected as the initial training site. The CIA put together a small unit to reactivate the base and to provide the highly specialized paramilitary training that the agency employs for similar units at certain military-covered facilities in the States, such as the one at Camp Peary, Virginia.

In the beginning, the CIA was unable to obtain properly qualified military doctors for Fort Gulick and therefore went to the Military Support Office at Headquarters, U.S. Air Force[7]

This action marked the formal entry of the U.S. military into the Bay of Pigs program in support of the CIA.

To keep the CIA-Cuban exile program in perspective and to understand the significance of how this prior planning had an impact later upon the administration of John F. Kennedy, it must be understood that these events were taking place while President Eisenhower was winding up his eight-year term in office. Eisenhower had had high hopes for his Crusade for Peace, based upon a successful summit conference in Paris during May 1960, and for a postsummit invitation to Moscow for a grand visit with Khrushchev. The visit to the Soviet Union was to cap his many triumphant tours of other countries, where the ever-popular Ike had drawn crowds of more than one million.

In preparation for the summit and its theme of worldwide peace and harmony, the White House had directed all aerial surveillance activity ("overflights") of Communist territory to cease until further notice and had ordered that no U.S. military personnel were to become involved in any combat activities, covert or otherwise, during that period.

Because of these restrictions, the support of this Cuban exile training facility began cautiously. Aircraft that had been ordered for a Cuban exile air force were being processed under the terms of an Air Force contract. In the Far East, an enormous overflight program that had been delivering vital food, medicine, weapons, and ammunition to the Khamba tribesmen (who were battling Chinese Communist forces) in the far Himalayas of Tibet was curtailed. Yet on May 1, 1960, a U-2 spy plane flown by Francis Gary Powers left Pakistan on a straight-line overflight of the Soviet Union en route to Bodo, Norway, contrary to the Eisenhower orders.

The U-2 came down in Sverdlovsk, halfway to its goal. Powers, alive and well, was captured by the Soviets. This incident destroyed the effectiveness of the summit conference and brought about the cancellation of the invitation to President Eisenhower to visit Moscow. It also ended Ike's dream of the Crusade for Peace.

The same man who was in charge of the Cuban exile program and the vast overflight program that supported the Khambas, Richard Bissell, deputy director of plans for the CIA, was the man who ran the U-2 program and who, ostensibly, sent the Powers flight over the Soviet Union on May 1, 1960.

Through this crescendo of events, the CIA kept the pressure on Vietnam[8] and moved the Cuban exile project along. On August 18, 1960, the President and a few members of his cabinet were briefed by the CIA on these developments, and a budget of $13 million was approved. Additionally, military personnel and equipment were made available for the CIA's use. Although the plan devised after Kennedy's election seemed to be the same as the original one approved by Eisenhower, those familiar with day-to-day developments noted a change. A number of Cuban overflights had been flown, usually in Air America[9] C-46 or C-54 transport aircraft. The crews were Cuban exiles. They were scheduled to hit selected drop-zone targets at night, based on signals from the ground. Few of these missions, if any, were ever successful, and reports reaching the Pentagon were that "Castro was getting a lot of good equipment free."

There were a number of over-the-beach landings from U.S. Navy ships that targeted sugar refineries, petroleum storage sites, and other prime targets for sabotage. These met with some success. But many exile teams disappeared and were never heard from again. The CIA and Cuban exile leaders either underestimated or did not believe in the total effectiveness of Castro's "block" system.[10] They could not get through its surveillance.

Faced with the reality of this situation, certain key CIA planners took advantage of the lame-duck administration to change the approved concept for the Cuban paramilitary operations. By midsummer, moves were designed to build a Cuban exile strike force to land on the Cuban coast. The three-hundred-man operation had grown to a three-thousand-man invasion. By June 1960, the CIA obtained a number of B-26 aircraft from the U.S. Air Force, each modified with eight .50-caliber aerial-type machine guns in the nose section. Those aircraft were aerodynamically "cleaner," with fewer antennas and protrusions to slow them down, and hence faster than the original World War II models. They packed tremendous firepower. Many of these B-26s had been used by the CIA in the aborted Indonesian rebellion of 1958[11] and were moved from Far East hideaways for use by the Cuban exiles.

The CIA had already consolidated its rather considerable covert air apparatus from air bases in Europe and Asia to a semisecret facility on Eglin Air Force Base, Florida. While this air force was being assembled at a modification facility in Arizona and an operations base in Florida, the CIA made a deal with Miguel Ydigoras Fuentes, president of Guatemala, and his close friend, Roberto Alejo Arzu, a wealthy landowner, to begin the improvement of a small airport at Retalhuleu in western Guatemala.

By summer 1960, around-the-clock construction was under way, under the management of a "nonexistent" firm known as the Cornwall-Thompson Company. Before long, a large assembly of C-46s and C-54s from Air America, along with the B-26s, took shape, and all further training was keyed to the landing operation on Cuban soil. While the Cuban program was being escalated, the CIA and its allies in the Pentagon took advantage of the political hiatus. They had so many covert programs under way and so many more planned that they had to make some arrangements for an enormous increase in available manpower.

The National Security Council's 5412/2 Committee, which was empowered to direct covert operations, had approved the limited use of military personnel for Cuban training. That approval opened the door to other cases and other clandestine operations. This is what CIA Director Allen Dulles used to call "peacetime operations," meaning clandestine operations. Some years later the Reagan administration—which included some of the same undercover operatives from the 1950s—referred to these clandestine operations as "low-intensity conflicts" by "special operations forces."

It is traditional that the uniformed armed forces of one nation are not to be used in or against another nation, except in time of war, without some specific agreement, such as the NATO plan. This generally means in time of a declared war. Up to 1960, as a result of the specific prohibitions of NSC 5412, the U.S. government honored this tradition, with very few exceptions, and limited the use of arms to specific actions. This is one reason why the Bay of Pigs tactical plan did not include any reference to "air cover" to be provided by U.S. forces.

Nations, and nationalism, survive because of the existence of the fragile structure called sovereignty. True sovereignty must be absolute. If sovereignty is not recognized by the entire family of nations—large and small, rich and poor, developed and underdeveloped—nationalism will crumble, and the larger nations will devour smaller ones before the last act, when those left will begin to devour each other, like scorpions in a bottle.

To be practical, we must admit that true sovereignty no longer exists. No nation today is free and absolutely sovereign. To be truly sovereign, a state must in no way be limited by external authority or influence. The United States is, in one way or another, under some degree of influence from other nations every day, and vice versa. The fact of the existence of the H-bomb and its uncontrollable power denies sovereignty to all nations. This fact has eroded sovereignty to the point that a small country, such as Israel, can boldly destroy a nuclear power plant in Iraq and a revolutionary camp in Tunisia, and demolish Lebanon, at will.

In today's matrix of nations, the power elite controllers[12] are attempting to structure something to take the place of nationalism and sovereignty in a "New World Order."

Thus, we have had the increasing use of military forces in nonmilitary roles, as in the indiscriminate carpet bombing of defenseless Cambodia. The CIA has been the leading edge of this change, and by 1960, during the transition period, it saw a way to make elements of the military available to itself for its ever-increasing "covert" operations. Of course, in this context the whole idea of "covert," "clandestine," or "secret" operations became ridiculous. Such operations could not be kept secret; they were called "secret" to avoid accounting for the vast sums of the "black" budget expended to support them and as a means of disciplining the media and any possible whistle-blowers.

The first step in this move for military support was for the CIA to join with the Office of Special Operations in the Office of the Secretary of Defense, where Lansdale and other CIA agents were assigned, to completely rebuild and enlarge the army's Special Forces units—the

Green Berets of Vietnam in the 1960s. The army's Special Forces units had been allowed to decline, and morale had deteriorated at Fort Bragg.

Then a sudden change occurred. Lansdale, who had returned from Vietnam after completing his job as chief of the Saigon Military Mission and confidant of President Ngo Dinh Diem, found a way to bypass the conventional U.S. Army channels to reinvigorate the army's Special Forces with the help of the CIA and friends in the Defense and State departments. He won approval to activate a new Special Forces school and to increase the size of the Special Forces center at Fort Bragg for U.S. troops and selected personnel from foreign armies.

He could not be sure of top-level U.S Army approval and support for his bold plan, so he went around them. While everyone else had become occupied with the final days of the presidential campaign, Lansdale, his longtime associate Col. Sam Wilson, and this writer flew to the U.S. Army Civil Affairs and Military Government School at Fort Gordon, Georgia, in October 1960, for a meeting with its commanding officer. During this meeting, Lansdale arranged to get a copy of the curriculum of that school, which—in the space of one week—we converted into a "Cold War" curriculum for use at the Special Forces center.

Lansdale, the CIA, and their Special Forces associates rushed this curriculum into print. The then deputy secretary of defense, James Douglas, cut the ribbon for the center, which became known as the Army Special Forces John F. Kennedy Center. The President-elect, ironically, had nothing to do with it.

This ceremonial opening was so hurried that "instructors" were reading and "teaching" from lesson guides they had never seen before, and the foreign "students" were so few in number that they were rushed from one classroom to another while Deputy Secretary Douglas was being shown Special Forces weapons—the longbow, the crossbow, flechettes,[13] and so forth.

Not to be outdone during this crucial lame-duck period, the CIA's deputy director for plans, Richard Bissell, made more moves. The departing members on the 5412/2 Committee would no longer have any interest in the covert Cuban exile training program. They would be glad to forget the many failures as the Cuban exiles, time after time, did not accomplish their projected goals in Cuba.

On November 4, 1960, with the election set to take place four days later, the CIA dispatched a cable to the Bay of Pigs project officer in Guatemala, directing a reduction of the guerrilla training and the introduction of conventional training of an amphibious and airborne assault force. This was named "Operation Trinidad," after the beach on which the invaders were originally supposed to land.

CIA officials made this major change on their own, without specific approval. They knew that if Nixon became President, he would go along with their decision anyway, since he had been the most vehement anti-Castro agitator at the top level.[14] When JFK reappointed Allen Dulles as CIA director, they figured they could go ahead with invasion planning.

With Dulles continuing as head of the CIA, agency leaders were confident they could work with, or around, Kennedy, and they contrived to lock him into as many programs as possible. This agency's momentum accelerated during the postelection period. Dulles briefed the President-elect on November 29, 1960, and the new plan was formally presented to the outgoing NSC 5412/2 Committee on December 8. There is no record of that Special Group's approval on December 8, but the CIA continued with Operation Trinidad. (This plan was discussed with members of the Joint Chiefs of Staff between January 11 and 19, 1961.)

I was the last officer to brief the outgoing secretary of defense on the subject of Operation Trinidad on his final day in office, while a major blizzard raged over Washington. It can be stated emphatically that the final tactical plan for the invasion that was approved by President Kennedy on Sunday, April 16, at about 1:45 P.M. could well have succeeded. It was based fundamentally on the prior use of four Cuban exile-piloted B-26s to destroy Castro's small combat air force. The first attack had been made on April 15 and had put most of those planes out of commission. Only three remained intact.

The concept behind the Bay of Pigs tactical plan was similar to that of the 1956 British-French clandestine attack on Nasser's air force in Egypt, which destroyed his entire combat air force first, making it possible for Gen. Moshe Dayan's Israeli army to dash across the Sinai to the Suez Canal without attacks from the air. This similar plan for the Cuban brigade was sabotaged[15] from the inside, however, after JFK had approved it that Sunday afternoon of April 16.

Zapata, the beach on the Bay of Pigs, had been selected on purpose because there was an airstrip there suitable for B-26 operations against Castro's ground forces. It was isolated and could be reached only via causeways or the narrow beach itself.

The brigade could take over the airstrip after securing the beachhead, and B-26s flown by Cuban pilots operating from that strip could have overwhelmed any Castro force approaching via the causeways. But this excellent tactical plan was predicated upon the total destruction of Castro's entire force of combat-capable aircraft.

Thus, a second attack was scheduled to knock out Castro's three remaining aircraft at dawn on Monday before the brigade hit the beach and alerted Castro's air defenses. It was absolutely essential that those three aircraft be eliminated first. Kennedy understood that key element of the strategy when he made the decision, on Sunday, to proceed with the Monday, April 17, landing, specifically approving the dawn air strike by four B-26 bombers from Nicaragua to wipe out those last three jets.

The overall second phase of the plan, now called "Operation Zapata," included a Cuban government-in-exile, on the beach if necessary, after the brigade had held Cuban soil for at least seventy-two hours. It had been planned that the Cuban government-in-exile would call upon the Organization of American States (OAS) for support of the brigade immediately and that the United States, with nominal OAS assistance, would sustain the brigade and its new government.

With this show of strength and determination, the CIA forecast that tens of thousands of Cubans would rise to join the brigade and revolt against Castro. In short order he would either be killed, flee, or surrender. This was the plan. But between the time of Kennedy's approval at 1:45 P.M. Sunday and the time for the release of the B-26s from the Hidden Valley base at Puerto Cabezas, Nicaragua, the vital dawn air strike to destroy Castro's three remaining T-33 jets was called off by President Kennedy's special assistant for national security affairs, McGeorge Bundy, in a telephone call to General Cabell.[16]

At about 1:00 A.M., April 17, my home phone rang in Virginia with a call from Nicaragua. It was an old friend, the CIA commander at Puerto Cabezas. He was upset. He told me that the dawn air strike had been delayed. He said, "Anything after a two A.M. departure will destroy the whole plan, because our B-26s will not be able to arrive before sunrise. The brigade will hit the beach at dawn. This will alert the air defenses and the T-33s, and we'll lose our targets on the ground."

He urged me to call General Cabell at the Operation Zapata office and, using OSO/OSD authority, demand the immediate release of the B-26s. I could hear the planes' engines running in the background of the telephone conversation. He suggested, "If I get on my bike and ride across the field, the Cubans will take off without orders." Later, we both wished he had done that. I was unable to reach General Cabell, and

Allen Dulles was out of the country. The Bay of Pigs operation came that close to a chance for success.

After that call, I reached the CIA's Zapata office and suggested they release the B-26s "on Kennedy's orders" or the whole effort would fail. The CIA's tactical commander told me that the situation "is in the hands of" the President's special assistant for national security affairs, McGeorge Bundy; Deputy Director of Central Intelligence Charles P. Cabell; and Secretary of State Dean Rusk.

We all understood that if the B-26s in Nicaragua did not leave very soon, the entire plan would fail. We learned later that someone else had called Nicaragua and said not to worry, other B-26s would knock out the T-33s. This is one reason so many B-26s were shot down later that day. The pilots believed there would be no air opposition—least of all from those superior T-33s.

As a result of that top-level cancellation, those three T-33 jets, scarcely to be considered combat aircraft, yet ever so much better in aerial combat than the relatively slow B-26, shot down sixteen brigade B-26s, sank the supply ships offshore, and raked the beach with heavy gunfire. They alone were responsible for Castro's victory over the brigade. That cancellation of the dawn air strike had created Kennedy's defeat and brought the whole burden down on the shoulders of the new President.

There was much about that sabotaged plan, which damaged Kennedy so drastically, that is similar to the sabotaged flight of Gary Powers's U-2 spy plane over the Soviet Union on May 1, 1960, which destroyed Eisenhower's Crusade for Peace. Neither defeat had been the result of a normal or expected turn of events. Some of the same men, in high places, were in key positions in both projects, and Nixon had worked closely with all of them. We have wondered why, in 1964, Nixon believed that Castro had "become the most momentous figure in John F. Kennedy's life" and why he believed that Lee Harvey Oswald was the lone assassin and that Castro had been Oswald's hero. These are important questions. We have just read how Castro came into JFK's life; the Lee Harvey Oswald scenario will come later.

Over the years since that fiasco on the Cuban beaches in April 1961, there have been many explanations for its failure, some reasonably accurate and some totally wrong. President Kennedy was quick to accept overall blame for the failure of Operation Zapata. Some have said that JFK himself caused the failure because "he denied U.S. air cover" for the embattled men on the beach. As part of the objective of this book, it is important to analyze this operation and to get as close as possible to a reasonable and factual answer to the question "Who caused the failure of the brigade's invasion of Cuba, and how did it happen?"

First of all, there's the subject of air cover for the men on the beach by U.S. military aircraft manned by U.S. military personnel. On previous pages I have written with some detail that the National Security Council had established the policy that U.S. military forces cannot be used operationally in peacetime. This was established policy when Kennedy became President, and he knew it. Therefore, the U.S. Marine Corps officers who drew up the invasion plan for the CIA, and for the Cuban exile brigade, were not allowed to include any supporting role for the U.S. military. Still, this posed no real problem for them, as long as they could predicate the tactical plan on the fact that all of Castro's combat-capable aircraft would have been eliminated before the men hit the beach.

With this stipulation in the plan, the CIA came to my office in U.S. Air Force headquarters and requested a number of modified World War II B-26 bombers. By means of intelligence data and aerial photographs, it had been determined that Castro had ten combat-capable aircraft. Therefore, on April 15—two days before the landing—a group of these modified B-26s flew over the Havana area and destroyed seven of these aircraft. Three T-33 jet aircraft had flown to a base in the Santiago area. That afternoon one of the CIA's U-2 spy aircraft located them parked wingtip to wingtip on a small air base.

The brigade was scheduled to hit the beach at dawn. The President had been well briefed on the significance of that prelanding air strike and had directed that B-26 attack. But, as we have seen, it was never carried out. Why wasn't that crucial air strike flown, after the President had specifically directed that it be done?

This failure has been erroneously blamed on President Kennedy for three decades in various contrived stories, some of which appear to have a bearing on the overall assassination story.

A most unusual article, "The Brigade's My Fault," appeared on the op-ed page of the *New York Times* on October 23, 1979. It contained an elaborate and confusing confession. Its author was McGeorge Bundy, the former special assistant to Presidents John F. Kennedy and Lyndon B. Johnson and the man the "Cuban Study Group" (to be identified below) determined had made the call that directed General Cabell of the CIA to cancel the B-26 bomber strike against Castro's last three combat aircraft.

In this article, Bundy wrote about the "brigade in Cuba" and "the famous brigade, a unit of about 2,600 men." He revealed his top-level views of the intelligence community of that time: "But in fact, like other people, the intelligence community usually has more on its plate than it can handle."

He recalled all those major programs the CIA had under full steam when the Kennedy administration came to Washington in 1961, then wrote: "So I have to consider that there was a staff failure—which means mostly me."

He leaves no question about it as he writes that after eighteen years of contemplation, "The Brigade's My Fault." Kennedy had never placed the fault for the brigade on anyone but himself. Eisenhower had done likewise with the U-2 affair.

On April 22, 1961, JFK had directed Gen. Maxwell Taylor, in association with Attorney General Robert Kennedy,[17] Admiral Arleigh Burke, and Allen Dulles, to give him a report on the "Immediate Causes of Failure of Operation Zapata," that is, the Bay of Pigs. That elaborate report by Taylor was submitted to JFK in the form of a lengthy letter on June 13, 1961.

The existence of that report has been denied by those principals and was one of the best-kept secrets of the Kennedy years.[18]

However, during 1979, the same year when Bundy wrote his op-ed piece, a book about the Bay of Pigs appeared, written by Peter Wyden, formerly editor of the *Ladies' Home Journal*. In Wyden's book there are several quotes that he attributes to the "so-called Taylor Report," and with that revelation the long-buried report became public. Wyden mentions McGeorge Bundy no less than seventeen times and quotes liberally from the long-missing Taylor Report. This is undoubtedly why, in October 1979, Bundy finally made his long-overdue statement. He most assuredly had read the Wyden book[19] and had heard people discussing the critical role he played in the strange Bay of Pigs drama.

Wyden had stated rather specifically about Bundy:

Bissell's former student, Mac Bundy, agreed in 1977 that the air strength was not only too small; it was much too small, but he pointed out that the planners said nothing about it. . . . He felt that the cancelled strike was only a marginal adjustment.

Bundy blamed himself in one respect: "I had a very wrong estimate of the consequences of failure, the mess."

Bissell, Bundy, and Wyden were all referring to a few specific lines from the Taylor Report that placed the blame for the defeat of the brigade on one telephone call. Keep in mind that Kennedy had approved the dawn air strike at 1:45 P.M., April 16, 1960.

This quote is from the Taylor letter, paragraph 43: "At about 9:30 P.M. on April 16, Mr. McGeorge Bundy, Special Assistant to the President, telephoned General C. P. Cabell of CIA to inform him that the dawn air strikes the following morning should not be launched until they could be conducted from a strip within the beachhead."[20]

No wonder Bundy admitted he had "a very wrong estimate of the consequences." First of all, U-2 photos taken late Saturday, April 15, showed the three T-33 jets parked wingtip to wingtip on a small airstrip near Santiago, Cuba. One eight-gun B-26 alone could have wiped them out on the ground. The CIA's operational commander at Puerto Cabezas was sending four B-26s to do the job that one could have done easily— provided the T-33s were caught on the ground. The brigade was scheduled to hit the beach at sunrise. That would alert Castro's air warning system and put the T-33s in the air. As reported by Wyden, the Bundy call to Cabell stating that no air strikes could be launched until after the brigade had secured the Giron airstrip constituted a total misreading and a complete reversal of the approved tactical plan.

The dawn air strikes were essential to destroy the three T-33s on the ground—the only way the slower B-26s could destroy them. With them out of the way, Castro would have had no combat aircraft. The brigade would have been subject to no air attacks, their supply ships would have been safe, and the "air cover" issue that some revisionists have raised would have been totally irrelevant. This was the plan JFK had approved; Bundy misunderstood it—or did he?

There is one more thing to add about the McGeorge Bundy article. Bundy had no doubt seen the Wyden book. He realized then that, after eighteen years, the "never written" Taylor "Letter to the President" had finally been released. Bundy saw the undeniable evidence that it was he who had canceled the dawn air strike and caused the failure of the brigade's gallant effort. There was nothing he could do to alter those facts except counterattack. He used a clever Freudian gambit: He let his mind think one thing and his fingers write another.

His op-ed article says, "The Brigade's My Fault." Any alert reader seeing that title would immediately connect it with the Bay of Pigs brigade and its failure. But Bundy is clever. He instead wrote a rather nonsensical, slightly offbeat, and quite disparaging article on the subject of the 1962 Cuban Missile Crisis. He didn't say one word about the Bay of Pigs. He used the word "brigade," but in a contrived context of the later event. It was clever, but it doesn't wash—especially not after the release of the Taylor Report, written right before the eyes of Robert F. Kennedy, who reported the group's findings to his brother every day.

During the Cuban Missile Crisis of October 1962, the problem Kennedy faced concerned the Russian "technicians," that is, rocket experts, and not a "brigade." The "brigade" was at the Bay of Pigs. Bundy furnishes two numbers of military unit strength, 22,000 and 2,600. Neither one is pertinent to anything, and neither represents a "brigade" of anything.

With Bundy's clever article in the *Times*, one is reminded of Richard Nixon's equally clever article in *Reader's Digest*, "Cuba, Castro and John F. Kennedy," and then of Gerald Ford's gratuitous article in *Life* magazine, scooping the report of the Warren Commission with his "Piecing Together the Evidence."

Not one of these articles is completely true. They all have a special scenario to build, and all are revisionist. They are all written by men who have held high positions—two by ex-Presidents and one by the man who was formerly the national security assistant to two Presidents. They are, one way or the other, closely involved with that most important subject: the death of John F. Kennedy.

T E N

JFK and the Thousand Days to Dallas

THE ASSASSINATION of President John F. Kennedy has been a never-ending puzzle for researchers and assassination "buffs." They can tell you the name of the street where Lee Harvey Oswald lived while he worked in Minsk in the Soviet Union or the precise weight loss of the so-called Magic Bullet that the Warren Commission says passed through both President Kennedy and Texas governor John Connally before it mysteriously came to rest among the sheets on a stretcher in Parkland Hospital. This research has become such a mad game that few people ever think of basic facts and causes. Who ordered the murder of President Kennedy? Why was it done, and for whose benefit? Who manages and perpetuates this omnipresent cover-up, even today?

On the other side of the coin, those who have created the entrancing cover-story scenario have provided so many precious and diversionary "golden apples" that many researchers have taken the lure and stopped to examine every one of them. As an example: It is clear from the abundant evidence that Lee Harvey Oswald did not kill President Kennedy. Then why study Oswald and that whole matter to absurdity? Such actions are an utter waste of time and serve to obfuscate the truth.

The murder of President Kennedy required the simultaneous existence and application of three fundamental factors:

136

1. the decision and the power to do it;

2. the professional mercenaries or "mechanics" to carry it off precisely as a team effort; and

3. the application and maintenance of the cover-story scenario to assure continuing control of the government of the United States of America thereafter.

The first two requirements were relatively simple ones and were the work of professionals. Once the decision had coalesced within the power elite, the die was cast. The "mechanics" were from "Murder Inc.," the international specialist group that is maintained by the government, just as ex-President Lyndon B. Johnson confirmed in his interview with Leo Janos that appeared in the July 1973 issue of the *Atlantic Monthly* magazine. The continuing cover story, on the other hand, was difficult to create and manipulate and is by far the most important factor. It is this third factor that reveals the nature of the top echelon involved and the power and skillful determination of the plotters who benefited by gaining control of the presidency.

After all, the members of this cabal were able to control a commission created by a President and headed by the chief justice of the United States. They obtained the written endorsement of two men who later became Presidents: Ford and Nixon. They have controlled the media and congressional activity, to the extent that the assassination has never been investigated adequately. And they have controlled the judicial system of the state of Texas where by law a trial for the murder of President Kennedy should have been, and must still be, convened. The book is never closed on murder.

Why, then, was Kennedy killed? What brought about the pressures that made murder of the President essential, no matter what it cost? This chapter will probe this subject within the scope of the parameters of that time and will attempt to link the assassination with the Vietnam War—a link that unquestionably exists.

On November 8, 1960, Sen. John F. Kennedy was elected President of the United States of America by a margin of 112,000 votes—a one-half-vote-per-precinct edge, the slimmest victory margin for the presidency since 1884.

Just over a thousand days later, President Kennedy was shot dead in the streets of Dallas by the closely coordinated rifle fire of a team of hired guns—or, to use the CIA terminology, "mechanics." Pressures that had built during the election had become even greater during those intervening three years. Someone else wanted to take over control of the presidency before JFK could be reelected in 1964, and wanted it badly enough to kill and to put up with the eternal burden of maintaining the cover-story scenario—that one lone gunman, from a sixth-floor window of the Texas School Book Depository building, did it with three shots from an old, Italian-made rifle with an unreliable telescopic sight. To maintain that cover story has taken real power; and those responsible for the assassination have that power.

It is relatively easy to assassinate a President; there are ways to beat the defenses. "Providing absolute protection for anyone is an impossible task," as the Secret Service men themselves say.[1] After all, on November 22, 1963, when JFK died, the Secret Service did not own a single armored automobile for the protection of the President. The FBI owned four of them; but the Secret Service had never asked for one.

The actual killing of the President is relatively simple, but shielding the gunmen and those who hired them, arranging for their safe and undetected removal from the scene, creating a "patsy" (the word used by Oswald himself before he, too, was murdered) to take the blame, and releasing a cover-story scenario in those early hectic moments and keeping it intact for the next several generations takes a cabal with the power and longevity of a great machine. The deft way it has been orchestrated reveals the skill of the plotters and indicates that those responsible included top-level government officials, plus their power-elite masters. The fact of conspiracy is revealed by the discovery of such circumstances.

More important by far, this cover story was not designed for the sole purpose of concealing the identity of the killers and their supporting team. It was designed to make possible the total takeover of the government of the United States of America and to make it possible for this cabal to control a series of Presidents from Lyndon B. Johnson to the present day. Look at the record.

What created this murderous cabal? What were the enormous conflicts that brought about the murder of a young and extremely popular President? Kennedy had just established the first plank in the platform for his reelection with his promise to bring one thousand men home from Vietnam by Christmas of 1963 and to have all Americans out of Vietnam by the end of 1965. His trip to Texas with Johnson and Connally marked the beginning of his 1964 reelection campaign. The cabal could wait no longer. The die had been cast, and the shots had to be fired in Dallas that day.

There can be only one reason powerful enough to cause the almost spontaneous coalescence of such a cabal for that single purpose. That reason was the fear of Kennedy's all-but-certain reelection. The alternative was to take control of the power of the presidency at all costs. In raising the age-old question *"cui bono?"*—who benefits?—we must examine the nature of the fatal pressures that enveloped the days of the Kennedy administration; and we must understand how they stood in the way of other plans by other peoples in their relentless drive for world power.

The American public has been led to believe that the mystery of the President's assassination was supposed to have been resolved by the massive investigation of the crime by those prominent members of the commission established on November 29, 1963, by the new President, Lyndon Baines Johnson, one week after the death of JFK. On that troubled day, LBJ called his trusted friend and confidant, J. Edgar Hoover, longtime director of the FBI, to the White House for a heart-to-heart discussion. LBJ and Hoover had lived across the street from one another in Washington, D.C., for nineteen years. Hoover had been a frequent visitor to the Johnson ranch on the banks of the Pedernales River in Texas. They were the type of friends who got along by necessity. They needed each other; they understood each other; they had been through fire together. They knew where many bodies were buried along the corridors of power.

On this day, LBJ sorely needed the ear and advice of his old comrade. A record of this meeting is contained in a memorandum written and signed by Hoover on the day of the meeting. As Hoover reported, Johnson asked him if he "was familiar with the proposed group he was trying to get to study my [Hoover's] report" on the JFK murder. Hoover had responded in the negative. Johnson said he hoped the "study" could get by "just with my [Hoover's] file and my [Hoover's] report."

Then Johnson asked Hoover what he thought of the proposed members of the group. He listed the names: Allen Dulles, John McCloy, Gen. Lauris Norstad, Congressmen Hale Boggs and Gerald Ford, and Senators Richard Russell and John Sherman Cooper. "He [Johnson] would not want [Sen.] Jacob K. Javits" for reasons not explained, wrote Hoover.

President Johnson did not discuss with Hoover the name of the man he wanted to head the group, Chief Justice Earl Warren; and for some reason, General Norstad was able to remove himself from the final commission list.

Following this meeting, President Johnson, by Executive Order 11130, dated November 29, 1963, "created a commission to investigate the assassination on November 22, 1963, of John Fitzgerald Kennedy, the 35th President of the United States."

The President directed this commission "to evaluate all facts and circumstances surrounding the assassination and the subsequent killing of the alleged assassin and to report its findings and conclusions to him."[2]

Note that Johnson's directive required this commission to do no more than "evaluate all facts" and "report its findings." Neither of these is conclusive. The commission served to deter legal action in Texas and silenced the threat of a major congressional inquiry. From the very first day of the creation of the Warren Commission, it had before it the inference that the alleged assassin was the man Jack Ruby had killed in Dallas while the alleged killer was being moved from one jail to another. The commission may have begun its investigation with the FBI "study... and its files and report"; but by the time it published its own twenty-six-volume report, in September 1964, it had been carried away by the entrancing cover story designed by the power cabal... the same cover story that lives today.

The first thing that President Johnson ought to have done was to demand that a trial for the murder of JFK be held in Texas. The fact that a man named Lee Harvey Oswald was dead was no barrier to the legal requirement. Oswald did not kill JFK. He was the "patsy" of the cover-story scenario. It would have been utterly impossible for the Dallas police to explain what truly incriminating information they had that was of sufficient merit to warrant the arrest of that young man while he was seated in a distant theater. Certainly the members of the Warren Commission were competent enough to understand that. Instead, they were the victims of great pressure brought to bear by those orchestrating the cover-up.

Because it is apparent that enormous pressure at the highest level had been generated during those thousand days of the Kennedy era, from November 8, 1960, to November 22, 1963, it is important that the "Days of Camelot" be reviewed and analyzed.

The very word "Camelot" as a definition of the Kennedy "thousand days" needs review. During the 1962–63 period, the U.S. Army had a typical contract study named "Camelot" under way in a "think tank" group that was associated with the American University in Washington. Because of some of the Kennedy-period treatment of the army, or what the army perceived that treatment to be during the JFK-McNamara days, there were many army officials who were quite vocal about their dislike of both men and of their policies. Not surprisingly, then, this study by the members of that army-contract think tank was unfriendly to Kennedy. It used the word "Camelot" in a derogatory sense, and its title was purposely intended to be a bit of a sarcastic rebuke of the President. It certainly was not intended to praise his name and record. Interestingly, this derogatory term has now lost that meaning for most and has become a public symbol of Kennedy and the presumed style and grace of his presidency.

It all began with the romantic election. Kennedy was viewed as a virtual messiah. Such was the power of the Kennedy charisma that the wife of a famous member of the Kennedy entourage was heard to say during the intermission of a play at the old Warner Theater, shortly after the Kennedy inauguration, "Isn't all this just marvelous? It is just like the break between B.C. and A.D."[3]

By the closing days of Dwight Eisenhower's second term as President, the giant multinational business machine that had engineered his travels from SHAPE (Supreme Headquarters Allied Powers, Europe) via the presidency of Columbia University to the presidency of the United States had learned that the ever-popular "Old Man" could be tough. Eisenhower left office on the wave of a substantial federal budget surplus and with a tip of his cap to the dangers of the military-industrial complex. As a result, these master manipulators had held billion-dollar items back from the budget of 1961–62, knowing full well that they could do better with a reliable old friend as President in 1961. They expected that new President to be Richard M. Nixon.

Nixon had always been the special friend of big business. As he likes to tell it, while he was still in the navy during World War II, he responded to a want ad in a Los Angeles newspaper that had been placed there by a moneyed group seeking a young, malleable candidate to run for Congress. With their financial help, he won that election. The remainder of his storied political life was lived under the shadow and tutelage of moneyed power centers.

What Nixon does not say is how he got into a position to take on that role in the first place. In 1941, he worked in the Office of Price Administration beside another up-and-coming young lawyer, Irving S.

Shapiro. There they both learned the ways of serving big business and the value of an "anti-Communist" stance. (Shapiro, son of an expatriate Lithuanian, went on to become the Justice Department lawyer in a widely publicized trial against the eleven top leaders of the U.S. Communist Party.[4] From there, he moved upward step by step in the DuPont Company, until he reached the position of chairman.) Nixon attacked Alger Hiss and Helen Gahagan Douglas viciously on his way to the House of Representatives, thence to the Senate, and the vice presidency.

Though his years of public life gave Nixon some popularity, they did not win him the presidency against John F. Kennedy in 1960. Thus, the many big-money projects deferred from the Eisenhower era were heaped upon the shoulders of President Kennedy. The greatest of these multi-billion-dollar packages, as described in previous chapters, was to be the war in Vietnam. It had been kept almost dormant during 1960, but it was ready to flare up on call.

Just before the inauguration, when President Eisenhower spoke privately to Kennedy, he informed him that his only concern in Southeast Asia would be the tiny kingdom of Laos. Military activity in Laos was already a public issue. In contrast, *Time* magazine had carried only six articles about Vietnam during 1960. Although the conflict in Vietnam had been moved along clandestinely since 1945, it was still just simmering when Kennedy came into office.

The CIA's anti-Castro planning was expedited. Just after the election, the CIA had made its move to increase its secret Cuban project from a small, three hundred-man operation to a three thousand-man, "over-the-beach" assault. By the time of the inauguration of Kennedy, the momentum of that effort was (as CIA Director Allen Dulles and CIA Deputy Director for Plans Richard Bissell put it, as a threat to JFK) harder to contain than to just let the Cuban exiles loose in an attempt to free their country themselves. Kennedy was getting his baptism of CIA pressure.

There were even bigger budget matters bottled up in anticipation of a Nixon inauguration. For several years, the air force had wanted a new jet fighter aircraft. This dream plane was called the "Everest" fighter, after Gen. Frank Everest, its staunchest supporter. The navy needed one also. However, Eisenhower, determined to go out with a budget surplus, would not allow the awarding of any major contract that could be charged to his term. By the time of Kennedy's inaugural, there was the promise of a $2–$4 billion air force budget item that could be used for the biggest military aircraft procurement award ever made. The entire aviation industry knew this, and pressures ran high in an attempt to win that prime contract.

Robert S. McNamara had been named to be Kennedy's secretary of defense. A World War II air force statistician and Harvard Business School professor, he had more recently been the president of Ford Motor Company, where (as part of a group known at Harvard as the "whiz kids") he had gone directly from his air force duties right after the war. McNamara had become president of the Ford Motor Company on November 9, 1960, the day after Kennedy's election.

McNamara was not familiar with aircraft or with the complex system of procurement used by the military, but he had a pretty good idea of what the availability of $4 billion meant politically. He announced he would make the award after careful study.[5]

Before long, the contest for the jet fighter had been narrowed to the Boeing Aircraft Company and a joint proposal presented by General Dynamics and the Grumman Aircraft Company. The aircraft the military desired was called a "Tactical Fighter Experimental," or TFX. The air force wanted an extremely unconventional aircraft, with wings that could be swept back in flight for higher speed.

Then McNamara sprang a surprise. He took some of the navy's procurement money and added that to the total and said this would represent "more bang for the buck" because of what he called "commonality." He believed that even though the air force and navy specifications differed widely, there ought to be enough "common" parts to lower the unit aircraft cost. By this time, the total program had been increased to 1,700 aircraft—235 of which would be for the navy—for a total initial procurement cost of $6.5 billion.

This was the largest single procurement contract ever put together in peacetime. Kennedy and his inner circle had their own ideas of what they were going to do with the disposition of that vast amount of money. They were a bold and politically savvy group. The election of November 1960 had been too close for comfort. They looked ahead to November 1964 and realized that $6.5 billion (or more) would pave a lot of streets on the road to reelection.

So Kennedy added Labor Secretary Arthur Goldberg, a wise old World War II OSS veteran, to the TFX team. He had not confided in Goldberg before the Bay of Pigs decision, a mistake he was not going to repeat. Goldberg had an idea. It was to use this $6.5 billion potential in every possible way, in selected "politically" marginal counties throughout the United States, to strengthen the Democratic party. Goldberg and McNamara began to work together. McNamara set up a suite of offices, one corridor ring in from his own in the Pentagon, with a staff that had nothing else to do than to plot the course of the TFX source selection program.

I had an office a few doors down the hall from this new suite, and I visited them frequently to join its chief, Ron Linton, and other Pentagon "whiz kids" for lunch. I noticed that the walls of this suite of offices were lined with maps of the United States showing all the states and counties. They were political maps. In short order, at Goldberg's suggestion, one set of those maps was colored to show every county that Kennedy had carried in 1960 and every county that had gone to Nixon.

Then the staff of this office, working with Department of Labor statistics, made detailed studies of each of the major proposals for the TFX. A proposal is an enormous stack of paper. Quite frequently a single proposal for some military item would arrive at the Pentagon in a large delivery truck. This process of "mapping" the proposals included the prime contractors, that is, Boeing or General Dynamics/Grumman, and from them right on down to the smallest subcontractor. These contractors were plotted on county maps. Goldberg's team marked the site of each facility, taking into account how many people it would employ, how much money would be spent there, how much new construction was involved, and every other political consideration.[6]

In a short time it was possible to get a visual plot of the impact of the award of a Boeing contract on one set of maps and of the General Dynamics/Grumman contract on another. Through confidential handling of copies of these charts, senators, congressmen, and local politicians throughout the Democratic organization were able to capitalize on the outcome of these proposals. Within no time, word that these charts were being developed in McNamara's office reached the contractors themselves.

I happened to visit the office one day when word had been received from one of the prime contractors that it planned to open a new facility in a remote county in Utah. That county had been a Republican county in 1960. Needless to say, the process of wooing future Republican votes in this manner was repeated all over the country. Six and a half billion dollars is a lot of money, and it goes a long, long way in a campaign.

While the studies of the political impact of the award of this huge contract were being made, McNamara was forced to draw out the routine source selection process. He had two of the nation's industrial giants, with their vast array of subcontractors and sub-subcontractors, locked in the biggest battle in corporate history. He managed to string out four full evaluation studies, each one of which nitpicked every item in each proposal, before he sent the whole package to the Source Selection Board, the final, ultimate arbiter, made up of senior officials from both services.

Later, during the 1963 senatorial hearings on the award of this contract, Gen. Curtis LeMay, chief of staff of the air force, told a Senate Investigations Subcommittee chaired by Sen. John L. McClellan that some 275,000 man-hours of work had been poured into this selection process.

The selection could have been made during Eisenhower's presidency. It certainly could have been made in 1961. Everything had been ready for a quick decision, in favor of Boeing, right after the Kennedy inauguration. But, with the addition of the navy money and the Goldberg-McNamara political selection concept, the decision was pushed back month after month in every county across the nation while the politicians wrung every ounce they could out of this process—and to hell with the aircraft companies and the services. The Kennedy team had, as always, its eye on the election of 1964.

Finally, on November 23, 1962—more than two years after the election—the decision of the Source Selection Board was made. Most of the senior officials at that meeting came away believing that the decision had been made in favor of Boeing. Eugene Zuchert, the secretary of the air force, confided to a few friends that evening that the decision had been made in favor of Boeing.

Behind the scenes, however, another decision had been made, and it overruled the entire military system. Any major change of the military procurement system, especially as it pertains to a $6.5 billion contract, is bound to have the impact of someone attempting to rewrite the Holy Bible. It cannot be done without an intense, prolonged, and very heated argument.

McNamara knew that he and Kennedy were playing with fire. On the Friday afternoon that he received the choice of the Source Selection Board in favor of Boeing, McNamara already knew the results of the final political survey of the two proposals, that is, the Goldberg comparison. It indicated clearly that the General Dynamics/Grumman proposal would get a greater return for the Democrats at the ballot boxes.

Moreover, he had an additional major problem to resolve on his own.

He had to be sure that the choice he was going to make would indeed fly. McNamara basically did not know one aircraft from another. He had a man on his staff, Alfred W. Blackburn, who was an experienced test pilot; Blackburn had been hired in 1959 by the Defense Department's Bureau of Research and Engineering specifically for the TFX project. Blackburn, however, favored the Boeing proposal, so McNamara could not discuss his personal problem with him.

To play this card, McNamara called an old friend and asked for the name of a man who could vouch for the design of the General Dynamics model. This friend suggested Lockheed's Kelly Johnson, head of the famous "Skunk Works," a shop where many of the finest aircraft built by Lockheed had been designed. Johnson had designed the CIA's U-2 spy plane, among others. McNamara had the General Dynamics specifications delivered to Johnson and asked him to verify their suitability. Johnson studied the aircraft designs carefully.

The fate of the $6.5 billion TFX project had been placed in the hands of a man who had devoted a lifetime to building superior aircraft, and to building them in direct competition with both Boeing and General Dynamics. Even at this stage of the game, fate played its part.

Years before, Roger Lewis, chairman of the board and president of General Dynamics, had worked at Lockheed. He and Kelly Johnson had been good friends, and still were in 1962. Lewis was an old aircraft professional who had been around the business since its golden years in the 1930s. Kelly looked over the General Dynamics design very carefully—no doubt thinking how much this meant to his old associate.

Johnson called McNamara and told him that the plan from General Dynamics was acceptable, and he assured McNamara that the aircraft would fly. Later, Roger Lewis was to say in a rather low key manner, "The company expects to produce an exceptional aircraft and that its qualifications to do so are unparalleled."

With the Goldberg review in hand, and supported by the call from Kelly Johnson confirming the airworthiness of the design, McNamara scheduled a meeting for November 24, 1962, to announce the decision. He ignored the vote of the Source Selection Board and all its senior military members and announced his choice of the General Dynamics design. With that he authorized the start of the engineering-design work, wind-tunnel testing, construction of a model of the plane, and all the other actions essential to the development of a total weapons system.

On April 8, 1963, during a period of intense controversy, McNamara authorized the issuance of a contract from the air force procurement offices at Wright Patterson Air Force Base, which in turn authorized General Dynamics and Grumman to turn out twenty-two test models of the TFX.

Gen. Curtis LeMay later testified that no one from the original air force–navy evaluation teams on up to the final air force–navy board that recommended the Boeing design—and this included himself—had ever recommended the General Dynamics model. The members of the Source Selection Board, which had voted for Boeing, were stunned by the development. Al Blackburn, who had worked on the project since 1959, resigned. This is to say nothing about the shocked feelings at Boeing and its long list of subcontractors.

The decision sent tremors throughout the entire aeronautical industry and the business world. If Boeing, traditionally the number-one defense contractor, could be set aside, anyone could be excluded from any contract, for what seemed to be arbitrary political reasons. LeMay added, "I was surprised that the decision was made without consultation. I don't consider this the normal procedure. I thought we had such a clear-cut and unanimous opinion all up and down the line that I was completely surprised at the decision."[7]

In the face of the heated opposition, McNamara held his ground. He said he had chosen the General Dynamics model of the TFX because that company's proposal showed a better understanding of the costs involved and offered a minimum divergence from a common design for air force and navy versions of the fighter. Of course, this only added fuel to the fire, because this was the very reason the services did not like the General Dynamics version. They all knew that a carrier-based aircraft had to be designed much differently from a land-based one.

In testimony before Congress, McNamara came back again and served notice on the generals and admirals, saying that the TFX decision process was a sample of a new policy. He said that the day had passed when the services would be allowed to develop their own weapons systems. He added that he picked General Dynamics over Boeing because Boeing had fudged and actually had planned to build different planes for the navy and the air force.

In the heat of battle, the Kennedy forces were pressing their point firmly, but cloaking it in equable terms. In contrast to some of the Pentagon civilian hierarchy of earlier days—for example, Charlie Wilson of General Motors, Tom Gates of Morgan Guaranty Trust, and Neil McElroy of Lever Brothers—the McNamara staff was pure Ivy league: Roswell Gilpatric, Cyrus Vance, Eugene Zuckert, and Paul

Nitze. They were neither military specialists nor industry favorites. Because of Kennedy they had been given the power to make these decisions despite the desires of the old military-industry team in high places. It was precisely those men in high places who were upset. It was those men and their associates who began to believe, and proclaim, "Kennedy has got to go!"

Gilpatric, a New York banker who was McNamara's deputy, was sent out to make an important speech to a bankers' convention on April 9, 1963. Its title, "The Impact of the Changing Defense Program on the United States Economy," was actually more pertinent than his audience expected it to be. He spoke about the TFX decision to bankers—and, of course, to the news media—at a time when this was a white-hot subject.

In an early paragraph, he revealed the scope of his subject. The new Kennedy policy was a blockbuster. Gilpatric said—and when he did, windows rattled in defense installations all over the world—"I have not the slightest doubt that our economy could adjust to a decline in defense spending." He was touching on a sacrosanct subject: Can any nation afford, or exist, with peace?

Having dropped that bomb, he moved along to a rationale for the TFX decision. He noted, "The shifts of defense spending within the budget can create intense problems in individual communities." If his listeners understood what he meant, they knew he was getting very close to the Goldberg procurement policy. "We do try to make a special effort to give work," he said, "where it can be done effectively and efficiently, to depressed areas."

But translate the reference to "depressed areas" to mean "areas that voted for Nixon and therefore are needed in the Democratic column," and you're closer to the truth.

Then Gilpatric made a daring comment: "The fundamental fact we all have to bear in mind is that the Department of Defense is neither able nor willing to depart from the requirements of national security in order to bolster the economy, either of the nation as a whole, or of any region or community."

Despite this statement, that is precisely what the implementation of the Goldberg policy had just indrectly done. As though he believed no one would perceive the real message, Gilpatric added (perhaps for the edification of Boeing and its host of allies in and out of the military), "In the award and management of contracts we have undertaken a wide range of steps to improve the whole process. . . . The handling of the TFX contract illustrated several of the techniques being worked out for use on development contracts where particularly acute problems have arisen in the past."

Then Gilpatric closed with: "Mr. McNamara and I, after an acceptable TFX proposal was offered, had to make a judgment between these two proposals. . . the air force and navy will get a better buy for the taxpayers' dollars than would have been forthcoming if the contract had been let earlier. . . ."

Gilpatric made these statements during a time of intense Senate hearings on the TFX. You will note how carefully both he and McNamara avoided any direct mention that they had arbitrarily gone along with the Goldberg formula augmented by the assurances of Kelly Johnson at Lockheed.

Indeed, Kelly Johnson's role in this selection has not been mentioned elsewhere. I was a friend of Roger Lewis's, president of General Dynamics, and was told this account of the "Skunk Works" role by Mr. Lewis himself.

As noted earlier, Kennedy's thousand days were marked by repeated and violent eruptions among power-elite elements within the government and its multinational corporate environment, and this is one that stands out. It is chillingly coincidental that Kennedy's murder in Dallas one year later occurred not too many miles from the Fort Worth factories where the TFX, and quite incidentally the Bell helicopters for Vietnam, were being built.

There was a subtle reasoning behind the TFX decision. Jack Kennedy, Bobby Kennedy, McNamara, Goldberg, and many others of the inner circle were not at all concerned about the final outcome of an aircraft-to-be called the TFX. Kennedy was a World War II veteran and had been a member of Congress for most of the years since that time. He had seen nearly $3 trillion poured into the military-industrial machine during those years, and he had seen those weapons systems come and go.

To the Kennedy circle, the TFX, the Skybolt, the Dyna-Soar, the atomic-powered aircraft, and all the rest that had fallen into their laps with the election were just what Kennedy, Goldberg, and McNamara took them to be: devices that could be used to direct money into political districts that needed it for their own benefit and to assure the election of a Kennedy for years to come. This is why Gilpatric made the speech he did to the assembled bankers, and this is why McNamara said that the day had passed when the services would be allowed to develop their own weapons systems.

The services and the great industries for whom the military establishment existed were staggered by these developments. They had never encountered such a serious challenge. The one-two combination of punches they had suffered had them on the ropes. On January 17, 1961, they had heard Dwight Eisenhower, in a farewell address to the nation, urge vigilance regarding the dangers to liberty implicit in a vast military establishment and caution against the power of the military-industrial complex.

Now they had a President who was not just talking about that danger, but was taking their dollars away to use them as he chose. This was the underlying significance of that TFX decision.

Let's return to a closing statement by "Ros" Gilpatric in his bankers' speech of April 9, 1963: "I have not the slightest sympathy for the view sometimes heard that this country couldn't afford disarmament." Now, why was that on his mind, and on the minds of the entire Kennedy inner circle, at that particular time? The answer is quite startling. The Kennedys were counting on at least eight years in office to move mountains. At the same time, their determined opposition was keeping an eye on the same clock. The 1964 election was rapidly approaching.

At the beginning of this book, reference was made to a novel by Leonard Lewin, *Report From Iron Mountain on the Possibility and Desirability of Peace*. It happens that the book concerned a reputed top-level study that was officially commissioned in August 1963 but in fact dated back to early 1961. In other words, the study process started, according to Lewin, right after the inauguration, with the arrival of John F. Kennedy and his new administration.

A purported member of the Iron Mountain Special Study Group believes that the group's mission was delineated by McNamara, William Bundy, and Dean Rusk. The members of the Kennedy circle were concerned that no really serious work had been done by any government instrumentality in planning for peace. The report contains a most portentous line: "The idea of the Special Study... was worked out early in 1963.... What helped most to get it moving were the big changes in military spending that were being planned...."

The chronology of these developments, which are very cleverly woven into this novel by Lewin, is important. It began with the inauguration. The first big-money item was the TFX. That orchestrated solution was stretched from the inauguration to November 1962. The reaction of the military, of the aeronautical industry, and of Congress was predictable. Then, in April 1963, McNamara announced that things had changed. A few days later, Gilpatric made his important speech, and the Special Study Group was selected in August 1963. The Kennedys were on their way. They were going to ride on the TFX $6.5 billion into a second term, and then they were going to prepare America for peace. The Vietnam War and its hundreds of billions of dollars in expenditures were nowhere in their plans.

Could America really afford the Kennedys?

This Kennedy agenda began to surface with the TFX decision and was confirmed by the existence—known to very few—of the Special Study Group for "the possibility and desirability of peace." Nothing, absolutely nothing, could have had a greater impact on the enormous military machine of this nation than the specter of peace. This Kennedy plan jeopardized not hundreds of millions, not even billions, but trillions of dollars. (The Cold War has cost no less than $6 trillion.) It shook the very foundation upon which our society has been built over the past two thousand years.

As the *Report From Iron Mountain* says:

> War itself is the basic social system. It is the system which has governed most human societies of record, as it is today.... The capacity of a nation to make war expresses the greatest social power it can exercise; war-making, active or contemplated, is a matter of life and death on the greatest scale subject to social control.... War-readiness is the dominant force in our societies.... It accounts for approximately a tenth of the output of the world's total economy.[8]

John F. Kennedy and his advisers were playing a dangerous game as they expertly moved along the calendar toward reelection in 1964. Kennedy had accepted the challenge. The duel, perhaps the greatest in the history of this country, had begun. To begin with, he needed a strong plank upon which to build his platform for reelection. He chose Vietnam, the cessation of all American military involvement there.

As his first step, Kennedy sent Gen. Maxwell Taylor and Secretary McNamara to Saigon in late September 1963. They returned to the White House and presented him with their voluminous report on October 2, 1963. In part that report said: "It should be possible to withdraw the bulk of U.S. personnel by that time...."

"That time," as stated clearly in their report, was the end of 1965. One thousand troops were already slated to come home in time for Christmas 1963.

Kennedy planned to get out of Vietnam and to turn the war over to a new leader in South Vietnam. This was the first order of business. To his adversaries, this confirmed the nature of the course he had chosen. They began to move, to move swiftly and with finality.

Ngo Dinh Diem, the first president of South Vietnam, was killed on November 1, 1963, and Kennedy was killed on November 22, 1963.

Former Presidents Gerald Ford and Richard Nixon have written that President Kennedy was killed by a lone assassin named Lee Harvey Oswald. The Warren Commission reported the same thing.

That was not the way it happened at all.

ELEVEN

The Battle for Power: Kennedy Versus the CIA

PRESIDENTIAL POWER: Does it come with the office, or must the incumbent fight for it every step of the way? As James David Barber states in his book *The Presidential Character*:[1] "Political power is like nuclear energy available to create deserts or make them bloom. The mere having of it never yet determined its use. The mere getting of it has not stamped into the powerful some uniform shape."

John F. Kennedy came to the office of the presidency with style and enough experience to know that he would have to fight to wrest political power from entrenched interests of enormous strength. If anything hit President Kennedy harder than the utter defeat of the Cuban exile brigade on the beaches of the Bay of Pigs, it was the realization that he had let himself be talked into that operation by inexperienced men in the CIA.

Kennedy blamed himself and believed that he should not have authorized the invasion. On the other hand, the Cuban Study Group (see below) concluded that the cancellation of the crucial air strike was the cause of the failure of the Zapata operation.

CIA director Allen Dulles had not been there at the time of the final decision making or at the time of the invasion itself. He was on vacation. This was a most unusual absence by the man responsible for the entire operation.

153

In his book *Kennedy,*[2] Ted Sorensen makes a good case for his doctrine that "the Kennedys never fail." However, Kennedy did fail in his attempt to gain full control of the CIA and its major partners in the Defense Department. It was the most crucial failure of his abbreviated presidency. He recognized his adversary during his first term, and as he related confidentially to intimate acquaintances, "When I am reelected. I am going to break that agency into a thousand pieces." He meant to do it, too, but the struggle cost him his life.

Former President Harry S. Truman was deeply disturbed when he learned of the murder of Jack Kennedy in Dallas. That experienced old veteran of political wars saw an ominous link between the death of the President and the CIA. One month after that terrible event, just time enough to get his thoughts in order and on paper, Truman wrote a column that appeared in the *Washington Post* on December 21, 1963. He expressed his doubts about the CIA directly:

> For some time I have been disturbed by the way the CIA has been diverted from its original assignment. It has become an operational and at times a policy-making arm of the government. . . .
> I never had any thought that when I set up the CIA that it would be injected into peacetime cloak-and-dagger operations. Some of the complications and embarrassment that I think we have experienced are in part attributable to the fact that this quiet intelligence arm of the President has been so removed from its intended role that it is being interpreted as a symbol of sinister and mysterious foreign intrigue and a subject for Cold War enemy propaganda.

Truman's characterization of the CIA as "a symbol of sinister and mysterious foreign intrigue" is, unfortunately, quite accurate. That "foreign intrigue" involved Cuba, Castro, and John F. Kennedy, at least in the minds of Richard Nixon and Gerald Ford, as is evidenced in their later writings about the assassination. And it was Lyndon B. Johnson who said the government operated a "Murder Inc." in the Caribbean.

It is absolutely astounding that when the thoughts of these four presidents turned to the murder of JFK, they all wove a fabric of sinister intrigue that included the CIA in the scenario of his death. These men were telling us something. It is time we listened to and learned from what they have said.

The power of any agency that is allowed to operate in secrecy is boundless. The CIA knows this, and it has used its power to its own advantage. Only three days after the disastrous Cuban defeat, Kennedy set up a Cuban Study Group headed by Gen. Maxwell Taylor to "direct special attention to the lessons which can be learned from recent events in Cuba."

With that action, which received little notice at the time, the President declared war on the agency. The Cuban Study Group was one of the most important creations of the Kennedy presidency, and it was the source of one of the major pressure points on the way to the guns of Dallas on November 22, 1963.

President Kennedy was seriously upset by the failure of the CIA and the Joint Chiefs of Staff to provide him with adequate information and support prior to his approval of the brigade landing at the Bay of Pigs. He was also upset by the results of the total breakdown of CIA leadership during the operation that followed that landing.[3]

Kennedy's good friend Supreme Court justice William O. Douglas, in recalling a discussion he had with Kennedy shortly after the disaster, said:

> This episode seared him. He had experienced the extreme power that these groups had, these various insidious influences of the CIA and the Pentagon, on civilian policy, and I think it raised in his own mind the specter: Can Jack Kennedy, President of the United States, ever be strong enough to really rule these two powerful agencies? I think it had a profound effect... it shook him up!

Can any President "ever be strong enough to really rule" the CIA and the Defense Department? Eisenhower had learned that he was not strong enough when a U-2 went down in the heart of Russia despite his specific "no-overflight" orders in 1960.

Kennedy set out to prove that he was "strong enough," and he might have done so had he had a second term in office. Instead, he was first overwhelmed and then murdered.

Each member of the Cuban Study Group was chosen for a particular reason. Gen. Maxwell Taylor, for example, had been in retirement since he had differed, in public, with the Eisenhower policy concerning the strength of the U.S. Army and had resigned as its chief of staff. He had not been involved in any way with the decision-making process for the Cuban invasion. In fact, Kennedy had never met General Taylor prior to 1961.

To augment the military side of the study group, Kennedy selected Adm. Arleigh Burke, considered by many to be the finest chief of naval operations the navy has ever had. Admiral Burke had been among the

Joint Chiefs of Staff who had been most closely involved in the military elements of the Bay of Pigs planning process and support preparation. The actual tactical training for the invasion had been placed in the hands of a U.S. Marine Corps colonel; the transport ships had been assembled in the Norfolk, Virginia, area; and much of the logistics support had been channeled through the inactive navy base at Elizabeth City, North Carolina. All these steps had involved considerable navy support.

Another appointee to the study group was the scorpion in the bottle, the President's brother and attorney general, Robert F. Kennedy.

Kennedy's next choice for the group was Machiavellian in its political implications. He appointed CIA director Allen W. Dulles, the man who in November 1960 had flown to Palm Beach with his deputy, Richard Bissell, to give the President-elect his first official briefing on the plan for the overthrow of Castro. It was Dulles who, on January 28, 1961, gave another briefing on the developing plan to the newly installed President, along with Vice President Lyndon B. Johnson, Secretary of State Dean Rusk, Secretary of Defense Robert S. McNamara, and the chairman of the Joint Chiefs of Staff, Gen. Lyman Lemnitzer, among others.

Now, Kennedy had decided to have Allen Dulles sit through the ordeal of this detailed study from beginning to end, to relive the whole scenario as General Taylor interrogated selected officials who had been connected with the operation.[4]

Despite the fact that Allen Dulles was the director of central intelligence when the plan was first presented to President Eisenhower in March 1960 and that he was the man who briefed Kennedy before and after his inauguration, Dulles had not been present at the White House on April 16, 1961, when the final discussions took place and when the go-ahead decision had been made by the President. Dulles was also not in Washington during the crucial period of the invasion itself to control the activities of his agency. He had taken that weekend off for a sojourn in Puerto Rico.

There is a businessmen's group, the Young Presidents Organization, that is closely affiliated with Harvard Business School and with the CIA. It is made up of men who are presidents of their own companies and under forty years of age. The CIA arranges meetings for them with young leaders in foreign countries for the purpose of opening export-import talks and franchising discussions.

The Young Presidents Organization met in Puerto Rico on the

Former President Harry S Truman visiting John F. Kennedy shortly after the new President's inauguration. Truman later wrote that the CIA had become "a symbol of sinister and mysterious foreign intrigue."

Shortly after the Bay of Pigs disaster, Supreme Court Justice William O. Douglas said, "This episode seared him [Kennedy]. He had experienced the extreme power that these groups had, these various insidious influences of the CIA and the Pentagon, on civilian policy, and I think it raised in his own mind the specter: Can Jack Kennedy, President of the United States, ever be strong enough to really rule these two powerful agencies?"

The President's brother, Attorney General Robert F. Kennedy (lower left), a member of the Cuban Study Group, scrutinized Allen Dulles's (lower right) every move during the post-Bay of Pigs investigation.

June 28, 1961

NATIONAL SECURITY ACTION MEMORANDUM NO. 55

TO: The Chairman, Joint Chiefs of Staff

SUBJECT: Relations of the Joint Chiefs of Staff to the President
in Cold War Operations

I wish to inform the Joint Chiefs of Staff as follows with regard
to my views of their relations to me in Cold War Operations:

a. I regard the Joint Chiefs of Staff as my principal military
advisor responsible both for initiating advice to me and for responding to requests for advice. I expect their advice to come to
me direct and unfiltered.

b. The Joint Chiefs of Staff have a responsibility for the defense
of the nation in the Cold War similar to that which they have in conventional hostilities. They should know the military and paramilitary
forces and resources available to the Department of Defense, verify their
readiness, report on their adequacy, and make appropriate recommendations for their expansion and improvement. I look to the Chiefs to
contribute dynamic and imaginative leadership in contributing to the
success of the military and paramilitary aspects of Cold War programs.

c. I expect the Joint Chiefs of Staff to present the military viewpoint in governmental councils in such a way as to assure that the
military factors are clearly understood before decisions are reached.
When only the Chairman or a single Chief is present, that officer
must represent the Chiefs as a body, taking such preliminary and
subsequent actions as may be necessary to assure that he does in
fact represent the corporate judgment of the Joint Chiefs of Staff.

d. While I look to the Chiefs to present the military factor without reserve or hesitation, I regard them to be more than military men
and expect their help in fitting military requirements into the over-all
context of any situation, recognizing that the most difficult problem in
Government is to combine all assets in a unified, effective pattern.

[signature]

This historical and seldom cited document, signed by President Kennedy after the
Bay of Pigs investigation, was sent directly to the Chairman of the Joint Chiefs of
Staff, bypassing the Secretary of State and the Director, Central Intelligence. The
Secretary of Defense was given a copy.

As can be noted, the President made the Joint Chiefs of Staff his advisor in
peacetime replacing the CIA. This one order created as much opposition to Kennedy
as anything else he did during his administration.

The original memorandum was on two pages, in precisely the language shown
here.

The Cairo Conference, Nov. 22–28, 1943, featured, seated from left, Generalissimo Chiang Kai-Shek, President Franklin D. Roosevelt, Prime Minister Winston L. S. Churchill, and Madame Chiang. Madame Chiang not only traveled to Cairo with her husband, but participated in the sessions. Her brother, T. V. Soong, was reported to be the wealthiest man in the world at the time, and the man who kept the generalissimo in power. The author was in Cairo at the time and served as a pilot for American and British delegations.

Premier Josef Stalin, President Franklin D. Roosevelt and Prime Minister Winston L. S. Churchill met publicly at Tehran, November 28–December 1, 1943. Historians have failed to note that Generalissimo and Madame Chiang Kai-shek were in Tehran and both participated in the conference. On November 27th, the author flew the military aircraft that transported their staff delegates from Cairo to Tehran. Because of the strong Chinese representation in Tehran the agenda of the conference had much to do with Far East planning.

White House Report

U.S. TROOPS SEEN OUT OF VIET BY '65

PACIFIC
STARS AND STRIPES

AN AUTHORIZED PUBLICATION OF THE ARMED FORCES IN THE FAR EAST

FIVE-STAR EDITION   10c DAILY

龍和二十個年一月二十五日國際現局外到達4 近875年773 号 目刊
(昭和34 年4月21日第3 種郵便物認可)   15c WITH SUPPLEMENTS

Vol. 19, No. 276   **Friday, Oct. 4, 1963**

Koufax, L.A. Top N.Y. 5-2

Compiled From AP and UPI

NEW YORK—Lefthander Sandy Koufax set a World Series strikeout record Wednesday as he pitched the Los Angeles Dodgers to a 5-2 victory over the New York Yankees in the first game of the fall classic.

Catcher John Roseboro powered the Dodgers to the win with a three-run homer into the right field stands off New York starter Whitey Ford capping a four-run outburst in the second inning. Bill Skowron, a former Yankee, drove in the other runs with two singles.

Koufax, 23-5 during the regular season, struck out 15 Yankees, one more than Carl Erskine of the Brooklyn Dodgers did against the Yankees, 10 years ago in the day.

Roseboro set another Series record with a total of 18 putouts on strikeouts and fouls to smash the mark held by Mickey Cochrane of the Detroit Tigers and Roy Campanella of the old Brooklyn Dodgers.

The Yanks, who managed to get only 6 hits off Koufax, scored all their runs in the eighth inning on a homer by Tom Tresh.

The crowd of 69,000 at Yankee Stadium also saw the team strikeout mark set. The total of 25 strikeouts for the two teams bettered the old mark of 22 established by the St. Louis Cardinals and the St. Louis Browns in 1944.

SANDY KOUFAX

President Kennedy gets a firsthand report on the situation in the Republic of Vietnam from General Maxwell D. Taylor (left), chairman of the Joint Chiefs of Staff, and Defense Secretary Robert McNamara. (AP Photo)

WASHINGTON (UPI) — The White House said Wednesday night after hearing a report from a two-man inspection team that the U.S. military effort in the Republic of Vietnam should be completed by the end of 1965.

The White House said the situation in the Southeast Asian country was "deeply serious."

The statement came after President Kennedy met for nearly an hour with the full Security Council to hear a detailed report on the Vietnamese situation from Defense Secretary Robert S. McNamara and General Maxwell D. Taylor, chairman of the Joint Chiefs of Staff.

McNamara and Taylor returned to the U.S early in the day after an on-site survey.

Highlights of the White House statement:

1—The U.S. government will continue to support the people and government of south Vietnam in their battle against the aggression of the communist Viet Cong.

2—McNamara and Taylor conceded that improvements could be made in the current military program but they thought progress had been made recently

(Continued on Back Page, Col. 2)

JFK Signs Military Pay Bill

WASHINGTON (AP) — President Kennedy signed Wednesday, with "great pressure," a bill granting an average 14½ per cent pay increase to most of the 2.7 million men and women in the U.S. armed forces.

In a cabinet room ceremony, Kennedy used more than a dozen fountain pens to sign the measure, which will cost the government $1.2 billion a year. It is the biggest military pay boost in history.

Kennedy said that while he is impressed with new and powerful weapons, he is mindful

(Continued on Back Page, Col. 1)

1931 GANG KILLINGS

Valachi Fingers Genovese

WASHINGTON (AP)—Joseph Valachi Wednesday linked Vito Genovese, the man he says now runs a U.S. criminal syndicate from a prison cell—to the violent deaths of two gangland bosses.

Tracing the history of the symbol cate known as La Cosa Nostra,

Valachi did not name Genovese as the actual killer but said the Senate investigations subcommittee...

1) The shooting of Giuseppe Massaria near the Bar in Coney Island N.Y. restaurant in April 1931 a set up by "Charles Lucky, Vito Genovese"

and Ciro Terranova.

2) Salvatore Maranzano gunned down the following September, had been on a meeting that day in Lucky.

Massaria and Maranzano at the time were leaders of rival

(Continued on Back Page, Col. 2)

Weather

Tokyo Area Forecast
Friday: Cloudy....
Saturday: Partly cloudy...
Wednesday's Temperatures: High 73,
Low 67
(STAF Weather Central, Fuchu AB)

Significant elements of the McNamara-Taylor Report on the situation in Vietnam, given to President Kennedy on October 2, 1963, became White House policy with the official publication of National Security Action Memorandum #263, October 11, 1963. Most important was that which promised to withdraw the bulk of U.S. personnel by the end of 1965.

Had John F. Kennedy lived, Americans would not have fought and died in Vietnam during that terrible 1965–1975 warfare. The cost: up to $550 billion and 58,000 American lives.

General Maxwell Taylor (left) and Secretary of Defense McNamara discuss their "Vietnam Trip" report with the President, October 2, 1963. It is the leather binder under the file folders.

The President approved "presently prepared plans to withdraw 1,000 military personnel by the end of 1963" and to "train Vietnamese so that essential functions now performed by U.S. military can be carried out by Vietnamese by the end of 1965. It should be possible to withdraw the bulk of U.S. personnel by that time." These quotations, which prove that President Kennedy positively planned to get all Americans out of Vietnam, are from the official White House document, National Security Action Memorandum #263, October 11, 1963.

The New York Times and Bantam Book version of the Pentagon Papers totally reverses this to read, "President Kennedy, who inherited a policy of 'limited-risk gamble,' bequeathed to Johnson a broad commitment to war." There is no reliable basis for that revision of Kennedy's policy.

In an action unprecedented in U.S. history, almost the entire Kennedy Cabinet had flown to Hawaii, en route to Japan, for a series of conferences, November 20, 1963. Those shown here are (left to right) Orville Freeman of Agriculture, Douglas Dillon of the Treasury, Dean Rusk of State, Stewart Udall of Interior, Luther Hodges of Commerce, Walter Heller of Council of Economic Advisors, and Willard Wirtz of Labor. Others who attended the Honolulu conference were McNamara of Defense, McGeorge Bundy, National Security Advisor, and Presidential Press Secretary Pierre Salinger. Looking back at that meeting and at the list of those in attendance, it appears that somehow something most important, other than the conference agenda, must have caused them all to leave Washington at that crucial time, i.e., two days before the President's death.

This famous photo of the "tramps" picked up by Dallas "police" shortly after the assassination of President Kennedy is, according to the author, one of the most important bits of evidence of the nature of that crime and coverup of November 22, 1963.

Note that (a) the two "policemen" carry shotguns, not rifles, (b) their caps are different (one white chinstrap, one black), (c) both of their caps differ from a true Dallas policeman's. In addition, one has a Dallas police shoulder patch (not visible in this photo) and the other does not. These "policemen" and the "tramps" are actors in neat clothes and new shoes. In this photo, one of a set of four pictures, these "police" were leading the men to the sheriff's office at Dealey Plaza. City cops have nothing to do with sheriff's offices. These "cops" have not handcuffed these dangerous presidential killers.

During 1959, the author received an urgent request from the Director, Central Intelligence, Allen W. Dulles, to provide support and assistance to prevent the overthrow of a friendly Far East government. This secret operation proved to be a success. The CIA sent a commendation to the Chief of Staff, U.S. Air Force, for Lieutenant Colonel Prouty that resulted in the award of the Legion of Merit citation and medal. This was presented by Lieutenant General John K. Gearhart.

Soon after, the author was promoted to the grade of colonel, and assigned in 1960 to the Office of Special Operations, a section of immediate office of the Secretary of Defense, where he became the senior Air Force officer responsible for the provision of military support of the clandestine activities of the CIA, among other duties. This office was headed by General Graves B. Erkstine, USMC (Retired), and was the office of assignment for Edward G. Lansdale of the CIA.

CITATION TO ACCOMPANY THE AWARD OF

THE LEGION OF MERIT

TO

LEROY F. PROUTY, JR.

Lieutenant Colonel Leroy F. Prouty, Jr., distinguished himself by exceptionally meritorious conduct in the performance of outstanding service to the United States from July 1955 to February 1960 as Chief, Team B, Deputy Director for War Plans, Deputy Chief of Staff, Plans and Programs, Headquarters, United States Air Force. Throughout this period, Colonel Prouty demonstrated outstanding ability to formulate and implement plans and operations on a global scale, designed to support and further the aims of the United States. His skillful evaluation of all factors involved in the conduct of the Air Force program for which he was responsible contributed materially to the development of the Air Force and the nation's cold war planning, and subsequently to the furtherance of national and international policy and security. Colonel Prouty's exceptional display of knowledge, initiative, loyalty and devotion to duty reflect great credit upon himself and the United States Air Force.

weekend of April 15 and 16, 1961, and Dulles was the principal speaker. Why he accepted—and kept—that appointment at such a crucial time has never been properly explained. Did he prefer to have the Bay of Pigs fail? Did he choose to embarrass the new President?

As Maxwell Taylor's "Letter to the President" on the Cuban disaster later stated: "There was no single authority short of the President capable of coordinating the actions of the CIA, State, Defense, and the USIA [U.S. Information Agency]."

Because of the absence of its director, the CIA's secondary leaders— officials with no combat or command experience—made "the operational decisions which they felt within their authority." For decisions above them, they were supposed to go to the President. "Mr. Bissell and General Cabell were immediately available for consultation" but, it is crucial to note, there "were usually emissaries sent to obtain" higher approvals. "Emissary" was a far cry from "commander," as Dulles's responsibilities required. This task fell far short of effectiveness, as the Taylor letter noted: "Finally, there was the failure to carry the issue to the President when the opportunity was presented and explain to him with proper force the probable military consequences of a last-minute cancellation."

In his letter, General Taylor suggested forcefully that after General Cabell had received the call from McGeorge Bundy to cancel the bomber strike planned for dawn on the seventeenth to destroy the last three combat aircraft in Castro's skimpy air force, someone ought to have gone directly to the President to explain the absolute necessity of the air strike against these three T-33 jet trainers.[5]

That was the issue. In its guarded language, Taylor's letter never mentioned the Dulles absence, but it discussed this "breakdown of leadership" during the study group meetings with both Allen Dulles and Bobby Kennedy present. We may be sure it did not go unnoticed by the President during those after-hours meetings with Bobby and his other "Irish Mafia" friends.

At about 9:30 P.M. on April 16th, Mr. McGeorge Bundy, Special Assistant to the President, telephoned General C. P. Cabell of the CIA to inform him that the dawn air strikes the following morning should not be launched....

In that volatile environment of the Cuban study group, the direct relationship between the failure of the CIA command element to cope with the air strike issue and the absence that weekend of Dulles, the man responsible for the success of the anti-Castro program, became the biggest issue.

For the study group, the sequence of issues became quite clear:

1. The President had approved the landings and the air strike to destroy the last three combat aircraft in Castro's air force at dawn before the brigade hit the beach.

2. Later that evening, McGeorge Bundy had canceled the air strike by calling Cabell. (There is a school of thought that raises the possibility that it was Cabell himself who canceled the air strike, for reasons that quite ominously have an impact upon plans for the President's assassination in Dallas in 1963.)

3. Cabell and Bissell, in Dulles's absence, were inherently unqualified to carry the issue back to the President to "explain to him with proper force the probable military consequences of a last-minute cancellation."

4. The Cuban Study Group added: "This failure was a consequence of the restraints put on the anti-Castro air force in planning and executing its strikes, primarily for the purpose of protecting the covert character of the operation. These restraints included the decision to use only the B-26 as a combat aircraft because it had been distributed widely to foreign countries; the limitation of prelanding strikes to those which could be flown from non-U.S. controlled airfields under the guise of coming from Cuban strips, thus eliminating the possibility of using jet fighters or even T-33 trainers; the inability to use any non-Cuban base within short turnaround distance from the target area (about nine hours were required to turn around a B-26 for a second mission over the target from Nicaragua); prohibition of use of American contract pilots for tactical air operations; restriction on ammunitions, notably napalm; and the cancellation of the strikes planned at dawn on D-Day. The last mentioned was probably the most serious as it eliminated the last favorable opportunity to destroy the Castro air force on the ground. The cancellation seems to have resulted partly from the failure to make the air strike plan entirely clear in advance to the President and the Secretary of State, but, more importantly, by misgivings as to the effect of the air strikes on the position of the United States in the current UN debate on Cuba. Finally, there was the failure to carry the issue to the President when the opportunity was presented and explain to

him with proper force the probable military consequences of a
last-minute cancellation."

The members of the study group saw this cancellation as the clear cause
of the failure of the whole anti-Castro program that had been initiated in
March 1960. To fortify their own professional findings, they called
before them a man who had been instrumental from the earliest days in
these decisions. This man was a key Cuban exile named Manuel
Antonio de Varona, premier of Cuba before the Batista regime.[6]

The CIA tried to monopolize him. Nixon wooed him, as did
Kennedy. Finally, he came to the Cuban Study Group and told the
whole story. Needless to say, he played all sides, as all "contras" do.

De Varona made the following statement before the Cuban Study
Group: "I would like to state that we would be in Cuba today if it was not
for the lack of air support that our forces suffered. All those who've
returned said that but for three airplanes,[7] they would have been
successful in their invasion attempt."

Dulles was the man on the spot. There is no record of what he said
behind those closed doors, but a record was unnecessary. Bobby
Kennedy was always there. Despite this maneuver by the Kennedys,
however, Dulles still controlled the moves. Few people have the
experience to know how such things work under the cloak of secrecy.
This is the great weapon of the CIA, and it is why the CIA cannot be
stopped—short of eliminating all of its money. All the people who
worked on the Bay of Pigs project—Cuban and American—did so
under deep cover. CIA agents and military supporting-cast members all
had pseudonyms and lived cover-story lives. The Cubans with whom
they worked had no idea who these agents were, and their own
American associates did not know their true names and identities.

Thus, after the anti-Castro program had failed and all participants
had been dispersed, they themselves did not know who had been there
with them. This gave Allen Dulles the key role within the study group.
General Taylor had no alternative but to ask Dulles for the names of
people—CIA, military, and Cuban—who could be called to testify
before the group.

Dulles weeded out the ones who could tell too much and padded the
list with those who knew very little. Although Bobby Kennedy sat there
and listened to all of the dialogue, he had no way of realizing that he was
hearing a carefully structured scenario. The book he wrote several years
later revealed how little he really knew about some of the actual
activities.

This advantage enabled Dulles and the CIA to shift the blame to the Joint Chiefs of Staff and the military. Dulles kept quiet about the shortcomings of his own agency and made it appear that Kennedy's denial of the employment of U.S. Navy fighter aircraft as "air cover" was the real reason for the failure of the project. (Since 1961, in fact, the CIA has mounted a vigorous and comprehensive propaganda and revisionist campaign designed to ensure that the public is afforded no opportunity to discover the true facts.)

The CIA had kept the various elements of the Cuban exile groups apart. Many of them were of different political backgrounds and social levels and did not get along with each other. Thus, these diverse groups were trained in widely separated camps. When it came time to set sail for Cuba, the CIA put some units in the forefront of the brigade and landed them on the beach. At the same time, other units were "lost" at sea and never reached Cuba. Obviously they were the first to return to their separate base in Louisiana. Their emotional story of the failure to use their units on the beaches has led to much of the misunderstanding of the tactics of the operation. The CIA played this up and blamed the U.S. military for the oversight.

It happens that the Louisiana elements of the Cuban exile groups and their "mercenary" American trainers became suspect during the investigation of President Kennedy's assassination in 1963. Many of them had been recruited in the later, and much larger, anti-Castro program Mongoose under the CIA's most experienced paramilitary leader, Gen. Edward G. Lansdale.

All this made a good cover story later, because the individual selected to be the "patsy" in Kennedy's murder was a former U.S. Marine Corps enlisted man named Lee Harvey Oswald. He was born in New Orleans and had been active there with a Fair Play for Cuba organization during the early 1960s. Many assassination theorists have carried this presumed assassin's trail from Dallas through the "Oswald" scenario to New Orleans and thence to Cuba and Castro himself. This is a futile exercise, because Oswald was only the "patsy," not the murderer. Yet this trail of diversionary "golden apples" (as we recall them from Greek mythology) continues to divert the unwary and the overeager.

In an earlier chapter, I mentioned an unusual article that appeared in the *Reader's Digest* of November 1964 in which the author, Richard Nixon, tied Cuba, Castro, and John F. Kennedy together. Nixon is one of those, as is Ford, who, for various reasons, want the American public to believe Oswald was the "lone assassin." A single assassin does not have to have a motive for murder; a conspiracy must have a *why*. The "lone assassin" scenario is a cover story to preclude a conspiracy and its inevitable *why*.

At another time, Nixon wanted the American public to believe that he and Henry Kissinger had valid reasons for their genocidal bombardment of Cambodia with B-52s. This decision is also woven into the tapestry of history.

This orchestration of hidden motives and public smoke screens caused Kennedy to underestimate the power and skill of the CIA. He did not get to the root of the disaster of the Bay of Pigs invasion, and as a result he, too, became a victim of the sinister power of those agencies of the government that operate in total secrecy, knowing that they do not have to account to anyone for their actions and expenditures.

None of this should be taken to mean that Kennedy was not wise to the ways of Washington or that he could not mount extremely shrewd political maneuvers of his own. He was, and he did—but, despite this experience, he was up against impossible odds.

When he created the Cuban Study Group, he made it appear as if he were investigating a failed operation and nothing more. But this was not quite the case. It was only part of the story. Kennedy's precise instructions to General Taylor were: "... to study our governmental practices and programs in the areas of military and paramilitary guerrilla and antiguerrilla activity which fell short of outright war with a view to strengthening our work in this area."

It was at this time that Kennedy began his campaign against the CIA and its allies of the military-industrial complex, a campaign that reached its climax with his publication of National Security Action Memorandum #263 on October 11, 1963, and that was aborted by his murder. The above statement was the Cuban Study Group's real directive, and it is what Kennedy wanted to discover for himself, then and for the future. Kennedy did not like what he found when he came to the White House. As he moved to 1600 Pennsylvania Avenue, a huge tidal wave that had been set in motion many months earlier loomed up to engulf him and his new administration.

The new President had been critical of the way covert operations had functioned during the 1950s. As a long-term member of Congress, he was fully aware of the record of failed intelligence operations throughout the years. With the Bay of Pigs disaster as a case study, Kennedy directed General Taylor to dissect the entire system and to come up with something better. This was an issue that divided the study group and widened the abyss between Kennedy and Dulles. Yet Kennedy continued to make use of Dulles in his desire to probe the real depths of the murky business of intelligence and clandestine operations.

By the middle of June 1961, the Cuban Study Group had gathered a remarkable series of documents. For decades since, these key materials have been concealed, ignored, and sometimes purposely misinterpreted. To fully understand the forces at work during Kennedy's presidency, it is necessary to lift the curtain of secrecy on a part of top-level government activity that is seldom, if ever, represented accurately.

The work of the Cuban Study Group was unequaled in its level of confidentiality. Even the word for its classification is so secret as to be relatively unknown: The group worked under the rarely used "ultrasensitive" label, that cosmic world above "top secret."

The reason for this lies in the delicacy of certain types of intelligence activities, namely, covert operations by one government against another. Even the use of the word "against" is not always accurate. Sometimes the target is an otherwise friendly, allied government, when it is deemed essential to acquire information or to confirm information that cannot be obtained by any other means.

For example, the United States has flown the U-2 over many friendly countries, such as Israel, to confirm certain situations with our own eyes and ears.

Although it is always assumed that national sovereignty is inviolate, in today's world national sovereignty has become an archaic and unworkable sham. It does not exist even among the great powers, and it is continuously violated—secretly. It has always been the unwritten rule that any covert U.S. operation must be performed in such a manner as to remain truly secret or, failing that, that the role of the government in the operation must be able to be plausibly disclaimed. The U.S. has spent untold tens of millions of dollars to "sterilize" entire aircraft and other equipment, so that if such a plane on a secret mission crashed while within the bounds of the target country, no one would be able to find the slightest evidence in the wreckage to incriminate the United States. All labels, name tags, and serial numbers are removed in such circumstances, and the crew uniforms are even made out of non-U.S. fabric to enhance denial. Weapons used are "sterilized" at a special underground facility overseas and are foreign-made.

Under the provisions of the National Security Act of 1947, the CIA operates at the direction of the National Security Council. The intent of this law is to place the origin for any covert operation at the top. This neutralizes and eliminates lesser matters and emphasizes the importance of those that the NSC actually originates and directs.

The NSC can direct any designated department or agency—not necessarily the CIA—to carry out a covert operation. These operations are normally done on a small scale, or else they could not be kept a secret. Being small, they can usually be handled by the CIA, sometimes augmented by the resources of the Defense Department.

These are legal considerations that, by the way, serve to underscore the foolhardiness and deceit of those activities that have been under way in Central America and the Middle East in recent years. Over the years, especially during the 1950s, when Allen Dulles was director of central intelligence and his brother, John Foster Dulles, was secretary of state, this legal precision had become more and more vague. Allen Dulles became accustomed to taking proposals that originated with the agency to the NSC—in those days to the "10/2" or "5412/2" Committee—for its approval.

In most cases, he would receive the committee's approval, sometimes with stipulations. But it was the CIA that had originated these plans, not the NSC, and this is a highly significant point with respect to the law.

The difference between a plan of highest national interest that originates within the NSC and is then given to the CIA "by direction of the NSC" and a plan that is originated within the CIA and then presented to the NSC for its "approval" can be enormous. It raises fundamental questions, such as "Who runs this government?" and "Is the government being operated under the law?"

These questions were foremost in Kennedy's mind when he became President. It was in March 1960 that the anti-Castro program was devised by the CIA and that the deputy director for plans, Richard Bissell, had briefed President Eisenhower and his NSC. At that time, Bissell had gained their approval for a rather modest program. It was the CIA that took this approval and turned a program intended to support small over-the-beach landings and paradrop operations into an invasion of Cuba at the Bay of Pigs.

Kennedy inherited the accumulated actions of one full year of this program. He had such strong convictions about it that he did not approve the invasion until the day before it actually took place. The CIA had launched its invasion fleet, small though it was, a full week before the day of the landing. The President was therefore faced with a virtual fait accompli before he had an opportunity to make a decision. Even then Kennedy knew he had been had, and it did not take him long to confirm it.

Moreover, the enormity of the various schemes that had been set in motion long before he was elected was staggering. By May 1960, for example, after the anti-Castro program had begun, the stage was prepared for the entry of American troops into the Vietnam War. The master war planners took advantage of the period when the country was involved with a presidential election—when the powers of the presidency were at their lowest ebb. Eisenhower was not told what was going on, and it would be some time before the new President would be able to do anything about it, once he was informed.

After eight years of peace, the national mood for détente was strong, and an incident was needed to reverse this. Such an incident was conveniently provided.

On May 1, 1960, a CIA U-2 spy plane piloted by Gary Powers was launched on what would have been its longest flight ever, directly across the Soviet Union from Pakistan to Norway. When it crash-landed in the heart of Russia, and Eisenhower accepted the blame, Khrushchev concluded Eisenhower had deliberately wrecked what had been planned as the "ultimate summit conference" in Paris.[8] This incident served to reverse the trend toward détente that had been carefully orchestrated by Khrushchev and Eisenhower, the two aging World War II veterans. With the summit conference disrupted, the road to Saigon, and disaster, was clear.

The following recapitulation will demonstrate how meticulously the road to Saigon was planned by experts in the war-making business. In order to set this plan irrevocably into motion, the powers-that-be formulated a counterinsurgency plan for Vietnam. The events that followed the formulation of this plan constitute an intriguing series of incidents.

Just prior to Kennedy's election, the U.S. Army Special Warfare Center at Fort Bragg, North Carolina, was rejuvenated. A new curriculum was written that combined counterinsurgency with pacification tactics that were already being employed by the French forces in Algeria and with Civic Action programs borrowed from the U.S. Army's Civil Affairs and Military Government school at Fort Gordon, Georgia.

This new Special Forces Green Beret school at Fort Bragg received substantial aid from the CIA, as well as from the Office of Special Operations in the Office of the Secretary of Defense. The strength of the forces was increased, and the Special Warfare Center opened a new counterinsurgency school for U.S. and foreign military students in November 1960.

President Kennedy was elected on November 8, 1960. Two days later, on November 10, Kennedy asked Allen Dulles to stay on as the director of central intelligence.

It was announced on November 11 that three battalions of President Diem's elite guard had taken part in a coup d'état at the presidential palace in Saigon and that the incident was quickly suppressed by Diem's forces. Under the cover of that contrived action, President Diem ordered the arrest of what was known as the Caravelle Group, eighteen political opponents of the Diem brothers' dictatorial regime. These eighteen men had in no way participated in the "coup." But they had published a scholarly "Manifesto of the Eighteen," and for this they were thrown in jail.

Edward G. Lansdale was a leader in the development of the counterinsurgency plan for Vietnam, author of the new Special Forces curriculum for the Special Warfare Center at Fort Bragg, and an old friend of President Diem's. He took advantage of Kennedy's election and of Dulles's reappointment to make a sudden, unannounced trip to Saigon. The trip was for the purposes of winning Diem's support and cooperation for the counterinsurgency program in Vietnam and of furthering Lansdale's own chances, with Diem's and Dulles's support, of being named ambassador to Saigon by Kennedy.

During this politically important visit, which set the stage for so many of the events that followed, Lansdale wrote a stirring report on the situation in Vietnam for his boss, the secretary of defense. This report was brought to the attention of key members of the new Kennedy team at the time of the inauguration.

In late January 1961, Lansdale was summoned to the White House to meet with President Kennedy and officials from the Departments of Defense and State, new people who had come in with the inauguration. He was warmly greeted by the President and commended for his excellent report. Kennedy also informed him that he could expect to be sent back to Vietnam in a high capacity.[9]

On April 12, 1961, a memo was written by Kennedy adviser Walt Rostow that was supportive of the Lansdale report. Lansdale, on April 19, submitted another memo of his own to his new boss, Secretary of Defense Robert S. McNamara. Up to this time, Lansdale's strongest support had come from Allen Dulles and Ngo Dinh Diem. For more than a year, the anti-Castro project and the counterinsurgency program for Vietnam had been running simultaneously.

On April 20, 1961, the brigade was defeated in Cuba. The coincidence—or, perhaps, the coordination—of the dates of the surrender of the brigade at the Bay of Pigs and the abrupt turn toward Saigon is noteworthy, for the Americanization of the warfare in Vietnam also began on April 20, 1961.

For it was on that same date, April 20, 1961, that President Kennedy, distraught over the disaster in Cuba, accepted the counterinsurgency program for Vietnam and directed Deputy Secretary of Defense Roswell Gilpatric to make recommendations for a series of actions to prevent the Communist domination of the government of Vietnam. Gilpatric and Lansdale headed a task force established to carry out those instructions from the President.

April 20, 1961, was the day Kennedy began to understand how the CIA and the Defense Department operated in this amazing world of clandestine operations. It was also the day Allen Dulles's influence in the Kennedy administration ended. With the eclipse of Dulles and the CIA, Lansdale's dream of being ambassador to Saigon collapsed.

Kennedy adopted the concept of counterinsurgency as his own, as he shifted his thoughts and energies from the failure in Cuba to the future in Indochina. The wheels of the counterinsurgency juggernaut were picking up speed. In April 1961, the director of the Joint Staff,[10] Gen. Earle Wheeler, and Secretary McNamara decided to create a new section within the structure of the Joint Staff that would be dedicated to counterinsurgency and special activities. The counterinsurgency element of that office was to be the cap on all military services in support of the counterinsurgency program for Vietnam. The special activities were a combination of special operations—that is, the military support of the clandestine activities of the CIA—and special plans, that is, the special art of military cover and deception.[11]

To balance the rapid growth of the U.S. Army Special Forces program and its new Special Warfare Center at Fort Bragg, Gen. Curtis E. LeMay, chief of staff of the U.S. Air Force, announced that on April 1961, a combat-crew training squadron had been activated at Eglin Air Force Base in Florida. The mission of that special squadron included counterinsurgency, unconventional warfare, and psychological warfare operations. Shortly thereafter, this cadre was expanded significantly to become a Special Air Warfare Center that included an Air Commando wing and a Combat Applications group. Without delay, Special Air

Warfare units from the center at Eglin were deployed to South Vietnam.[12]

It should be noted that both the Green Berets of the Army Special Forces and the Air Commandos of the Air Force had been developed and trained in close cooperation with the CIA, and upon their arrival in South Vietnam they operated under the control of CIA agents. They were very special organizations. They were what President Reagan later duplicated during his administration with some of the same people in Central America. But what Reagan was unable to create was a Nicaraguan George Washington. The first thing Lansdale had done in Vietnam was to create a "Father of his Country," in the person of Ngo Dinh Diem.

By the end of April 1961, a revised counterinsurgency program[13] had been submitted to President Kennedy, without the Lansdale material. Kennedy lost no time in implementing many of its recommendations. The first troop movement, the deployment of a four-hundred-man Special Forces group to South Vietnam, was made to accelerate the training of the South Vietnamese army. This move was directed by President Kennedy under the terms of National Security Action Memorandum (NSAM) #52, issued on May 11, 1961.

By April 20, Kennedy knew that if he was ever going to gain full control of the CIA, he would have to understand what went wrong with the anti-Castro program and what he had to do to take over control of the counterinsurgency program for Vietnam. This accounts for the strong directive he wrote to Gen. Maxwell Taylor on April 21, 1961.

With the collapse of the brigade in Cuba, Kennedy lost no time in getting to the heart of the matter. On June 13, 1961, Maxwell Taylor forwarded his "Letter to the President." It was a most remarkable document. Kennedy and his inner circle studied it carefully, and on June 28, 1961, President Kennedy issued one of the most important and unusual directives to leave the White House under any President since World War II.

This directive, National Security Action Memorandum #55, said in part, "I wish to inform the Joint Chiefs of Staff as follows with regard to my views of their relations to me in Cold War Operations:... The Joint Chiefs of Staff have a responsibility for the defense of the nation in the Cold War similar to that which they have in conventional hostilities."

This is a revolutionary statement when one considers who wrote it and the circumstances under which it was promulgated. The Cold War was a massive global struggle that existed only in vague terms. A "Cold

War operation," however, was a very specific term that referred to a secret, clandestine activity. Traditionally, the uniformed services of this country have not been authorized to become involved in clandestine activities in peacetime. Therefore, with NSAM #55, President Kennedy was making the Joint Chiefs of Staff—the military forces of the United States—responsible for the Cold War, just as they would be responsible for a real, declared state of war among nations. This was a radical departure from the traditional rules of warfare among the family of nations.

Kennedy was directing that U.S. military forces be used against any Cold War adversary, whether or not there had been a declaration of war. This was a revolutionary doctrine, especially for the United States, and if these presidential directives (NSAM #55 was accompanied by two others, NSAM #56 and #57) had become operationally effective, they would have changed drastically the course of the war in Vietnam.

They would effectively have removed the CIA from Cold War operations and limited the CIA to its sole lawful responsibility, the coordination of intelligence. In many situations, these directives would have made the chairman of the Joint Chiefs of Staff the day-to-day counterpart of the secretary of state.

At the same time, these documents stated the Kennedy position, clearly setting forth his battle plan. Kennedy was taking charge, if he could, and he was relying upon the Joint Chiefs of Staff for assistance. He did not know it at the time, but with the issuance of these directives, he had only eighteen months left to win his battle against the CIA and its allies, or to die in the attempt.

It was an odd twist of fate that led Kennedy to choose the Joint Chiefs of Staff over the CIA to become his strong right arm. He did this because of the strength and courage of Maxwell Taylor's letter. By midsummer, Taylor had become Kennedy's military and intelligence adviser in the White House. Kennedy appointed him to be chairman of the Joint Chiefs of Staff in October 1962. It was Maxwell Taylor—not Jack Kennedy or anyone else in the White House—who, representing the members of the Cuban Study Group, actually wrote the paragraphs in NSAM #55 that are cited above. Those words, along with many others like them from the same series of documents, were taken absolutely verbatim from that long-hidden "Letter to the President" that Taylor wrote on June 13, 1961.

Why did Taylor, Burke, and Dulles, all members of the Cuban Study Group, unanimously put those words into the mind of Jack Kennedy?

Why did Kennedy accept them and publish them with his signature without delay?

Having been given such vast powers by their President, where were the Joint Chiefs of Staff when the guns were fired in the streets of Dallas only eighteen months later? Where was Lansdale? Where was Allen Dulles? Why was Kennedy so alone and unprotected by the time he made that fateful trip to Texas in 1963?

Kennedy asserted a power of the presidency that he assumed he had, but when his orders were delivered to the men to whom they were addressed, he discovered that his power was all but meaningless. His directives were quietly placed in the bureaucratic files and forgotten. There have been few times in the history of this nation when the limits of the power of the President have been so nakedly exposed. I was the briefing officer for the chairman of the Joint Chiefs of Staff, to whom NSAM #55 was addressed. I know exactly what he was told about that series of documents, and I know what he said about them during that meeting. During that meeting, I was told to have them put in the chairman's file, where they remained. Gen. Lyman L. Lemnitzer did not choose to be a "Cold Warrior."

In the great struggle between Kennedy and the entrenched power sources of Washington, as personified by the CIA and its allies in the Defense Department and the military-industrial complex, the President learned that his weapons were powerless and his directives unheeded. Beginning in July 1961 he set out to change that situation.

TWELVE

Building to the Final Confrontation

BARELY TWO MONTHS after the humiliating defeat of the Cuban exile brigade on the beaches of the Bay of Pigs, President John F. Kennedy attempted to put a halter on the maverick CIA. On June 28, 1961, three top-level White House directives, National Security Action Memoranda (NSAM), were published.

One of them, NSAM #55, entitled, "Relations of the Joint Chiefs of Staff to the President in Cold War Operations,"[1] was signed by Kennedy and sent directly to the chairman of the Joint Chiefs of Staff, Gen. Lyman L. Lemnitzer. This was a most unusual intragovernmental procedure. Ordinarily it would have gone to the chairman via the secretary of defense, with copies to the secretary of state and the director, central intelligence, because of its subject. Without doubt, this directive was the most important single act of the first year of the Kennedy presidency. He had determined to limit the CIA's role in clandestine activities, perhaps eliminate it altogether. This was the first in a series of such top-level policy directives issued by Kennedy that culminated in NSAM #263, issued one month before his murder.

These papers, and their actual authorship, were concealed for years. Although parts of them appear in the so-called Pentagon Papers, they do not appear there as a unit or with their correct titles and language. As far as I know, they have never before this work been linked with their source document, the Cuban Study Group report contained in a "Letter

170

to the President" from Gen. Maxwell Taylor to John F. Kennedy dated June 13, 1961. This is discussed in greater detail elsewhere in this book.

The White House did make a copy of NSAM #55 available separately to the secretary of defense. No copy was sent to either the secretary of state or to the director of central intelligence. Kennedy's no-nonsense policy directives marked the first steps in his ambitious plan to change the course of Cold War operations, which, for the most part, had been made the responsibility of the CIA since that agency's creation in late 1947. These remarkable documents led directly to the later Reagan decision to do away with Eisenhower-period "plausibly deniable" covert operations and to come out into the open with Cold War operations, such as his action against Grenada and the overt F-111 air strikes against Libya. The Bush administration has continued this "overt" policy with its attack on Panama and the Desert Storm operation.

Whether or not this new military policy has been formally proclaimed the official guideline of the United States, it is being practiced today, as evidenced by the Gulf War. This policy means, in effect, that national sovereignty no longer exists and that a nation's independence and borders are no longer sacred.

As this newer doctrine becomes more widely implemented, the traditional family of nations will dissolve into a shambles of raw power. From now on, no one will be safe. There is no sanctuary. Everyone, everywhere, is someone's potential target. There is no place to hide.

This doctrine, quite literally adopted from the writings of Mao Tse-tung, first attained prominence and a measure of legitimacy under the signature of John F. Kennedy, who clearly and unhesitatingly stated his intentions in the opening sentences of NSAM #55 to the chairman of the Joint Chiefs of Staff. (To repeat, this directive was not written by JFK. We learned later that it was written by Gen. Maxwell Taylor, who was familiar with the studies of Mao's writing done by the U.S. Army.)

> I wish to inform the Joint Chiefs of Staff as follows with regard to my views of their relations to me in Cold War operations:
>
> a. I regard the Joint Chiefs of Staff as my principal military adviser responsible for initiating advice to me and for responding to requests for advice. I expect their advice to come to me direct and unfiltered.
>
> b. The Joint Chiefs of Staff have a responsibility for the defense of the nation in the Cold War similar to that which they have in conventional hostilities.

As used in these directives, the term "Cold War operations" generally referred to covert operations, although it was not entirely limited to secret activities. What was new about this policy was that the President was bringing the experienced military Chiefs of Staff into an area of operation that traditionally, as under the terms of the March 15, 1954, NSC Directive #5412, had been declared to be outside the scope of the uniformed services in peacetime. A first step in this direction had taken place in 1957, when the chairman of the Joint Chiefs of Staff was made a member of the NSC #5412 "Special Group" that had been empowered to approve clandestine operations.

It must be noted that these policy statements that JFK signed arose directly from a study of the Bay of Pigs operation. President Kennedy had directed an essential, covert air strike against Castro's last three combat aircraft. As noted, that strike did not take place. Others, unwitting of the stipulations of NSC #5412, have charged that Kennedy ought to have provided U.S. military "air cover" for the Cuban exile brigade on the beach, when it came under attack by Castro's last three jet aircraft. Those who make this charge do not realize that the NSC had prohibited the utilization of regular military forces in support of clandestine activity and that that prohibition had established the parameters of the overall strategy.

With this in mind, Kennedy emphasized this factor when he stated, "The Joint Chiefs of Staff have a responsibility for the defense of the nation in the Cold War similar to that which they have in conventional hostilities." He was making it possible, when necessary, to turn to the Joint Chiefs of Staff for just such purposes as had previously arisen at the time of the Bay of Pigs operation.

Thus, his NSAM #55 is an important statement, and much could be said about it as it has reappeared during succeeding administrations. In conventional hostilities, as defined by Clausewitz[2] or in the traditional sense, the military establishment takes over from the diplomats and is made responsible for total war against the citizens, territory, and property of the enemy, in every possible way. Converting this doctrine for application during time of peace, albeit during the Cold War, has the effect of raising the Cold War to a higher and more overt level and prescribes a role for the U.S. military that it has never had before. When these three directives hit the Joint Staff,[3] the wheels within wheels of the Pentagon began to grind. The situation was exacerbated by the fact that no immediate explanation for this significant policy change had reached the CIA or the Department of State.

Within the bureaucracy, whenever a major shift in policy occurs, the first thing that is done is to dispatch secret investigators in all directions to discover the origin of the new policy and to determine what the change means. A new President and a new presidential staff rarely come equipped with insiders of sufficient experience to produce such major changes on their own in one swift stroke. It was thought that Ted Sorensen, the President's counsel, and Bobby Kennedy must have been the source of these directives. This was not so.

The Pentagon, the CIA, and the Department of State—each for its own reasons—probed the White House. They were unable, however, to find any person, or any prior work, that gave clues to the origin of these very special papers. The problem was made worse by the fact that very few copies of these NSAMs had been made available to anyone. The true source was not discovered for many years, and therein lies a story of great importance, one that has threaded its way through the Cold War era for decades. During this period the whole concept of warfare, the role of the military, and the nature of the modern nation-state have been drastically altered, at a cost, to United States citizens alone, of no less than $3 trillion.

In the process of attempting to implement the policy he had promulgated with these three directives on June 28, 1961, President Kennedy created an explosive force within the environs of the government and its allies such that the resulting mass went critical on the streets of Dallas on November 22, 1963.

It all began with one of the best-kept secrets of World War II. As this secret is exposed, it will reveal how it happened that select elements of the U.S. Army and their CIA associates became interested in the undercover warfare tactics written and practiced by the Chinese Communist leader Mao Tse-tung.

This secret originated from the fact that while historians have openly revealed that Winston Churchill and Franklin D. Roosevelt had gone to the Tehran Conference in late November 1943 to meet with Joseph Stalin for a discussion of grand strategy for the prosecution of the war against Nazi Germany, they have failed to note that Chiang Kai-shek and his wife, May Ling, and a special Chinese delegation had accompanied them from Cairo,[4] where Churchill, Roosevelt, and Chiang had been meeting. This was a most important summit meeting not only for the purposes of advancing war planning in Europe but for much longer range planning in the Far East, planning that has spilled over into the Cold War era with the Korean and Indochinese warfare of later years.

This select Chinese delegation had a delicate task to perform that involved Stalin and could not be made public for several reasons. Whereas the Soviets, British, and Americans were locked in battle against Germany in Europe and the Chinese, British, and Americans opposed the Japanese on the mainland of China and in the Pacific, the Chinese forces of Chiang Kai-shek had a more complex problem. While Chiang was faced by an external force from Japan, his men were threatened also by the formidable Chinese Communist army under Mao Tse-tung. The British and Americans wanted Chiang to put more pressure on the Japanese on the mainland. But if he moved troops facing Mao, in China, to engage the Japanese, he would expose the rear elements of his army. Therefore, he could not move his army from its positions against Mao's forces in order to aid the Allies against the Japanese and hope to survive the threat of the Chinese Communists.

The other part of the problem was that as British and American forces were moved in increasing numbers onto the mainland of China to help Chiang against the Japanese, it was inevitable that somewhere along the line they would encounter Chinese Communist forces that were ideological allies of the Soviets—who were, in turn, the military allies of the British and Americans.

Such complex affairs do not digest well in time of war, when the friend-versus-enemy scenario is supposed to be as clear as black and white. This is why the four powers could not meet publicly at one time in one place, and this explains why there had to be two conferences, one in Cairo and one in Tehran. And it further explains why the Chinese met secretly with Stalin in Tehran and how the three Pacific allies—the United States, Great Britain, and Chiang Kai-shek's Chinese—won a concession from Stalin to have him prevail upon his ideological ally, Mao Tse-tung, to withhold his forces from further pressure on Chiang, at least until the war with Japan ended. (Mao finally defeated the Nationalists in Nanking in 1949.) Such intricate diplomacy in the heat of the war demanded true statesmanship all around.

It is not within the scope of this book to venture into the areas of diplomacy and political intrigue that grew out of this most important meeting. Rather, we shall pursue its impact upon the development of a new trend in U.S. military doctrine that emerged and shaped itself during the Cold War years. Elements of this doctrine became evident in the NSAM #55, #56, and #57 series of presidential directives that John F. Kennedy issued in June 1961 as he initiated his objective of bringing the CIA under his effective control by putting the military into the "Peacetime Operations" (clandestine) business.

Following the Tehran and Cairo conferences, American military aid to and participation with the Chinese on the mainland increased enormously. A group of B-29 Super Fortress bombers was flown from the United States via Africa and the Middle East to bases in the Assam Valley wartime airport complex of eastern India. From there they were flown to advance bases in China for direct operations against the Japanese home islands.

It was during the post–Tehran Conference period that selected American military leaders ran up against conditions in China that were totally uncharacteristic of the military practices and doctrine of the United States. In China, military force was deeply involved in a political role at the same time as it was fighting a conventional war against the Japanese and a civil war with Mao. This necessarily political role of the military opened the eyes of the more traditional U.S. military observers.

The United States had sent a number of its finest military leaders to China. The army was under the command of Gen. Joseph W. Stilwell. The air force units were commanded by the legendary Gen. Claire Chennault of "Flying Tigers" fame. A number of these officers and their key subordinates came home from the war in Asia deeply impressed with what they had experienced there. Two things stood out above all others: the impact of the atomic bomb and the writings and revolutionary military doctrine of Mao Tse-tung.

Looking back at World War II, and even before it, U.S. military men—for the most part—regarded warfare as something that took place overseas, beyond our borders. They viewed military service as a totally nonpolitical function. This, they found, was also generally true of the military traditions of our British and French allies in Europe—until, that is, the closing period of the war. Then things began to change.

After the surrender of Italy, the U.S. Army began to help the Italians, who had been under Fascist totalitarian rule for a generation or more. They needed help not only to obtain food, shelter, and clothing but also to restructure local governments.

The U.S. Army began a program of "Civil Affairs and Military Government." American servicemen, making use of their civilian skills, pitched in to get public water supplies flowing again, to get transportation rolling, and even to form a political structure that could take over the local administrations. This function spread all over Europe as cities and towns were liberated, one after the other, by the advancing U.S. armies.

The U.S. Army was getting into politics. But it was someone else's politics. This new role for the army came at a fortuitous time. Two cities had been totally leveled by atomic bombs in faraway Japan. If the future of warfare was going to face up to reality, it would have to recognize that whole countries, or at least major regions of countries, would be totally devastated by nuclear weapons and their lethal fallout.

During the late 1940s and early 1950s, the War Colleges, where military doctrine is developed, began the study of nuclear weapons and their immense power, with the idea of placing these weapons into wartime Grand Strategy. If the entire span of the evolution of warfare had created a spectrum based upon weaponry from hand-held clubs at one end across to the B-29 bomber at the other, then it might be said that the nuclear weapon extended that spectrum of power almost to infinity.

The curriculum of each of these schools for senior officers contained major segments on nuclear warfare. "War Plans"—those very formal and fundamental plans designed to implement Grand Strategy and used in the budgeting process to ensure the availability of men, money, and matériel essential to carry out and fulfill those plans in time of war— were being developed that contained major segments dedicated to "poststrike" activity.

This new nuclear-age strategy recognized a type of warfare initiated by a sudden exchange of nuclear weapons, followed by a time of shock and stagnation. The urban areas of the Soviet Union, it was contemplated, would be devastated, and transportation and communications would be totally disrupted. The daily activities of the surviving population would be at a standstill, with no voice of leadership from the Kremlin; the survivors would be on their own. War Plans forecast that the first nation that could introduce, by airlift, its military forces into this shocked and devastated area and that could reestablish law and order, along with a new political and economic system, would seal victory.

For this purpose, the newly established CIA was brought into the war-planning activity and visualized as a fourth force in wartime. The CIA was asked to oversee the development of these special activities in peacetime and to manage their operation in time of war. Similarly, the air force was ordered to create a huge, global air transport system that could be rapidly augmented at the outbreak of war by CRAF (Civil Reserve Air Fleet) aircraft from the airlines. This huge air armada would airlift the army and essential supplies into enemy zones that had been specifically avoided by nuclear strikes to be sanctuaries and rallying zones following the nuclear deluge.

Those army "Special Forces" units, created for this purpose to work with the CIA and its "stay-behind" assets, would begin to create a government that would include a new economic and political system. As the lead element of these forces, the U.S. Army was directed to create, in peacetime, a Special Warfare section, to train Special Forces; and, once it had trained them, to disperse them to strategic locations around the world. The CIA had been directed to do everything possible to establish networks of foreign agents, in peacetime, far behind the borders of potential enemy countries. With the outbreak of war, the CIA would activate these "stay-behind" networks in preparation for the arrival of U.S. armed forces.

The air force created Air Re-supply and Communications (ARC) Wings, vast flying organizations trained and equipped to work with the army's Special Forces and the CIA. These ARC Wings possessed airborne printing facilities that could be operated in flight. They were able to make areawide blanket leaflet drops to provide the psychological-warfare edge and the communications substitute required to reorganize a stunned and disorganized populace. This was the grandiose plan that emerged out of the merger of the World War II atomic bomb and "Civil Affairs and Military Government" experiences of World War II. On reflection, it is amazing to see how these two widely divergent concepts became a Grand Strategy war plan; and how then, by adding the superlative ingredient of elements of the Mao doctrine, they were shaped expertly to become the Cold War doctrine and the tactics of the Vietnam era, among other applications. For example, this planning was behind the "Strategic Hamlet" concept that will be described later.

It is even more fascinating to see how all this has been shaped in the hands of later administrations and applied as a main theme of the military action concept of the 1980s and 1990s. Yet with all this development, there was one thing lacking. This new doctrine needed eyes and ears and, if possible, reliable contacts within the denied areas of Soviet, or other potential-enemy, territory.

The relatively new CIA, concentrating for the most part on its mission of intelligence, had none of the bases, military equipment, manpower, storage sites, etc., required for such a task. Faced with this dilemma—it sorely wanted to be the Fourth Force, but did not possess the wherewithal to pull it off—the CIA made a characteristically clever and self-serving decision.

The agency placed the burden of support right back on the military system. As the years passed, the CIA amassed enormous stockpiles of War Plans–authorized equipment in warehouses, ostensibly to await either a military exercise to flex its muscles or the real thing. This is the way the CIA got its toe in the door to flesh out its early clandestine operations.

It is an old military truism that "if you have the weapons, they will be used," and, indeed, as the years rolled by, these weapons were used, by the CIA.

These two strategic concepts, one gleaned from the China of Mao Tse-tung and the other arising out of the wartime devastation of Europe, began to merge with the nuclear reality. American military officers with Asian experience began to soak up the European concept of Civic Action and Special Warfare. This change of direction became the central theme of the warfare in Indochina during the 1960s and 1970s and later became the dominant theme of President Reagan's military policy, as evidenced in Central America, Africa, and the Middle East.

In earlier days, such "Peacetime Operations" were secret, and every attempt was made to keep them that way. Today they are called "covert," but they are as overt as the attacks on Libya, and they are, of course, readily attributable to the United States. This situation marks the end of the principle that honored national sovereignty among the family of nations. By 1958, senior military officers at the Army War College heard lectures on these subjects presented by the new breed of U.S. military strategist. An excerpt from one such lecture given by Edward G. Lansdale follows:

Mao Tse-tung explained the importance of the Communist politico-military forces in the new modern warfare. Their main purpose deals with the army-people relationship for winning over people to unite with the armed forces. They can be adopted by all other armies and especially guerrilla forces. There are those who cannot imagine how guerrillas could survive for long in the rear of the enemy. But, they do not understand the relationship between the people and the army. The people are like the water and the army is like the fish. How can it be difficult for the fish to survive when there is water?

This is straight out of Mao Tse-tung's *Little Red Book*. In other words, all of a sudden the teaching of Mao, the Chinese Communist leader, had become part of the doctrine of the new U.S. military strategy. This example of the "fish in the water" was repeated thousands of times in thousands of lectures. The voice of Mao was raised again and again at the Army War College, to wit:

> There are often military elements who care for only military affairs but not politics. Such one-track-minded military officers, ignoring the interconnection between politics and military affairs, must be made to understand the correct relationship between the two. All military actions are means to achieve certain political objectives, while military action itself is a manifested form of politics. There are of course differences between political and military affairs, each with its special characteristics, but the one should not be disconnected and isolated from the other.
>
> The world today is already in a new era of evolution and today's war is already approaching the world's last armed conflict. This is also a fact which should be understood. The majority of mankind, including the 450 millions of China, is already engaged or preparing to engage in a great, just war against the aggressors and oppressors of the entire world. No matter how long this war is going to last, there is no doubt that it is approaching the last conflict in history. After such a prolonged, ruthless war, there will emerge an historically unprecedented new era for mankind in which there will be no more wars.

These are the written comments of one of the greatest military leaders of modern times. He is defining the Cold War in terms of real war. It was heady stuff for the leaders of the U.S. Army. They knew it did not have immediate application within the United States, but they saw ways to create armies of this type in other countries, particularly in the emerging Third World nations.

The next step on the road to full implementation of this new doctrine involved the joining of the teaching of Mao with the curriculum of the Civil Affairs and Military Government School at Fort Gordon, Georgia, and the creation, from this merger, of the new Special Warfare doctrine of 1960.

From army platforms such statements as "the kind of peace we have today is too important to entrust to the career diplomats and professional economists" became common as senior army officials began to see that the U.S. Army had a Cold War role. As explained by these lectures,

"With U.S. guidance and help, the politico-military actions of Southeast Asian armed forces can be decisive in building strong, free nations, with governments responsive to and representative of the people."

It did not take much imagination to see the way things were going. This new doctrine proposed that somehow a strong army—for example, one under a powerful leader such as Gen. Augusto Pinochet of Chile— was supposed to build "representative" government. This new doctrine visualized a national army suspended somewhere between the people on the one hand and the seat of government on the other—truly the "fish" (army) in the "water" (people).

Despite the planners' optimism, they were never able to demonstrate an army that operated that way (least of all General Pinochet's). Once an army has developed the power, it uses it. The seat of government becomes engulfed by this new army, and the people are subjugated. Tradition in military circles is always stronger than mere words.

Mao wrote those ideas about his army while he was the rebel leader. Once in power, and with that army under his control, the tables were completely turned. He became as dictatorial as all the rest. To those who are not students of the evolution of warfare and the history of war, some of these developments in U.S. military doctrine since World War II may seem complex and obscure. Essentially the regular armed forces of the United States have always been regarded as a base or cadre upon which the much larger forces required for overseas warfare could be built. The role of the regular armed forces, between wars, has been to train and equip themselves for war, and no more.

In the past, the United States has never used armed forces, during peacetime, for political or diplomatic reasons, other than for an occasional show of force externally. And certainly there is no role for these forces within the borders of this country, with a very few exceptions: to aid police or the Secret Service or in the event of national disasters and emergencies. Therefore, the emergence of U.S. military doctrine tailored to the policies of Chairman Mao is quite a departure, especially when flavored with the "Civil Affairs and Military Government" concept.

The U.S. armed forces have, for the most part, been cautious about this role. But over the years they have associated themselves with the armed forces of Third World nations, in support of this concept of the army being the "fish" in the "water" of the populace. Tens of thousands of leaders in the armed forces of Third World countries have attended U.S. military schools and colleges where they have been taught to adopt an Americanized version of Mao's ideas of the politico-military relationships. Where the concept has been put into practice, certain military elements, including U.S. Army Special Forces, have been under the direction of the CIA. This was the case in Indochina between 1954 and 1965, and this is how it happened that the tactics of the Vietnam War were so closely allied with these Maoist ideas.

In other examples, covert operations were run, as much with a blank checkbook as anything else, to build up a new, popular military leader, as in the case of Ramon Magsaysay in the Philippines. As described in earlier chapters, Magsaysay's CIA-supported rise placed him at the head of the military forces in the Philippines. The CIA knew that the military there could be relied upon to build a "strong government responsive and representative of the people." And the fact is that once Magsaysay reached that level of military power, he also became the head of state, with the support of a strong army. His "fish" did not stay in the "water" for long.

Other examples of the theoretical application of these principles have involved such countries as Iran, Chile, Guatemala, the Congo, Indonesia, Tibet, Vietnam, and Laos, and many other nations in Africa, Latin America, and the Middle East. In every case where the intent was to create a model "Mao-defined" army, it has failed. In spite of this, however, proponents of the doctrine continued their work.

There was a singularly economic reason for this. Since World War II, the Department of Defense had become the perennial biggest spender in the government. If such a level of spending was to be continued, Cold War or not, there had to appear to be some reason for the vast procurement orders other than for actual warfare; and, perhaps even more important, there had to be some way to consume military hardware so that it would have to be replaced from new procurement. (This is one explanation for the growing size of the so-called black budget—the part of the federal budget that is secret and not accounted for by its recipients.)

It is quite customary to find that for every defense dollar spent on new military equipment, ten more dollars are spent for support during its military "life of type." These same figures, perhaps even higher on the average, apply to the military hardware that is sent as "military aid" to other countries and maintained and consumed overseas.

On such a scale, a modest $50 million order may grow to $500 million over time. With this in mind, it is essential—from the point of view that the industrial complex supports, and in turn is supported by, the military—to have as broad a base as possible throughout the world in the armed forces of as many countries as possible.

Such a situation can create many extremes. At one time, for example, Egypt was firmly in the "Communist" camp and purchased its military matériel from the Soviets. However, the Soviet manufacturers were notoriously poor managers of essential follow-up supply requirements. The CIA sent an official letter to the Defense Department suggesting that it might be wise for some armament suppliers to acquire Russian-made spare parts and to produce them for the Egyptians. It did not make any difference who was going to get military hardware or whose it was as long as the dollars flowed through the industry.

After this "Mao doctrine" had been developed and preached at the War College level during the late 1950s by U.S. military experts steeped in Asian military lore, two of them wrote one of the most influential military documents of the past half century as part of the work of a Special Presidential Committee for President Eisenhower. Army General Richard G. Stilwell,[5] who served as a member of this committee, and Air Force general Edward G. Lansdale were the principal authors of this report. It was introduced into the White House on May 15, 1959, under the title "Training Under the Mutual Security Program (With Emphasis on Development of Leaders)."

The two generals were sponsored effectively by Allen W. Dulles, the director of central intelligence, and by the resurgent Army Special Warfare elements at Fort Bragg, North Carolina. In this important report, intended "for the President's committee business only," the authors set forth the doctrine "governing the employment of the military instrument, in peace and in war." It was most influential during the Vietnam War and in other Third World developments since that date.

During the spring of 1959, the CIA had skillfully extricated the Dalai Lama from Tibet ahead of the invading Chinese Communist army (which, of course, used the same doctrine that had been adopted in the White House), and the CIA was setting up a massive overflight program of support for the Tibetan Khampa tribesmen, who were fighting a losing battle against the Chinese.

Gen. Maxwell Taylor, who served as chief of staff of the U.S. Army, from 1955 through 1959, had just resigned because of differences with Pres. Dwight D. Eisenhower over army policy matters. This was the climate in which the new U.S. military doctrine reached the White House. In deference to the general-purpose civilian Mutual Security

Program, this long report paid lip service to "the essentiality of properly trained and motivated manpower" without using the word "military," although any observant reader could see through this thin smoke screen.

It should be kept in mind that this was the context of army thinking at the time Gen. Richard Stilwell announced that an area to be discussed was "the exploitation of MAP [Military Assistance Program]-supported military establishments in furtherance of political stability, economic growth, and social change."

Here the new doctrine raised its horns. The military would be used to further "political stability, economic growth, and social change" in peacetime. This was a totally revolutionary role for the U.S. military. For military forces in most Third World nations, such a function was unheard of. The doctrine was focused on the military of those countries in what the report called "the middle third of the world."

To educate its readers and to underscore this point the report stated:

It is not enough, however, to restrict leadership inputs to U.S. norms. Except in specifically defined circumstances, our Armed Forces have no operative responsibilities within national frontiers; conforming generally to the precepts of Western democracies, they are not an integral part of the mechanism for maintenance of law and order. The prevailing concept is expeditionary—an instrument of latent power—unentangled domestically, ready for projection abroad should the exigency arise. Not so for the great bulk of the forces of the new nations. Their role has additional dimensions and their missions are actual as opposed to contingent. They are a key element in the maintenance of internal security and are largely determinant of whether stability or instability characterizes the routine of government. The Officer Corps is perforce deeply involved in domestic affairs. Those who lead, or are destined to lead, must therefore acquire qualifications and attributes beyond the criteria which identify the successful commander in combat.

Finally, the ranks of the Officer Corps in most less developed countries are a rich source of potential leaders of the national civil service, the professional class, and other nonmilitary sectors. Here one finds a high degree of discipline, dedication, and political moderation. Moreover, one must reckon with the possibility— indeed probability—that the Officer Corps, as a unit, may accede to the reins of government as the only alternative to domestic chaos and leftist takeover. Both considerations point to a program for selection and preparation of promising officers for eventual occupation of high level managerial posts in the civil sector, public and private.

In the field of general education, as in the development of national leadership, the military establishments can play a significant role.

During the Cold War, the full significance of these statements may not have been clear to many readers, because our concern with the threat of "Communism" and the Soviet Union was all that mattered. However, as these words are read in the nineties, they take on an altogether new significance as the policy statement of the military organizations of the world under a New World Order.

This introductory material was woven into the Mutual Security Program report to create a bridge from the more normal nonmilitary and political elements of the work to the revolutionary Cold War military doctrine. It served as a palliative for the civilian sector, both at home and abroad. But as the report moved along into a presentation of its military-sector concepts, it began to sound more and more like Chairman Mao and his political-military army that was deeply involved in the internal affairs of the state.

This subject was significant in the Eisenhower era, and it grew more controversial and dynamic during the aborted Kennedy period. It has become even more significant during the years since then. Despite the passage of decades since the doctrine was first introduced, some of the same military officers who developed and promoted these concepts— with the strong backing of the CIA —are even today in high-level positions where they are able to promote it and influence top-level policy more than ever before.

The quotes involving military subjects that are taken directly from this report serve as a reminder of how something novel in 1959 and 1960 has come to be taken as an accepted philosophy, especially now that the Cold War is over and the military and its industrial friends are forced to look for new fields to conquer. Although the following extracts, taken from the section headed "New Roles for the Military," were written in the 1958–59 time period, they appear to have been for today's consumption:

In the past year, a number of informed and thoughtful observers have pointed out that MAP-supported military establishments throughout the less developed areas have a political and so-

THE JOINT CHIEFS OF STAFF
WASHINGTON, D.C. 20301

26 December 1963

SUBJECT: Letter of Appreciation

TO   :   Colonel Leroy F. Prouty
          Chief, Special Operations Division
          Office of the Special Assistant for
          Counterinsurgency and Special Activities,
          Joint Staff

    1. On the occasion of your departure from the Joint
Staff, I wish to express my appreciation for your outstanding performance of duty as Chief of the Special
Operations Division of the Office of Special Assistant
for Counterinsurgency and Special Activities. Particularly
noteworthy has been your enduring achievement in planning
and developing an effective program for control and
direction of important activities of mutual interest
to several departments of the US Government. Throughout
your duty with the Office of the Special Assistant for
Counterinsurgency and Special Activities, your unique
knowledge and appreciation of the inter-relationship
of political and military factors have contributed
materially to the achievement of national objectives.

    2. Your careful preparation of special studies on a
variety of most sensitive subjects has formed a major
element in accomplishing the missions assigned to SACSA
and to the Joint Chiefs of Staff Organization. Your
special studies concerning interdepartmental relationships, military assistance and special activities in the
Cold War have had a direct and beneficial influence on
subsequent military plans and programs.

    3. You take with you both the gratitude of your
associates and the confident hope that in your forthcoming responsibilities in civilian life you will profit
from the same high standards that have characterized your
outstanding service with the Organization of the Joint
Chiefs of Staff.

                                    V. H. KRULAK
                                    Major General, USMC

This "Letter of Appreciation" was given to the author by his boss on the Joint Staff,
Major General V.H. Krulak, USMC. He had served under General Krulak for two
years and had been directed to establish the Office of Special Operations in the Joint
Staff by the then Director of the Joint Staff, General Earle Wheeler, shortly before
that time.

    The Office of Special Operations was created to provide a system for all military
services to provide special support for the clandestine operations of the Central
Intelligence Agency.

President, John F. Kennedy, and the Joint Chiefs of Staff as he inherited them from President Eisenhower on January 25, 1961. From left: Generals David M. Shoup (Marine Corps), Thomas D. White (Air Force), and Lyman L. Lemnitzer (Army and Chairman), President John F. Kennedy, Admiral A. Burke (Navy) and General George H. Decker (Army).

The author worked under General Lemnitzer for nearly two years and learned to know him well and to respect him highly. Lemnitzer was a traditional "old soldier," not a "cold warrior." His friend and confidant was General Shoup, who shared much the same views. The author served, as Chief of "Team B" (code for Special Operations), under General White on the Air Staff for three years, 1957–1960. At the age of eighteen, General White was the youngest man ever to graduate from West Point. Admiral Burke, Chief of Naval Operations, gets the author's vote as the finest of all CNO's. He served on President Kennedy's Cuban Study Group with General Maxwell Taylor, Allen W. Dulles, and Bobby Kennedy. General Decker, a brilliant fiscal expert, graduated from Lafayette College in 1924.

In Oliver Stone's 1991 movie *JFK*, about the assassination of President John F. Kennedy, November 22, 1963, actor Kevin Costner played the part of New Orleans District Attorney Jim Garrison, and actor Donald Sutherland played the part of "Man X."

During his January 15, 1992, speech at the National Press Club, Oliver Stone revealed the identity of "Man X," saying, "So many people have asked me 'Who is Man X?' Let me just say that Man X exists. He is here today on the podium. He is Fletcher Prouty." Fletcher Prouty is seated second to right of podium, looking at Stone.

L. Fletcher Prouty

Photo: Harris & Ewing

Colonel Prouty and General Abrams are life-long acquaintances, and natives of Springfield, Massachusetts.

The author, commissioned in the U.S. Cavalry, reported for active duty during July 1941 with the 37th Armored Regiment of the 4th Armored Division. The first officer he reported to was Captain Creighton W. Abrams, adjutant of the 37th Armored Regiment. General Abrams became one of the greatest combat commanders of World War II. He was named Commander of U.S. Armed Forces in Vietnam in 1968 by President Johnson and continued in that capacity under President Nixon. He became Chief of Staff, U.S. Army, in 1972.

The author flew from Okinawa to the Japanese Air Base "Atsugi" on September 1, 1945, the day before the official Japanese surrender. He flew in U.S. Marines, a part of the elite guard for General Douglas MacArthur.

Atsugi became a U.S. Naval Air Station. The CIA established a Far East Headquarters for its U-2 "Spy Plane" operations at Atsugi. Lee Harvey Oswald served at Atsugi with a complement of U.S. Marines during 1957–1958. Customarily, marines on such highly classified duty are carefully selected and have outstanding records. Oswald had U-2 and radar experience.

August 22, 1945. Japanese generals from the campaign in Manchuria whitewashed this Japanese bomber and painted a red cross on it. They flew to Yontan Air Base, Okinawa, to surrender to American forces rather than to the Russians or Chinese.

August 23, 1945. The author in front of the Japanese "Betty" bomber at Yontan Air Base, Okinawa. Note the red cross symbol of surrender.

During this period, August–September 1945, a 500,000-man Japanese invasion force stockpile of U.S. military materiel was reloaded from Okinawa onto U.S. Navy transport vessels. The harbormaster told the author that one half of that enormous shipment was being sent to Korea, and that the other half was going to Indochina. Both became "Cold War" period war zones.

A giant mushroom cloud rises over Nagasaki on the southern island of Japan after "Fat Man," the first combat-ready, five-foot-diameter implosion sphere in a tactical bomb, was dropped by an Air Force B-29 of the 509th Composite Group from Tinian in the Marianas Islands.

"In the twenty-one short days from July 16, 1945, the date of the 'Trinity' test in New Mexico, through Potsdam and Hiroshima to August 9th, the date of Nagasaki, the fate of the world was changed for all time.

"International control of nuclear weapons means world government, nothing less."—Bernard J. O'Keefe, the man who was responsible for readying and releasing the "Fat Man" bomb over Nagasaki, from his book *Nuclear Hostages*, Houghton Mifflin Company, 1983.

The author (left) with Captain Ed Clark and Captain Harry Rogers at Tokyo International Airport, 1954.

The author returned to the Far East during July 1952. He became commander of the 99th Air Transport Squadron of the Military Air Transport Service.

During those years, Colonel Prouty met Edward G. Lansdale and members of his special CIA operation in Manila during 1953-1954, and flew some of them to Saigon when they were transferred there to establish the CIA's Saigon Military Mission in 1954.

cioeconomic potential which, if properly exploited, may far out-
weigh their contribution to the deterrence of military aggression.

This is due, in part to "... the growing realization that armies are often
the only cohesive and reliable non-Communist instrument available to
the fledgling nations" and that "armies... are the principal Cold War
weapon from the shores of the East Mediterranean to the 38th Parallel
(Korea)."
Then the report drives home its point that the armed forces operate in a
never-never land somewhere "between government and populace."

> It is not enough to charge armed forces with responsibility for the
> military aspects of deterrence. They represent too great an
> investment in manpower and money to be restricted to such a
> limited mission. The real measure of their worthiness is found in
> the effectiveness of their contribution to the furtherance of
> national objectives, short of conflict. And the opportunities there-
> fore are greatest in the less-developed societies where the military
> occupy a pivotal position between government and populace. As
> one writer has phrased it, "... properly employed, the army can
> become an internal motor for economic growth and sociopolitical
> transformation."

Later in the report, that same thesis is sounded again: "The maintenance of internal security constitutes a major responsibility of these
armed forces...."
The report states: "...a key requirement may be direct military
action against armed dissidents; consequently, appropriate elements of
the army should be equipped and trained for unorthodox warfare."
It reaches a climax with the following statements of U.S. military
policy, concealed in 1959 behind a Third World policy. This affirmative
presentation at the White House level shows how thoroughly the new
U.S. military doctrine—albeit for other nations, the authors say—
followed the teachings of Chairman Mao.[6]

> Here is the ultimate test of the armed forces. Their role, in the
> countries under discussion, is unique. They are at once the
> guardians of the government and the guarantors that the govern-
> ment keeps faith with the aspirations of the nation. It is in their
> power to insure that the conduct of government is responsive to
> the people and that the people are responsive to the obligations of
> citizenship. In the discharge of these responsibilities, they must be

prepared to assume the reins of government themselves.... We have embraced the struggle for the minds of men...."

The report continues and endorses the "Formulation of a Military Creed." It cites: "the unique responsibilities of the military forces—one might almost say armies—in the development of political stability and national unity" and talks about "the relationship of the military instrument to the state and to civil power."

This Eisenhower White House Report takes on full color when we recall that Chairman Mao had launched, in 1957—only two years before this report was written—the Great Leap Forward, which was an attempt to decentralize the Chinese economy, such as it was, by establishing a nationwide system of people's communes.

At the same time, the CIA, augmented by the U.S. Army and the Department of State and assisted by experts from the Department of Agriculture, was working with the Diem government of South Vietnam to establish hundreds of similar communes, then called "Agrovilles" and later "Strategic Hamlets," in South Vietnam.

And in May 1959, this White House presidential committee had suggested in the same report: "Military equipment and labor can expedite completion of village communal projects.... Only thus can an enduring relationship be established among the government, the military, and the people themselves."

Mao's doctrine, even in the Great Leap Forward, found itself flowing from the pens of U.S. military officers in the form of revolutionary ideas. The nations they describe are to be sliced up into three distinct entities: the people, the government, and the military. What kind of country is that? They do not say. But their new U.S. military doctrine was thrust upon the emerging government of Vietnam, and their concept of Cold War (peacetime) operations permeated the highest levels of government at the time Kennedy was inaugurated in January 1961.

There is a strangely contrived side to all this. As Mao Tse-tung had said: "The world today is already in a new era of evolution and today's war is already approaching the world's last armed conflict.... No matter how long this war is going to last, there is no doubt that it is approaching the last conflict in history."

By the mid-1950s, significant elements of the U.S. military establishment had begun to accept the fact that a nuclear war was impossible and that the Cold War was the best scenario for those who saw some form of warfare as essential to the existence of the nation-state.

In several earlier chapters, *Report From Iron Mountain on the Possibility and Desirability of Peace* was cited as a novel of crucial importance. It stated that a nation-state could not survive without warfare, and this work about a top-level study commissioned in August 1963 described an attitude that had begun to surface right after the inauguration of John F. Kennedy.

The members of Kennedy's inner circle were concerned that no serious work had been done to plan for peace in the world, and such discussions were heard in the Pentagon. The commissioning of the study in *Report From Iron Mountain* illustrates this concern.

The reader will understand that the author, Leonard Lewin, has a perfect right to characterize his work as a "novel." I have spoken with Lewin at length. He is a well-informed man who was well aware of the situation in Washington as pictured in the Lansdale/Stilwell report in 1959 and its progression into the Kennedy era, with its Pentagon offices filled by Phi Beta Kappas and other men of experience and learning. The most interesting part of both "reports" is the many ways in which they overlap and agree with each other; and, even more important, how they have survived the contrivances of the Cold War and have become thoroughly modern military doctrine.

Chairman Mao predicted all this. Many good strategists in the U.S. military also foresaw it, so they designed the parameters of the new type of military doctrine and a new type of constant warfare that would, for the most part, take place in the territory of relatively powerless Third World nations.

Thus, in the process of stamping out "Communist-inspired subversive insurgency" or other bogeymen foes, millions of defenseless little people were murdered, as though some monstrous Malthusian bulldozer had been mindlessly set in motion to depopulate Earth. Classic examples of this was the massive slaughter in Cambodia, the Iran-Iraq war, and subsequently "Desert Storm" and other related hostilities in the Middle East.

It just happened that Kennedy put a man he had never met, Gen. Maxwell Taylor, on the Cuban Study Group after the Bay of Pigs disaster. Taylor had been the chief of staff of the U.S. Army when the Mutual Security Program report was written. No man was better prepared to further that philosophy. It was written in accordance with his guidance. He believed and endorsed this new doctrine that members of his army staff had developed.

The Cuban Study Group was the source of the report that had been given to the President on June 13, 1961, that in turn became National Security Action Memoranda #55, #56, and #57 on June 28. They hit the Pentagon like a thunderclap and caused a muffled roar from the State Department and the CIA. General Taylor was their author. (I have acquired a copy of the original work, and these documents will be discussed in detail in chapter 15.)

Shortly thereafter, General Taylor moved into the White House as military adviser to the President. This created a rather anomalous situation. President Kennedy had just sent NSAM #55 to the incumbent chairman of the JCS, General Lemnitzer, saying that he wanted his advice on Cold War matters, then he placed General Taylor in the White House for practically the same purpose. That October, the President sent General Taylor to Vietnam for a military report on the situation there. One year later, in 1962, Taylor was made chairman of the Joint Chiefs of Staff, where he remained until 1964, when he left to become ambassador to South Vietnam.

THIRTEEN

The Magic Box, Trigger of the Expanded War in Vietnam

THIS IS THE STORY of a people who endured war for thirty years, who were driven from farm and home, and who had no way to get food, water, and the other necessities of life other than by banditry.

As veteran bandits they became good fighters—so good that we credited their success to Ho Chi Minh, to General Giap, to Mao Tse-tung, to the Soviets, and, at times, to our own doves. They fought to eat, to live. Some called them the Vietcong. In their own country they were known as the "dangerous brothers" rather than the enemy. They were terrorized refugees in their own homeland, the beggars, the people of a ravaged land.

If a person were to fly over the hills of Indochina, he might be reminded of the Green Mountain State of Vermont. He would see similar lush, rolling hills that pull a blanket of green up one side, over the top, and down the other. But the Vermont hills were not always that way, not always peaceful; read Kenneth Roberts's great book of our own Revolutionary War, *Northwest Passage*. To the early American war heroes and to the British invaders, Vermont was a nightmare, a green hell. So, too, was Vietnam to the American GI and to the CIA's underground warriors.

Glorified in the pages of *National Geographic* magazine as the home of the carefree, naked, little brown man, Vietnam has for centuries been considered one of Earth's garden spots, a place where man had only to exist to live comfortably. Deep in the forest on the mountains, the Rhade (Rah-Day) tribesmen have lived for hundreds of years. They grow crops. They raise chickens and pigs. They have been lumbermen. They lived easily with the French for generations and managed to coexist with neighboring tribes, because they were strong. The Rhade are a closely knit, self-disciplined group.

After the great defeat of the French at Dien Bien Phu by the Vietminh army under General Giap, the French lieutenant of police left the Rhade area, taking with him his family and his few belongings. In his place a Rhade corporal took over the police powers, and things continued about the same, except that European-style law and order ended. The village elders, or Huong-ca, resumed their political functions under their own traditional council.

The French padre stayed only a few more months. When he departed, European religion and medical care went with him. Then the French overseer at the lumber mill took off, and work there stopped, for with him had gone the European economy. With the cessation of the only real income-producing enterprises of the area, contact with the outside world was severed almost entirely. Now and then a Chinese trader would come with his few coolies, bringing salt, cloth, blades (axes, knives, machetes), and news. But the Chinese merchants, too, came less frequently. The Rhade farmers had to work all the harder to produce the extra provisions that the elders would have to take to the central village over the mountain to trade for necessities.

In a country where tall grasses and bushes shoot up about as fast as they can be cut down, it is nearly impossible to grow a crop in the fields. A field that has been standing uncultivated abounds with such a thick cover of grasses that the tiny sprouts of seedlings can never grow. These tribesmen farm by cutting, slashing, and burning the forest to get to cleared earth and luxuriant soil. They have learned from their forefathers to kill the trees at the margin of the forest and then, hurriedly, to plant their scant seeds in this new, bare ground. If the farmer diligently fights the inroads of the grasses and weeds, he may have a farm for several years. But if he turns his back, the grasses take over. This battle is eternal.

The Rhade have worked hard to clear more ground and to harvest more crops. But crops alone do not make an economy. Produce must be moved to market; there must be a place where one can buy and sell. Without this, produce rots. When the French and Chinese no longer came to the Rhade regions, the produce rotted, and the basic economy staggered to a halt.

When a basic economy deteriorates in a marginal area—in Indochina, in Africa, or in Oklahoma—the people must move on. When war, pestilence, flood, drought, or some other disaster strikes a primitive society, the people must search elsewhere for food and other necessities. Often this search becomes banditry, and banditry, that last refuge of the desperate and starving—is a violent business—so violent that in this case it led the uninitiated to believe that there was a wave of "Communist-inspired subversive insurgency" in the land, under the command of General Hunger.

During the early, amateurish days of the ten-year Diem dynasty, in that newly defined piece of real estate that was called South Vietnam, there was considerable misinterpretation. Little did Ngo Dinh Diem, that foreign mandarin and erstwhile Father of His Country, realize that by issuing an edict removing French influence he was bringing an end to law and order, such as it was. Nor did he realize that by promulgating a second edict banning the Chinese, he was causing the basic tribal economy—marketplace bartering and produce movement—to vanish.

The French did not return; neither did the Chinese. But one day the old padre came back. The tribesmen turned out to greet the familiar face. This fragile gentleman had new clothes and new shoes, and he rode into the village in a jeep. The Rhade had not seen such a thing since the return of the French after the Japanese had gone—the French lieutenant and his family had arrived in a jeep back in the mid-1940s. The padre dismounted and spoke to his old friends. Then he introduced the young driver of the jeep, explaining that this young white man was American, not French, and that the other passenger was a Vietnamese from the faraway city of Saigon.

The padre said that the French no longer governed the country but that a great man named Ngo Dinh Diem was the president of this new bit of land called "South Vietnam" and that his palace was in Saigon.

The padre avoided mention of Ho Chi Minh and the northern government. He knew it would be useless to try to explain that Ho Chi Minh's Nationalist government was not the government of all Indochina. It would be too complicated, it would not be believed, and the Rhade would not care much one way or the other anyhow. The Rhade had lived in their ancestral areas for centuries and cared little for the outside, whether it was represented by Japanese, French, American, Vietminh, or Saigonese officials.

The padre, the young American, and the Vietnamese official returned many times. After a while, the American was welcomed without the priest and often stayed for weeks. He was interested in animal husbandry and agriculture. He brought with him some poultry and a new breed of hog that he taught them to raise. He carried with him new seeds and tried over and over to encourage the Rhade to plant them as he directed. On countless occasions he would persuade the villagers to dig holes in the fields and to plant the seeds as he had learned to do at the university in Ames, Iowa.

He never did understand the Rhade farmers and their primitive "slash and burn" farming. And they never could explain to this young expert that the seeds could not grow in that heavy grassland of the open fields. In any event, the American became a familiar figure, and his hard work and gifts of chickens, pigs, candy, and cigarettes were always welcome. Then one day he came with the Magic Box.

The padre, the American, and the Huong-ca sat in earnest discussion all that day. The Magic Box rested on the hood of the jeep while several young men dug a hole in front of the patriarch's hut. They were unaccustomed to the American's shovel, and work progressed slowly. Meanwhile, the American felled a tree and cut out a section to be used as a post. This post was put into the hole and the dirt replaced.

Now a tall, sturdy, upright pedestal stood in front of the chieftain's hut. To this, the American affixed a tin roof as shelter. Then he removed the shiny jet-black Magic Box from the jeep and nailed it firmly to the post, about four feet above the ground, just the right height for the Huong-ca and above the prying hands of the children.

After the box was secured, the padre told the villagers all about the Magic Box and how it would work, about the wonders it would produce to save them from communism. He told them that this box was a most miraculous radio and that it would speak to their brothers in Saigon. It was, in their language, powerful medicine.

At the same time, he warned that only the village patriarch could touch the box. If anyone else did so, the kindly government in Saigon would be most angry, and the village would be punished. The padre told the villagers that whenever they were attacked, the patriarch should push the big red button on the box, and that was all.

At this point in their Village Defense Orientation Program, the Viet soldier and the American interrupted the padre and ordered him to repeat that if the village was attacked by the Communist Vietcong from the forest—emphasizing the "Communist Vietcong"—the patriarch was to push the button. To the Viet soldier and the American, the men in the forest were not starving and frightened refugees; they were the enemy.

Because the elderly padre knew that these native people had never heard of the Vietcong, he explained that his friends called all bandits from the refugee camps in the forest "Vietcong" and that the Vietcong were to be greatly feared because they were the puppets of the National Liberation Front, who were the puppets of Hanoi, who were the puppets of the Chinese, who were the puppets of the Soviets, ad infinitum.

The padre explained that when the patriarch pushed that shiny red button on the Magic Box, the powerful gods of Saigon would unleash vengeful armies through the air, and the dreaded Vietcong would be blasted by bombs from airplanes and napalmed from helicopters. And the village would be liberated and pacified. He also told them that every village that had been selected by the Father of His Country in Saigon to receive the Magic Box would forever thereafter be furnished food, medicine, and special care.

The Rhade would receive these "benefits" whether they wanted them or not. For they knew only too well that the villages that had plenty of food and medicine and that were the special elect of Saigon were always the first targets for the starving bandits. They knew enough to know that they would live in fear of the Magic Box and its munificence.

Ever since the day when the padre had returned with the American, the village had received special medicine and food relief. The "Extended Arms for Brotherhood" program of the new president in Saigon was caring for these tribesmen. Shortly after the first time this extra food had been delivered, the village had been visited by some young men from the camps in the woods. They sat with the patriarch all day and quietly but firmly explained that they came from a refugee camp that was hidden in the hills and that was caring for thousands of homeless natives from the south (Cochin China) who had been driven from their homes by the Diem-backed police and hordes of northern (Tonkinese) invaders.

These people had fled from their wasted homes. They had been enemies in every new region they came to, and now, terrorized and starving, sick and dying, they had had to turn to that last resort of mankind, banditry and pillage. These countless refugees, in their own homeland, had fled the careless deprivations and brutal massacres of the benevolent forces of Saigon. They wished to be peaceful, but they desperately needed food and medicine. They demanded that the village share some of its plentiful goods with them. This arrangement, although unappealing to the village, was accepted, and for a while it kept a fragile peace between the two worlds. However, the refugee numbers swelled, and their demands became greater and greater.

It wasn't long before the Saigon political observer and the padre reported to the American that they suspected that the patriarch was collaborating with the "enemy." This sharing of their meager goods with the refugees was called "the payment of tribute" by the Vietnamese. The refugees had become the "enemy," and the Americans' word for "enemy" was Vietcong.

The political leader had explained to the patriarch that collaboration with the Vietcong meant death for him and removal of the village people to a Citizens' Retraining Camp or a "Strategic Hamlet," as the Americans liked to call it. No matter what their benefactors chose to call these displacement centers, they were prisons to the natives.

The more or less peaceful demands of the refugees became adamant orders as their needs increased. What had begun as a reluctant sharing of food became submission to force and banditry. The ranks of the refugees swelled as the exodus from such areas as the no-man's-land of the once-prosperous and fertile Mekong Delta area of the Camau Peninsula turned into a vast and relentless human wave.

A situation not unlike that of the Native American migrations westward took place. Each tribe, displaced from its ancestral homeland by the white man, became marauders and attackers in the territory of the next Indian nation. Thus it was that tens of thousands, even hundreds of thousands, of once-peaceful, docile, and reasonably well-to-do rice farmers became the feared, terrorized bandits called the Vietcong.

Several nights later, the village was raided. The dogs barked, chickens and pigs ran about, the food huts were ransacked and burned, and several young men of the village were kidnapped. For the first time since the installation of the radio, the old man crept out of his hut and stood before the Magic Box. In the deep darkness of the forest night, the red glow of the buzzer filled the sky with its talismanic power. The chieftain had often wondered what would really happen if he pushed that red button. Even though the padre had told him of the wonders that would take place when he did push the warning device, he had never been able to fully comprehend it all.

The political observer had warned the patriarch of the punishment he would suffer if he turned in a false alarm. At times the red-eyed Pandora's box proved too much for the villagers, and they dared the patriarch to push the button. He had steadfastly resisted these temptations. But now, in the heat of a raid by the starvation-crazed refugees, he stood before the box, knowing that he would be calling down the might of the Village Self-Defense Forces and that he would bring down the full wrath of the dread People's Arms of Brotherhood[1] upon his village.

Yet if he did not push that button, he and his people would suffer the fate of collaborators. He had no real choice. It was his turn, and that of his village, to become part of this war that was being made in Saigon with the expert advice of the American men of goodwill.

He called upon the wisdom of his ancestors. Banditry, pillage, and rape were not unknown in Asia. Whenever starvation, pestilence, and war had ravaged the land, the thin veil of civilization had been torn away, and the destitute had turned to banditry as the last stage of community life before surrendering to the relentless death of the ravaged.

Hunger is the general of these armies. Hunger provides a terrible motivation of its own. It needs no ideological boost from Moscow or Peking. The blind, ignorant actions of General Hunger are all it takes to create a war. In a lawless, unorganized society, this was the natural and inevitable reaction. This is especially true in a country where the natives eat by nibbling most of the day. They do not sit down to a hearty three meals a day. Tropical peoples eat a bite at a time, and as a result their stomachs are small, and they have very little fat. For these people, starvation sets in much faster than it does for the people to the north, who are fatter and who eat at longer and more regular intervals. Thus, the time between deprivation of food and the driving necessity to eat is much shorter, and such people strike out hard for food as soon as their supply is wiped out. This explains why napalm, bombings, and defoliation tactics created more instead of less war and created it in a short time. The victims were deprived of food and had to fight for it, without delay. The people who had raided the village were of this hungry, refugee populace.

As the patriarch sought the wisdom of his ancestors, he found nothing to explain this new terror, that is, the unknown "Vietcong." Bandits and refugees he understood. But the ideological dilemma posed by his new friends, the American and the Saigon political activist, made him, the patriarch, their enemy if he rationalized and sympathized with the refugees, even under duress. This left him no alternative.

He knew that many other elders had resisted the refugees and had been slain by them out of the necessity for food. He knew that others who had sympathized with the refugees had been brutally taken to retraining camps (prisons) by the political observers and had suffered cruelly there. He knew that there was no hope. No alternative. The food, the medicine, and "Operation Brotherhood" from Saigon had sealed the fate of the villagers and doomed them to the dread final tactic called "Pacification." He pushed the glowing red button. The Magic Box did the rest.

A sleep-dulled South Vietnamese Special Forces elite trooper saw the flickering warning light on the situation map. Grid Code 1052 was hostile! Grid Code 1052: The village of Thuc Dho in Rhade territory was under attack. There was no two-way capability with the village radio equipment, no way to discuss the attack or to evaluate the warning from the village chieftain. Any signal was hostile in the Village Defense Network, and "hostile" meant "retaliate." The system could say only that there was an attack and automatically identify the location. It could not say that the "attack" was nothing more than a small raid by a few starving natives intent on stealing food.

The Viet trooper took one look at the American Green Beret soldier of the Special Forces "A" Team who was sleeping in a native hammock nearby. He knew that after two minutes the flickering red light would cease automatically. On so many other occasions when the American had been out in the village drinking beer with the other "A" Team members and with the young girls of the "White Dove Resistance Sisters," he had let other warning lights flicker out without sounding the alert. He realized that the Pandora's box problem caused many red-light alerts. He knew, too, that some elders, eager to flaunt their powers before the villagers, would push the button to bring out the helicopter patrols.

He understood that the desperate villagers, half-crazed by starvation and by bandit raids, were often "spooked" into pushing that glaring red eye on the Magic Box. And he knew that even when attacks were real, the Magic Box did not save the villagers. It simply brought on more retaliation, the dreaded wrath of a war of recounter in which the aggressor creates his own enemy. By the time the forces got there, the village would have been burned to the ground. The people would have been killed or be hiding in the forest, so that when the "avengers" arrived the chances were better than even that the villagers would be miscast as the enemy anyhow.

They appeared to be "enemy" on both sides, and the general rule was to shoot at anyone who ran, regardless of who that person might be. From such a "rescue" the villagers had but one alternative, and that was to flee with the refugees and become "Vietcong," or "enemy" in their own homeland.

The trooper wrestled with these thoughts. Just then the American rolled over in the hammock and his rifle, which had been leaning against it, fell to the floor. He leaped to his feet. The Vietnamese trooper snapped into action and pointed to the glowing red alert signal, the warning from the Magic Box in Grid Code 1052, the Rhade village of Thuc Dho.

The Green Beret veteran of Fort Bragg's stern indoctrination grabbed the single-sideband radio mike and called Division Alert. In minutes, sirens sounded and engines began to roar. Truckloads of South Vietnamese Special Forces—the elite civilian, CIA-trained troops of Ngo Dinh Nhu—roared off into the early-morning quiet of Ahn Lac Air Base.

Helicopter maintenance crews readied the ungainly craft. Twenty pilots dashed to the briefing room. Twenty crews were being assembled. This one was going to be all-out; it was the first attack reported from the Rhade zone.

Intelligence had predicted a vast enemy buildup in the area, including a reportedly heavy preparatory movement on the trails of Laos. The dread border of Cambodia was seen to be a beehive of activity. Everything pointed to a massive National Liberation Front/ North Vietnamese masterstroke against a new attack zone.[2] The enemy must be stopped now with a resolute counterattack.

As the semitropical dawn burst in all its pink brilliance over Ahn Lac, twenty helicopters stirred up a hurricane of dust as they prepared for the convoy flight to Thuc Dho. Six of the choppers were gun carriers; the remaining fourteen carried 140 armed troops. As the briefing ended, the pilots were told that the refueling stop would be at Thien Dho because the loaded helicopters could not fly a greater than one-hundred-mile radius mission without refueling. The entire flight would be convoyed. This meant that cruising speed would be fifty-five knots for the cargo craft to assure the ability to autorotate safely to the ground in the event of engine failure at the planned "nap-of-the-earth" flight level. In convoy, with formation and linkup, this would mean an average out-and-back ground speed of twenty-five to thirty knots. Therefore, the returning choppers would RON (Remain Overnight) at Thien Dho after hitting the target.

The 280-mile round trip with midpoint touchdown at Thuc Dho and out-and-back refueling would take two days. This meant twenty choppers to take 140 men 140 miles in two days. Cheap for the price of avenging the attack on Thuc Dho? Hardly!

The Village Self-Defense Network helicopter force was an incredible organization. Each helicopter could carry ten armed men one hundred miles in one day. With a one-hundred-mile radius for the helicopter and a convoy speed of twenty-five knots, it would be four hours each way, for a total of eight hours in the air.

Since army/civilian helicopter maintenance was operating at a commendable 49 percent in-commission rate, it took no fewer than forty choppers to assure the availability of twenty for the Thuc Dho mission. The forty helicopters were supported by two aviation companies of about two hundred men each, a total of four hundred men.

These companies were in turn supported by a supply squadron and a maintenance squadron of two hundred men each. And all of these squadrons were supported by housekeeping units, transportation units, base-defense units, fuel-storage units, and fuel-delivery units. Never before in the history of warfare had so much been expended to accomplish so little as was being demonstrated by sending 140 fighting men in response to the flashing red light of the Magic Box of Station #1052.

While the chopper convoy was en route to Thuc Dho, advance-scout aircraft were dispatched to reconnoiter the area for a landing zone. This is no small task in this kind of country. The rotor blades of each Huey are fifty-five feet long. A helicopter must touch down on level ground, since any unequal or nonlevel touchdown, one in which a corner of the landing gear touches first, creates a destructive situation as a result of the dislocation of the center of force around the vertical axis of the craft.

The Huey is built especially strong to resist any uneven landing force, but fully loaded, with the rotors whirling at full power, the strain can be dangerous. Spotter aircraft must find an area large enough to accommodate several Hueys at a time, to assure the protection of massed firepower in the event of an ambush and to reduce costly fuel consumption.

By the time the choppers had refueled at Thien Dho and were back in the air, scout aircraft were able to report a landing site at an abandoned farm a half mile from Thuc Dho. It was estimated that three choppers could touch down at one time, in trail. It was also reported that although smoke was still rising from the village, there had been no enemy action against the spotter aircraft and no enemy sighted. Two troop choppers and one armed Huey had maintenance troubles and were forced to remain at Thien Dho. The remaining twelve troop-carrier choppers skimmed the earth at about fifty-five knots as the five gunships weaved across the course to Thuc Dho at full speed.

In the direct sunlight of early afternoon, the airborne force arrived at Thuc Dho. The spotter aircraft fired smoke flares to mark the landing zone. The gunships hovered over the area, ready to suppress any movement below with direct machine-gun fire. Meanwhile, the convoy began to form a circle around the zone as the first three choppers settled into the field to disembark thirty men.

Then, quickly, the choppers leaped upward, whirling dust and straw into the air, just before the next three Hueys landed with the next wave of troopers. These pilots were experienced and wasted no time. Crewmen saw to it that the silent South Vietnamese Special Forces elite troops jumped out immediately. The crewmen, too, were experienced and recalled stories of earlier days when untrained troops had to be ordered out at the point of a gun and a few well-placed kicks. In the commotion and difficulty of this maneuver, the second and third choppers of the third wave had touched blades as they neared touch-down. Both machines had disintegrated.

As the last wave settled on the field, two circling gunships opened fire into the high grass near the forest. This was the opening action. The troopers on the ground flattened out and fired rapidly and blindly. The spotter aircraft lobbed flares to mark the hostile target. The circling, unarmed Hueys began to back away. At that instant, two of them dropped back to the ground. Old hands recognized the pattern!

When the old H-19s were being used over the rice fields of the Camau Peninsula, the natives had learned that a crude bow held by the feet of a man lying on his back in the grass could be most effective against low-flying choppers. The arrow was a heavy stick that trailed wire, rope, or even a vine. Since the rotor is the most vulnerable part of the helicopter, this crude weapon, fired to "hang" this hazard in the air, brought down many a chopper. First reports indicated engine or rotor failure, since there was no gunfire or other hostile action observed.

The remaining gunships were nearly out of ammunition, and all the choppers were low on fuel, so the convoy, now down to thirteen Hueys, left the surveillance to the spotters and sped back to the refueling base.

At Thuc Dho, 120 men, plus a few injured Huey crewmen, were pinned down in the high grass. Gunfire from the ambush site was sporadic. Sixteen of the 120 were of a Green Beret "A" Team. The radio man was in contact with the spotter aircraft, which directed them to the village. Here in the smoldering ruin of grass huts there was not a sign of life. Even the half-starved dogs were gone. With only a few hours of daylight left, the "A" Team lieutenant placed his troops into defensive positions for the night. Thuc Dho had been regained. The Magic Box had proved its value.

In the early-morning hours when the first word about Thuc Dho had been relayed to the Division Combat Center, it was also relayed to USMACV (U.S. Military Assistance Command—Vietnam) Headquarters in Saigon.

Here all Village Self-Defense Forces information was collated into a report that was sent directly to the Pentagon. With the twelve-hour time differential, the Pentagon and the intelligence community were able to compile all data relayed from Southeast Asia into an early-morning briefing for the President and his immediate staff.

This material from intelligence sources, Combat Center input, U-2 and satellite reports, a master weather report, and certain domestic information were put together at the prebrief in the Command Center in the Joint Chiefs of Staff area at the Pentagon.

Thus the day begins for official Washington. The briefing of yesterday's events sets up today's work and tomorrow's operations. Intelligence input replaces diplomacy and advance planning as the source of "things to do."

However, on this special day in early December 1960, there happened to be some new faces at the prebrief. They were the secretary of defense designate and certain of his transition staff. The alarm from Thuc Dho was mentioned quite routinely by an army officer at the early-morning prebrief. The secretary of defense designate, absorbing the first flavor of Vietnam, requested full elaboration on this action at the briefing the following day. This special highest-level interest was duly noted by all service chiefs and their attending staff members. During the day a flood of messages filled the air to and from Saigon, placing top priority on the action at Thuc Dho.

The army arranged for a full supply and manpower buildup for the area. The air force announced heavy surveillance and bombing of all supply lines to Thuc Dho through Laos and the northern routes. Thuc

Dho appeared in all news releases. Helicopter reinforcement and supply became a maximum effort.

Meanwhile, Green Beret "A" Team troops established their base, set out the area perimeter, and sent South Vietnamese Special Forces scouting teams to establish contact with the "enemy." The efforts of these elite troops were ineffectual. The "enemy" had slipped away. A few elderly villagers, along with young children, were found cowering in holes and huddled in the forests.

When interrogated concerning the attack and the whereabouts of the village patriarch and the able-bodied men, the captives stared in ignorance. Most of all, they were confused when asked about the "enemy." They kept referring to the "Viet Kha"—the Vietnamese term for "beggars": the refugees—but the overzealous interpreter translated this to mean the Vietcong. This confirmed for the eager lieutenant that he had stumbled upon a major Vietcong encampment.

The lieutenant radioed along this valuable information, plus the routine body count, enriched to include those killed by bombardment and napalm. At this early stage of the operation, confirmation of any casualty figures was not required. The lieutenant estimated the enemy strength as a reinforced battalion or perhaps a regiment. All the dead were Vietcong. They had to be.

It was from such on-the-spot information that the briefing material was prepared by Saigon to be sent to Washington. Sensing the military's concern with this action as a result of the secretary designate's request, the intelligence community stepped up its own input.

Although it was no secret, it was not generally known that Ngo Dinh Nhu's elite Special Forces were under the absolute control of the CIA. Since they were, it was in the interest of the intelligence community to assure that the role of these elite troops be at least the equivalent of the U.S. Army's. Saigon's CIA headquarters outdid itself building up all information available about Thuc Dho. The U.S. Army Special Forces "A" Team, all Fort Bragg trained, were bona fide army soldiers, but their commander, a rather unorthodox major, was a CIA man on an army cover assignment.

Along with South Vietnamese Special Forces officers and civilians under cover of the South Vietnamese Army, this major was among the first to reach Thuc Dho in the early wave of more helicopters on the second day.

The Pentagon prebrief was prepared, as usual, using data gathered from sources all over the world. Information on space, from the Congo, from India (where border skirmishes presaged later troubles)—all such data except that on Cuba—was kept to a minimum. The key item on the agenda was Thuc Dho. Extra chairs were placed in a second row around the polished walnut table behind the military chiefs for the CIA and Department of State guests in the Command Center.

By eight-ten the room was almost full. Everyone there had a clearance that surpassed "top secret"; all were admitted on a "need to know" basis. Three of the Joint Chiefs were there. The usual Office of the Secretary of Defense contingent was there. Everything pointed to a full account of the action at Thuc Dho. It should be recalled that as of that moment in December 1960, only one month after the election of John F. Kennedy, the troubles in Vietnam were much less serious than they would become later, and all this attention was something special at the time.

For most of those present, part of this great drama was impressing and winning over the new defense secretary and, through him, capturing the eye of the new administration. The secretary designate, Robert S. McNamara, was particularly interested in the "reported" Vietcong battalion or regiment. If, as reported by the captive villagers, the battalion had fled into the woods, and if, as reported by the Green Beret (CIA) major, the battalion was now surrounded in the woods by the elite South Vietnamese Special Forces troops, then why wasn't the Vietcong battalion being flushed out, then annihilated or captured?

Discussion of this question was limited somewhat by the fact that the army briefing officer had been ordered to stick to his notes. Then a general, in the second row behind his army chief of staff, rose to report that he had a message, just in from Saigon, saying that the elusive Vietcong battalion had slipped through the South Vietnamese cordon and that, according to army spotter-plane forward observers, there was no one in the woods. As he completed this report, he glanced at the CIA representatives in the audience.

The secretary designate grasped the significance of what had been said and fired another question at the briefing officer and at the room in general. "If we can create the capability to go to the aid of a beleaguered village, as we have done at Thuc Dho, but then having done this we find the village vacant and the enemy fled, how can we ever expect to win the war? We must destroy the enemy."

An acorn had been planted, and a vast oak grew. Immediately one of the CIA men half-raised a hand, slid his feet out from under his chair, and prepared to rise. He was not the usual prebrief attendee; he was the chief of the supersecret Far East branch himself, an old Asia hand.

"Sir," he said, "that is a most searching question. It gets to the root of our problem. We have been trying to control a Communist-inspired war of national liberation in South Vietnam that has spread out of control throughout the land. Diem's forces are much too green. They do not like war, even for their own homeland. And we who have put so much effort into Laos, Thailand, and South Vietnam feel that the advisory role of the U.S. military forces does not go far enough. The Strategic Hamlets and the Village Self-Defense Forces are not enough.

"You have seen the example of Thuc Dho. Fortunately, the village had been prepared by one of our agents and they had a transmitter that linked them to the Village Self-Defense Network. As a result we were able to strike back at once. But this is too little. No network is any good if it is full of holes. We must organize every hamlet, every village, every tribe. Then this Communist-supported enemy can be driven from this peaceful country and these little people can be left to choose their own destiny in peace."

The secretary designate bought it.

By January 1961, an "Advanced Counterinsurgency Course," designed specifically to train thousands of Green Berets for Vietnam, had been hastily lifted from the Civil Affairs and Military Government School at Fort Gordon, Georgia, and put at Fort Bragg. One of the last official acts of the outgoing deputy secretary of defense, James Douglas, was to visit Fort Bragg to bless this new school.

But the corner had been turned. Quietly and efficiently, the orders went out. One of the key items was the radio transmitter. The one at Thuc Dho had been a test unit. Within weeks a special order for thousands of these transmitters had been placed with the manufacturer and given the highest priority. Shortly after the inauguration of President John F. Kennedy, these transmitters were being bolted to posts in village after village to augment and facilitate the Strategic Hamlet campaign.

Not too many months later, the new secretary of defense, Robert McNamara, made his first visit to South Vietnam. Thuc Dho was now a model. By the time the secretary saw it, the villagers, the South Vietnamese Special Forces elite troops, and the American Green Berets had worn paths through the area rehearsing and reenacting the famous attack for visiting dignitaries.

The once-lush hills had been dug up by bombs, seared by napalm, defoliated by chemical genocide. But the center of interest was always the black plastic box with the red eye, the famous Magic Box number 1052, the trigger of the expanded war in Vietnam.

NOTE: There were many such villages as described in this story. Thuc Dho is a name created to represent a typical one. The story was compiled from the author's personal trips to Vietnam and liaison with the CIA between 1955 and 1964.

FOURTEEN

JFK Makes His Move to Control the CIA

As a member of the U.S. House and Senate, John F. Kennedy was an experienced politician. As the son of the U.S. ambassador to the Court of St. James's during the days just before the start of World War II, he was made privy to the ways of foreign policy and to the world of big business. He was the son of one of the wealthiest and most powerful men in America. But as the newly elected President of the United States, he discovered that he had to start all over again. The stakes in the game played at the White House were much higher and more complex than those in any of his previous endeavors, and the flow of events during the closing months of the Eisenhower era had not made his task any easier.

Eisenhower's repeated illnesses, perhaps his age, and particularly the heartache he suffered as a result of the collapse of his dream of a meaningful "Crusade for Peace"[1] created a "lame duck" period of deeper than usual dimensions. A counterinsurgency plan for Indochina had been set in motion, and the buildup of the army's Special Warfare program at Fort Bragg had gotten under way.

On the big business side, proponents of the U.S. Air Force's "Everest" Tactical Fighter Experimental (TFX) aircraft development project were rushing plans to have that selection made before the pro-business Eisenhower team left Washington. In 1960, the TFX was visualized as the biggest single aircraft procurement order ever placed—running as high as $6 billion.

At the same time, life seemed relatively quiet in Vietnam as the principal skirmishes, both military and political, took place in nearby Laos. All of these pent-up pressure points exploded after Kennedy's inauguration and proceeded to overwhelm his new and relatively inexperienced administration.

Barely one week after taking office, Kennedy received a personal report from Col. Edward G. Lansdale, the CIA's longtime and most important Southeast Asia agent, regarding his recent trip to Saigon. Lansdale also offered a second briefing on the counterinsurgency plan for Indochina. Later, Kennedy approved the counterinsurgency plan, which expanded South Vietnamese forces at a rather leisurely pace.

This plan provided South Vietnamese president Ngo Dinh Diem with the financial support for a twenty-thousand increase in his army (then standing at one-hundred fifty-thousand men) as well as support for his counterguerrilla force, then known as the Civil Guard.[2]

Between January and May 1961, the new President was kept busy with, among other things, the anti-Castro project, which had grown in the hands of CIA opportunists from a cycle of sporadic para-drop raids on Cuba to a full-blown, over-the-beach invasion plan. According to the invasion plan approved by President Kennedy, Castro would have had no combat aircraft remaining by dawn on the morning of the invasion.

However, a key bomber strike that was supposed to destroy the last three aircraft on the ground was called off. This strike had been approved by President Kennedy only the afternoon before the landing. The delay of this mission was found by the Cuban Study Group to be the primary cause of the failure of the invasion.[3]

Deeply angered by this CIA disaster, Kennedy set up a unique Cuban Study Group to discover what had happened to cause the failure and to make plans for the future actions of his administration in the Cold War arena. This group left its mark on the nascent Kennedy administration. During its tenure, Jack and Bobby Kennedy made up their minds that Allen Dulles, along with other top-level CIA staff, must go.[4] As a result of the study-group experience, Bobby Kennedy, a military neophyte, became enchanted with the experienced, educated, and sophisticated Gen. Maxwell Taylor.[5]

Each evening after returning from the Pentagon, where he had witnessed General Taylor's masterful control of the investigation of the Bay of Pigs operation and his development of paramilitary plans, Bobby

Kennedy would discuss all of that information, augmented by Taylor's ideas of Army Special Warfare, with his brother and other close advisers.

Concurrently, the President had asked Roswell Gilpatric, the deputy secretary of defense, "to work up a program for saving Vietnam." Lansdale became executive director of Gilpatric's Vietnam task force and assumed the role of governmentwide coordinator and manager of the concept of counterinsurgency.

This development only seemed fitting, since it was Lansdale, his friend Gen. Richard Stilwell, and their close army and CIA associates who had done so much to launch this new Cold War military doctrine during the Eisenhower period (much of it as we have seen, derived from elements of the teachings of Chairman Mao Tse-tung).

In his own autobiography, *In The Midst of Wars*, Ed Lansdale writes about his own wealth of knowledge and depth of experience with the works and teachings of Mao Tse-tung:

> I arrived in Washington in late January [1953] and made the rounds of talks with policy-makers.

> I found myself quoting Mao Tse-tung to them, from one of his lectures to military officers in a Yenan cave classroom early in World War II. Mao had said: "There are often military elements who care for only military affairs but not politics. Such one-track-minded officers, ignoring the interconnection between politics and military affairs, must be made to understand the correct relationship between the two. All military actions are means to achieve political objectives, while military action itself is a manifested form of politics"

> I would note that it didn't matter that Mao had cribbed his lectures from Sun Tzu, Clausewitz, and Lenin. Asian Communist doctrine currently was heeding Mao's words in its warfare, and we, on our side, had to learn to be more flexible in meeting it.

You will recall the many excerpts from the special White House committee report of May 1959 entitled "Training Under the Mutual Security Program" that are included in chapter 12. That report was written by General Lansdale and General Stilwell. They cited references to the teachings of Chairman Mao and recommended them as a pattern for the new armies they visualized "in the Third World." In this connection, one must keep in mind that when one teaches such policy

for another country, he is likely to be convinced that it would work and
do well in his own country also. This is the great lesson of our review of
this report and of the reminder how important the Communist teaching
of Mao Tse-tung has become in American military doctrine and
training. It could be used here.

Because a major objective of this book is to analyze the events that
brought about the murder of John F. Kennedy and the seizure of power
in this country at that time, it may be well to note that in the eight-page
index of Lansdale's book there are six references to Mao Tse-tung—and
not one single mention of John F. Kennedy.

By May 3, 1961, the extremely flexible Kennedy administration had
changed horses in midstream. The Gilpatric-Lansdale draft for Vietnam
of late April was shelved, and a newer State Department draft of May 3
(presumably written by George Ball) was approved by the President.
Lansdale's Defense Department recommendations were eliminated
completely, and Fritz Nolting, a man with close CIA ties (if not himself
actually a full-fledged CIA agent), had become ambassador to Saigon.
Lansdale's star had been eclipsed, and the Dulles-Cabell-Bissell team
was fading fast as Gen. Maxwell Taylor became man of the hour in the
Kennedys' eyes.

By the end of May 1961, Vice President Lyndon B. Johnson was in
Saigon to conduct a fact-finding mission and to deliver a letter from
President Kennedy to Ngo Dinh Diem. Johnson had been authorized to
raise the matter of stationing U.S. troops in South Vietnam. Diem did
not want them at that time; the Diem government had other things on
its mind.

As described in earlier chapters, Diem had been dependent upon
and personally close to Lansdale ever since Diem had returned to the
Far East from exile. He had spent a lot of time working out plans with
Lansdale during the latter's lengthy visit to Saigon after Kennedy's
election in late 1960. Diem and his CIA-oriented brother, Ngo Dinh
Nhu, were perplexed by the rapid changes and developments on the
banks of the Potomac that so dramatically affected Dulles, Lansdale,
and the CIA. Diem became suspicious of the Kennedy administration
and its representatives. He was reluctant to accept new faces, new ideas,
and a new strategy, despite the fact that he was repeatedly assured that it
was all for his own good.

From the middle of 1959, Diem had begun the creation of commune-
like "Agrovilles" that were planned as small communities in which all
essential amenities were provided. As noted, the greatest single factor

underlying the serious unrest in the new nation of South Vietnam was the infiltration of more than one million Tonkinese (northern) refugees who had been transported south by U.S. sea and air assets. These people, many of whom came to fill key posts in the Diem government as the years progressed, needed a place to live. In Diem's mind, these Agrovilles, designed and supported with American funds, were to provide a place to live for as many of these invading strangers as possible.

For many reasons, this plan failed miserably after fewer than twenty-five Agrovilles had been carved out of a no-man's-land in the destitute countryside. Thus the open-commune Agroville, based on a design concept from Chairman Mao Tse-tung, became the heavily barricaded Strategic Hamlet of 1961 in the Kennedy era. The Strategic Hamlet was designed, out of necessity, to overcome two serious problems: It was engineered as much to keep the settlers in as to provide security for them against attack from the outside by starving bandits, usually called the Vietcong. By 1961, South Vietnam was overrun with displaced, starving natives and by equally displaced and starving Tonkinese.

Viewed from the eye of the maker of Grand Strategy, with his Malthusian incentives, the situation "to engender warfare" in Vietnam could not have been better. As Alberto Moravia wrote in his book *The Red Book and the Great Wall, an Impression of Mao's China,* "More is consumed in wartime in a day than is consumed in peacetime in a year."

It is all too easy to forget that this conflict in populous, wealthy (by Asian standards), and placid Indochina had been set in motion back in 1945, when Ho Chi Minh arrived in Hanoi accompanied by his associates from the U.S. Office of Strategic Services[6] and armed with American weapons from Okinawa. These were the weapons used by the Vietminh to control much of the region from 1945 to 1954. These same weapons, especially the heavy artillery, had made it possible for them to defeat the French at Dien Bien Phu. At that time, what remained of the $3 billion arms aid the U.S. had provided to the French was added to Ho Chi Minh's U.S.-supplied arsenal.

By modern standards, the United States had provided a more than adequate arms supply to the man whom it would, after the stage was set, call "the enemy." During 1962, Michael Forrestal, a senior member of the National Security Council staff and a close friend of Jack Kennedy's, visited Vietnam with Roger Hilsman from the Department of State. They wrote a report to the President, saying, "The vast bulk of both recruits and supplies come from inside South Vietnam itself." That was their bureaucratic euphemism for saying that the Vietminh's weapons were American-made. Of course they were.

Another top-level official stated, "Throughout this time no one had ever found one Chinese rifle or one Soviet weapon used by the Vietcong." He noted that all weapons taken from the Vietcong (bandits) by the United States were either homemade (mainly crude but effective land mines) or previously acquired from the Diem government or the United States.

It is little wonder that the Diem brothers found the Kennedy administration difficult to accept. The actions of supplying weapons to both sides, on top of the forced movement of more than one million Tonkinese from the north to the south via U.S.-supplied navy vessels and aircraft, constituted "make war" tactics, in the Diems' eyes.

It was in this climate that the Kennedy administration welcomed the post–Bay of Pigs report from Gen. Maxwell Taylor and his assignment as military adviser to the President in the Kennedy White House. On October 11, 1961, the President directed General Taylor and Walt Rostow, a foreign policy adviser, to travel to Saigon.

Rostow had stated, in the fall of 1961, that it was "now or never" for the United States in Vietnam. Bill Bundy, formerly with the CIA (if "formerly" ever applies to CIA agents) as a Far East expert and, in 1961, deputy secretary of defense, said there was a 70 percent chance to "clean up the situation." He advised a preemptive strike, an "early and hard-hitting operation." Neither of these men were military experts. They were just trying to show muscle and daring.

Taylor was a little more patient and, under the guise of a "flood relief" project, recommended that a small number of U.S. servicemen be introduced into Vietnam. Kennedy agreed and in all later public pronouncements referred to them as "support troops."

Meanwhile, Robert S. McNamara and his former Ford Motor Company "Whiz Kids" were gearing up to get into the act. Everyone wanted to be known as a military expert. McNamara did not have any experience with warfare; he knew little, if anything, about Indochina. He was a precisionist. He liked things to be orderly and to be explained in "case study" detail. One of his first decisions, based upon a preinaugural briefing in the Pentagon, was to order the use of a defoliant spray in Vietnam. He turned this idea, his own, over to the Advanced Research Projects Agency (ARPA), the high-powered organization of technicians that had sprung up in the Pentagon in the wake of the Sputnik surprise, where it came under the wing of an old bureaucratic professional, Bill Godel.

Making use of the postelection hiatus in senior government employee activity, Godel had jumped from the Office of Special Operations in the Office of the Secretary of Defense, where he had worked under Gen. Graves B. Erskine, USMC (Ret'd), along with Col. Edward G. Lansdale and myself, to the greener pastures of ARPA.

During its first days, this defoliant project was known as Operation Hades; shortly thereafter, it was given the name Ranchhand. No one gave the project much consideration, and the ordinary defoliant used by the railroads was given a try. In the normal course of business, it never occurred to anyone that this defoliant would prove to be dangerous. As was customary with many projects at this time, the Ranchhand project was approved by McNamara, Roswell Gilpatric, Robert Kennedy, U. Alexis Johnson, Mike Forrestal, Dick Helms and Maxwell Taylor.

The aircraft assigned to this project had been left over from other projects, and their modification for spraying purposes did not prove difficult. No one had any concern for the consequences of the decision to defoliate. As events showed later, the use of harmful defoliants served little, if any, practical purpose in Vietnam. As a matter of fact, the "enemy" found it useful to burn the dead leaves and flee in the clouds of smoke, so it had more use from their point of view than for regular Vietnamese forces.

During May 1961, McNamara set up a project monitoring system called the Combat Development Test Center (CDTC). This process was characteristic of McNamara and his concept of operation. The objective of the CDTC was to place one office "at the front" in Saigon and the other close to the seat of power, and money, in the Pentagon. They were connected by a direct communication channel. As each problem arose and was identified in Saigon, it was numbered and wired immediately to the Pentagon. Thus, if there was a problem with "the action of the M-16 carbine" in combat, it was given a number in serial order and sent to the Pentagon, where #1156 would be given priority treatment.

Many people, myself included, used to read the lists of the CDTC priority projects every day. One unusual thing about CDTC projects was that their size, complexity, cost, or combat utility made no difference in their serial listing and treatment. All were equal, one after the other.

One day, I read a project that stated: "Elite troops of the Palace Guard are suffering from malnutrition on the Cambodian border." These "elite troops" were CIA and Filipino trained, and they were normally assigned to the palace to guard President Diem and his family. As part of their training they were getting "field combat" experience on the troubled Cambodian border.

For some reason, they suffered malnutrition while on this duty. Without delay, ARPA, the Pentagon manager of the CDTC project, set up a conference in the Pentagon for nutrition specialists from three leading universities. These specialists were next flown to Hawaii for Indochina briefings, then to Saigon, and thence to the Cambodian border. There they learned that the "elite troops," for the most part Tonkinese, could not eat the food prepared for them in Saigon and flown to them on the border. It lacked a native sauce that, to the Tonkinese, was essential.

The ARPA team arranged to have the sauce prepared in enormous quantities and, for lack of a better alternative, run through a nearby soft-drink bottling plant. The bottles were packed in wooden crates, airlifted to the border, and paradropped to the starving troops. End of case—almost.

Some months later, I observed a new CDTC project much farther down the numbered list. It read, "Elite troops of the Palace Guard are suffering malnutrition on the Cambodian border." ARPA handled each case by rote. It called a conference of nutrition experts—in the random process, these were different people—and flew them to Saigon.

In Saigon, they were told about the earlier project and shown the large-scale production facility and bottling plant. All seemed in order. Nevertheless, they asked to be flown to the border. There they found the starving troops. The problem was not difficult to discover.

When the cases of special sauce had been paradropped, the glass bottles were smashed. The troops were not allowed to eat anything for fear of broken glass. There was the problem. Back to Saigon.

Now the experts looked for a cannery. The nearest available one was at the San Miguel brewery in Manila. It was disassembled, flown to Saigon, and reassembled. The special Tonkinese sauce was made in the same vats and then canned at the new facility. This time, when the sauce was air-dropped to the troops, it survived the impact. The team of nutritionists declared the project a success and returned to their separate campuses. ARPA closed the project without ever looking back and turned to the next case. This was how the modern war was being fought in the halls of the Pentagon—"Whiz Kid" style.

Other examples were not so amusing. A Washington lawyer with ready and frequent access to the White House had made a trip to Florida, where he saw some massive machines clearing land in great swaths. As rows of these monster machines moved forward in teams, one beside the other, they chewed up everything in their way and left behind bare ground about as smooth as a tennis court. This lawyer was told that such machines were used in Latin America in the upper Amazon Basin, where they chewed their way through the rain forests, producing pulp for paper manufacture and leaving behind nothing but bare, dead ground.

When he returned from Florida, this quick-thinking lawyer went to see McNamara, after having paid a tactical call on the President, and suggested that an array of these enormous machines, set loose at the no-man's-land of the 17th parallel in Vietnam, could remove everything on the ground and leave nothing but bare earth. He suggested that the bare earth be networked with electronic devices that would permit the instant detection of anything that moved. This became a CDTC project, and before long it became the multi-billion-dollar "electronic battlefield."

In a similar but more costly deal, another astute planner learned that one of the major problems in Indochina was its lack of ports adequate for seagoing cargo vessels. Through all the early years of the war, almost all supplies delivered by ship had to be off-loaded in the inadequate river port of Saigon, far from the sea. (It is something like the minor port of Alexandria, Virginia, far up the Potomac River near Washington.)

This man rented a large office on Connecticut Avenue in Washington and had a huge replica of the Cam Ranh Bay (Vinh Cam Ranh) area on the coast of Vietnam constructed on a set of large tables. He filled it with water, and it looked like the real thing. It was his idea that the natural, shallow bay could be dredged and that huge plastic bags could be submerged, with weights, and used for the storage of large quantities of gasoline and jet fuel.

The weight of the seawater on these plastic bags would pump the lighter petroleum through pipes to a seaside storage site. His estimate for this project ran to about $2 billion. McNamara and his CDTC people put the project up for bid. A huge consortium of general contractors worked together on the project, and before it was done, that original $2 billion project had multiplied in cost many times over. This was the part of the Vietnam War that was rarely seen and is still seldom realized. After all, the $220 billion direct cost of the war—perhaps an overall cost of $500 billion—had to have been spent somewhere... somehow.

The Kennedy team had decided on the priorities. They had learned from the failure of the Bay of Pigs operation that they could not trust the CIA, and they had learned from Gen. Maxwell Taylor that the only way to fight the kind of war they inherited from the CIA in Indochina would be to do it with the kind of paramilitary tactics as waged by the U.S. Army Special Warfare units.

Because all earlier U.S. Special Forces troops had been serving in South Vietnam under the operational control of the CIA, Gen. Maxwell Taylor had proposed in his letter to President Kennedy on June 13, 1961, that National Security Action Memoranda #55, #56, and #57 become the basis of a new order of things. Kennedy had agreed without delay, and by late 1961 he had installed General Taylor in the White House as his special military adviser.

Not long after that, Taylor and Rostow made their trip to Saigon and returned with their proposal to introduce U.S. "support troops" into Vietnam under the cover of a "flood relief" action. Kennedy approved of this modest recommendation, and a new era was begun—one based upon an even greater change in Washington.

Allen Dulles, Gen. C.P. Cabell, and Dick Bissell were out. Ed Lansdale's star was in eclipse, and a new internal battle was under way in the murky halls of the windowless Joint Chiefs of Staff area of the Pentagon. The fight began with the establishment of the Office of the Special Assistant for Counterinsurgency and Special Activities and the arrival of its boss, Maj. Gen. Victor H. "Brute" Krulak of the U.S. Marines.

Gen. Lyman L. Lemnitzer, the man to whom National Security Action Memorandum #55 had been addressed and delivered, made sure that all of the service chiefs had had an opportunity to read and study these unique presidential papers and then ordered them to be securely filed. Lemnitzer and his close friend Gen. David M. Shoup of the U.S. Marine Corps were traditional soldiers. They had never been "Cold Warriors" or Cold War enthusiasts. Nor were they proponents of an Asian ground war.

It bothered Lemnitzer not at all to observe that Kennedy had created the office of "military adviser to the President" and had placed Taylor in that office. By the end of 1962, General Lemnitzer was on his way to the NATO command in Europe, while Kennedy, Taylor, and all the others had become mired in the quicksands of Southeast Asia.

When President John F. Kennedy published National Security Action Memorandum #55 on June 28, 1961, "Relations of the Joint Chiefs of

Staff to the President in Cold War Operations," he directed the Joint Chiefs to "present the military viewpoint in government councils." This did not work. The U.S. military establishment was neither designed nor prepared to engage in peacetime covert operations, nor did it wish to be. As a result, this type of activity remained with the CIA by default.

The CIA, however, is no more prepared to wage clandestine warfare than is the military establishment, except for one point: The CIA is always able to incite an incident sufficient to require U.S. action and involvement. The CIA can do this because it has, or is able to create, intelligence assets. The CIA is the first agency of the government to make contact with "rebel" or "insurgent" parties.

CIA spooks prowl the bars and meeting places of other countries in search of just such information. One may overhear, or participate in, a conversation with some natives who are making derogatory remarks about the government in power, as Contra leaders did in the case of Nicaraguan president Daniel Ortega.

The agent races to his "back-channel" communication system,[7] reports directly to his boss in CIA headquarters, and then is urged to obtain more information and to broaden his sources; this is why the agent was sent there in the first place. So he gets more information, even if he has to encourage or generate it. This leads to the beginning of a clandestine operation. It is a reaction process, not a planned affair.

At this point, we recall National Security Action Memorandum #57, "Responsibility for Paramilitary Operations," wherein it states: "A paramilitary operation...may be undertaken in support of an existing government friendly to the United States [as in the case of El Salvador] or in support of a rebel group seeking to overthrow a government hostile to us," as in Nicaragua.

Those lines were written by Gen. Maxwell Taylor in his post–Bay of Pigs investigation letter to President Kennedy on June 13, 1961. They have always been the doctrine of the CIA and its close allies in the Army Special Warfare program.

With few if any changes, they were also the basis of the doctrine being promulgated by Assistant Secretary of State Elliot Abrams, the key policy official for plans regarding paramilitary operations in Nicaragua.

In the same memorandum, there is an important but little-noticed definition that plays directly into the hands of the CIA, even though Kennedy was attempting to refocus this type of activity onto the Joint

Chiefs of Staff. It said, "Small operations will often fall completely within the normal capability of one agency; the large ones may affect State, Defense, CIA, USIA [United States Information Agency], and possibly other departments and agencies." What this says and what it means are clear enough. How it is applied becomes the problem.

All clandestine operations begin "small." Thus, the proposed operation, when presented to the National Security Council for a decision, was sent to the CIA, because the operation was seen to be "small." But no operation can remain "small" once the CIA begins to pour into the fray tens of millions of dollars and the tremendous military assets of the United States.

Over the years, the CIA has developed an efficient system of obtaining military equipment, manpower, overseas base facilities, and all the rest, ostensibly on a reimbursable basis, in order to carry out covert activities. The reimbursement is made by transferring hidden CIA funds in the Department of Defense accounts to DOD, thereby repaying all "out-of-pocket" expenses of the military. This complex but effective system has been in effect since 1949. For example, in Indonesia in 1958, the CIA was able, quite easily, to support a rebel force of more than forty thousand troops by using U.S. military assets. So what is "small"? And if it is not "small," if it has got large enough to be transferred to the Department of Defense, how will that be done? How can anyone rescue the situation after it has got out of hand?

At what point should U.S. military forces be prepared, for example, to enter into paramilitary action in Nicaragua or Africa? It is an old military axiom that "as soon as the blood of the first soldier is shed on foreign soil the nation is at war." The activities in Nicaragua were "small" when they began after the ouster of Anastasio Somoza in 1979. The CIA mined a harbor. It supported antigovernment Contra rebels. It spent $20 million for related purposes. Before long, it had spent another $27 million and eventually went on to spend more than $100 million.

Inevitably, this action in Nicaragua would cross the line from "small" to "large." Inevitably, American blood would be shed, and inevitably regular military forces would be called in to bail the Contras out, just as they were called into Vietnam in 1965 after the CIA and the OSS had worked there for two decades to escalate that conflict.

There are two enormous problems with this method of handling such activities:

1. The action initiated by the CIA is a reaction to some minor and, perhaps, misleading event, and

2. It is based upon a totally false definition of the problem.

"Reaction," by definition, implies the lack of a plan and of an objective. This was the single greatest strategic failure of the Vietnam conflict. The United States had no reasonable military objective; it simply reacted to the situation it found there.

A false definition of the problem is the greatest failing of American administrations and explains why such adventures are rarely, if ever, successful and productive. Any military activity instigated as no more than a reaction to some minor event lacks the element of strategic planning that is needed to attain an objective.

The Third World or less-developed countries were poorly defined. Despite decades of propaganda that would have had us believe they lived in either the "Communist" or "pro-West" sphere, they were not dedicated members of the bipolar "Us or Them" political scheme.

The distinguishing feature of these smaller countries is that they are not broad-range manufacturers or producers. They do not make typewriters, radios or televisions, coffeepots, fabric, automobiles and trucks, etc. Their biggest business, as a nation, is the import-export business. Therefore, much of their national revenue is derived from customs fees, and much of their private wealth is derived from individual franchises for Coca-Cola, Ford automobiles, Singer sewing machines, and so forth. They are totally dependent upon such imports and exports.

In such an economy, the ins, regardless of politics, control these lucrative franchises, and the outs do not. This creates friction. It is based on pure economics and greed and has nothing to do with communism or capitalism.

Therefore, if the ins solicit franchises from businesses in the United States, they are called friendly and pro-Western. If they turn to other sources, they are designated the enemy. If they are the enemy, we have labeled them Communists.

The leaders of the Contras, who used to serve Somoza in Nicaragua, wanted their valuable U.S. franchises back. For this they were willing to kill. For this the CIA helped them kill. The CIA supported them because it supports U.S. business.

This may be an oversimplification, but only to a degree. The basic motivations are always the same. Money lies at the root—in the scenario above, the enormous amounts spent on military matériel for the Contras and for the follow-on U.S. troops provided more than adequate incentive for those who intended to make war in Nicaragua.

In Vietnam the money spent amounted to more than $220 billion. This is why an in-depth recapitulation of the Vietnam era is important in shedding light on the events of today. We have seen it all before. And we have had to pay for it all before, not only with dollars, but with the lives of 58,000 Americans who never returned from that tragic conflict.

FIFTEEN

The Erosion of National Sovereignty

IN HIS NOVEL *Report From Iron Mountain on the Possibility and Desirability of Peace,*[1] Leonard Lewin writes: "War fills certain functions essential to the stability of our society," and adds, "War is virtually synonymous with nationhood. The elimination of war implies the inevitable elimination of national sovereignty and the traditional nation-state."

Lewin has told me his book is a novel and that he had a serious message to deliver to the public. I was assigned to the Office of the Secretary of Defense in 1961, at the time Thomas Gates left the office and Robert McNamara arrived. Along with McNamara came a group of dedicated and intelligent men who, for the most part, were not highly experienced in the military and such things as Grand Strategy and the utilization of modern military forces and modern weaponry. Despite this, as I got to know them better—men like Ed Katzenbach, who had been dean at Princeton—we would take part in luncheon discussions that sounded much like Lewin's writing. This is what was said in the halls of the Pentagon. What Lewin wrote is true to life, and we all would do well to heed his words.

Novel or not, these were serious words that weighed heavily on the causes of the escalation of warfare in Indochina in the 1960s and 1970s. They represent the classic views of a cabal of leaders in our society who fail to see any reason other than war for the existence of man. The very fact that certain select individuals of the Kennedy and Johnson administrations were said, by Lewin, to be thinking such thoughts in the face of the reality of the hydrogen bomb shows that this temporal world of ours has been changing faster than its leaders and the public can accommodate.

And since then, with the lessons of such things as the overt invasion of Grenada, the attack on Libya, the Contra attempt to overthrow the Ortega government of Nicaragua, the use of U.S. military forces to augment the national police of Bolivia, American military aid to the rebels in Afghanistan, the attack on Panama, the "Desert Storm" fighting against Iraq, and the recent creation of a regular U.S. Special Warfare Force for the pursuit of "low-intensity conflict"[2] all over the world, respect for the concept of national sovereignty has fallen to a dangerous low in the world family of nations. This is a revolutionary development.

Knowledgeable grand strategists of the power elite realize today that there cannot be a true, all-out war in a world society equipped with thousands of hydrogen bombs. But Grand Strategy requires that warfare be waged for the purpose of attaining the highest national objective— Victory. No nation can go to war knowing full well that the prosecution of that war with hydrogen bombs will inevitably lead to the elimination of all mankind and to the destruction of Earth as a living system. These strategists have been looking for an alternative. Perhaps Chairman Mao was correct in his forecast: "No matter how long this war is going to last, there is no doubt that it is approaching the last conflict in history."

As this realization has permeated the various levels of world leadership, those in positions of genuine power face the chilling reality of this truth. Their game of nations, their house of cards, is already showing signs of falling apart. Principal among these fading truths is the very evident decay of national sovereignty. Without sovereignty there can be no nation-state, and without the state, what remains? A New World Order? Perhaps.

In the *New York Times* of July 16, 1986, James Reston wrote, "The Congress has returned from its July Fourth recess to a capital that is changing in subtle ways." He noted that leaders of both parties have been forced to wonder how the United States could have lost its lead in the trade markets of the world. The United States is now the world's leading debtor nation. Reston observed that officials in Washington were finding their pet theories being murdered by the brutal facts and were beginning to wonder what went wrong.

To the question that many were asking, "What went wrong?" he responded, "What we are seeing is just the beginning of a philosophical inquiry about the assumptions of the past—even the validity of the sovereign nation-state."

Reston has not been the only one showing concern over this important subject. The fate of our own nation and of the family of nations hangs in the balance.

During an informal presentation at the National Press Club, a reporter asked the speaker, Richard Perle, then an assistant secretary of state under Reagan and a frequent voice of the Reagan administration on such matters, whether or not he thought the administration had been willfully disregarding national sovereignty. It was the only question Perle evaded and left unanswered during the meeting. He had no other choice. He could scarcely have honestly claimed that the administration did recognize and did honor the principle of national sovereignty. This is evidence of Reston's "philosophical inquiry." On a subject of such magnitude, a response is not easy.

On the other hand, Walter Wriston, formerly chief executive officer of Citicorp, the nation's biggest banking organization at that time, raised similar questions in his book *Risk and Other Four-Letter Words*.[3]

People of all nations have long since adjusted to the grim reality that an intercontinental ballistic missile can travel from the Soviet Union to the United States, or a reverse path, in about thirty minutes, carrying enough explosives to render society unlivable.... We now have a less visible but perhaps equally profound challenge to the unlimited sovereign power of nation-states in the technical reality of global communications.

What we are witnessing and participating in is a true revolution, and like all revolutions it is creating political unease.

Wriston cites "communications" as a "challenge...to sovereign power" perhaps equal to that of ICBMs. Obviously, both serve to severely limit the undivided power of nation-states. Once that power has been divided, it is, by definition, no longer sovereign.

Things were not always this way. In fact, the concept of sovereignty itself is of rather recent origin. During the sixteenth century, the French political philosopher Jean Bodin defined sovereignty as the ultimate location of that power "which legally commands and is not commanded by others." He wrote, "Sovereignty is what distinguishes the state from any other kind of human association." It is neither size nor might, nor the lack thereof, that counts on the world plane: "A state remains a state as long as it is sovereign. . . . Sovereignty determines the structure of the state." It is basically unitary and indivisible. The jurisdiction of the state cannot be divided, and the state is supreme within its own boundaries.[4]

These have been reliable and respected definitions and ideas until rather recently. It may be that this international obligation to honor the concept of sovereignty "no matter the size and power of the state" has led to the utilization of deep secrecy to cover those small, secret operations carried out by one state within the borders of another. The operative state believes in sovereignty as a foundation of the intangible structure of the family of nations; it carries out a covert operation for reasons of presumed necessity, hoping that it will not be discovered and exposed. If exposed, the operative state hopes that it may be able to disclaim, quite plausibly, its sinister and unwelcome role in the affair. This has been the unwritten policy among nations for centuries.

It may be said, with few exceptions of any significance, that this was the policy of the Eisenhower administration and its predecessors. It may also be said that this was why the Eisenhower administration from time to time directed the CIA, rather than the uniformed military establishment, to plan for and carry out such operations, even though the military possessed the experience and the assets required for such activities and the CIA did not. Within the terms of such a policy, the requirement for secrecy outweighed other considerations. In other words, the administration took a gamble and placed its chips on the CIA.

By the last years of the Eisenhower era, the CIA had overleaped its bounds. Its vast operations in Indochina, Tibet, and Indonesia and its U-2 spy-plane flights over the Soviet Union had seriously compromised this policy because the operations could not be kept secret, if for no other reason than their size and duration.

The Kennedy administration inherited this situation, and the early exposure of this practice caused by the disaster on the beach at the Bay of Pigs in Cuba brought things to a head. Kennedy's new policy signaled a direct turnabout of the assignment of responsibility for covert operations from the CIA to the military.

In June 1961, when this new policy was announced, Gen. Lyman L. Lemnitzer was the chairman of the Joint Chiefs. He and the service chiefs were traditionalists. (The chiefs at that time were Gen. George Decker for the army, Adm. Arleigh A. Burke for the navy, and Gen. Thomas D. White for the air force. Lemnitzer's good friend and confidant, Gen. David M. Shoup, commandant of the Marine Corps, also attended meetings of the Joint Chiefs.) These men all believed that warfare and the utilization of military forces was a formal affair and that the military services were not to be used in any other country, large or small, in violation of that state's sovereignty. They also believed that the utilization of military forces within the borders of the United States, save for accepted emergency situations, was also a violation of the state's sovereignty, that is, its power to govern and command.

In this climate, General Lemnitzer and the service chiefs studied each of the NSAMs from the White House with considerable care.

Not long after NSAM #55, "Relations of the Joint Chiefs of Staff to the President in Cold War Operations," had been signed by President Kennedy, it was delivered to the secretary of the Joint Staff. Discussion of NSAM #55, #56 and #57 was scheduled on the "Joint Chiefs' agenda" for an early meeting.

The Joint Chiefs of Staff meet regularly in the Gold Room in the heart of the windowless JCS area of the Pentagon in the depths of that vast building. The agenda for each meeting is selected with care, running from routine unclassified items to those of the very highest classification. The military service and the Joint Staff briefing officers are notified well in advance that they are on the agenda for that date.

In the Gold Room, the chairman and the service chiefs sit at a large table with ranking staff associates from each service. Rows of special staff members are seated behind them. As a result of the security classification pecking order, these extra staff officials leave after the briefing on their special subject has been given and before the next-higher level of classification begins. As the morning proceeds, both tables thin out with the departure of these officials.

On that day in July 1961 when the Joint Chiefs met on these directives, the briefing began with the definition of "Cold War operations." They are secret, clandestine operations sponsored by the highest authority of the U.S. government "in support of an existing government friendly to the United States, or in support of a rebel group seeking to overthrow a government hostile to us." "Cold War Operations" are distinct from "Secret Intelligence Operations."[5] Both of these types of operations are a violation of the sovereignty of some state, sometimes even of a friendly state that may unwittingly become involved in the action.

Although such operations had been carried out by the U.S. government, in one way or another, since 1948 (and of course during World

War II), it was surprising to see how little the Joint Chiefs actually knew about them and how little close-in experience they had in this area of operations.

One of the prominent members of the U.S. Senate,[6] a member of that select group which is always informed of such CIA activities before they take place, told me one day when I had been sent to tell him about one of these operations, "Keep it short. What I don't know about it won't hurt me." I had learned that by "short" he meant, "Don't tell me anything." That was Senate "oversight" in the 1950s. The JCS felt much the same way and had limited their participation in both the planning and operation of such activities as much as possible.

As the discussion of NSAM #55 broadened, General Lemnitzer and General Shoup—both of whom had commanded military units on Okinawa that had provided extensive support for the huge CIA activity that took place against the government of President Sukarno of Indonesia in 1958—admitted that they had not realized that that was what had been done with the planeloads of weapons and other war matériel they had furnished in response to a "classified" request made by a CIA agent in U.S. military uniform. It did not take long to see that these military men, all chiefs of their services, were not Cold Warriors and did not intend to be.

They listened intently to the President's statement: "I regard the Joint Chiefs of Staff as my principal military adviser responsible both for initiating advice to me and for responding to requests for advice. I expect their advice to come to me direct and unfiltered."

They had rarely been included in the special policy channel—which Allen Dulles had perfected over the past decade—that ran from the National Security Council (NSC) to the CIA for all clandestine operations. They did not want to be involved. Their services, of course, inevitably got involved whenever CIA operators approached the individual services for support, such as weapons from the army, airlift from the air force, or sealift from the navy. But despite this logistical support they rarely, if ever, participated in the overall operational planning with the CIA—even for such complex "secret" activities as the Bay of Pigs invasion of Cuba.

After the chiefs had been briefed on the key elements of the directives, copies were given to each of them personally for safekeeping. NSAM #56, "Evaluation of Paramilitary Requirements," had been delivered to the secretary of defense by the White House. It required the compilation of an "inventory [of] the paramilitary assets we have in the United States armed forces." This task had been assigned by Secretary McNamara to that longtime CIA operator Gen. Edward G. Lansdale.

The third presidential directive, NSAM #57, "Responsibility for Paramilitary Operations," was a document of great potential. As written, the primary thrust was contained in an enclosure that proposed the establishment of a Strategic Resources Group for initial consideration of all paramilitary operations and for approval, as necessary, by the President.

Despite this quite specific language defining the role of this new group, the covering letter contained a recommendation that "the Special Group [5412 Committee] will perform the functions assigned in the recommendation to the Strategic Resources Group."

For an important paper from the White House, the language of the covering letter came as quite a surprise. The message of the directive was carried in the enclosure, yet it was negated completely by the sentence cited above that assigned the responsibility for "paramilitary operations" back to the system used by the National Security Council and the CIA since 1954. The confused language that did this was a "recommendation" about a "recommendation."

We know that the basic paper (the enclosure) was written by Gen. Maxwell Taylor. The letter that reversed the Taylor procedure was written and signed by McGeorge Bundy. In this connection, it is interesting to recall that it was McGeorge Bundy who had made the telephone call to Gen. Charles Cabell, the deputy director of the CIA, on the evening before the Bay of Pigs invasion, canceling the essential air strikes against the last of Castro's combat aircraft, even though President Kennedy had approved those same air strikes that very afternoon. Later, Bundy, with his brief message, again reversed a decision of the President as affirmed in NSAMs #55 and #57: "I regard the Joint Chiefs of Staff as my principal military adviser responsible both for initiating advice to me and for responding to requests for advice."

By concluding that the Special Group would "perform the functions" of the new Strategic Resources Group, NSAM #57 left the former Cold War operations system in place with one stroke of the McGeorge Bundy pen. This circumscribed the role of the Strategic Resources Group designed by General Taylor. (The supersecret 5412 Committee had been created early in the Eisenhower years and had become the compliant tool of the CIA.)

The JCS recognized this loophole immediately and slipped through it. They did not want the job of clandestine Cold War operations. With its toe firmly in the door as a result of the loophole in NSAM #57, the CIA began an argument that effectively neutralized that directive and the others. NSAM #57 said, "Where such an operation [clandestine] is to be wholly covert or disavowable, it may be assigned to CIA, provided that it is within the normal capability of the agency."

This seemed to make it clear that a small and covert operation would still be assigned to the CIA, despite NSAM #57. Then the directive added: "Any large paramilitary operation wholly or partly covert which requires significant numbers of militarily trained personnel, amounts of military equipment which exceed normal CIA-controlled stocks and/or military experience of a kind and level peculiar to the Armed Services is properly the primary responsibility of the Department of Defense with the CIA in a supporting role."

It seemed to me, and many others, that this language made it indisputably clear what the President wanted. On the contrary, the CIA, with the support of certain willing military leaders (such as those with the Army Special Warfare elements), began a long series of meetings to discuss such questions as "What is a small covert operation? What is a large one?" They, of course, battled to stake out as big a claim as possible. Their arguments progressed to the subject of the eventual transfer of such operations from an embattled CIA to the larger and more experienced military.

This question was raised: "Suppose the CIA begins a certain Cold War operation with a small, covert activity that leads through a normal sequence of events to a large operation that becomes a major military conflagration far beyond that agency's capability? When and how will the transfer of the responsibility for that operation from the CIA to the military take place, and at such a time is there any chance, at all, that the operation can be kept secret and plausibly deniable?"

These arguments, plus the natural desire of the JCS to remain uninvolved, doomed this series of presidential directives to the files. The CIA and its allies prevailed. This had important results, especially with reference to the future of the war in Vietnam—and later in the situations in Central America and the Middle East, where almost identical progressions were taking place.

Gen. Maxwell Taylor became chairman of the JCS in October 1962 and ambassador to the South Vietnamese government in July 1963. Since he himself had written these papers and originated the concept of the Special Resources Group, he knew that the concept, at least, had the support of the President. What eventually came about in Vietnam, when the first U.S. troops under direct military command landed at Da Nang in March 1965, was a direct result of the policy outlined in NSAM #57.

The warfare in Indochina that had begun in 1945 under the Office of Strategic Services had become too big for the CIA. With the landing of the U.S. Marine battalions, under the command of a marine general, the nature of the warfare that had been carried out under the aegis of the CIA changed. It took twenty years for the clandestine work of the CIA to achieve that level—and it was not accomplished during JFK's lifetime.

Returning to the time of the original briefing of these three presidential documents, especially that of NSAM #57, in July 1961, the Joint Chiefs wondered how these new policy ideas had reached the President. Some thought that Ted Sorensen, the President's counsel, and, perhaps, Bobby Kennedy were responsible for them. Some suspected that Walt Rostow and Bill Bundy may have come up with the concept. If they had been able to discover the source of these documents, they would have been better able to evaluate their true significance.

This question of the document's source was an interesting one. During my study of them, I had come to the conclusion that Sorensen and Bobby Kennedy may have put them together, Bobby having attended all of the meetings of the Cuban Study Group. My guess was wrong. As we discovered later, these directives had been written by General Taylor, and a small, select staff.

Many years later, I invited Admiral Burke to lunch, along with a lawyer friend. I asked the admiral directly if the Cuban Study Group had ever issued a "report" to the President after the conclusion of its lengthy deliberations. He said, "No. The only report our group made to the President was oral." Furthermore, he noted that Bobby Kennedy had attended all of the meetings. His inference was that with Bobby in the room, there was no need to report the findings to his brother, whom Bobby saw and spoke to every day.

His response was technically true. There was no "report." But he shaded the facts. The admiral's response leaves open another possibility. General Taylor, with the consent of the other members of the Cuban Study Group, may have written his lengthy "Letter to the President" (described earlier) on his own in order to present his personal views about the way this nation should carry out Cold War operations. After all, he was the military expert among that group and the others were not. In view of the situation at that time, this may be the correct interpretation of these important events. The admiral and the others on the group hid under the fine point that General Taylor delivered a "letter" to the President, not a formal report. This famous "report" was discovered nearly a generation later at the Kennedy Library in Cambridge, Massachusetts, filed under "Letters," not "Reports."

The President had recalled General Taylor to active duty on June 26, 1961, two days before he signed NSAM #55, and said that he would be his "military representative for foreign and military policy and intelligence operations."

Continuing his behind-the-scenes plan to downgrade the CIA, the President signaled his acceptance of the "Report on the Defense Intelligence Organizations" that had been written by a group headed by Gen. Graves B. Erskine, U.S. Marine Corps (Ret'd), the longtime head of the Office of Special Operations in the Office of the Secretary of Defense. President Kennedy announced his intention, on July 11, 1961, to establish the Defense Intelligence Agency (DIA). Changes were in the wind.

Following this announcement, on August 1, 1961, Secretary McNamara created the DIA. Its first leader was Air Force General Joseph F. Carroll, formerly an agent with the FBI. This was followed, between August 16 and August 25, 1961, by a large recall of Army Reserve and National Guard troops, ostensibly in support of pressures in Europe. On September 6, 1961, 148,000 more men were recalled to active duty, with 40,000 of them sent to Europe.

By the end of September the President had announced that John McCone would be the new director of central intelligence after Allen Dulles left the CIA. Dulles, who had been the director since February 1953, left the CIA on November 29, 1961. This marked the end of the Dulles decade. There would never be another like it.

When the going gets rough, the agency professionals circle the wagons and get tough. They began their next moves as soon as Kennedy announced his selection of McCone to replace Allen Dulles. McCone had come from the world of big business. He had no military or OSS experience, although he had been deputy to the secretary of defense for several months in 1948 and under secretary of the air force during 1950 and 1951. The CIA turned this lack of experience to its advantage. McCone could be made into an executive figurehead, while the straight-arrow army general, Maxwell Taylor, could be maneuvered into a most useful paramilitary role.

To get these plans started, a long orientation trip around the world was scheduled for McCone. The great significance of such a trip is that the new DCI would be isolated from all other contacts and kept in the company of no one but the agency's best for an extended period. The CIA's number-one spokesman and craftsman at that time was Desmond Fitzgerald, head of the agency's Far East Division. He was selected by the "Gold Key Club," the inner circle of the hard-line CIA professionals, to accompany McCone on this trip. (It is significant that such a crucial choice as the selection of Fitzgerald was made by this inner circle, not by members of the old guard.)

Before leaving, Fitzgerald came over to the Pentagon for a meeting with key officials in clandestine business. He revealed plans for this trip that would include stops at major CIA stations and a special tour of South Vietnam. Certain villages were to be prepared, like movie sets, so that McCone would believe he was seeing Vietnamese combat action in "real time" and up close. The object of his visit to Vietnam was to have him exposed to as much CIA action as possible and to have him meet Ngo Dinh Diem and other selected leaders who had been working with the CIA for decades.

As the Pentagon meeting broke up, the CIA's Desmond Fitzgerald said that the trip had been timed to provide for lengthy briefing sessions—in the air, where there would be no interruptions and no other expressed viewpoints and where the CIA would have weeks to totally indoctrinate (or, as some said, brainwash) the new director. McCone would not only hear about worldwide political activities, but he would get a good rundown on the key people in the new CIA headquarters at Langley, Virginia. Not long after McCone's return from the trip, he was sworn in as the new director of central intelligence, and shortly after that he appointed Richard Helms, a longtime careerist, to the position of deputy director, plans (clandestine operations), and Ray Cline as deputy director, intelligence. Both were old associates of Des Fitzgerald.

A new era in the CIA had begun, and a new secret team was in control. At the close of 1961 there were 2,067 American servicemen in Vietnam; by the end of the decade there would be more than half a million. As we look back on that decade, we see the record of revolutionary changes. As David Halberstam has written, "Those who had failed, who had misled the Presidents of the United States the most, would be rewarded, promoted, given ever more important and powerful jobs."

Many of these same men have played similar roles for later administrations in Latin America, Africa, and the Middle East. We cannot but be alarmed at the bewildering innocence of American citizens. Actions of these administrations reflect a policy that began to take shape during the latter years of the Eisenhower era and was then quite clearly documented in those Kennedy National Security Action Memoranda. As presidential administrations come and go, the bureaucracy lingers on to perfect its ways, and this is nowhere more sinister than in the domain of the CIA and its allies throughout the government. The CIA has learned to hide behind its best cover—that is, that it is an intelligence agency—when actually it devours more money, more time, more manpower, and more effort in support of that part of its organization responsible for its covert "Fun and Games" activities all over the world (not to mention within this country).

When one analyzes such activity carefully, he must realize that the essence of covert operations directed and carried out by the government of the United States, from the top down, is the denial of the international concept of nation-state sovereignty, the principle upon which the family of nations exists.

This situation has been brought about by the existence of the Earth-destroying hydrogen bombs, by the uncontrolled and uncontrollable growth of world-around communications, by the runaway power of transnational corporations, and by a new economic system of corporate socialism. All of these factors threaten and destroy sovereignty, as is evidenced by the events that have occurred in the Soviet Union since 1990.

Is the sovereignty of the nation-state worth saving? Lest the significance of such revolutionary change be underestimated, consider the words of Arnold Toynbee, the eminent British historian and friend of the United States, as quoted in the *New York Times* of May 7, 1971:

To most Europeans, I guess, America now looks like the most dangerous country in the world. Since America is unquestionably the most powerful country, the transformation of America's image within the last thirty years is very frightening for Europeans. It is probably still more frightening for the great majority of the human race who are neither Europeans nor North Americans, but are Latin Americans, Asians, and Africans. They, I imagine, feel even more insecure than we feel. They feel that, at any moment, America may intervene in their internal affairs, with the same appalling consequences as have followed from the American intervention in Southeast Asia.

For the world as a whole, the CIA has now become the bogey that communism has been for America. Wherever there is trouble, violence, suffering, tragedy, the rest of us are now quick to suspect the CIA had a hand in it. Our phobia about the CIA is, no doubt, as fantastically excessive as America's phobia about world communism; but in this case, too, there is just enough convincing guidance to make the phobia genuine. In fact, the roles of America and Russia have been reversed in the world's eyes. Today America has become the nightmare.

This is what the destruction of sovereignty and disregard for the rule of law means, and it will not stop there. With it will go property rights—as we have witnessed in Eastern Europe and the former Soviet Union—and the rights of man.

SIXTEEN

Government by Coup d'État

THE YEAR WAS 1964. Pres. John F. Kennedy had been shot dead months before by bursts of "automatic gunfire"[1] in Dallas by "mechanics," that is, skilled gunmen, hired by a power cabal determined to exert control over the United States government. Lyndon B. Johnson, JFK's successor, had been only a few feet under the bullets fired at Kennedy as he rode two cars back in that fatal procession.[2]

By 1964 Johnson was becoming mired in the swamp of the Indochina conflict. Kennedy, who had vowed to "break the CIA into a thousand pieces," was dead. LBJ, who heard those fatal bullets zing past his ears, had learned the ultimate lesson; and for good measure, Richard Nixon was in Dallas on that fatal day, so that he, too, had the fact of this ever-present danger imprinted on his memory for future use by his masters.

During those fateful years, other events revealed the ubiquitous hand of the rogue elephant that is the CIA. Within a year of President Kennedy's death, the CIA was on the move again. Following an abrupt coup d'état engineered by the CIA, Victor Paz Estenssoro, the president of Bolivia, fled from La Paz to Lima, Peru.

This coup established Gen. René Barrientos Ortuño as the new president. The man Barrientos replaced is the same Paz Estenssoro who again served as president of Bolivia in 1986 and who was much disturbed when U.S. antidrug campaign troops showed up in his country with armed helicopter gunships and automatic weapons.

232

From long experience, Paz knew what it meant to have weapons in the hands of outsiders who might at any moment permit them to be used by his enemies to threaten the government. It had happened to him before, more than once. Paz was an old hand in the game of international intrigue and power politics; his experience predated World War II. Before the outbreak of that war, the German Nazi machine had built a vast underground spy network throughout Latin America structured around the German airline Lufthansa and its affiliated companies. It was operated in much the same manner as the CIA's huge proprietary corporation, Air America, was decades later, and it acted in support of a Nazi spy network.

In 1941, Paz, who already had a political record as the Bolivian minister of finance, sided with the Nazis and was arrested for promising to deliver the oil fields of his country into the hands of the Germans. He had been the leader of the pro-Nazi National Revolutionary Movement and was connected with four Bolivian newspapers that operated under the domination of Hitler's propaganda chief, Joseph Goebbels.

On that day in November 1964 when Paz fled Bolivia to seek refuge in the elite San Antonio district of Lima, three men met in the dimly lit barroom of the old, regal Hotel Bolívar, adjacent to the Plaza St. Martín. I had just walked across that sunlit plaza and entered the same barroom through its street-level doorway. I heard those men speaking English and immediately recognized them, even though my eyes had not adjusted enough to the dim lighting to see them.

In our silent profession we learn never to approach anyone in strange surroundings until we are certain the coast is clear. I went to the bar, where I stood in brighter light and ordered the Peruvian national drink, a Pisco Sour. One of the three men came to the bar beside me, ordered drinks, took out a cigarette, and prepared to light it. "Do you have a light?" he asked. The bartender, hearing me say no, lit the cigarette. A normal conversation had opened. All was clear.

I returned with the man to his table and joined the others. The three had just finished an assignment in Bolivia and were on their way back to Washington. They had engineered the coup d'état against Paz and installed General Barrientos as president. It had been that easy.

During the 1964 political upheaval in Bolivia, it had been decided by the U.S. National Security Council that Paz must go and a new man placed in his shoes. The man chosen for this role, Barrientos Ortuño, was a popular young air force general. He was to be given the "Robin Hood" treatment by the CIA to increase his popularity, just as the CIA had done for Ramon Magsaysay in the Philippines, for Ngo Dinh Diem in South Vietnam, and for a host of others around the world.[3]

Control of a small Third World country is always tenuous at best. Paz was an old hand and knew the business. The man at the top must constantly be ready for an attack. He must maintain absolute control over all weapons, and particularly over all ammunition, in his country. In Bolivia at that time, Paz had put control of all weapons in the hands of relatives and reliable friends who commanded the civilian militia as an elite palace guard.

They maintained an edge over the armed forces by controlling all ammunition—absolutely. Soldiers of the Bolivian army and air force had weapons and were trained with live ammunition; after a day on the firing range or other maneuvers, their unit leaders had to turn in a shell case for every round fired. There was strict accountability not only for every weapon but for every single bullet.

The task for the CIA—to overthrow Paz and replace him with Barrientos—was clear, and it was simple. All that had to be done was to put more ammunition into the hands of Barrientos's regular troops than Paz could get into the hands of his own civilian militia, and to do it quickly and by surprise.

This was done under the cover of an openly declared joint exercise involving United States and Bolivian army and air force units, scheduled to take place in outlying regions of Bolivia. This exercise, in 1964, was designed much as the antidrug campaign in Bolivia would be in 1986. The military maneuvers served to raise the political stature of Barrientos and to cover the secret delivery of tons of ammunition to his troops.

All of the U.S. Air Force aircraft employed in support of this exercise were "clean"—they had taken no part in the delivery of ammunition. The CIA used a contract Super Constellation aircraft from Air America to fly the ammunition to a remote landing ground in Peru. From there it was flown across the border in CIA-controlled light aircraft to several smaller magazines scattered throughout Bolivia.

On the day before the coup, CIA agents moved a sizable (in Bolivian terms) military force to the outskirts of La Paz. During the night its members were issued live ammunition, and at daybreak they infiltrated the city. The troops of the civilian militia were caught by surprise, with their weapons in hand but with no ammunition. Paz, yielding to good sense, quickly accepted the offer of a flight to Peru. The battle that never took place was over—except for one detail.

During the night, my friends, the three CIA operatives, had been hosts, that is, captors, of General Barrientos at a secret safe house. The dinner was bounteous, and the drinks flowed freely. When it was time to take the general to La Paz, they loaded him onto an old Bolivian Air Force C-47 (DC-3) for the final leg of his journey to power.

When the plane landed in a leaderless city, these CIA agents realized that El Presidente was far from being sober enough to assume his new duties. Cups of black coffee and a long, cold shower later, Barrientos was driven, in proper glory, down the main street to the cheers of his subjects, while the CIA men explained to him what had happened, his new duties and responsibilities, and some of the hazards of his new job.

Needless to say, my old friends were anxious when I spoke to them to get out of the city that now harbored Paz. Less than an hour later they were at the Lima airport and on their way to Panama. The CIA headquarters in Panama was, at that time, responsible for all clandestine activities in Latin America. The Bolivian coup was over. It had been a success, and the three CIA agents were ready for other assignments.

This is a picture of the CIA in action. This formula for the transition of leadership in less developed countries (LDCs)[4] has been used over and over again. In such countries the politics are very simple. It is always "Us" or "Them." The people of those countries have little, if anything, to say about it. The record of this type of activity goes back to World War II, and off the record it goes back much farther than that. The conflict in Indochina is the prime example in our time.

As the progression of events in Central America has demonstrated, the tactics of Vietnam have become the method of dealing with the problems of less-developed countries in the bipolar world. The big enemy has been said to be "communism," and the presumed threat the dire effects of the domino theory: Lose Vietnam and the rest of Southeast Asia would fall to communism; lose Nicaragua and there would be Communists right on the other side of the Rio Grande, if not in the streets of Houston.

Despite the changes in what was the Soviet Union, this kind of warfare isn't over yet. In Vietnam the United States won precisely nothing, but that costly war served the primary purposes of the world's power elite. For one thing, they benefited splendidly from the hundreds of billions of dollars that came their way. For example, more than ten million men were flown from the United States to Saigon by contract commercial airline flights, representing more than $800 million in windfall business for those airlines. And this is only the beginning. With each takeover, the victors gain access to the natural resources and human, low-cost, assets of the country.

As *Report From Iron Mountain on the Possibility and Desirability of Peace* found: "War fills certain functions essential to the stability of our society; until other ways of filling them are developed, the war system must be maintained—and improved in effectiveness."

According to Lewin, the "Special Study Group" that produced this amazing report voted to keep it under wraps, because the members of the group felt that:

The reader may not be prepared for some of its assumptions—for instance, that most medical advances are viewed more as problem than as progress; or that poverty is necessary and desirable, public postures by politicians to the contrary notwithstanding; or that standing armies are, among other things, social-welfare institutions in exactly the same sense as are old-people's homes and mental hospitals...that the space program and the controversial antimissile missile and fallout shelter programs are understood to have the spending of vast sums of money, not the advancement of science or national defense, as their principal goals, and that military draft policies are only remotely concerned with defense.[5]

Before we put the CIA-instigated Bolivian coup d'état behind us, we should note that the operational role stops with the completion of the overthrow of the government. Once that "dirty work" has been achieved and the operatives are out of town, a new band of intelligence experts takes their place.

One of the least-known divisions of the CIA is that headed by the deputy director of economics. This division moves into a country to work with a new regime and to begin the task of selecting and setting up new franchise holders for as many goods as possible to assure that they are imported from American companies and that those from other sources, formerly the Soviet sphere in particular, are excluded.

These new franchise holders are usually closely associated with the new President. They are members of his cabinet and other top government officials. The CIA screens and selects these new "millionaires" and arranges for them to meet with the various companies they will front for under the new regime. It might be said that this cleansing of the economic system is the real reason for most coups d'état, and that political ideology has very little to do with it. The ins (the men in the foreign government) are called "friends of the West" and "anti-Communist," but that is just for public consumption. On the other side of the coin, the outs are well aware of the system—having been the ins and beneficiaries of the same, or similar, largess under the prior administration.

But it happens that over a period of time an administration begins to believe that it is truly in power and that it actually runs the government. This leads its officials to make franchise arrangements with an ever-increasing number of sources. Some of the more daring, in an attempt to escape the severe financial and profit-making controls placed upon them and their government by U.S. manufacturers and by the canopy of international banks that is spread over all imports and exports to their country, attempt to make deals with other countries. They believe that they may be able to buy essential goods cheaper that way and to sell their resources and labor at better rates. To oversimplify, this is what Ferdinand Marcos was doing in the Philippines before he was ousted.

As such actions increase, the national leadership will be increasingly attacked by the United States on the grounds that it is turning toward communism and becoming a base for the infiltration of the Communist ideology and military system into the hemisphere. In other cases there are more or less "legitimate" coups d'état as internal opposition rises against an oppressive dictatorship. There could have been no more "anti-Communist" dictators than Rafael Leónidas Trujillo Molina, who ruled the Dominican Republic from 1930 to 1961 and then was assassinated with American aid, or Fulgencio Batista in Cuba and Anastasio Somoza of Nicaragua. All of these men, to cite a few, had been in power so long that they believed they could throw their weight around and extend their franchise selections to other countries. In such cases (Trujillo is the exception) the United States does not so much aid the insurgents as it just sits on its hands and lets the aged dictator be eliminated by others who want his job and the largess that goes with it.

Sometimes the United States gives the old leader a firm and friendly cue, as when Director of Central Intelligence William Casey visited the Philippines in 1985 and suggested to Marcos that he ought to "hold an election." As we have seen, such a suggestion is the kiss of death. It remained for President Corazon Aquino to heed the hints that poured out from the Office of the Deputy Director of Economics and other "friends" as she faced the task of rebuilding the franchise networks. This means big money to the country involved and to the United States and to the bankers who manage the finances in both directions.

According to a September 1986 article in the prestigious *Harper's*

Magazine, "The amount spent by the United States in 1985 on military operations in the Third World was $137.6 billion." These figures were compiled by the Coalition for a New Foreign and Military Policy, in Washington, D.C. That amount is more than 50 percent of the net cost of the Vietnam War—even though it was the total for only one year. Note also that this amount was only for military operations. This type of activity continues with or without the specter of communism.

This business of military and foreign aid is much more complex and much more important to the economic future of this nation than most people understand. According to R. Buckminster Fuller, who served as a consultant to the governments of many countries, including Brazil and the Soviet Union, the total cost of U.S. foreign aid from 1952 through 1979 amounted to $100 billion, in 1950 dollars.

In *Critical Path*,[6] Fuller stated (and the *New York Times* later printed substantially this same quote):

> Each new year's foreign aid bill had a rider that said that if American companies were present in the country being aided, the money [from foreign aid funds] had to be spent through those American companies.... Foreign aid paid for all the new factories and machinery of all the American corporations moving out of America. This became a fundamental pattern: first the 100 largest corporations, then the 200 largest corporations followed, then what Fortune calls the 500 largest corporations.... So the Wall Street lawyers simply moved their prime corporate operations elsewhere.... But the main objective of the Wall Street lawyers was for the corporations to get out from under the tax control of the American government.... This allowed the corporations to acquire gold equities while U.S. citizens and small domestic businesses could not do so.

Anyone who wishes to learn even more about the exploitation of the less-developed countries and the control of U.S. corporations should read Walter Wriston's book *Risk and Other Four-Letter Words*. As the retired CEO of Citicorp, Wriston knows the subject better than almost anyone else. The only problem is that the reader must understand Wriston's point of view. This is a man who promoted and fostered sending all of our savings to these LDC under the guise of "loans." They were strange loans indeed. Almost none of that money will ever return to the United States, and it is our savings and our pension plans—or rather, was.

Not only do we, the people of the United States, have no idea of what our personal objective and that of our country ought to be with respect to the rest of the world, but on top of that, we so frequently totally misunderstand the nations of the Third World, most of which, like Vietnam, have been created by design... the design of other powers... in recent centuries to divide ancient groups of people whose native societies are far older and far more experienced in many ways than we are.

Not long ago the United States celebrated its bicentennial. Many of these Third World social groups, such as those in Indochina, have histories that go back fifteen thousand years or more; as a people, they have survived for thousands of years on the same ground as that of their ancestors. Yet most of the national boundaries of those ancient lands, such as Vietnam, Saudi Arabia, Ghana, South Korea, and Iraq, are latter-day devices, creations that divide these ancient and quite homogeneous people.

When we speak of the failure to have and to understand our national objective, we must be able to define its meaning, especially in time of war. Some of the questions most frequently asked since the termination of warfare in Vietnam have been "Why were we there? What was our objective? What did we want to do there that caused us to enter that hostile area as far back as 1945? And what kept us there until 1975?"

It was that illustrious World War II armored brigade commander, Gen. Creighton W. Abrams, who asked the crucial question of President Johnson. He needed to know what this country's strategic objective was in Indochina. With that in hand, he and his staff would have be able to draw up a proper and effective military plan to win that war. Without such a statement from the President, the best that men like Abrams and Westmoreland could do was wallow in the quagmire of indecision while counting bodies on both sides.

General Abrams knew, as did most of the senior U.S. military officers, that if he had been turned loose with the forces at his disposal he could assuredly have captured Hanoi, and all of Ho Chi Minh's forces in the process. One of the most forceful statements of this belief has been made by the former Commander in Chief, Pacific, Adm. U.S.G. Sharp, in his book *Strategy for Defeat*.

But these men knew also that such a tactical achievement would not have brought with it victory; it would simply have caused the immediate escalation of warfare on an international scale. Any success they might have achieved on the border of China would have unleashed hordes of

Chinese armed and equipped with the modern weaponry of the Soviet Union, and there could have been no victory in a land war in Asia against hordes of well-armed Chinese.

Such an eventuality would have led inevitably to a so-called conventional war of such fury that the leaders of both sides would have been forced to weight the tactical necessity of the utilization of the hydrogen bomb.

At that point, there could be no such thing as "graduated" or "limited" warfare. The very heart of the meaning of warfare is that it is, and forever must be, all-out and unrestricted in its fury. There can be no referee in warfare. Furthermore, the progress, or direction, of the course of wide-open warfare is always unpredictable.

Therefore, if General Abrams had really been turned loose by his commander in chief in the White House, it would not have been long before the President would have been forced to make the decision to use the hydrogen bomb. Would he then have used that enormous destructive power against the North Vietnamese, against the Chinese, or against the ultimate foe, the Russians? Or perhaps, against all three? The response to that decision would have been immediate. The United States would have been made the target of Soviet retaliation. In that series of decisions, which appear to be all but inevitable, lies the power to bring about the destruction of Earth.

There it is! That is the real significance underlying General Abram's question to the President. Faced with these facts, and the dilemma they create, no President will ever again be able to order Americans to take part in an all-out, classic war. No President or his counterparts in nuclear-armed nations will be able to commit troops to battle in which the certain outcome will be global destruction.

There is a little-known secret about the war in Indochina that illustrates how dangerous the H-bomb threat actually was. There was a day when three U.S. Air Force F-84 fighter-bombers had been put on tactical alert at the Udon Thani air base in Thailand, just across the river from Laos. At that time the Vietminh were believed to be mounting an all-out massed campaign, in conjunction with opposition Pathet Lao forces, westerly across the Plaines des Jarres from Samneua (in northeastern Laos) toward the capital of Laos. It was also suspected that the Vietminh were planning a flanking attack into Cambodia on the way to a final strike at Saigon. Thus, although the Vietminh rarely massed their forces, it was believed they had a sizable army on the move.

The three F-84 aircraft were equipped with nuclear weapons. The year was 1960; this was the first time since the atomic bomb attacks on Japan in 1945 that these massive weapons had been readied for actual combat. Cooler heads, some shocked to the core by the very thought of such a possibility, prevailed, and the F-84s and their nuclear weapons were returned to their bases. As a result, a lower-level form of inconclusive warfare continued in Indochina for the next fifteen years.

Today this method of "no win" warfare is called the doctrine of "low-intensity conflict." Therefore, when we discover that $137.6 billion was spent by the United States for "military operations" alone in the Third World during 1985, we must understand that it has become the objective of "low-intensity conflict" to continue the wasting of money, the pointless killing of defenseless people, and the consumption or attrition of costly war matériel to make way for the procurement of more.

"Low-intensity conflict" is a way in which the hundreds of billions of dollars of armaments produced each year can be used, destroyed, and wasted this year in order that more may be procured and used next year. It is a general rule in the military procurement business that for every dollar spent for new weapons, ten more dollars will be spent on those same weapons for their maintenance and support during their "life of type."[7]

Much of this action is motivated by a misunderstanding of the true nature of what is called a "Third World nation" or "less-developed country." Although national sovereignty no longer exists as a fact in LDCs, and exists only partially in all other nations today, the rules of the "Game of States" require that the game be played as though sovereignty did exist. As a result, the LDCs are considered to be sovereign equals, as at the United Nations, that is, one state, one vote. Nothing could be further from the truth.

The true definition of "less-developed country" has nothing to do with politics, ideology, or military power. An LDC is a country that differs from others because it does not have the ability to produce or manufacture all of the things it needs or wants to survive, even at a relatively low level of subsistence.

As some scholars have put it, the LDCs do not have the "carrying capacity" for bare existence and real growth in modern times. Therefore, they must be "aided." As a result, the biggest business in a less-developed country, and the sole reason for its governmental power structure, is import and export. LDCs hope that they can export enough, in dollar values, to provide the money required to make payments on the interest on their national debt, with enough left over to pay for all the things they must import.

The government of such a country is a business monopoly over its people and its territory and is motivated much less by some political ideology than by the very pragmatic aim of controlling the import-export business. In most LDCs the customs activity and border patrol are the most important elements of the governmental structure, because they enable the political leadership to maintain its monopoly and to keep an accurate and absolutely essential account of everything exported and imported by the country, as well as its value.[8]

The government of an LDC makes its money by granting exclusive and monopolistic franchises to its friends, relatives, and true financial and traditional leaders of its national infrastructure, for everything from chewing gum and Coca-Cola to Cadillacs and F-16 fighter planes.

These franchise holders, the ins, are usually assured of becoming millionaires. Their franchises are obtained through contacts with select sources in the United States and other Western powers. They cover all the essentials required by the populace; there is no other way to obtain nonlocally produced goods, including foodstuffs, which must be imported. The same franchise system applies to the nation's exports.

The outs, on the other hand, are those who have been stripped of their franchises, usually as a result of a coup d'état, in favor of the ruling group. The term "political party" and the words "communism," "socialism," and "democracy" rarely apply in any of these LDCs. The outs are definitely on the outside looking in and represent an ever-present danger to the ins through the possibility of a coup d'état. In most LDCs there can be no meaningful campaigns and elections. In most cases, the votes, if elections are held, are counted by the armed forces, and the armed forces are the instrument of the in power group. Such controls leave little alternative to the outs other than the coup d'état method of power transition.

In all less-developed countries, the difference between the ins and the outs has little, if anything, to do with political ideology. The scenario exploited by the major powers divided the world into "Communist" and "the West" or some other structure. As far as each LDC is concerned, the game is quite simple: "Where do they buy—that is, where are the franchise materials produced and sold—and to whom do they sell their own resources, to include physical labor?"

The supremely powerful international bankers keep the books and balances for each side. They make these transactions possible by offering the loans, issuing letters of credit, collecting huge fees for their role in each transaction, and collecting the interest on the entire package. In many LDCs the total amount of interest paid to the banks and their international financing structure amounts to more than half of the total value of dollars earned by their exports. For this reason annual payments are seldom more than the interest involved and none of the principal. This is one reason why the principal never comes back to the United States.

The long-range future of such a system can mean only one thing: the eventual default of the total amount loaned and the loss of savings that had been deposited with the network of banks involved. For example, when the Chicago-based Continental Illinois Bank failed, a major share of its $47 billion holdings had come from 2,200 other financial institutions throughout the United States. Had the U.S. government not moved to take over these massive losses, the failure of that single "money center" bank would have taken down with it the majority of those other 2,200 financial institutions.

Of course, nothing operates along such uncomplicated lines. Among the "Western" powers there is steep competition. France vies to sell the Mystère fighter plane to each LDC at the same time the U.S. pushes its own aircraft. Deals are made, for example, by Japan with Brazil to purchase iron ore and, in the process, to construct a much-needed 1,100-mile railway line. In most LDCs vast amounts of raw materials and labor at low cost are traded for manufactured items.

All that is important here is to know that the struggle for less-developed countries is not a political contest such as Communists versus the West. It is, rather, a struggle for an import-export lock on each country, with the aim of creating markets and consumers, along with a maximized flow of dollars in both directions that includes a heavy overhead burden of interest for the bankers, who benefit likewise.

This understanding takes us back to the origins of the thirty-year war in Indochina and events of that era. In 1945, even before Germany had surrendered in World War II, certain OSS officials, among them Allen Dulles and Frank Wisner, had made contact with German leaders to create the anticommunism scenario that was to follow World War II.

Despite the fact that the Soviet Union had been our ally during World War II and had sacrificed more than 20 million of its people for that victory, elements of the U.S.-British coalition began the postwar "anti-Communist" battle cry before the actual surrender of Germany. This means that OSS and British agents were scheming with "the enemy" (Germany) while they were joined with "the friend and ally" (Russia).

As the business of World War II ended and the business of the postwar world moved into high gear, the key to the peacetime strategy called the Cold War was to be this division of the world's nations into two camps: "communism" and "the West."

Since that time, approximately $100 billion per year has been spent on foreign military aid, and in real dollar terms as of 1980, a staggering total of "$6 trillion has been legally transferred from the U.S. people's national capital account over to the capital ownership account of the stockholders of the one thousand largest transnational, exclusively American-flag-flying corporations."[9]

When so much money is loaned to the less developed countries and when the contacts that lead to the award of exclusive franchises for American-manufactured items are made, the next question is: To whom should these franchises be awarded by the American corporations involved? This question points to a need for a reliable American source in the LDCs who has information, that is, "intelligence," on all key families in the country. The CIA fills this role quietly and unobtrusively.

The CIA station chief in each less-developed country will create a list of key families who are close to the ruling power. In many instances, a son will be enrolled in the military of that country and will then, as a function of the U.S. Military Aid Program, be put on a quota of officers who have been selected to attend a "radar school" or other military course in the United States.

An August 20, 1986, article in the *New York Times* states, "The Defense Department's English Language Center here [Lackland Air Force Base in San Antonio, Texas], where military people from seventy foreign countries come to study English, is a barometer of United States military relations with others."

It goes on to say, ". . . the long-term benefit is the opportunity for us to influence other countries—this center is a vital link in American foreign policy."

Furthermore, the *Times* adds, "Beyond language, the center tries to expose the students to the United States. Tours to local banks, businesses, and the Lone Star Brewery are arranged, as are trips to Dallas and Washington."

What the *Times* did not add was that many, if not all, of these special students had been selected for this trip to the United States by the CIA's chief of station in the home LDC. Upon return, these students and their families will be looked upon as future franchise holders for the import of U.S.-made products. This effort is cloaked in the military uniform, but it has been arranged by the CIA for business purposes.

As with all good intentions, there are times when things go wrong. Despite all precautions, there comes a time when the in government is overthrown by the outs. In spite of all the propaganda, the new ins are rarely, if ever, "Communists," "socialists," or other ideologues. They just want to cancel all existing franchises, turn out the former franchise holders, and begin the whole process again. In such a system, it becomes necessary for the United States to side with one group or the other. Thus we have Ortegas, Castros, Ho Chi Minhs, and Garcías.

A check of the record would reveal that many later "enemies" had been, at one time or other, favorites of the CIA or OSS. A serious dilemma is thus created: The CIA would like to keep its role in these affairs secret, but how can it be secret when the present outs are only once removed—often, literally—from having been the ins? Both sides are well aware of the game played by the CIA and its friends in the American business community.

So, as we said earlier, when Paz was displaced by the CIA and when Barrientos was put in his place, Paz knew exactly what had happened and who had done it. And it was no surprise when, twenty-two years later, he regained the presidency of Bolivia.

Is Paz thinking, every day, that the CIA must be at work again, behind the cover of the so-called anticocaine project, to put bullets in the guns of the armed forces to once more run him out of town? Stay tuned. We'll see how it all ends.

After all, CIA Director Casey's suggestion to Marcos that he run an election worked like a charm. Marcos was out, and the franchises for products to be imported into the Philippines under the Aquino regime were all written anew. That is good business, and worth every penny of the $137.6 billion or so in annual foreign military aid—or is it?

SEVENTEEN

JFK's Plan to End the Vietnam Warfare

AS STATED IN EARLIER CHAPTERS, the Bay of Pigs operation mounted by the CIA against Castro and Cuba failed because of the cancellation of the air strike that Kennedy had ordered to destroy the final three combat-capable aircraft in the Cuban air force.

Here is an example of the failure of an administration to understand the employment of military power. This time the failure involved conventional equipment. On January 27, 1963, a report in the *Los Angeles Times* by Marvin Miles contained key information from an important member of the Kennedy administration:

> The discussion whether United States air cover was planned for the Bay of Pigs invasion is academic, in our opinion, whereas U.S. failure to properly assess the fighting capabilities of the T-33 jet trainer has serious implications.
>
> Attorney General Robert Kennedy acknowledged last week that underestimating the T-bird was a major mistake.
>
> "We underestimated what a T-33 carrying rockets could do," he said. "It wasn't given sufficient thought. They caused us a great deal of trouble."

This article is evidence that by January 1963, the Kennedys had realized that the cancellation of that crucial air strike was the major miscalculation behind the defeat of the exile brigade, just as Gen. Maxwell Taylor had reported to them. As Robert Kennedy said in the same article, "The plans and the recommendations obviously were not adequate." The Kennedy brothers agreed that they would not lay themselves open to that problem of underestimating enemy capability again.

But far away, on the other side of the world, Indochina, with all of its pitfalls, was looming over Camelot at 1600 Pennsylvania Avenue.

By mid-1961, the Kennedys realized that the mysteries of a national military strategy that was clouded by the reality of the H-bomb was as much a factor, in the theater of operations in Indochina, as the T-33 jets had been in the Bay of Pigs operation. In other words, any participation in a military action in a friendly Third World country was necessarily limited to the use of conventional weaponry. At the same time, military strategists know that war must always be an all-out, go-for-broke activity.

A war, by definition, cannot be limited. Furthermore, if limited warfare is attempted, it inevitably becomes a war without an objective. Such a war cannot be won, as we learned in Korea and would learn in Vietnam. Thus, as Clark Clifford so clearly predicted, a war in Vietnam, fought as it was without a military objective, had to lead nowhere. Kennedy knew that the introduction of U.S. military forces into Vietnam would create that insoluble problem. Despite this understanding, the low-level action Kennedy inherited in Indochina from the Truman and Eisenhower administrations existed, and the CIA continued in operational control there as it had since 1945, although now in a somewhat more diversified and obscure role.

By the end of 1961 President Kennedy's military adviser in the White House, Gen. Maxwell Taylor, had visited Vietnam and had rendered an important report on conditions there. The President accepted most of the Taylor recommendations, with the exception of his call for the introduction of U.S. ground forces "to help the Diem government with flood relief."

Also by the end of 1961, John McCone, appointed to replace Allen Dulles as the director of central intelligence, had been to Indochina and around the world on a most highly specialized orientation trip orchestrated by one of the CIA's best, Desmond Fitzgerald.

At the same time, it became quite clear to those most active in promoting military activity in Indochina that President Kennedy was not going to accept proposals to introduce U.S. armed forces into Vietnam for military purposes but that he might approve their use as advisers in a limited partnership with Diem's government. First, however, he wanted to learn more about conditions there.

Since most of Kennedy's advisers came from academic backgrounds, they were interested in learning more about the Vietnamese, their lives, and their traditional government. With two thousand years of cultural and political history, Indochina—and particularly that part called Vietnam—was a "traditionalist society." Its basic economic way of life was simple and efficient, sustained as it was by agriculture and fishing.

One of its most remarkable characteristics was that its peasant communities were cohesive social units that easily managed the behavior of their inhabitants. This social structure was based upon the clan, or "Toc," which consisted of all persons, male and female, of a common ancestry through the male line going back to the fifth ascending generation and forward to the third descending generation. This represented a total of nine generations and a time span of two hundred years or more.

Such a clan was headed by the senior male of the principal lineage, and his home served as its headquarters. The clan was sustained by the "cult of ancestors," and rites took place in an ancestral hall. As can be imagined, these clans were closely knit and generally remained in the same area century after century. They were quite isolated, and other than the payment of a head tax and a requirement of limited military service, they had very little contact with any central government.

These rice-growing peasants rarely traveled far from their own village, and most personal contact was with members of their own clan. With the exception of Saigon in the south, Hanoi in the north, and Hue, the old Imperial capital, near the middle, few places in Vietnam could have been considered to be urban. These clusters of families and clans constituted self-contained units of social conservatism that were strongly resistant to external influences. Yet, in their quiet way, they set the tone of the war. They had no use for outsiders.

At this time, the total population of Vietnam was approximately 30 million, with 14 million in the south. Of those in the south, about a million and a half were Chinese, and more than a million were recent "refugees," or invaders from the north. These northern Vietnamese were neither welcomed by nor well assimilated among southern clans. The southern Vietnamese recognized these invaders, who were mostly of the Catholic faith, by their more Mongoloid or Chinese features. But this was not the problem.

Shortly after establishing the South Vietnamese government under the leadership of Ngo Dinh Diem, the United States transported this enormous tide of northern refugees into the south. Diem was from a Mandarin background and from central Vietnam. He was a staunch Catholic who had been an exile in the United States and Europe under the sponsorship of the Catholic church for many years. A brother, Monseigneur Ngo Dinh Thuc, was the archbishop of Hue and the head of a Catholic clergy of two thousand, including four bishops who served in the provincial regions. This meant that President Diem and his government were much closer to the northern "invaders" than to the southern villagers and landowners.

This influx of over one million northern Catholics was, without question, one of the most inflammatory causes of hostility throughout South Vietnam, as the CIA and its allies intended it to be. The stable, nonmobile natives of the south were overwhelmed by these new arrivals, whom the Diem government favored and had settled on their land, into their established way of life and inflexible economic system.

Almost from the start of his regime, in 1955, Diem initiated land-reform measures by issuing new land ordinances. By means of magna-nimous-sounding actions, the traditional landowners were required to declare their uncultivated land; if they failed to bring any unused holdings into production, the government would seize the land and use it for the settlement of refugees from the north. In this manner Diem "legally" acquired an enormous amount of land for the actual resettle-ment of more than half a million "invaders." Such actions made no friends for Diem in the south and became the basis for much of the violent rioting, called "insurgency," that developed in later years.

By 1959 Diem had instituted another idea. He set up "Agrovilles," which were intended to be semirural communities in which all families could enjoy the amenities of the town and still have their basic garden property. This is an old idea; in fact, one of the underlying, unstated objectives of the thirty-year war in Indochina was to bring about the breakup of this ancient and traditional communal style of living.

The Agroville concept was a failure, primarily because of the continuing friction caused by the burden of the million-plus refugees. Then there was a new development. A plan for the "pacification" of the southernmost region of Vietnam, the Mekong Delta, was proposed to Diem in November 1961, just after General Taylor had left Saigon and returned to Washington.

It was sponsored by R.G.K. Thompson, a British civil servant who had come to Saigon from the position of permanent secretary of defense in Malaya. Diem had issued a request for experienced third-party (non-U.S. and non-Vietnamese) officials to assist him with counterinsurgency problems. Thompson came as part of the British Advisory Mission to Saigon. He began by laying out a plan for the "pacification" of the Mekong Delta region.

"Pacification" is a word that has an ominous meaning in some quarters. Although it may be confused with "pacify" (that is, to calm) or "pacifism" (that is, opposition to war), this is not what it meant in Indochina. There it had taken on a deadly meaning.

"Pacification" became a term drenched in blood. Borrowed from the French commandos in Algeria by U.S. Army Special Forces activists, it meant to hit an area as hard as possible in order that it would be reduced to rubble—that is, "pacified." "Pacification" became the battle cry of the dreaded Phoenix program that was operated under the direction of the CIA in later years.

Thompson may not have had that in mind when he sold the idea to Diem, but the Englishman, who had plenty of experience with pacification in the years of rebellion in Malaya, preached a program that could go either way. Thompson traveled to Washington and gave briefings, attended by this author, on the subjects of: (a) British methods of putting down the rebellion in Malaya and (b) his plan for the pacification of the Mekong Delta by the creation of Strategic Hamlets. These discussions were highly confidential. They centered on basic issues and matters of fundamental concern to the Vietnamese.

There has been a Malthusian movement, concealed at all times from the public, to uproot and destroy the existing and traditional system of communal society in many parts of the world. The activists of this movement fear the strength of the peasant and the ways of peasant life. They much prefer a society of dependent consumers. Indochina and Korea were their prime targets during the post–World War II decades.

Around the world and from ages past, "the peasantry consists of small agricultural producers who with the help of simple equipment and the labor of their families produce mainly for their own consumption and for the fulfillment of obligations to the holders of political and economic power."[1]

This means that there were two opposite views with respect to the development of Strategic Hamlets. To some, they were an attempt to permit the indigenous population to return to a way of life that had been interrupted by World War II. To others, they were places where the hundreds of thousands of refugees from the north could be settled, or where the residents of certain embattled southern areas could be protected from their local enemies, somewhat in the style of the old Indian palisades of early American times.

At the same time, there was another movement in Asia, little noticed in the West, that supported the concept of the "commune," or independent village. Mao Tse-tung had come to power in China in 1949 and had adapted Marxism to Chinese conditions by placing the peasantry, rather than the urban proletariat, in the revolutionary vanguard. This was why so many world leaders feared Mao and his work. Then, in 1957, he launched the "Great Leap Forward." This revolutionary concept, actually a step backward in time, was an unsuccessful attempt to decentralize the economy, chiefly by establishing a nationwide system of people's communes. This move flew in the face of Soviet communism, which—despite its Orwellian name—was actually an anticommune system, or a commune-annihilator system.

The play of this strange mix of ideas was not lost on the various members of the Kennedy administration. Thompson's briefings were well attended and hotly discussed. From the start, it was made clear that Thompson's charter would be limited to matters of "civic action" (another new term, developed from the World War II program of "Civil Affairs and Military Government"), which became a buzzword in Vietnam.

This Orwellian play on words had much to do with the way war-making policy developed in Vietnam. Whereas "civic action" meant just that when used in the context of Thompson's proposal, in other areas of the vast Pentagon universe "civic action" had been adopted by the army's Special Warfare section as an increment of what it called "unconventional warfare."

In Thompson's basic plan, the main governmental aim of the Strategic Hamlet program would be to offer an attractive and constructive alternative to Communist appeals. As noted above, the very choice of words assured that his concept would be received quite differently by various groups and interests.

Thompson's strategy, taken from his successful campaign in Malaya, was what he called "clear and hold" operations. An area would be cleared of opposition—that is, "pacified"—and then, as the Strategic Hamlet, held safely, and the natives would be allowed to return to their normal ways. The object of the Strategic Hamlet, as he proposed it, was to protect the villagers.

President Diem bought this British proposal, and it was, on the whole, enthusiastically received in Washington. A plan entitled "A Strategic Hamlet Concept for South Vietnam," drawn up in the State Department, was well received by General Taylor and presented to President Kennedy. It was at this time that the term "oil spot" entered the military vocabulary. This new concept not only espoused "clear and hold" operations but optimistically proposed that once an area had been cleared and held by the construction of a Stragic Hamlet, the pacified area would expand, like an oil spot on calm water. These new concepts moved forward, and before long everyone on the Vietnamese "desks" was talking "Strategic Hamlets," "oil spots," and "clear and hold." Then Gen. Lionel C. McGarr, the senior army man in Saigon, decided to move ahead with a "test area" where he could establish this new type of "pacification infrastructure."

By that time, early 1962, Diem saw Strategic Hamlets as a national program in which he could install his ambitious brother Ngo Dinh Nhu as the central figure. He had been assured by that time that the U.S. government would provide the financial support needed, along with U.S. military "advisers." Up until this time, during the seventeen years of U.S. support of the conflict, any U.S. military personnel sent to Vietnam had been placed under the operational control of the CIA, with the exception of those assigned to the regular MAAG (Military Assistance Advisory Group). As these new "advisers" came upon the scene in Vietnam, their tactic seemed to be "close with and destroy the enemy." The distinction between this approach and the Thompson concept, which had been approved by the President, became an important factor as the years marched on.

Meanwhile, there were many within the Kennedy administration who began to doubt the advisability of continuing blind support of the Diem regime. Diem made little effort to make his government more popular, and unrest among the people, particularly because of the burden of the 1,100,000 northern refugees, kept the pot boiling.

John Kenneth Galbraith, then ambassador to India and prone to exercise his writing skills on any subject, wrote to his friend, the President: "In my completely considered view... Diem will not reform either administratively or politically in any effective way. That is because he cannot. It is politically naive to expect it. He senses that he cannot let power go because he would be thrown out."

Despite the fact that such thoughts were common among administration officials, the McGarr test program, "Operation Sunrise," was launched in Binh Duong Province on March 22, 1962. The "clear and hold" aspects of the tactical situation were understood, but when it was learned that a new Strategic Hamlet was to be constructed, the whole project came to a halt.

Diem saw Strategic Hamlets as a means to institute basic democracy in Vietnam, where nothing like that had ever existed before. And he added his own Eastern flavor to the concept: "Through the Strategic Hamlet program the government intends to give back to the hamlet [read "commune" in Mao Tse-tung's model] the right of self-government, with its own charter and system of community law. This will realize the ideals of the constitution on a local scale which the people can understand."

To underscore how different Diem's concept was from that of the chairman of the Joint Chiefs of Staff, Gen. Lyman Lemnitzer, we need to see a line from the Pentagon: "The Strategic Hamlet program promises solid benefits, and may well be the vital key to success of the pacification program."

Assistant Secretary of State Averell Harriman added to the weight of these issues: "The government of Vietnam has finally developed, and is now acting upon, an effective strategic concept."

The under secretary of state, George Ball, commented "on the progressive development of strategic hamlets throughout South Vietnam as a method of combating insurgency and as a means of bringing the entire nation under control of the government."

And the secretary of defense, Robert McNamara, added: "The Strategic Hamlet program was the backbone of President Diem's program countering subversion directed against his state."

Nothing could underscore more clearly the conflict that existed on the two sides of the ocean. Diem saw the institution of "basic democracy," "self-government," and "community law." Everyone on the other side of the Pacific was talking about warfare of one kind or another. "Strategic Hamlets" had entered the Orwellian world of "pacification." In a strange and unique way, they symbolized the essential ideological difference between "the West" and "communism" as expressed in the "Cold War."

The new program at Binh Duong got off to a bad start. Only seventy families could be persuaded to volunteer for resettlement, a sign that those families were most likely northern Catholic refugees. Other people were herded forcibly into the hamlet, but they were supposed to have been paid for their former land and for their labor in building this new Strategic Hamlet. In this first hamlet alone, $300,000, provided through the U.S. mission in Saigon never reached the families. (One thing we must realize about the Vietnam War is that it created many illicit millionaires.)

By the time the hamlet was settled, it was discovered that most of the military-age males had disappeared. Startling figures reveal what this Strategic Hamlet program really was. First, there was the massive forced movement of more than one million northern Catholics to the south. This disrupted northern families and overburdened the south. Second, the Strategic Hamlet program further disrupted millions of southerners. These planned, insidious programs, so characteristic of the very roots of the Cold War itself, did as much to destabilize Indochina as the warfare that they caused. Although communism or the threat of communism was the usual excuse for the escalation of the war, the real "subversion" and "rioting" were directly related to these mass movements of a once-stable and immobile population from the north and its enormous impact upon the equally stable and settled people of the south.

In February 1963, a report was given to the President that was drawn to appear cautiously optimistic. It was based upon the expectation that all of the materials needed to complete the Strategic Hamlet program would be delivered during the year and that it was nothing more than the slow delivery of materials that had been delaying the success of the program.

In fact, there was little basis for this optimism. There is no way that such a revolutionary program could have been forced upon these ancient, land-oriented people, who had been uprooted from their ancestral plots and thrust, forcibly, into these new hamlets, whether or not the area around them was hospitable to them, to their traditional society, and to their farming methods.

Many considered these new hamlets to be the equivalent of concentration camps. Whereas they were planned as safe havens for the residents to help them protect themselves from raiding parties of starving hordes—then called "the Vietcong"—they actually became prisons for the inhabitants, who dared not leave these hamlets because of pressure from the government.

Knowing what we do now about the Strategic Hamlets, the million Tonkinese "refugees," and all the rest of the Saigon Military Mission's make-war mission from the CIA, it is staggering to realize that by September 2, 1963, Gen. Maxwell D. Taylor, then the chairman of the

Joint Chiefs of Staff, could write, in a memorandum to the President: "Finally, progress continues with the strategic hamlet program. The latest Government of Vietnam figures indicate that 8,227 of the planned 10,592 hamlets had been completed; 76 percent, or 9,563,370 of the rural population, are now in these hamlets."

The government provided food in vast quantities, medicine, and small-arms ammunition for the inhabitants of these Strategic Hamlets. Because of the enormous number of starving, homeless people wandering around the country, it was inevitable that they would direct their attacks at these well-supplied hamlets. It got so bad that the new hamlet residents would have to leave the hamlet at night as swarms of bandits pillaged these government stockpiles. They were afraid to live there because they were unable to withstand the ever-present threats from the outside.

Diem's idea of "pacification," with its "new democracy" and other benefits, never had a chance. Meanwhile, his brother Nhu began emphasizing government control of the peasantry, at the expense of "pacification" as it was understood in Washington. By this stage, the Kennedy administration had begun to experience serious doubts as to whether the Diem government was "winning the war," or even capable of doing so... on these terms and against that form of "close-in" opposition.

Keep in mind that it is difficult to think back to the Vietnam situation of 1961 and 1962 in terms of what we saw in Vietnam between 1965 and 1975. In 1962, what we now call the Vietnam War was a relatively low level paramilitary activity. All of the combat that in any way involved U.S. armed forces and U.S. personnel was a result of the "advisory" role approved by the President.

To certain military observers, it may have been safe to say that the war was going well, and even safe to predict a time when Diem's forces— with strong U.S. support—would be victorious. On the other hand, there was so much poor planning, corruption, and alienation of the native, indigenous peasants that it appeared there was no way Diem could win and that a Diem-controlled government would be a serious handicap. By the end of 1962, this latter position prevailed in the White House and even in some areas of the Pentagon and State Department.

As the reader will recall from an earlier chapter, helicopters were introduced by the CIA into Vietnam in December 1960. Between December 1960 and March 1963, more than $2 billion in U.S. assistance had been sent in support of the Diem government. By March 1963 the number of U.S. armed forces "advisers" in Vietnam had been increased to 12,000, and there had been sixty-two American deaths.

Up to March 1963, twenty of the helicopters in action in Vietnam had been destroyed by enemy fire, and sixty helicopters had been destroyed as a result of mechanical trouble; twenty-five of the sixty-two Americans who had died there had been killed in helicopter action.

March 1963 was a turning point in this long warfare in Vietnam. During that month the rules of engagement were officially modified to permit Americans to fire at the enemy if they felt themselves "endangered," without having to wait to receive enemy fire. As President Kennedy said at that time, "We are engaged in a civil conflict and a battle with communism."

He had dispatched "advisers" to Vietnam, but he fully recognized the reality of the situation and the position they were in.

Faced with the ambiguities of this situation and the misunderstandings of each other on both sides of the Pacific, by 1963 there arose a feeling within the Kennedy administration that the war should be turned over to Ngo Dinh Diem entirely; or, failing that, that Diem should be replaced. By midsummer 1963, Diem had become more intractable, and the latter view dominated.

During an interview with Walter Cronkite that was broadcast by the CBS television network on the evening of September 2, 1963, President Kennedy said: "I don't think that unless a greater effort is made by the government to win popular support that the war can be won out there. In the final analysis, it is their war. They are the ones who have to win it or lose it. We can help them, we can give them equipment, we can send our men out there as advisers, but they have to win it, the people of Vietnam, against the Communists."

During the broadcast the President made another comment that most Americans seem to have forgotten: "What, of course, makes Americans somewhat impatient is that after carrying this load for eighteen years, we are glad to get counsel, but we would like a little more assistance, real assistance."

These are very significant statements. Kennedy was saying, as John Foster Dulles had said in 1953, that Americans have been actively involved in Vietnam since 1945. But things were different then: In 1945, Vietnam had just been freed from Japanese wartime control; in 1945, Ho Chi Minh had declared the independence of a new Democratic Republic of Vietnam; in 1945 there was no government and no country of South Vietnam. The thought that the people of a place called South

Vietnam in 1963 had the capability to win a war of independence by themselves was preposterous then as it was when President Eisenhower first proposed the idea in January 1954.

It was in this uncertain atmosphere that the next summer of crises erupted in Vietnam. On May 8, 1963, a mass meeting was held in Hue, the ancient imperial capital of Vietnam, to commemorate Buddha's birthday. The government saw this demonstration as a challenge, and the Catholic deputy province chief ordered his troops to fire on the mob. Nine people were killed, and many were injured. The following day, in Hue, more than ten thousand people demonstrated in protest of the killings. On May 10 a manifesto was delivered by the Buddhists to the government in Saigon, and on May 30 about 350 Buddhist monks demonstrated in front of the National Assembly in Saigon.

Then, as feelings rose to a fever pitch, Madame Nhu, by now "the Dragon Lady" in the press of the world, exacerbated the problem by announcing that the Buddhists were infiltrated by Communists. Three days later, the press was alerted to be at a main downtown intersection at noon. On June 11, they were horrified to witness the first immolation suicide of a Buddhist monk in protest of Diem's treatment of his people. Thich Quang Duc's shocking death alarmed the world and electrified Vietnam.

Shortly after midnight on August 21, Ngo Dinh Nhu's U.S.-trained Special Forces shock troops, along with combat police, invaded Buddhist pagodas in Saigon, Hue, and other coastal cities and arrested hundreds of Buddhist monks. Nhu had decided to eliminate Buddhist opposition in his own way. More than fourteen hundred Buddhists, primarily monks, were arrested, and many of them were injured.

At the same time, President Kennedy had dispatched a new ambassador, the veteran Henry Cabot Lodge, to Saigon. After a brief stop in Tokyo, Lodge arrived in Saigon at 9:30 P.M. on August 22, 1963. This date marked the beginning of the most explosive and ominous ninety days in modern U.S. history.

On November 1, 1963, Ngo Dinh Diem and his brother Nhu were killed. On November 22, 1963, President John F. Kennedy died. On that date, November 22, 1963, the government of the United States was taken over by a superpower group that wanted an escalation of the warfare in Indochina and a continuing military buildup for generations to come. Within a few days after the assassination, the trends and policies of the Kennedy administration had started to be changed by the new Johnson administration to assure the achievement of these goals.

The warfare in Vietnam would go on to become a major military disaster—but at a good price: no less than $500 billion in total expenses.

Why did this happen? What had created all the pressure? Why was John F. Kennedy killed?

Around the time Henry Cabot Lodge arrived in Saigon, certain Vietnamese generals began talking with U.S./CIA contacts to determine what the reaction might be to a military coup d'état against the Diem regime. In particular, they were opposed to Ngo Dinh Diem's brother, Nhu, who was the head of the Strategic Hamlet program, and his wife.

Nhu had developed and controlled the CIA-trained Vietnamese Special Forces and had handpicked the generals who commanded the military units around Saigon. None of the plotters wished to attack that strength. Ambassador Lodge sent a message to Washington noting the disaffection with the Diem regime, and particularly with the Nhus, but underscoring that the Saigon generals were still strongly with the Diems.

At about this same time, Adm. Harry Felt, the commander in chief of the Pacific Command, called Washington in support of a strong stand against the Nhus, both Diem's brother and his outspoken wife. Admiral Felt, the senior military commander in the Pacific, was not directly responsible for activities in Vietnam because of the dominant CIA role there. Nevertheless, he followed all developments closely and had his own eyes and ears on the scene.

Shortly after the admiral's call to Washington, this author was called to Hawaii. After a long introductory discussion with Admiral Felt, I was asked to sit at a table in his office as members of his staff brought stacks of intelligence messages in for analysis.

I worked in his office for the entire week, reviewed hundreds of messages and letters, and had many talks with the admiral and his staff. He was vitally concerned with the intelligence situation. He believed that intelligence gathering in Vietnam was very bad and that commanders, both Vietnamese and American, were being forced to make decisions without sufficient military information and without knowing what the actual situation was. This was particularly true at that time. There was much controversy over the status of the actual military situation throughout the country. There was dissatisfaction over Nhu's deplorable attacks on the Buddhists. There were rumors of the possibility of the overthrow of Diem and his government, or at least the overthrow of the Nhus.

At the same time, as the U.S. government debated the pros and cons of getting rid of Diem and his brother, there was another unusual development. It became necessary to meet with leaders of the various factions who would support a coup. Such meetings had to be held secretly for the protection of all parties. Certain CIA agents were selected to attend the meetings. One of the men designated for this delicate responsibility was one of the most enigmatic characters of the thirty-year war: Lucien Conein.

Conein was serving in Vietnam in 1963 as a U.S. Army lieutenant colonel. He was not actually in the U.S. Army, but was a CIA agent assigned to Indochina under the notional cover of a military officer. Conein, born in France, had been educated in the United States. During World War II his duties with the OSS took him to China, where he worked with U.S. Army major general Gallagher, who operated with the nationalist leader of Indochina, Ho Chi Minh.

At the time of the Japanese surrender, it became necessary to fill the vacuum of leadership in Indochina, particularly in Hanoi, for the purpose of rounding up the Japanese troops still there and providing a rallying point for the people of Indochina, who had been under French colonization and later the Japanese occupation. General Gallagher was sent to Hanoi for this purpose and took with him Ho Chi Minh, Col. Vo Nguyen Giap, and the French-speaking Conein. This was 1945.

In early 1954, when Allen Dulles created the Saigon Military Mission for the purpose of infiltrating CIA agents into Indochina under the cover of the U.S. military, he chose his most experienced Far East agent, Edward G. Lansdale, to be in charge of that unit. Among those on the SMM team was Lucien Conein. While Lansdale spent most of his time that year in Saigon with the fledgling Diem administration, Conein was in Hanoi at the same time working against his old associates, Ho Chi Minh and General Giap.

The scope of the activities of the SMM, and of Lansdale and Conein, had been enlarged to include the mounting of "dirty tricks" against the Vietminh, who were led by Ho Chi Minh, and at times against the French. It has always seemed rather strange that the same man who had arrived in Indochina with Ho Chi Minh should have been the one sent back to Hanoi to employ his clandestine skills against the same Ho Chi Minh. Questions have arisen: Did the SMM really work against the Vietminh, or did it work against the French? And why?

At the same time, of course, the SMM was actively instigating the movement of the more than one million Tonkinese to the south.

All of this took place between 1954 and 1963. This same Lucien Conein, who had been designated as the go-between for the anti-Diem plotters—principally Gen. Duong Van Minh and newly installed U.S. ambassador Lodge—had since 1945 been one of the most important agents of the OSS and later the CIA in the Far East. His orders came from that agency. In 1963, nearly twenty years after arriving in Hanoi, he was being employed to encourage the apparatus being formed to eliminate Diem—the man whom the CIA had installed as leader of the new government of the south. This certainly raises a number of questions.

Why did the U.S. government, in 1945, before the end of World War II, choose to arm and equip Ho Chi Minh? Why did the United States, a few short years later, shift its allegiance from Ho Chi Minh to the French in their losing struggle that ended ignominiously with the battle of Dien Bien Phu? Why, after creating the Diem government in 1954 and after supporting that new government for ten years, did the United States shift again and encourage those Vietnamese who planned to overthrow it? And finally, why, after creating an enormous military force in Indochina, did the U.S. government fail to go ahead and defeat this same Ho Chi Minh when, by all traditional standards of warfare, it possessed the means to do so? The answers to these and related questions remain buried in closed files, along with so much other information of that time period.

Negotiations leading to the overthrow of Diem, particularly to the elimination of the Nhus, continued through August 1963 but were not conclusive. An August 31 message from Ambassador Lodge, however, came close to outlining the series of events that became the approved plan.

It had become clear that the war could not be won with the Diem regime in power in Saigon, that the Vietnamese people were not with him. But these conclusions failed to consider the impact of the one-million-plus Tonkinese Catholic "refugees" on the people of South Vietnam and of Diem's callous disregard for the welfare of the indigenous population. U.S. officials never seemed able to understand why the situation, political and military, was much worse in the far south, the Mekong Delta region, than it was in the north and central regions. After all, if the Vietminh in the north were behind the Vietcong enemy in the south, how did it happen that the people farthest from North Vietnam were the most hostile to the Diem government and those nearest to the

North Vietnamese the most peaceful? The answer never surfaced. Most of the one-million-plus refugees had been dumped into the southern districts south of Saigon. That was the simple, undeniable, and most volatile reason. They had become the "insurgents" and the fodder for the insatiable war machine.

Under the burden of these and other questions, President Kennedy set up a train of events that became vitally important and that revealed his own views and his future plans for Vietnam. In the aftermath of the showing of Oliver Stone's movie *JFK*, there were many top columnists, among others, who attempted to have the American public believe that the Kennedy administration had not produced any substantive body of historical fact concerning his plans for Vietnam. They were wrong— dead wrong. It is very interesting to speculate on why these columnists all "circled wagons" with their untenable stories even before *JFK* had been shown in the theaters. What is the source of their common bond?

In response to their contrived questions and to bring to light the facts of the matter, I shall present selected information from the public record and from personal experience. A recently published (1991) book, the *Foreign Relations of the United States*, 1961–63, volume 4, by the Government Printing Office, specifically covers "Vietnam, August–December 1963." This book contains the record of frequent meetings, studies, messages, and travels to and from Saigon by top U.S. officials at the White House, the Department of State, and the Defense Department during that period. These meetings often included Kennedy, McNamara, Rusk, General Taylor, and other high-level administration officials.

At that time my boss was Gen. Victor H. Krulak. He was assigned to the Joint Staff and worked closely with General Taylor and President Kennedy. A review of the above source book will reveal that he was involved in as many as thirty such meetings, messages, and trips on the subject of the future course of the U.S. government in Vietnam. Krulak and I worked closely, and I was involved in much of the preparation of this developing policy. A fact that I recall clearly was that Kennedy was the driving force of these meetings and the "idea man" behind the policy.

Because Kennedy attended a number of these meetings, it will be seen, quite readily, that he was deeply involved in Vietnam planning from 1961 until his death and that the climax of this work came between August and late November 1963. Chief among these records is the

Kennedy-generated National Security Action Memorandum #263 of October 11, 1963, which was developed as a result of the McNamara and Taylor trip to Vietnam during September.

First, the President dispatched General Krulak to Vietnam so that he would be completely up-to-date on matters there, with the purpose of Krulak's writing a "Trip Report" that would contain the new Kennedy policy and any last-minute items that the general would be able to pick up that might not have been apparent to JFK during the last round of meetings in Washington.

Accompanying Krulak was a senior Foreign Service officer, Joseph Mendenhall. What most people in Washington had not noticed was that of all the senior officers in the Pentagon at that time, Krulak had become the one closest to Bobby Kennedy, and through him, to the President. This was not only an official closeness; it was also personal. They understood one another and could work together.

Krulak and Mendenhall made a whirlwind four-day tour of Vietnam and returned with views so opposite from each other's that during the NSC meeting of September 10, President Kennedy asked, "You two did visit the same country, didn't you?" This kind of public small talk about their trip concealed the real significance of what Krulak actually had been asked to accomplish for the President—which unfolded with the next decisions from the White House.

Shortly thereafter, Kennedy announced that he was sending Secretary McNamara and General Taylor, at that time the chairman of the Joint Chiefs of Staff, on another fact-finding mission to Vietnam. Ambassador Lodge did not like the idea, but the President was adamant. The trip was announced on September 21. The two men left on September 23 and were back in Washington on October 2, with a massive report for the President.

On September 29, McNamara, Taylor, Gen. Paul Harkins, Lodge, and Admiral Felt had met with President Ngo Dinh Diem. The next day, most of them had met privately with the Vietnamese vice president, Nguyen Ngoc Tho. Tho was able to inform them about the failure of the Strategic Hamlet program and of the broad-based peasant disaffection with the Diem government. These were the last top-level meetings with President Diem, and from that day forward his days in Saigon were numbered. The decision to remove him had been made. But it had been planned to take effect quite differently than has generally been reported.

McNamara and Taylor left Saigon and returned to Honolulu for a one-day stop "to prepare their report." This was an interesting ingredient of such an official, top-level trip. They had spent a lot of time traveling; they had met people on an unbroken schedule all day long and into the night. And yet, when they returned to Washington, they stepped off the helicopter onto the White House lawn, carrying a huge, leather-bound, fully illustrated official report to the President containing all that they had done during the trip—a report written in one day, during their spare time. Could this be true?

It seems impossible; yet it happened then, and it has happened on other occasions. Let's see how this magic is performed.

When Krulak was sent to Saigon, the President knew that he would come home with all the current data essential for final decision making. But the President wanted to move the decision level up to the top. Therefore, he sent McNamara. While McNamara and Taylor were touring Vietnam, the President, Bobby Kennedy, and General Krulak were setting down the outline of their report—aided by frequent contact with McNamara in Saigon via "back-channel" communications of the highest secrecy—which would contain precisely the major items desired by the President, in the manner in which he wanted them. This report was written and produced in the Pentagon by Krulak and members of his SACSA staff, including this author.

Krulak is a brilliant man and an excellent writer. He set up a unit in his office to write this report. Teams of secretaries worked around the clock. The report was filled with maps and illustrations. It was put together and bound in leather and had gold-leaf lettering for President Kennedy. As soon as it was completed, it was flown to Hawaii to McNamara and Taylor so that they might study it during their eight-hour flight to Washington and present it to the President as they stepped out of the helicopter onto the White House lawn.

The Government Printing Office history text *Vietnam: August–December 1963* includes a brief note about this "Trip Report":

10. Final Report.

a.) Must be completed before return to Washington.
b.) Guides for report are proposed outline prepared by General Krulak and master list of questions consolidated by Mr. Bundy.
c.) To maximum extent, report will be worked out in Saigon. Layover in Honolulu is scheduled for completion of report.

Let no one be misled: This is simply the public record. That McNamara-Taylor report to Kennedy of October 2, 1963, was, in fact, Kennedy's own production. It contained what he believed and what he planned to do to end the Vietnam problem. More important, this Kennedy statement on Vietnam was the first and major plank in his platform for reelection in 1964. This was one of the rising pressure points that led to the decision to assassinate him. A Kennedy reelection could not be permitted.

This report, entitled "Memorandum for the President, Subject: Report of McNamara-Taylor Mission to South Vietnam," and the decisions that it produced played a most important part in the lives of Diem and his brother, in those of President Kennedy and his brother, and in those of the American public because of events that it set in motion. Some of the report's most significant items were:

[The Vietnamese were to]...complete the military campaign in the Northern and Central areas (I, II, and III Corps) by the end of 1964, and in the Delta (IV Corps) by the end of 1965...to include a consolidation of the Strategic Hamlet program.

...train Vietnamese so that essential functions now performed by U.S. military personnel can be carried out by Vietnamese by the end of 1965. It should be possible to withdraw the bulk of U.S. personnel by that time.

...the Defense Department should announce in the very near future presently prepared plans to withdraw 1,000 military personnel by the end of 1963.

Then, revealing the President's plan to remove the Diems from power:

...MAP and CIA support for designated units, now under Colonel Tung's control...will be...transferred to the field. [Col. Le Quang Tung led the CIA-trained Saigon Special Forces loyal to Nhu. This deflated Tung's power.]

This is a Vietnamese war and the country and the war must, in the end, be run solely by the Vietnamese.

With this report in hand, President Kennedy had what he wanted. It contained the essence of decisions he had to make. He had to get reelected to finish programs set in motion during his first term; he had to get Americans out of Vietnam. And he had to make a positive and comprehensive move early in order to accomplish both of these goals.

To achieve his ends, he send Krulak to Saigon first and then followed this with the "official" McNamara and Taylor visit. All of this was made formal with the issuance of National Security Action Memorandum #263 of October 11, 1963, particularly that section that decreed the implementation of "plans to withdraw 1,000 U.S. military personnel by the end of 1963."

Plans continued for the removal—but not the death—of Diem and his brother. Madame Ngo Dinh Nhu had left Saigon on September 9 to attend the Inter-Parliamentary Union meeting in Belgrade, Yugoslavia, with plans to extend the trip to Europe and the United States. With the intercession of the Vatican and the papal delegate in Saigon, Diem's brother, Archbishop Ngo Dinh Thuc, traveled to Rome.

These detailed plans carefully included arrangements for the departure of President Diem and his brother by commercial airliner from Saigon for Europe. This was the most delicate part of the removal plan. The two men actually were driven to the Tan Son Nhut airport, in Saigon, and boarded the [Super-Constellation] plane waiting for them. Then, for some totally unexplained and unaccountable reason, President Diem and his brother turned and left the plane while the few witting Americans on the scene looked on, stunned by their action.

The brothers hurried back to their limousine, which had not yet pulled away from the airport ramp, entered it, and drove back into Saigon and to the Presidential Palace at high speed. There they found themselves alone. Their longtime household and palace guards had fled as soon as they realized that Diem and his brother Nhu had gone. Without them, they were all marked men.

The brothers were alone. They had no troops at their call. All anyone in the government knew was that they were going on a trip. There was no fighting, as would have been normal had the plotters made a move against Diem.

This is how their removal was planned, and this is how close it came to success. But they had returned to an empty palace.

The stark realization struck Diem and his brother: They were alone and deserted in a hostile environment. A tunnel had been dug, for just such purposes, from the palace and under the river to Cholon. They ran through the tunnel to what they thought would be safety and ended up in the hands of their enemies. They were thrown into a small military van, and en route to some unknown destination, they were murdered.

EIGHTEEN

Setting the Stage for the Death of JFK

WHEN I BEGAN TO WORK with Oliver Stone as an adviser for the development of the script of the screenplay for his movie *JFK*, I realized that few Kennedy assassination researchers and writers had ever looked at the scene in Washington during 1961–63 for clues to the answers to the questions, "Why was President John F. Kennedy assassinated? What enormous pressures had arisen to create the necessity for a decision of that magnitude that would not only result in the death of Kennedy, but in the overthrow of the U.S. government?"

I discussed this subject with Stone and he became most interested in that side of the assassination scenario. I had already written letters to Jim Garrison, judge of the Court of Appeal in New Orleans, as I worked with him on his manuscript of his book, *On the Trail of the Assassins*. Garrison had become interested in the subject of my letters and had shown them to his editor, Zachary Sklar, at Sheridan Square Press. Sklar became the screenwriter for Stone's movie *JFK*, and he had discussed my letters with Stone also. It was Garrison who introduced me to Oliver Stone in July 1990.

The significance of all this was that I had introduced President Kennedy's Vietnam policy statement NSAM #263, into these discussions. It is my belief that the policy announced so forcefully by Kennedy in his earlier NSAM #55 and in NSAM #263 had been the major factor in causing the decision by certain elements of the power elite to do away with Kennedy before his reelection and to take control of the U.S. government in the process.

Kennedy's NSAM #263 policy would have assured that Americans by the hundreds of thousands would not have been sent to the war in Vietnam. This policy was anathema to elements of the military-industrial complex, their bankers, and their allies in the government. This policy and the almost certain fact that Kennedy would be reelected President in 1964 set the stage for the plot to assassinate him.

Strong evidence in support of this belief lies in the statements in the previous chapter that are transcribed directly from NSAM #263, and from a description of the deaths of South Vietnam's President Ngo Dinh Diem and his brother Nhu.

First of all, NSAM #263, October 11, 1963, was a crucial White House document. Much of it, guided by White House policy, was actually written by my boss in the Pentagon, General Krulak, myself, and others of his staff. I am familiar with it and with events which led to its creation.

Its cover letter authenticated that policy to the addressees. In this case, McGeorge Bundy prepared and signed the cover letter and dispatched it directly to the secretary of state, the secretary of defense, and the chairman of the Joint Chiefs of Staff. Official copies were made available to the director of central intelligence and the administrator, Agency for Internal Development. These formalities authenticated the President's decision that applied to specific sections of the "Memorandum for the President, Subject: Report of McNamara-Taylor Mission to South Vietnam," dated October 2, 1963.

In order to appreciate what had taken place with the publication of President Kennedy's policy I shall cite the few paragraphs of this NSAM #263 (Document 146 in the *Pentagon Papers*)

At a meeting on October 5, 1963, the President considered the recommendations contained in the report of Secretary McNamara and General Taylor on their mission to South Vietnam.

The President approved the military recommendations contained in Section I B (1-3) of the report, but directed that no formal announcement be made of the implementation of plans to withdraw 1,000 U.S. military personnel by the end of 1963.

After discussion of the remaining recommendations of the report, the President approved an instruction to Ambassador

Lodge which is set forth in State Department telegram No. 534 to Saigon.

What is unusual about this cover letter from McGeorge Bundy is the fact that, although it makes reference to the McNamara-Taylor report, it does not carry or cite an enclosure. Without the report itself in the record this cover letter of NSAM #263 is all but worthless. This fact has confused researchers since that time. The cover letter authenticates the fact that the President had approved only "Section I B (1-3) of the report." In other words, on that date, that was an official statement of the President's Vietnam policy. What does that section say? In the usual source documents of the Pentagon Papers the researcher will have to turn to another section to find Document 142, "Report of McNamara-Taylor Mission to South Vietnam." Here he will discover the cited sections (pertinent items extracted below):

IB(2) A program be established to train Vietnamese so that essential functions now performed by U.S. military personnel can be carried out by Vietnamese by the end of 1965. It should be possible to withdraw the bulk of U.S. military personnel by that time.

IB(3) In accordance with the program to train progressively Vietnamese to take over military functions, the Defense Department should announce in the very near future presently prepared plans to withdraw 1,000 U.S. military personnel by the end of 1963.

In brief, those sections above are the essence of the Kennedy policy that would take men out of Vietnam in 1963 and the bulk of all military personnel out by 1965. At that time, after nearly a generation of involvement in Vietnam, this was a clear signal that Kennedy meant to disengage American military men from Vietnam. This was the bombshell. It made headlines around the world.

On January 15, 1992, Oliver Stone made a speech at the National Press Club in Washington, D.C. This was about one month after the movie had opened in theaters across the country. In this speech Stone said, "Had President Kennedy lived, Americans would not have become deeply involved in the Vietnam War."

For his movie, and for having said things such as the above quote, Oliver Stone was attacked by leading journalists across the country. To this he responded, "Am I a disturber of history... [not] to accept this settled version of history, which must not be disturbed?... No, ladies and gentlemen, this is not history! This is myth! It is a myth that a scant number of Americans have ever believed. It is a myth that a generation of esteemed journalists and historians have refused to examine, have refused to question, and above all, have closed ranks to criticize and vilify those who do."

Stone was right. But the problem goes beyond that which he cited so eloquently. Our history books and the basic sources of history which lie buried in the archives of government documents that have been concealed from the public and, worse still, government documents that have been tampered with and forged. As I have just demonstrated above, this most important policy statement, NSAM #263, that so many historians and journalists say does not exist, has been divided into two sections in the Pentagon Papers source history. One section is no more than the simple cover letter, and the other section, pages away in the record, is presented by its simple title as a "report" with no cross-reference whatsoever to the fact that it is the basic substance of President Kennedy's Vietnam policy. Such things are no accident. The record of the Kennedy administration has been savagely distorted in basic government documents and by so-called historians who have accepted the myths to be found on the record.

I have cited these facts with care in order to demonstrate what the original presidential policy was and to compare it with what has been done with it since those days by those who wish to conceal and obfuscate the facts of the Kennedy administration by means of such grandiose "cover story" creations as the *Pentagon Papers*, the *Report of the Warren Commission*, and the whole family of historical publications both from governmental and private sources. As we have seen repeatedly, the cover-story aspect of the plot to kill the President is much the more serious and elaborate task of the whole plan. Furthermore, as we have seen as a result of Oliver Stone's movie *JFK*, the cover-story activity lives on today.

When the "Department of Defense Study of American Decisionmaking on Vietnam," as the *Pentagon Papers* study is called officially, was completed in January 1969, it was said to be highly classified and did not become available to the public until Daniel Ellsberg, who had worked in Vietnam with Lansdale and Conein, found a way to make the documents available to certain major newspapers in June 1971. While the Nixon administration was bringing charges against Ellsberg and the newspapers in order to suppress their use, Senator Mike Gravel obtained a complete set of these documents and, over a period of days, read them into the *Congressional Record* as a way of making them available to the public.

In his introduction to this four-volume compilation Senator Gravel said:

> The Pentagon Papers tell of the purposeful withholding and distortion of facts. There are no military secrets to be found here, only an appalling litany of faulty premises and questionable objectives, built one upon the other over the course of four administrations, and perpetuated today by a fifth administration.
>
> The Pentagon Papers show that we have created, in the last quarter century, a new culture, a national security culture, protected from the influences of American life by the shield of secrecy.

This was 1971. In 1991, after time enough to permit government historians to correct the brazen errors and omissions of the record of the Vietnam era, the Office of the Historian in the Bureau of Public Affairs of the Department of State has published a new document, "Vietnam August–December 1963." Even in this new publication, the presentation of NSAM #263 is unclear. On page 395 it publishes document #194, National Security Action Memorandum #263 in the form presented above. Then without any cross-referencing data whatsoever, on page 336, it presents Document #167: Memorandum From the Chairman of the Joint Chiefs of Staff (Taylor) and the Secretary of Defense (McNamara) to the President, Subject: Report of McNamara–Taylor Mission to South Vietnam. Then to further obfuscate the record, this State Department publication omits crucial elements of the trip report entirely. Instead of improving the historical record with the passage of time, the authors are further distorting it. There can be but one conclusion. Almost three decades later the cover story lives on, and records of the Kennedy era, in particular, are the hardest hit.

The deaths of President Ngo Dinh Diem and his brother Nhu in Saigon on November 1, 1963, were considered a Vietnamese internal affair during most of the decade that followed, but on September 16, 1971, President Richard Nixon made a statement that revived those events and put them in a different light. Sen. Harry "Scoop" Jackson of Washington, a strong possibility as the Democratic candidate against Nixon in 1972, had suggested that the United States might be in a position to exert discreet pressure upon President Nguyen Van Thieu of

South Vietnam to move toward a more democratic form of government and to settle the warfare in Indochina.

That same day, President Nixon, when questioned by Peter Lisagor of the *Chicago Daily News* about the Jackson statement, responded, "If what the senator is suggesting is that the United States should use its leverage now to overthrow Thieu, I would remind all concerned that the way we got into Vietnam was through overthrowing Diem, and the complicity in the murder of Diem; and the way to get out of Vietnam, in my opinion, is not to overthrow Thieu."

Nixon had put a match to the fuse, and the bomb was certain to explode. The "Pentagon Papers" had been published just three months prior to this exchange, and some of those carefully screened documents did appear to show that the Kennedy administration had had a role in the overthrow of Diem in 1963. But until this Nixon comment, no public official had openly suggested the Kennedy administration was guilty of complicity in Diem's murder.

It was not long after this press conference that a CIA agent, Howard Hunt, then working as a consultant to Charles Colson, Nixon's jack-of-all-trades, mentioned several of the highly classified messages contained in the Pentagon Papers, specifically those that referred to White House action relative to Diem's death. Hunt suggested to Colson that it might be possible to alter those messages, in White House files, so that anyone using them for research in later years would "discover" that President Kennedy had, beyond doubt, ordered the murder of President Diem.

Colson, the man who had said that he would walk over his own grandmother if it would help the reelection of Nixon, took no action to stop his crafty consultant from trying to see what he could do with those messages.

These events, among so many others at the time, underscored the nature of the pressures that had been brought to bear on President Diem in Saigon and President Kennedy in Washington during those fateful months of October and November 1963. They also demonstrated the deep animosity that still existed between Nixon and the Kennedys. As this example shows, there were in the Nixon camp those who would not stop at forgery to achieve their goal of destroying the Kennedy historical record.

This was a role played quite willingly by Howard Hunt, who was as bitter about the Kennedys as was Nixon. Despite the unclear account of the assassination of the Diems that appears in the Pentagon Papers, and because of the totally false record that resulted from the forgery of the White House records, the extent of the Kennedy role in U.S. govern- ment plans to remove the Diems from power has been stated clearly and authoritatively by those familiar with it.

As mentioned earlier, Diem had made it quite clear what his goals with the Strategic Hamlet program were. His position did not jibe with those who wanted to escalate the war in Indochina and who were not at all interested in the introduction of an ancient form of self-government into the battle-scarred countryside.

On top of this came Kennedy's desire to get the United States out of Indochina by the end of 1965, as evidenced by his orchestration of a series of events such as the Krulak-Mendenhall visit to Vietnam in September 1963. By late summer, and certainly by the time of the McNamara-Taylor trip, closely held plans had progressed for the removal of the Diems from Saigon. President Kennedy had reached the decision that the United States should do all it could to train, equip, and finance the government of South Vietnam to fight its own war, but that this would be done for someone other than Ngo Dinh Diem.

On the same day that the President received this McNamara–Taylor report, Gen. Tran Van Don had his first "accidental" (it had been carefully planned) meeting with the CIA's Lt. Col. Lucien Conein at Tan Son Nhut airport in Saigon. This was a meeting of great signifi- cance, and one that to this day has never been properly explained. General Don was the commander of the South Vietnamese army. He had been born and educated in France and had served in the French army during World War II. He and Conein were well acquainted.

Nearly twenty years later, in 1963, the CIA designated Conein, one of its most valuable agents in the Far East, to meet with his old friend of eighteen years, Gen. Tran Van Don, to arrange for the ouster of President Diem. Only ten years earlier, Gen. Edward G. Lansdale and Conein had worked hard to get Ngo Dinh Diem started as the newly assigned president of South Vietnam.

Conein's task was to stay close enough to key Vietnamese to assure them that the United States would not interfere with their plan to move in as soon as President Diem had left Saigon, and to keep Ambassador Henry Cabot Lodge and Conein's own CIA associates informed.

The plan prepared by the United States had been carefully drawn to leave Diem no alternative except to leave on this scheduled trip. There was much discussion and argument among members of the Kennedy administration, who knew of the President's intention to oust Diem once he had left the country. With Madame Nhu and Archbishop Thuc already in Europe, Diem and his brother were to follow to attend a meeting of the Inter-Parliamentary Union in Belgrade, Yugoslavia.

The evacuation plan, carefully orchestrated under Kennedy's direction, broke down, and Ngo Dinh Diem and his brother were murdered. There have been many accounts of this coup d'état. They do not tell the role that Kennedy played in the story, and many were created to cover the real plan and to protect those Vietnamese who had worked closely with the administration.

I was on duty in the Joint Chiefs of Staff section of the Pentagon on the day of the coup d'état. My immediate boss, General Krulak, knew the full details of the plan to remove Diem from the scene by flying him and his brother out of Saigon. Krulak remained in contact with the White House as developments in Saigon were relayed. I can recall clearly the absolute shock in our offices when it was learned that Diem had not left on the proffered aircraft for Europe.

One of the most important narratives of this event was written by Edward G. Lansdale in his autobiography *In the Midst of Wars*. Few Americans, if any, knew Ngo Dinh Diem and the situation in Vietnam from 1954–68 better than Ed Lansdale. He wrote:

As the prisons filled up with political opponents, as the older nationalist parties went underground, with the body politics fractured, Communist political cadre became active throughout South Vietnam, recruiting followers for action against a government held together mainly by the Can Lao elite rather than by popular support. The reaped whirlwind finally arrived in November 1963, when the nationalist opposition erupted violently, imprisoning many of the Can Loa and killing Diem, Nhu, and others. It was heartbreaking to be an onlooker to this tragic bit of history.

It was some time before the news became known that Diem had fled to Cholon and been captured and killed there. This news was flashed around the world; this was the story that everyone heard. The public never heard of the planned flight to Europe that the Kennedy administration had arranged for him.

Thus it was that the file of routine cable traffic between Washington and Saigon eventually became known with the release and publication of the Pentagon Papers. This is how it happened that Howard Hunt was able to locate certain top-level messages to and from the White House and Ambassador Lodge in Saigon that contained information referring to "highest authority"—the cable traffic code for President Kennedy.

None of these messages contained any reference to a plot to kill President Diem and his brother or came even close to it. Concealed within these messages were carefully worded phrases that gave Ambassador Lodge the information he needed in order to direct all participants into action and to begin the careful removal of the two brothers to Europe by commercial aircraft.

According to information that came out during the Watergate hearings, those files that had been forged to smear President Kennedy were put in Hunt's White House safe, where they remained until discovered by investigators later.

There is much about this episode that has become important upon review. There are those who have been so violently opposed to Jack Kennedy and all that he stood for that they have stooped to all kinds of sordid activities to smear him while he was alive, to attack his brother Bobby while he was still alive, and to hound Sen. Edward Kennedy to this day. Nixon's gratuitous reference to Kennedy's "complicity in the murder of Diem" after a decade of silence on that subject speaks for itself. The efforts of Howard Hunt and Chuck Colson (both employees of the White House at the time) to dig up old files in order to besmirch the memory of President Kennedy provide another example.

In an ominous way, the Pentagon Papers and Watergate episodes were cut from the same fabric, and most important, their exposure was a direct outgrowth of the nationwide dissatisfaction with the Vietnam War. Because the development of the war in Indochina had been spread out so long, since 1945, and because most of the events that brought about this terrible form of modern genocide in the name of "anti-communism" or "containment" were buried in deep secrecy or not even available in written records, Robert S. McNamara, then secretary of defense, directed, on June 17, 1967, that a task force be formed to collate and study the history of U.S. involvement in Vietnam from World War II to the present.

This project, which produced thousands of documents of all kinds from many sources, was the primary source of that group of more than four thousand documents that were surreptitiously released to various news media and called the Pentagon Papers. Almost four years later, on June 13, 1971, the *New York Times*, the *Washington Post*, and the *Boston Globe*, among others, started the serialization of the Pentagon Papers.

Few people have been more articulate on the subject than the then senator from Alaska, Mike Gravel:

> The Pentagon Papers reveal the inner workings of a government bureaucracy set up to defend this country, but now out of control, managing an international empire by garrisoning American troops around the world. It created an artificial client state in South Vietnam, lamented its unpopularity among its own people, eventually encouraged the overthrow of that government, and then supported a series of military dictators who served their own ends, and at times our government's ends, but never the cause of their own people.

In his brilliant introduction the senator included an extract from the works of the English novelist and historian, H. G. Wells, who once wrote:

> The true strength of rulers and empires lies not in armies or emotions, but in the belief of men that they are inflexibly open and truthful and legal. As soon as a government departs from that standard, it ceases to be anything more than "the gang in possession" and its days are numbered.

The publication of the Pentagon Papers became an event unique in American history. One day after their publication had begun in the *New York Times*, I received a call from the British Broadcasting Corporation requesting that I travel to London to participate in a series of programs, live on prime-time TV, with Daniel Ellsberg. I did travel to London and did take part in a daily series on the subject, but Ellsberg did not participate in the broadcasts, because his lawyer advised him not to leave the country at that time.

In this book, I have used various editions of the Pentagon Papers as reference material. They are useful and they are quite accurate as far as individual documents go, but they are dangerous in the hands of those who do not have the experience or the other sources required to validate and balance their content. This is because their true source was only marginally the Pentagon and because the clever selection of those documents by the compilers removed many important papers. This neglect of key documents served to reduce the value of those that remained to tell the story of the Vietnam War. From the beginning, the

Pentagon Papers were a compilation of documents designed to paint President John F. Kennedy as the villain of the story, and to shield the role of the CIA.

This vast stack of papers has been labeled the Pentagon Papers, but that is a misnomer. It is quite true that most of them were found in certain highly classified files in the Pentagon, but they were functionally limited files. For example, despite their volume—nearly four thousand documents—there are remarkably few that actually bear the signature of military officers. In fact, many of those that carry the signature of a military officer, or that refer to military officers, make reference to such men as Edward G. Lansdale, who actually worked for the CIA while serving in a cover assignment with the military. When such papers are removed from the "military" or "Pentagon" categorization, what remains is a nonmilitary and non-Pentagon collection. For the serious and honest historian, this becomes an important distinction. To be truly "Pentagon" Papers, the majority of them, at least, ought to have been written there.

In a letter to the then secretary of defense, Clark Clifford, dated January 15, 1969, Leslie H. Gelb, director of the Study Task Force that assembled the Pentagon Papers, said: "In the beginning, Mr. McNamara gave the task force full access to OSD [Office of the Secretary of Defense] files, and the task force received access to CIA materials, and some use of State Department cables and memoranda. We had no access to the White House files."

Despite this disclaimer, there are many White House files in the Pentagon Papers—and it was this group of documents, in fact, that was the source of the anti-Kennedy forgeries.

The files from which most of these papers were obtained were in that section of the Office of the Secretary of Defense called International Security Affairs. Although this office was in the Pentagon, it was lightly staffed with military officers, and most of its activities concerned other government departments and agencies, such as the CIA, the Department of State, and the White House. That is why its files consisted of papers that originated outside the Pentagon, giving the Pentagon Papers production an entirely nonmilitary slant.

Another reason for caution regarding the utilization of the Pentagon Papers as history is that, as Gelb said, "These outstanding people [those who worked on the task force] came from everywhere—the military services, State, OSD, and the 'think tanks.' Some came for a month, for three months, for six months...in all, we had thirty-six professionals working on these studies, with an average of four months per man."

That says it all! They had become experts in four months!

John Foster Dulles, formerly secretary of state, once declared that one of the most complicated periods in this nation's history began in Indochina on September 2, 1945. There is no way that this group, averaging "four months per man" in its studies in 1967, and 1968, was going to be qualified to present a true and accurate account of that war by the compilation of a scattering of papers that contained bits and pieces of the story.

This reveals one of my greatest misgivings concerning the accuracy of the study. There are altogether too many important papers that did not get included in this study, too many that were absolutely crucial to an understanding of the origins of, and reasons for, this war.

This has been a complaint of historians who have attempted to teach the facts of this war. They have found that the history book accounts of it have been written by writers who were not there, who had little or nothing to do with it—or, conversely, that they have been written by those who were there, but who were there for a one-year tour of duty, usually in the post-1965 period. Few of these writers have had the comprehensive experience that is a prerequisite to understanding that type of contemporary history.

Regarding the Pentagon Papers themselves, Senator Gravel wrote:

> The Papers do not support our good intentions. The Papers prove that, from the beginning, the war has been an American war, serving to perpetuate American military power in Asia. Peace has never been on the American agenda for Southeast Asia. Neither we nor the South Vietnamese have been masters of our Southeast Asian policy; we have been its victims, as the leaders of America sought to preserve their reputation for toughness and determination.

He added:

> The elaborate secrecy precautions, the carefully contrived subterfuges, the precisely orchestrated press leaks, were intended not to deceive "the other side," but to keep the American public in the dark....For too long they have been forced to subsist on a diet of half-truths or deliberate deceit by executives who consider the people of the Congress as adversaries."[1]

It is important to understand the Pentagon Papers' subtle anti-Kennedy slant. Nothing reveals this bias more than the following extract

taken from the section "The Overthrow of Ngo Dinh Diem, May–
November 1963."

At the end of a crucial summary of the most momentous ninety-day
period in modern American history, from August 22 to November 22,
1963, this is what the authors of the Pentagon Papers had to say:

> After having delayed an appropriate period, the U.S. recognized
> the new government on November 8. As the euphoria wore off,
> however, the real gravity of the economic situation and the lack of
> expertise in the new government became apparent to both
> Vietnamese and American officials. The deterioration of the
> military situation and the Strategic Hamlet program also came
> more and more clearly into perspective.
>
> These topics dominated the discussions at the Honolulu con-
> ference on November 20 when [Henry Cabot] Lodge and the
> country team [from Vietnam] met with [Dean] Rusk, [Robert]
> McNamara, [Maxwell] Taylor, [George] Ball, and [McGeorge]
> Bundy. But the meeting ended inconclusively. After Lodge had
> conferred with the President a few days later in Washington, the
> White House tried to pull together some conclusions and offer
> some guidance for our continuing and now deeper involvement in
> Vietnam. The instructions contained in NSAM 273, however, did
> not reflect the truly dire situation as it was to come to light in
> succeeding weeks. The reappraisals forced by the new information
> would swiftly make it irrelevant as it was overtaken by events.

Recall what had been going on during that month of November 1963.
President Ngo Dinh Diem and his brother had been murdered, and the
administration of South Vietnam had been placed in the hands of Gen.
Duong Van "Big" Minh. Then, in one of the strangest scenarios of recent
history, most of the members of the Kennedy cabinet had flown to
Honolulu, together, for that November 20 series of conferences. The full
cabinet meeting—even the secretary of agriculture was there—in
Hawaii was to be followed by a flight to Tokyo on November 22. Again,
almost all of the Kennedy cabinet members were on that flight to Tokyo.
They were on that aircraft bound for Tokyo when they learned that
President Kennedy had been shot dead in Dallas. Upon receipt of that
stunning news, they ordered the plane to return directly to Hawaii and,
almost immediately, on to Washington.

But consider here the strange and impersonal words used by this
"official history." The Pentagon Papers, in its long section on the events
of that tragic period, ends its own narrative report of those events by

saying: "But probably more important, the deterioration of the military situation of the Vietnamese position...."

What could have been the basis for that conclusion? What caused the Papers' authors to say that in 1968? Let's look at the record from the pages of their own work:

1) On September 11, 1963, Ambassador Henry Cabot Lodge had cabled to Secretary Rusk saying:

   "I do not doubt the military judgment that the war in the countryside is going well now."

2) On September 16, 1963, President Kennedy had written a personal letter to President Ngo Dinh Diem in which he said:

   "... the contest against the Communists in the last year and one half has gradually but steadily turned in our favor."

3) On September 29, 1963, Secretary McNamara and General Taylor met for three hours with President Ngo Dinh Diem in Saigon. As reported, President Diem said:

   "The war was going well, thanks in large measure to the strategic hamlets program... " Diem concluded his optimistic presentation by noting that "although the war was going well, much remained to be done in the Delta area" [where most of the Tonkinese had been sent].

4) Then we have the McNamara/Taylor "Trip Report" of October 2, 1963, that became the body of NSAM #263 on October 11, 1963, that concludes:

   #1. "The military campaign has made great progress and continues to progress.

   #2. "A program be established to train Vietnamese so that essential functions now performed by U.S. military personnel can be carried out by Vietnamese by the end of 1965. It should be possible to withdraw the bulk of U.S. personnel by that time.

   #3. "... the Defense Department should announce in the very near future presently prepared plans to withdraw 1,000 U.S. military personnel by the end of 1963.

   #6. "... We believe the U.S. part of the task can be completed by the end of 1965."

News of this "White House Report" was splashed across the front page of the U.S. armed forces *Pacific Stars and Stripes* newspaper of October 4, 1963, in banner headlines: U.S. TROOPS SEEN OUT OF VIET BY '65.

These are quotes taken from official documents of that time, all taking an optimistic view of the war by the leaders closest to it and including statements by President Kennedy and President Diem. The official Kennedy White House policy document, National Security Action Memorandum #263, was dated October 11, 1963, and there is no evidence that the situation, as perceived by Kennedy and his closest advisers, had changed over the next month. General Krulak was as close to the President and his policy as he had ever been, and I worked directly with General Krulak on the Joint Staff. We never heard of any changes in plans from the White House.

Just four days after Kennedy's death and less than sixty days after Kennedy published NSAM #263, which visualized the Vietnamization of the war and the return of all American personnel by the end of 1965, Lyndon Johnson and most of the JFK cabinet viewed the situation in an entirely different light. In Johnson's NSAM #273 they saw the military situation deteriorating ("the deterioration of... the Strategic Hamlet program") and all of a sudden saw the program as a failure. ("These topics dominated the discussions at the Honolulu Conference on November 20....")

This is a remarkable statement. On that date, John Kennedy was still alive and President of the United States. Yet this report says that his cabinet had been assembled in Honolulu to discuss "these topics"—the very same topics of NSAM #273, dated November 26, and a vital step on the way to a total reversal of Kennedy's own policy, as stated in the Taylor-McNamara report and in NSAM #263, dated October 2, 1963. The total reversal was completed with the publication of NSAM #288, March 26, 1964.

This situation cannot be treated lightly. How did it happen that the Kennedy cabinet had traveled to Hawaii at precisely the same time Kennedy was touring in Texas? How did it happen that the subject of discussion in Hawaii, before JFK was killed, was a strange agenda that would not come up in the White House until after he had been murdered? Who could have known, beforehand, that this new—non-Kennedy—agenda would be needed in the White House because Kennedy would no longer be President?

Is there any possibility that the "powers that be" who planned and executed the Kennedy assassination had also been able to get the

Kennedy cabinet out of the country and to have them conferring in Hawaii on an agenda that would be put before President Lyndon Johnson just four days after Kennedy's death?

President Kennedy would not have sent his cabinet to Hawaii to discuss that agenda. He had issued his own agenda for Vietnam on October 11, 1963, and he had no reason to change it. More than that, he had no reason at all to send them all to Hawaii for such a conference. It is never good practice for a President to have key members of his cabinet out of town while he is on an extended trip. Why was the cabinet in Hawaii? Who ordered the cabinet members there? If JFK had no reason to send them to Hawaii, who did, and why?

Keep in mind, through this series of vitally important questions, that we are piling circumstance upon circumstance. It is the body of circumstantial evidence that proves the existence of conspiracy.

As soon as the Honolulu conference broke up, these same cabinet members departed from Hawaii on an unprecedented trip to Japan. No one has explained why the Kennedy cabinet was ordered to Japan at that time.

This trip to Japan was not some casual event. Someone had arranged it with care. A reading of newspapers from late November 1963 reveals that extracts of speeches supposedly given by some of these cabinet officers in Japan were made available and then printed, for example, even in the Washington, D.C., *Star*.

We all know now that these cabinet officers did not reach Japan and that their VIP aircraft returned to Hawaii. Why would newspapers in the United States print extracts of their speeches as though they actually had gone to Japan and delivered those speeches? Who had set this trip up so meticulously that even such details as the press releases appeared to validate the presence of the cabinet members in Japan when in fact they never went there?

Continuing this account of the period, the chronology prepared by the authors of the Pentagon Papers lists the following:

> 22 November 1963: Lodge confers with the President. Having flown to Washington the day after the conference, Lodge meets with the President and presumably continues the kind of report given in Honolulu.
>
> 23 November 1963 NSAM #273: Drawing together the results of the Honolulu Conference, and Lodge's meeting with the President, NSAM #273 reaffirms the U.S. commitment to defeat the VC in South Vietnam....

These are astounding statements, considering that they were written sometime in 1968, when everyone knew that the most important fact of those two days was the assassination of President Kennedy on November 22, 1963. This massive compilation of official documents produced by Secretary McNamara's "task force... to study the history of United States involvement in Vietnam from World War II to the present" (1969) totally ignored the assassination.

The Pentagon Papers say simply, "Lodge confers with the President," as though it were just another day in the life of a President. Which President? Didn't that matter? What a way to dismiss Kennedy and his tragic death! This entire section of the Pentagon Papers, which were commissioned to be a complete account of the history of the Vietnam war period, cannot find a word to say about that assassination. This official history simply skips all mention of the death of the President of the United States and tells the story of the death of Diem as though it had occurred in a vacuum.

Why do you suppose Leslie Gelb, director of the Pentagon Papers Study Task Force, chose to close his "Letter of Transmittal of the Study" with this quote from Herman Melville's *Moby-Dick*: "This is a world of chance, free will, and necessity—all interweavingly working together as one; chance by turn rules either and has the last featuring blow at events."

Then, as if to introduce some reality into the study, he closes with this remarkable thought: "Our studies have tried to reflect this thought; inevitably in the organizing and writing process, they appear to assign more and less to men and free will than was the case."

This sounds more and more like the "God throws the dice" syndrome. What could Les Gelb have been thinking about when he saw "chance" taking "the last featuring blow at events?" Did the Vietnam War happen by "chance"? Was President John F. Kennedy killed by "chance"? That takes a strange view of history. When Oliver Stone's movie asked, "Why was Kennedy killed?" I doubt that anyone in the audience would have answered, "By chance."

This "Letter of Transmittal" of January 15, 1969, was addressed to Clark M. Clifford, secretary of defense and a man we have quoted frequently during this work.

These questions and the subjects they unfold are the things of which assassinations and coups d'état are made. The plotters worked out their plans in detail as they moved to take over the government that Kennedy had taken from them. As a result, every other public official became a pawn on that master chess board. Assassinations and coups d'état permeate and threaten all levels of society.

These may be entirely speculative questions, but they are based upon a close reading of the subject and firsthand knowledge of the times. They are presented here for the consideration of the reader. Let the record speak for itself. It is unfortunate that most historians have not looked more carefully at Kennedy's NSAMs from NSAM #55 in July 1961 through NSAM #263 in October 1963; or at NSAM #273 of November 26, 1963, and its draft of November 21, 1963, or at the enormous pressures that all of these documents created. If anyone had wished to zero in on the key to the source of the decision for the "Why?" and the "Who?" of that assassination, he would not have needed to go much further.

In concluding this chapter, it may be well to add a few more words. I was on Okinawa in 1945 and observed the shipments of arms being loaded onto U.S. Navy transport vessels for shipment to Haiphong Harbor in Indochina, where, as we have seen, they were given to Ho Chi Minh under the auspices of the OSS.

I was in Vietnam many times during 1952, 1953, and 1954. I saw that serenely beautiful country go from a placid recreation area for wounded and hospitalized American soldiers fighting in Korea to a hotbed of turmoil after the defeat of the French forces at Dien Bien Phu, the division of the country into two parts, the forced movement of more than one million Catholic northern Tonkinese to the south, and the establishment of the Diem administration. During this period I had frequent contact with the members of the CIA's Saigon Military Mission.

Then, from 1955 through 1963, I was in the Pentagon. I served as chief of special operations for the U.S. Air Force for five years, providing air force support of the clandestine operations of the CIA. I was assigned to the Office of Special Operations in the Office of the Secretary of Defense for the next two years, and then I was directed to create the Special Operations Office for the Joint Chiefs of Staff in order to bring that military support work under the guidance of a single "focal point" office. I headed that office until 1964, when I retired after the death of President Kennedy.

By the fall of 1963, I knew perhaps as much as anyone about the inner workings of this world of special operations. I had written the formal directives on the subject that were used officially by the U.S. Air Force and by the Joint Chiefs of Staff for all military services.

Therefore, it seemed strange when I was approached after I had come back from a week spent reading intelligence papers in Admiral Felt's headquarters in Hawaii, during September 1963, and informed that I had been selected to be the military escort officer for a group of VIP civilian guests that had been invited to visit the naval station in Antarctica and the South Pole facility at McMurdo Sound. This group was scheduled to leave on November 10, 1963, and to return by the end of the month.

Although this trip had absolutely nothing to do with my previous nine years of work, except that I had supported CIA activity in Antarctica over the years, I appreciated the invitation and looked forward to the trip as a "paid vacation."

After we went to the South Pole and returned to Christchurch, New Zealand, a member of the VIP party, a congressman, asked me if I would like to go with him on a two-day side trip to the beautiful New Zealand Alps and to the Hermitage Chalet at the foot of Mount Cook, the highest mountain in the country. I said yes.

On the first morning of our visit I was about to have breakfast in a dining room of rare beauty, offering as it did a dazzling view of Mount Cook and the nearby range. I had secured a table for the two of us and had ordered coffee. The public-address announcer had been reading off the list of passengers to be taken to the top of Mount Cook by small aircraft for the ski ride back down when he broke off his announcements to say: "Ladies and gentlemen, the BBC have announced that President Kennedy has been shot...dead...in Dallas."

That is how I learned of the assassination of the President and of the start of the strange events surrounding that murder and the takeover of our government as a result of that brazen act.

I have always wondered, deep in my own heart, whether that strange invitation that removed me so far from Washington and from the center of all things clandestine that I knew so well might have been connected to the events that followed. Were there things that I knew, or would have discovered, that made it wise to have me far from Washington, along with others, such as the Kennedy cabinet, who were in midair over the Pacific Ocean en route to Japan, far from the scene?

I do not know the answer to that question, although many of the things that I have observed and learned from that time have led me to surmise that such a question might be well founded. After all, I knew that type of work very well. I had worked on presidential protection and knew the great extent to which one goes to ensure the safety of the chief executive. Despite all this, established procedures were ignored on the President's trip to Dallas on November 22, 1963.

It seems that those who planned the murder of the President knew the inner workings of the government very well. This fact is made evident not so much by the skill with which the murder of the President was undertaken as by the masterful cover-up program that has continued since November 22, 1963, and that terrible hour in Dallas's Dealey Plaza when the warfare in Indochina moved from a low-intensity conflict, as seen by President Kennedy, to a major operation—a major war—in the hands of the Johnson administration.

NINETEEN

Visions of a Kennedy Dynasty

BY NOVEMBER 1963, the Kennedy administration had begun to weave subtle changes into the fabric of American life and politics. John F. Kennedy, the first Roman Catholic U.S. President, had been elected to office in November 1960 over the incumbent vice president, Richard M. Nixon, by the narrowest margin in history. As his third year in office drew to a close, Kennedy sensed that his popularity had increased and that his chances for reelection in 1964 were good.

He had not left the possibility of his reelection to fate. From the beginning of his presidency, he had poured billions of Defense Department contract dollars into a savvy plan that benefited the voting districts of the country that were most important to him. He was skillfully changing the method of assigning military contracts, much to the alarm of the powerful arms industry.

By 1963, Kennedy was telling confidants what some of his actions would be following his reelection. One of his memorable statements was that he planned to splinter the CIA into a thousand pieces and scatter it to the winds. Another was that he would end American military participation in the conflict in Indochina.

He was pragmatic enough to know that once he was reelected, he could do things more effectively than he could with the uncertainties of the election process ahead of him. He sensed the nation's growing discontent with the undercover warfare in Indochina. He saw this discontent as part of a pattern of rebellion against the Cold War.

Furthermore, as the son of the former American ambassador to the Court of St. James's in London, President Kennedy's interests and instincts were always slanted more toward Europe than to the lands of the Pacific Basin. This, too, created friction among the strong and growing "Pacific Rim" interests of the financial and industrial world.

Kennedy understood the will of the people. He was building an administration designed to respond to that will. Not since the days of Franklin D. Roosevelt had a President so moved a nation—and the world, for his popularity didn't end at the shores of the Atlantic and the Pacific. He was recognized, admired, and loved as few leaders have been. However, as his popularity increased and as his reforms began to take root and grow, other forces came into play. Powerful interest groups began to join in a cabal against the young American President.

On November 22, 1963, less than a year before his probable reelection to four more years as President, John F. Kennedy was struck down. From all indications, he was killed by a team of gunmen hired as part of a detailed plot to terminate the Kennedy political initiatives— which had the appearance of establishing a political dynasty—and to direct the powers of the presidency back into Cold War activities and into the hands of more amenable "leaders." There can be no doubts: The Kennedy murder was the result of a coup d'état brought about by a professional team equally skilled in the field of "cover story" and deception activities as it was in murder. We may recall that Lyndon Johnson said, in 1973, "We had been operating a damned Murder Inc. in the Caribbean" (or, as they call them in the CIA, "Mechanics").

What were the circumstances that led to such drastic action?

Kennedy's plans for reelection were based in large measure on the allocation of billions of Defense Department dollars available in the Tactical Fighter Experimental (TFX) construction program. This money was going to states and counties that had had the closest balloting during the 1960 election. The $6.5 billion TFX budget made it the largest government contract ever put together in peacetime.

In the process of divvying up the funds, Kennedy had made it clear to the gnomes of the military-industrial complex that he was in control and that they were not. This raised the pressure for the ultimate confrontation between the President and a cabal of extremely powerful financial and industrial groups.

During the Kennedy years, people within the government and their close associates in academia and industry discussed frequently and quite seriously many of the major questions phrased by Leonard Lewin in

Report From Iron Mountain. I had been assigned to the Office of the Secretary of Defense before the Kennedy election and was there when the McNamara team of "Whiz Kids" arrived. Never before had so many brilliant young civilians with so many Ph.D.s worked in that office. It was out of the mouths of this group that I heard so frequently and precisely the ideas that Lewin recounts in his "novel." A brief sampling will show these words' power on the thinking of that era:

> Lasting peace, while not theoretically impossible, is probably unattainable; even if it could be achieved it would most certainly not be in the best interests of a stable society to achieve it.
>
> War fills certain functions essential to the stability of our society; until other ways of filling them are developed, the war system must be maintained—and improved in effectiveness.
>
> War is virtually synonymous with nationhood. The elimination of war implies the inevitable elimination of national sovereignty and the traditional nation-state.
>
> The organization of a society for the possibility of war is its principal political stabilizer....The basic authority of a modern state over its people resides in its war powers.

There is no hard evidence that this political philosophy was that of President Kennedy or of senior members of his administration. Indeed, the Kennedy administration had already undertaken several courses of action that showed a clear intention to slow the forward thrust of the Cold War. One of these, of course, was spelled out in NSAM #263, which announced plans for the Vietnamization of the war in Indochina and the scheduled, early withdrawal of all American personnel.

It appeared to many that the process of accommodation that Khrushchev had initiated with Eisenhower, which had failed because of the U-2 affair, had actually begun to take root with President Kennedy. There were other major shifts in direction attributable to President Kennedy as his administration matured in office. The U.S. space program was an example.

As early as May 25, 1961, Kennedy had made a speech stating that a goal of this country was to land a man on the moon "before the decade is out." He had declared that one of the objectives of Project Apollo was to beat the Russians. He was talking about a plan that had been conceived during the last years of the Eisenhower administration to orbit satellites and to "beat the Russians in the space race." A 1958 study by the Rand

Corporation had forecast that the United States would land a man on the moon.

In 1958, NASA employed nine thousand people; in 1963 that number reached thirty thousand. Project Apollo was projected to cost $40 billion. Then, in a surprising turnabout, President Kennedy appeared before the United Nations on September 20, 1963, and offered to call off the moon race in favor of cooperation in space exploration with the Soviets.

News of this offer was received with horror in certain powerful circles. Clare Booth Luce, wife of Henry Luce (founder of the Time-Life Corporation) and herself highly influential in the Republican party, called this "a major New Frontier" political blunder and economic Frankenstein."

With Kennedy's announcement that he was getting Americans out of Vietnam, he confirmed that he was moving away from the pattern of Cold War confrontation in favor of détente. He asked Congress to cut the defense budget. Major programs were being phased out. As a result, pressure from several fronts began to build against the young President. The pressure came from those most affected by cuts in the military budget, in the NASA space program, and in the enormous potential cost—and profit—of the Vietnam War.

Kennedy's plans would mean an end to the warfare in Indochina, which the United States had been supporting for nearly two decades. This would mean the end to some very big business plans, as the following anecdote will illustrate.

It was reported in an earlier chapter that the First National Bank of Boston had sent William F. Thompson, a vice president, to my office in the Pentagon in 1959, presumably after discussions with CIA officials, to explore "the future of the utilization of the helicopter in [clandestine] military operations" that had been taking place in Indochina up to 1959.

A client of that bank was Textron Inc. The bank had suggested to Textron officials that the acquisition of the near-bankrupt Bell Aircraft Company, and particularly its helicopter division, might be a good move. What the bank and Textron needed to determine was the extent of use of helicopters by the military and by the CIA then and the potential for their future in Indochina.

Both parties were satisfied with the information they acquired from the Pentagon and from other sources in Washington. In due time the acquisition took place, and on October 13, 1963, news media in South

Vietnam reported that an elite paramilitary force had made its first helicopter strike against the Vietcong from "Huey" Bell-Textron helicopters. It was also reported in an earlier chapter that more than five thousand helicopters were ultimately destroyed in Indochina and that billions of dollars were spent on helicopter purchases for those lost and their replacements.

Continuing the warfare in Vietnam, in other words, was of vital importance to these particular powerful financial and manufacturing groups. And helicopters, of course, were but one part of the $220 billion cost of U.S. participation in that conflict. Most of the $220 billion, in fact, was spent after 1963; only $2–$3 billion had been spent on direct U.S. military activities in Vietnam in all of the years since World War II up to and including 1963. Had Kennedy lived, it would not have gone much higher than that.

It is often difficult to retrace episodes in history and to locate an incident that became crucial to subsequent events. Here, however, we have a rare opportunity.

The success of the deal between the First National Bank of Boston, Textron, and Bell hinged on the escalation of the war in Indochina. A key man in this plan was Walter Dornberger, chief of the German Rocket Center at Peenemünde, Germany, during World War II and later an official with the Bell Aircraft Company. Dornberger's associate and protégé from Peenemünde, Wernher von Braun, who had been instrumental in the development of the army's Pershing and Jupiter rocket systems, became a central figure in NASA's plans for the race to the moon. Such connections among skilled technicians can be of great importance within the military-industrial complex, as they generally lead to bigger budgets for all related programs.

Kennedy had announced a reduced military budget, the end of American participation in Indochina, and a major change in the race to the moon. It takes no special wisdom or inside knowledge to understand that certain vested interests considered the Kennedy proposal to defuse Vietnam and these other major budget items to be extremely dangerous to their own plans.

The pressure brought to bear upon Kennedy was intense, but some sort of major event was needed that would stir emotions and trigger action. It is very likely that the death of President Ngo Dinh Diem of Vietnam and his brother, Ngo Dinh Nhu, on November 1, 1963, in Saigon was one of those events. There were at least eight or nine more that, in retrospect, indicate that a plot against Kennedy had begun to unfold.

For example, in an unprecedented action, almost the entire Kennedy cabinet traveled to Honolulu for that conference on November 20, 1963, with Henry Cabot Lodge, then ambassador to Saigon.

Meanwhile, President Kennedy and Vice President Lyndon Johnson had left Washington for a goodwill visit to Texas. On November 21, the President and his party spent the night in Fort Worth, a city that had given him a particularly warm welcome because it was a major recipient of TFX aircraft contract funds and was scheduled to get the multi-billion-dollar Bell helicopter business.

Both of these trips were highly unusual. The Honolulu trip removed most of the Kennedy inner circle—a cabinet quorum—from Washington. To then extend such an absence with a trip to Tokyo by virtually the entire group would have been hard to justify on any grounds, at any time.

At the same time, the swing through Texas by the President and vice president directly violated a long-standing Secret Service taboo on events that brought both men together in public appearances.

Whatever the answers to these apparent mysteries, it is an unavoidable conclusion that the master scenario of the planned coup d'état had been set in motion, at the highest levels, well before the President set out for Texas. On the morning of November 22, the presidential party made the short flight from Fort Worth to Love Field, Dallas, and debarked from Air Force One for a rousing parade through the city.

As the presidential motorcade began its procession through the streets of Dallas, we note that many things which ought to have been done, as matters of standard security procedure, were not done. These omissions show the hand of the plotters and the undeniable fact that they were operating among the highest levels of government in order to have access to the channels necessary to arrange such things covertly.

Some of these omissions were simple things that are done normally without fail. All windows in buildings overlooking a presidential motorcade route must be closed and observers positioned to see that they remain closed. They will have radios, and those placed on roofs will be armed in case gunmen do appear in the windows. All sewer covers along the streets are supposed to be welded to preclude the sewer's use as a gunman's lair. People with umbrellas, coats over their arms, and other items that could conceal a weapon are watched. The list is long, but it is sensible and routine.

These things were not done that day in Dallas.

By 1963, the Secret Service had many decades of experience in the task of protecting presidents. There were ironclad procedures and policies that had been established ever since the Secret Service was given protection of the President and his family as its main responsibility by Congress following the assassination of President William McKinley in 1901.

Because the Secret Service is a relatively small organization, it customarily calls upon local police, the local sheriff's office, state police, the National Guard, and the regular military establishment for assistance as necessary. There is even a special course, called "Protection," for personnel of selected military units to familiarize them with this responsibility. In this day of high technology, it has become a profession of great precision and expertise.

In a bureaucracy, it is more difficult to arrange for some office not to perform its duties than to let it do them. Such duties are automatic and built into the system. Therefore, when a unit does not perform its duties in accordance with custom and regulations, it is a signal that something highly unusual has occurred. In the case of the killing of President Kennedy, certain key people had been told they would not be needed in Dallas. Some were told not to do certain things, while others were simply left out altogether.

It is not always easy to obtain positive proof of a conspiracy, even when many facts point to its existence. The power of the conspirators may be such that they can squelch usual legal procedures. Thus, the public, if it is to know the truth, must discover what happened from details and circumstantial material supporting the case. Then, from whatever valid evidence becomes available, the public can eventually determine the nature of the conspiracy and the identity of those behind it.

More than 120 years ago, Special Judge Advocate John A. Bingham observed:

> A conspiracy is rarely, if ever, proved by positive testimony. Unless one of the original conspirators betrays his companions and gives evidence against them, their guilt can be proved only by circumstantial evidence. It is said by some writers on evidence that such circumstances are stronger than positive proof. A witness swearing positively may misrepresent the facts or swear falsely, but the circumstances cannot lie.[2]

In something as routine as the providing of protection for the President during a parade through a major U.S. city such as Dallas, the presence of variations in the routine can reveal the existence and the skill of the plotters. Let us review certain facts concerning the events surrounding President Kennedy's death.

The Warren Report contains testimony by Forest Sorrels of the Secret Service. Sorrels said that he and a Mr. Lawson of the Dallas Police Department selected "the best route... to take him [the President] to the Trade Mart from Love Field." This is a legitimate task. But was the route Sorrels chose truly the "best route" from a security standpoint? Why was that specific route chosen?

The route chosen by Sorrels and the Dallas police involved a ninety-degree turn from Main Street to Houston Street and an even sharper turn from Houston to Elm Street. These turns required that the President's car be brought to a very slow speed in a part of town where high buildings dominated the route, making it an extremely dangerous area. Yet, Sorrels told the Warren Commission, this "was the most direct route from there and the most rapid route to the Trade Mart."

What Sorrels did not say was that such sharp turns and high buildings made the route unsafe. Why did he and the police accept that hazardous route, especially when it was in clear violation of security regulations?

President Kennedy was shot on Elm Street just after his car made that slow turn from Houston. Many have considered this to be a crucial piece of evidence that there was a plot to murder the President. It is considered crucial because the route was selected by the Secret Service, contrary to policy, and because this obvious discrepancy has been ignored by the Warren Report and all other investigations since then. The conclusion that has been made is that it was part of the plot devised by the murderers; they had to create an ideal ambush site, and the Elm Street corner was it. Furthermore, no matter what route was selected for the presidential motorcade, the Secret Service and its trained military augmentation should have provided airtight protection all the way. This they did not even attempt to do, and this serious omission tends to provide strong evidence of the work of the conspirators. Someone, on the inside, was able to call off these normal precautions.

According to the Secret Service's own guidelines, when a presidential motorcade can be kept moving at forty miles an hour or faster (in most locales), it is not necessary to provide additional protection along the way. However, when the motorcade must travel at slower speeds, it is essential that there be protection personnel on the ground, in buildings, and on top of buildings in order to provide needed surveillance. These personnel would have discovered, for instance, that before the shooting

many windows in the Texas Schoolbook Depository Building were
open, as on-the-spot photos revealed.

So few of the routine things were done in Dallas. Incredibly, there
were no Secret Service men or other protection personnel at all in the
area of the Elm Street slowdown zone. How did this happen? It is
documented that Secret Service men in Fort Worth were told they
would not be needed in Dallas.

The commander of an army unit, specially trained in protection and
based in nearby San Antonio, Texas, had been told he and his men
would not be needed in Dallas. "Another army unit will cover that city,"
the commander was told.

I have worked with military presidential protection units. I called a
member of that army unit later. I was told that the commander "had
offered the services of his unit for protection duties for the entire trip
through Texas," that he was "point-blank and categorically refused by
the Secret Service," and that "there were hot words between the
agencies."

I was told that this army unit, the 316th Field Detachment of the
112th Military Intelligence Group at Fort Sam Houston in the Fourth
Army Area, "had records on Lee Harvey Oswald, before November 22."
It "knew Dallas was dangerous," the commander told my associate in
explaining why he had offered his services, despite a call to "stand
down." Like an old dog, he'll do his tricks without further instructions.
Telling him "not to do his old tricks" would be futile.

This leaves an important question: Why was the assistance of this
skilled and experienced unit 'point-blank refused'? Who knew ahead of
time that it would not be wanted in Dallas?

There were no Secret Service men on the roofs of any buildings in the
area. There had been no precautions taken to see that all windows
overlooking the parade route in this slowdown zone had been closed.
The man alleged to have killed the President is said to have fired three
shots from an open window on the sixth floor of the building directly
above the sharp turn at the corner of Houston and Elm streets.

The availability of that "gunman's lair," if it was occupied at all,
violated basic rules of protection. It overlooked the spot where the car
would slow down. The building had many open windows at that time.
No Secret Service men were covering that big building, and no Secret
Service men were on the roofs of adjacent buildings to observe it or
other such lairs. And no military units were in Dallas for that duty.

Why did the Secret Service men do everything wrong or omit doing things that were customary and were required for protection? Had they actually been told they were not needed? If so, who had the power and know-how to tell the Secret Service such a thing? Obviously, ·that authority had to have come from a very high level.

The official scenario of the President's murder is patently absurd, for many reasons. The Warren Commission was required to base its entire story on a script that said there was only one gunman, that this gunman fired three shots from a single-shot Italian rifle from a corner, sixth-floor window, and that only these three shots were fired. The FBI and the Secret Service told the same story. They both reported three shots, fired by a single gunman, from the same rifle.

There are twenty-six volumes of the Warren Report. Most of that report is obfuscation and irrelevant data. If there was more than one gunman, if any shots were fired from any other location, or if there were more than three single shots, the entire house of cards fabricated by the Warren Commission and its allies, such as the FBI, the Secret Service, the armed forces, and the Dallas Police Department, among others, collapses.

It follows, then, that if the report is proven wrong on any of these key points, there must clearly be a conspiracy involving perpetrators of a master plan not only to do away with the President and to take control of the government of the United States but also to maintain the most elaborate cover-up of the century. Since all of this information is on the record, let's examine some key elements of the Warren Commission scenario.

The alleged lair of the gunman was six floors above the turn that the President's car made onto Elm Street. Unforeseeably, a Dallas resident named Abraham Zapruder had stationed himself on a low stone structure to take color movies of the President's motorcade. He was a little higher than ground level and to the right front of the Texas School Book Depository building. Because of Zapruder's eyewitness film, it is possible to mark precisely the location of the President's car at the time of the first shot and to time the intervals between the shots.

Even at a slow speed and a moderate distance, a rifleman must follow the target and lead it to compensate for movement. From the distance and height of the sixth-floor window, it would not have been an impossible shot—had it not been for the foliage of a large tree that stood between the gunman's lair and the President's car, as shown in the spot news photos, such as the one taken by Altgens, a professional news cameraman.

The frame speed of Zapruder's camera is known. The film captured the rotation of the tires and the movement past the spaced white lines in Elm Street. These items make it possible to ascertain with precision where the President was and to determine that he was concealed by that big tree at the time of the first shot. No marksman could have followed that moving target through the foliage and fired three shots in quick succession and have two of them hit his target with precision. To think that is possible is preposterous.

Moreover, an experienced gunman—a former marine, we'll say— would not have selected a place where he had to peer through a tree if he was planning to shoot the President of the United States.

In an attempt to prove that the gunman had been able to shoot the President through the tree, the FBI had a camera mounted in the sixth-floor window and aimed it through a telescopic sight. The bureau arranged for an automobile with four passengers to move slowly down Elm Street while the camera took pictures, ostensibly to show what the gunman saw. In these photographs, it is possible to see the cross hairs of the telescopic sight zeroed in on the back of the target victim from that window and through the tree.

The FBI did not mention that this was a trick of photography. A telescopic lens may be focused on a distant target and will appear to see "through" intervening obstructions, such as leaves. In the same way, the eye can focus on a distant target through a screen door; it sees the distant target and doesn't notice the screen. But although this can be done by the human eye and by means of a cameraman's trick shot, it cannot be done by a rifleman peering through branches and leaves, as any hunter can tell you. It's the bullet, not the lens, that has to crash through the branches and leaves; such obstructions knock it off its course.

This simple bit of FBI skullduggery with the tree, the telescopic lens, and the camera is a classic example of how a real crime can be hidden by a skillful cover-up. As this becomes obvious, we wonder who, at what high level of the administration, had the power to engage the FBI in such a plot and its cover-up. This is the heart of the matter as we dig further into the Kennedy assassination.

A memorandum by FBI director J. Edgar Hoover on November 29, 1963, cites a discussion he had on that date with President Johnson. (A copy of this memorandum is held by the author.) Hoover wrote:

The President then indicated our conclusions are:

1) He [Oswald] is the one who did it;
2) After the President was hit, Governor Connally was hit;
3) The President would have been hit three times except for the fact that Governor Connally turned after the first shot and was hit by the second....

In summary, the President and the director of the FBI had concluded that Kennedy was hit once and Connally twice. That is a total of three bullets. As we know, the Warren Commission Report states that one bullet that went through the President's body also hit Connally and that another bullet hit the President's head and killed him. And the report recognizes that one bullet missed both men and hit a bystander. This also is a total of three bullets and requires all the trickery of the "magic" bullet scheme.

If we think about this for a moment, we realize the importance of the Johnson-Hoover conversation. President Johnson was stating his conclusion only one week after the murder. He had been two cars behind President Kennedy. He heard those shots, and his account that day completely contradicted what would later become the official scenario.

This important memorandum begins with a recapitulation of a conversation between Hoover and Johnson in which they discussed the selection of the men to be asked to serve on the Warren Commission. As quoted by Hoover, Johnson himself disproved the Warren Report's "three-bullet" finding.

Hoover wrote, "I stated that our ballistics experts were able to prove the shots were fired by this gun; that the President was hit by the first and third bullets and the second hit the governor; that there were three shots...." (Note that in the above "three-bullet" scheme, Hoover wrote, "...indicated our conclusions" was that two bullets hit Connally and only one hit the President.)

That simple statement, by itself, throws out the validity of the Warren Report. It does not account for the "near-miss" bullet that hit a curb and injured a bystander named James Tague, as will be described below. That was an undeniable fourth shot. Furthermore, ample evidence proves beyond the slightest doubt that neither the Warren Report nor even this Hoover memorandum was correct. The stories are equally invalid. Both were contrived.

The Warren Commission murder scenario states that three shots were fired. Any change in that number destroys the commission's entire case.

Yet the most cursory of analyses of this "three-bullet" contrivance does ruin the case. There had to have been more than three shots and more than one gunman.

One bullet hit the President in the back. (This can be established, beyond doubt, by the fact that both Kennedy's suitcoat and shirt have holes in the back below the right shoulder blade.) Without going into the autopsy details, we will simply accept that as bullet number one. One bullet hit the President in the head, shattering his skull. Gov. John Connally of Texas, who was sitting in the car on a jump seat just in front of the President, said it had the effect of "covering the car with brain matter." That is bullet number two. One bullet missed and has been acknowledged by the Warren Commission as a clear miss. That is bullet number three.

Unfortunately, the members of the Warren Commission were confronted with the fact that at least one bullet hit Governor Connally. There was no fourth bullet, or so they said. The commission members bulldozed their way through this dilemma by ramming bullet number one (which hit Kennedy in the back) through the President, out a small aperture in his throat area, through the air (in a circuitous path), and into the governor's back, crashing through a rib, out into the air, crashing through the governor's wrist, out into that clear Texas air again, and then back into the governor's thigh, where to this day a few small fragments remain.

As if the flight of this "magic" bullet were not fantasy enough, the Warren Commission asserted that someone found this much-traveled projectile lying on a stretcher in Parkland Memorial Hospital, where Kennedy and Connally had been taken. The Warren Commission published photographs of that bullet, and the bullet itself may be seen "live" in the National Archives. Miraculously, the magic bullet is unscathed, except for a slight mark where someone cut away a tiny bit for identification purposes. This historic specimen, moreover, shows no evidence of missing those bits that John Connally still carries with him in his injured thigh.

The story of bullet number one's magic flight is preposterous. But it is valuable for illustrating how certain the perpetrators of this crime were of sufficient power to arrange for the murder of the President, for the extensive cover-up, and for the abject reduction of the chief justice to the role of puppet for purposes of issuing the cover-up report. Even more unnerving has been their ability to foist such a story on the American public for nearly thirty years and to make it stick by having every President since Kennedy vouch for it. This alone is a definition of the location of and the magnitude of that anonymous power center.

The magic-bullet scenario has survived more than a generation of attacks, investigations, and doubt. It remains the official story, a story that very few, if any, government officials and major news media representatives contest. Examples such as these prove that this crime was committed not only to kill the President but to take over the powers of the government. The cabal knew that whatever it contrived as the explanation for the crime could never be contested. This murder has never been tried in a Texas court, as law requires.

The Secret Service, the FBI, and the Warren Commission had to admit that one of the three bullets fired by their "lone gunman" missed. This admission was forced upon them by the fact that James Tague, a bystander, was struck on the cheek by a fragment of the bullet or by a bit of the granite curbstone struck by that errant round. In either case, Tague was photographed with blood running down his cheek by an alert news cameramen. He also photographed the curbstone where Tague stood that day, and those photographs show the bullet strike on the stone.

This left the Warren Commission with only two bullets to account for the injuries to Kennedy and Connally cited above. They were further constrained by the "fact" that someone had "found" only three shell cases at the scene of the alleged gunman's lair. Once all of these bits of evidence, real and contrived, had become public, the commission had to weave its story accordingly. It handled the Tague item rather casually. The members of the Warren Commission agreed that Tague had been struck by a fragment and that Tague's injury was the result of a "near miss." It said nothing about where Tague was standing.

Most readers of the Warren Report assume that Tague was standing close to where the President's car passed on Elm Street. They think it was an actual near miss and that the path of the bullet could not have been far from the others that were fired. The readers assume that if the commission was going to credit this gunman with the uncanny ability to shoot through the foliage of a tree and hit a moving target with two out of three shots, then he must have been good enough to have a very "near" miss with the wasted shot. That was not the case, however, and therein lies another key factor in the ingenious plot to kill the President.

Tague was standing on a curb on Main Street, not Elm Street. He was more than one full block away from the President's car. Let's draw a line from the point of impact on that curbstone back to a position within a circle with an eighteen-inch diameter around the President's head and shoulders. If we project that line back to some firing point, we have placed that gunman in a window on the second floor of the Dal-Tex building, behind the President's car.

On the other hand, if we draw a line from that same point of contact with the curbstone back to the alleged lone gunman's lair on the sixth floor of the Book Depository building, we discover that the bullet would have traveled about twenty-two feet above the President's car and as much as thirty-three feet to its right. Obviously, this bullet is hardly a "near" miss. The path of the Tague bullet reveals that the true location of at least one gunman at Dealey Plaza was in a second-floor window of the Dal-Tex building. In this location he would have had a logical field of fire from the rear of the car, with no intervening tree. The caliber of a professional "mechanic" or hit man is such that he would select only the best position. That Dal-Tex window is an ideal sniper's location.

It is noteworthy that on Saturday, November 23, 1963, the curbstone with the mark of the bullet strike on it was removed and replaced. Oswald, the supposed lone gunman, was then in custody. Who benefited by removing this evidence? The answer begins to be clear: those who wanted to maintain the scenario of a lone gunman. Yet the idea of a sixth-floor location of a lone assassin is absurd. The final, fatal, and shattering shot—as clearly and starkly revealed by the Zapruder film—came from ground level and from a position in the direction of the grassy knoll that gave the gunman a close-in, clear shot at Kennedy's head. The fact that brain matter was splattered backward, over the trunk of the car, onto the motorcycle policeman riding to the left and rear of the car, and even as far as onto the grass to the left and rear of the car, fortifies the conclusion that the shot came from the right, from in front of the car, and from ground level.

What happened to the Zapruder film provides further insight into how the wily plotters arranged their cover-up. That night, November 22, 1963, a *Life* magazine official negotiated with Zapruder for the rights to the film in his camera. Later, when a series of still photographs was printed to show the tremendous impact of that bullet on the President's head, someone had cleverly reversed their sequence to make it appear that the head had been thrust forward, not backward.

Not long after the publication of that series of pictures, a researcher, Harold Weisberg, noted that these crucial moving picture photos had been reversed and did not match the sequence of the actual movie strip film. This was truly astonishing.

This meant that, somehow, someone had either caused the FBI to change the sequence or had caused *Life* magazine to arrange the pictures in an order to make it appear that the President's head had been struck from the rear—from the direction of the lone gunman's sixth-floor lair, and not from the front, where the actual killer had been.

This crafty reversal of the photographic sequence reveals that the case was carefully monitored by skilled agents who could control certain key activities of the bureaucracy (the military and Secret Service), the Warren Commission (including its staff assistants), and the news media, which have remained under this control since that date.

But perhaps the most incredible aspect in this plot to murder the President, to take over control of the administration of the U.S. government, and to cover up any related actions for as long as necessary, is the ability of the conspirators to reach as far as the chief justice of the United States in order to lend credence to the cover-up scenario.

Nothing reveals the extent of this control more than the following words from a January 27, 1964, meeting of the newly created Warren Commission. The members were discussing the problems they foresaw in having to deal with the Secret Service, the FBI, and the state of Texas, where the murder trial should have taken place.

John McCloy, a member of the commission, said of one such problem, "I can see the difficulty with that [differences between the Secret Service account and the report from the FBI], but on the other hand, I have a feeling we are so dependent upon them [the FBI and the Secret Service] for our facts."

J. Lee Rankin, the commission's general counsel, said, "Part of our difficulty in regard to it [the murder] is that they [the FBI and the Secret Service] have no problem. They have decided that it is Oswald who committed the assassination. They have decided that no one else was involved. They have decided."

Sen. Richard B. Russell then said, "They have tried the case and reached a verdict on every aspect."

Congressman Hale Boggs agreed: "You have put your finger on it."

With reference to the thousands of "further inquiries" the commission would have to make, Rankin said he assumed the response from the FBI and Secret Service would be "Why do you want all that? It is clear."

As you will recall, in the Hoover memorandum of November 29, 1963, the new President, Lyndon Johnson, said the murderer was Oswald. Hoover concurred and stated there were three shots. Those two men had decided. Setting up the Warren Commission after that was itself a mere gesture. The Warren Commission did not investigate what had happened; it merely took prepackaged, precooked data and published its prescribed report, as it had been ordered to do.

Going back to the meeting of the Warren Commission on January 27, Senator Russell gave his view of the probable response from the FBI and the Secret Service: "You have our statement. What else do you need?" McCloy then offered his version of what the FBI and the Secret Service would say: "We know who killed Cock Robin."

Those statements illustrate the troubled climate under which the members of the Warren Commission operated.

The commission was created by executive order on November 29, 1963, the same day Hoover and Johnson met to discuss how the investigation would be handled. A first get-together of the commission took place on December 5, 1963. Official hearings began on February 3, 1964. The commission received a five-volume report from the FBI on December 9, 1963, and another report from the Secret Service on December 20, 1963.

Of particular interest is the fact that during the November 29 meeting between President Johnson and J. Edgar Hoover, Johnson told his good friend and longtime neighbor that, in Hoover's words, "he wanted to get by just with my [Hoover's] file and my report."

An important result of the announcement of the formation of the Warren Commission was the derailing of a planned independent congressional investigation of the assassination. Johnson told Hoover on November 29 that he wanted to "tell the House and Senate not to go ahead with the investigation."

Waggoner Carr, the Texas attorney general, and Preston Smith, the lieutenant governor of Texas, were two of Johnson's first visitors after he became President. The visit occurred on November 24. It would be interesting to know whether they decided then not to hold a trial for the murder of Kennedy, even though it was committed in Texas. It should be noted that at almost the exact time Johnson, Carr, and Smith were conferring in the White House, Jack Ruby (Rubenstein) shot Lee Harvey Oswald at Dallas Police Department headquarters, a murder shown on nationwide TV.

According to Hoover, in the November 29, 1963, memorandum, the Dallas "chief of police admits he moved Oswald in the morning as a convenience and at the request of motion picture [television] people who wanted daylight."

Only essential police and the TV crews were permitted at headquarters—yet somehow Jack Ruby gained entrance. Hoover's words in the memorandum about this tense scene are important:

> [Ruby]... knew all of the police officers in the white-light district... that is how I think he got into police headquarters. I said [to Johnson] if they [police] ever made any move, the pictures did not show it, even when they saw him [Ruby] approach and he got right up to Oswald's stomach; that neither officer on either side made any effort to grab Rubenstein—not until after the pistol was fired.

This is no place to examine all of the evidence available of this skillfully managed killing of a President, but it may be clear from the examples provided here that the Warren Commission's "findings" would be more accurately labeled a "contrived scenario."

If we have come to the conclusion that Lee Harvey Oswald was made the "patsy" for the murder of the President, we must consider again the atmosphere under which the men on the Warren Commission operated. They had been selected and appointed by the President, after a discussion with FBI director J. Edgar Hoover.

During that discussion, as related in Hoover's November 29, 1963, memorandum, Johnson stated, "I [Hoover] was more than head of the FBI—I was his brother and personal friend... he did want to have my thoughts on the matter to advocate as his own opinion."

The commission members were appointed immediately following this Johnson-Hoover conversation—the very same day, as a matter of fact. It was said that they had a clear charter to investigate and to solve this terrible crime. The commission was authorized by Congress to use subpoena powers. The members, all listed here, were experienced in the pathways of supergovernment:

> Chief Justice Earl Warren; former Director of Central Intelligence Allen Dulles; Congressman (later President) Gerald R. Ford; Congressman Hale Boggs (who later mysteriously disappeared in a light-plane crash in Alaska); Sen. Richard B. Russell; Sen. John Sherman Cooper; John J. McCloy, former president of the World Bank.

As a note of interest:

1. It was Allen Dulles who overlooked President Eisenhower's

express orders not to involve Americans in Vietnam, with the creation of the Saigon Military Mission (1954).

2. Allen Dulles was in charge of the CIA's U-2 spy plane operations and of the flight that crash-landed in the Soviet Union on May 1, 1960, causing the disruption of the Paris Summit Conference. Eisenhower had specifically ordered all overflights of Communist territory to be grounded before and during that period.

3. The Bay of Pigs operation was planned under Dulles's leadership, and his failure to be "on duty" that day may have been a contributing factor in its failure (April 18, 1961).

4. Dulles was a member of the Cuban Study Group that reviewed that ill-fated operation (1961).

5. Dulles was a member of the Warren Commission (1964).

If any men, in or out of public life, could have solved this murder, these seven men should have been able to do so. But they did not. In blunt language, as we have said throughout this work, they didn't even try. Why not? What power structure was so strong that it could emasculate a presidential commission?

A presidential commission is not a court of law, and its processes are not a reasonable substitute for a court. The Warren Commission was given subpoena power, but for some reason it did not use the time-honored adversarial process of cross-examination. The fact that Walter E. Craig, president of the American Bar Association, had been asked to attend the hearings and to "advise the commission whether in his opinion the proceedings conformed to the basic principles of American justice" and that he was "given the opportunity to cross-examine witnesses" had little, if any, bearing on the course and outcome of the commission's work. Craig never took advantage of this opportunity to cross-examine witnesses.

The commission never really considered the possibility that anyone other than Oswald, by himself, had committed the crime.

The President was murdered in Dallas, Texas. By law, the crime of murder must be tried in the state where it is committed. It remains to be tried today. There is no statute of limitations on the crime of murder.

Why hasn't the case been tried? Oswald is dead, but that does not preclude a trial. He is as innocent of that crime as anyone else until a court of law has found him guilty. Given the available evidence, no court could convict him. These experienced men on the Warren

Commission, particularly the chief justice of the United States, had to have known that. The least they could have done was to order that a trial be held in Texas.

Why did Texas authorities permit the removal of Kennedy's body from Texas? Why did they not hold an official autopsy? Why did Dr. James Humes, the man who did an autopsy at Parkland Memorial Hospital in Dallas, burn his original notes? The answers to these questions, and to so many others like them, are, unfortunately, quite obvious. Anyone who came in touch with this case became shrouded under the cloak of secrecy that has covered it for decades. Even now, countless thousands of records are locked away.

At this point many of us ask, "Who are the people who set up this crime? Who shot the President, and who has been able to maintain the cover-up for three decades?"

To these questions, there are at least two responses, each on a different yet complementary level. First, "Who?" We shall never know. Throughout history, there is adequate evidence to accept the existence of an almost mythical and certainly anonymous power elite. Buckminster Fuller does his best to describe it; Winston Churchill used the term "High Cabal"; Dr. Joseph Needham, of Cambridge University and a great China scholar, wrote that the Chinese recognize the existence of a power elite that they refer to as "the Gentry." In the case of the Kennedy murder, there has been no way to pierce its cloak of anonymity, because neither the government of the state of Texas nor the federal government will take positive legal action.

Second, "Who fired the shots and who covered up the crime?" Lyndon Johnson came as close as anyone has when he said that "we had been operating a damn Murder Inc." These are the skilled professionals. We shall never discover who they are. The "cover story" is another thing. It has been a masterpiece, all the way from the Lee Harvey Oswald role to statements made by high officials today. One thing we must understand is that the cover story has its band of actors. Many of these actors came from the Cuban exile groups in Miami and New Orleans and were prepared in the huge Operation Mongoose infrastructure that was established ostensibly to eliminate Fidel Castro. Any who are alive today are shielded by the mantle of the cabal.

The entire plot may be likened to a play, a great tragedy. There are the authors. They created the plot, the scenario, the time, the characters, and the script. Then there are the actors who carried out the scenario as mercenaries. In this case they would have been a band of skilled men who do such things regularly on a worldwide basis for money and protection. In the ultimate sense, they are expendable.

There are colonies of such experts that are maintained by certain governments, or by select instrumentalities of governments, and by other powers. They are used for such activities regularly.

Who can command the absolute power sufficient to create such a scenario, and who can put it into operation? The following items will serve to illustrate the extent of the power these people wield.

The murder of President Kennedy and its accompanying pageantry was witnessed, on film, TV, radio, and in print, by hundreds of millions around the world. David Lawrence, writing in the *New York Herald Tribune* on November 26, 1963, observed, "Thanks to the inventions of man, instantaneous communication throughout the world has been made possible. No such wide coverage on the same day, simultaneously with the occurrence of a news event, has been achieved in the past."

This was true, of course, with respect to the communications capability, but was the information that traveled around the world the truth of legitimate news, or was it more like a mixture of real news items and orchestrated propaganda that had been prepared and written even before the crime took place?

For those of us who just happened to be in far-off Christchurch, New Zealand, for example, the Kennedy assassination took place at seven-thirty on the morning of Saturday, November 23, 1963.

As soon as possible, the *Christchurch Star* hit the streets with an "Extra" edition. One-quarter of the front page was devoted to a picture of President Kennedy. The remainder of the page was, for the most part, dedicated to the assassination story, from various sources. Who were those sources, and how could so much intimate and detailed biographic information about Oswald have been obtained instantaneously? The answer is that it wasn't obtained "instantaneously." It had to have been prepared before the crime, and like everything else, prepackaged by the secret cabal.

This "instant" news, available so quickly and completely in far-off New Zealand, is a most important detail of the murder plan. This newspaper ran an "Extra" edition that was on the streets before noon in Christchurch. It ran news items filed by experienced on-the-spot reporters in Dallas, who reported that the President was hit with a "burst of gunfire." A few lines below, it said, "Three bursts of gunfire, apparently from automatic weapons," were heard.

Another reporter quoted Sen. Ralph Yarborough, who had been riding in the procession, as saying, ". . . at least two shots came from our right rear." As confirmed by photographs made at that time, the "right rear" of Senator Yarborough's position could not have been the alleged lone gunman's lair six floors above.

NBC-TV reported that the police took possession of "a British .303-inch rifle . . . with a telescopic sight." That was not the Italian rifle of the Warren Report.

Another account in this same newspaper stated that "the getaway car was seized in Fort Worth, Texas." Whose getaway car? Oswald never left Dallas.

This type of sudden, quite random reporting is most important, because one can usually find the truth of what occurred in these early news reports. Later, the "news" will be doctored and coordinated and will bear little resemblance to the original, more factual accounts.

Experienced reporters travel in the presidential party. They know gunfire when they hear it, and they reported "bursts" of gunfire. They reported "automatic weapons." They reported what they heard and saw. They did not yet have propaganda handouts.

Neither the FBI nor the Secret Service reported such action. Since automatic weapons were never found, it becomes apparent that the reporters on the scene had heard simultaneous gunfire from several skilled "mechanics" or professional killers and that this gunfire had sounded like "bursts" of "automatic weapons."

This reference to "three bursts of gunfire" and "apparently from automatic weapons" that I read first on the front page of the *Christchurch Star* provides a most important clue. It shows how on-the-spot news coverage creates real facts that are much different from the preprepared cover story, and the after-the-fact *Report of the Warren Commission*.

Another factor is important. On-the-spot news coverage benefits from that "instantenous communications throughout the world . . . simultaneously with the occurrence of a news event" that David Lawrence mentioned in the *New York Herald Tribune*.

During early on-the-spot news bulletins CBS made use of these same words: "Three bursts of automatic gunfire, apparently from automatic weapons, were fired at President Kennedy's motorcade in downtown Dallas." These same lines were repeated in subsequent CBS bulletins of that date.

Another point can be made from this bulletin. Although the gunmen may have used "automatic" weapons, it is more likely that what the reporters heard that day was the well-coordinated fire from at least three gunmen in different locations, and that they fired at least three times each.

This is an old firing-squad and professional hit-man ploy. It serves to remove the certain responsibility from each gunner as a psychological cleanser. If three men are to fire, they all know that two guns are loaded and one gun is firing blanks. The gunmen do not know who had the bullets, or who had the blanks. Each man can choose to believe that he did not kill the victim; and each man can swear an oath that he was not the killer.

It is relevant to note that these on-the-spot bulletins did not contain the previously written "Lee Harvey Oswald" data that had been fed to the world press and that I read in New Zealand.

Nowhere does the Warren Report mention the precision control of several guns, yet it is hard to discount the first, eyewitness reports from experienced men.

On the other hand, almost one-quarter of that front page in Christchurch was taken up with detailed news items about Lee Harvey Oswald. An excellent photograph of Oswald in a business suit and tie was run on page 3. This odd photograph appeared in no other files.

At the time this edition of the *Star* went to press, the police of Dallas had just taken a young man into custody and had charged him with the death of a Dallas policeman named J. D. Tippit. They had not accused Oswald of the murder of the President and did not charge him with that crime until early the next morning. Yet a long article put on the wires by the British United Press and America's Associated Press had been assembled out of nowhere, even before Oswald had been charged with the crime. It was pure propaganda. Where did those wire services get it?

Nowadays, Oswald is a household name throughout the world, but in Dallas at 12:30 P.M. on November 22, 1963, he was a nondescript twenty-four year-old ex-marine who was unknown to almost everyone. There is no way one can believe that these press agencies had in their files, ready and on call, all of the detailed information that was so quickly poured out in those first hours after the assassination.

In the long account in the *Christchurch Star* about Lee Harvey Oswald—which included that fine studio portrait in business suit, white shirt, and tie—these press services provided, and the *Star* published, some very interesting information.

According to the account, Lee Harvey Oswald:

"defected to the Soviet Union in 1959"
"returned to the United States in 1962"
"has a [Russian] wife and child"
"worked in a factory in Minsk"
"went to the USSR following discharge from the Marine Corps"
"became disillusioned with life there [in the USSR]"
"Soviet authorities had given him permission to return with his wife and child"
"had been chairman of the Fair Play for Cuba Committee"

...and much more.

The statement by David Lawrence of the *Herald Tribune* that "instantaneous communications throughout the world has been made possible" is true. It is possible to send news around the world "instantaneously." But what of the content of that news? Can information on some young unknown be collected and collated "instantaneously"?

By what process could the wire services have acquired, collated, evaluated, written, and then transmitted all that material about an unknown young man named Lee Harvey Oswald within the first moments following that tragic and "unexpected" event—even before the police had charged him? How could they have justified the collation of such news until *after* the police had charged him with the crime?

There can be but one answer: Those in charge of the murder had prepared the patsy and all of that intimate information beforehand.

Strangely, the FBI, the Secret Service, the Warren Commission, and the Dallas police force instantly declared Oswald to be the killer. They never considered any other possibilities. The evidence was never examined. In newspapers around the world, even as far away as Christchurch, New Zealand, the headlines blared that Oswald was the President's murderer.

If one believes the information in the wire-service article, is it possible also to believe that Lee Harvey Oswald, alone, was the murderer of President John F. Kennedy?

That is such a powerful question that one wonders why it hasn't been asked more often by those who have recourse to excellent sources, tenacious investigators, and wide experience—the moguls of the media themselves. How can the press of the world have lived with this fantasy it inherited from clandestine propaganda sources before Kennedy's body was cold? How has this story been contained for more than twenty-eight long years? We must wonder what has happened to our once-free press.

We must also wonder at the chilling effect this assassination has had on succeeding presidents.

Lyndon Johnson was riding in a car behind President Kennedy in the Dealey Plaza motorcade. Johnson was seared by that event. During his November 29, 1963, conversation with J. Edgar Hoover, Johnson asked, "How many shots were fired" and "Were any fired at me?" We may be sure that he thought during his years as President about those shots that went right over his head. As any soldier can tell you, such an experience provides an excellent education.

We have noted in an earlier chapter that, despite frequent denials, Richard Nixon was in Dallas during those fateful moments, attending a meeting with executives of the Pepsi-Cola Company. According to the general counsel of that company, Nixon and the others in the room knelt in a brief prayer when they heard of Kennedy's death. Despite this, there were many news stories in which Nixon denied that he was in Dallas at the time of the assassination. Why did Nixon tell so many different, false stories about his whereabouts at that time—all placing himself outside Dallas?

Although Nixon may not have heard those guns of Dallas, there can be no question that they were never far from his mind, especially during the hectic years of his own presidency. Some people say Nixon became paranoid. That would be understandable.

Gerald Ford, who became President after Nixon left office, was a member of the Warren Commission. He attended more of its meetings than any other member. He knows the details of the murder of Kennedy well. Add to that his own experience when an assassin fired at him while he was President. He, too, knows the sound of bullets and understands their lesson.

President Reagan was not in Dallas and was not a member of the Warren Commission, but he was a member of the Rockefeller Commission that studied CIA activities in the United States. He learned about allegations concerning the assassination of President Kennedy and of the CIA's role in foreign assassination attempts as a member of that commission. Then, on the steps of the Washington Hilton in 1981, he, too, was felled by an assassin's gun. On that day, if not before, he learned how the game is played.

Four days after Kennedy's death, on November 26, President Lyndon B. Johnson met with his new presidential team, most of whom had served with JFK. Only four days after the assassination in Dallas, LBJ listened to a briefing on warfare in Indochina, which had been the subject on the agenda of the November 20 conference in Hawaii. This briefing and the agenda formulated at the November 20 conference in Honolulu, before President Kennedy's death, marked a major turning point in the Vietnam War.

Whereas Kennedy had ordered, in NSAM #263 of October 11, 1963, the return of the bulk of American personnel by the end of 1965, the November 20 agenda and the November 26 briefing moved in direct opposition to Kennedy's intentions and paved the way for the enormous escalation that took place after his death. President Johnson's NSAM #288 of March 1964 completed the full turnabout.

On March 8, 1965, U.S. Marines landed on the shores of Vietnam at Da Nang. Before long, there were 550,000 American troops in Vietnam. Fifty-eight thousand U.S. soldiers would die there. Before that "no-win" conflict would end, more than $220 billion would be poured into the coffers of the war makers.

It had been evident that great pressures were building against President Kennedy. The Kennedy administration, especially with the near certainty that the President would be reelected, was diametrically opposed to many of the great power centers of our society. He had to go. The government had to be put in the hands of more pliable "leaders."

A nation with the strength and determination to rise and demand an investigation into the death of President Kennedy—as well as the deaths of Robert Kennedy and Martin Luther King—will have the strength to survive and prosper.

Does America have that strength? I believe it does. More than any other country, America represents the cause of freedom, for all of mankind. For that reason, for ourselves and for others, it is vitally important that the truth of the events in Dallas on November 22, 1963, be told.

TWENTY

LBJ Takes the Helm as the Course Is Reversed

ON NOVEMBER 22, 1963, President John F. Kennedy flew to Dallas, Texas, to deliver a major speech at the Trade Mart. He did not live to deliver that speech. What follows are extracts from the speech that he had planned to deliver and an analysis of events that followed:

> I want to discuss with you today the status of our strength and our security because this question clearly calls for the most responsible qualities of leadership and the most enlightened products of scholarship. For this Nation's strength and security are not easily or cheaply obtained, nor are they quickly and simply explained. There are many kinds of strength and no one kind will suffice. Overwhelming nuclear strength cannot stop a guerrilla war. Formal pacts of alliance cannot stop internal subversion. Display of material wealth cannot stop the disillusionment of diplomats subjected to discrimination.
>
> But American military might should not and need not stand alone against the ambitions of international communism. Our security and strength, in the last analysis, directly depend on the security and strength of others, and that is why our military and economic assistance plays such a key role in enabling those who live on the periphery of the Communist world to maintain their independence of choice. Our assistance to these nations can be

painful, risky and costly, as is true in Southeast Asia today. But we dare not weary of the task. For our assistance makes possible the stationing of 3–5 million allied troops along the Communist frontier at one-tenth the cost of maintaining a comparable number of American soldiers. A successful Communist breakthrough in these areas, necessitating direct United States intervention, would cost us several times as much as our entire foreign aid program, and might cost us heavily in American lives as well.

In a nutshell Kennedy planned to say much about the reasons for his policy in Southeast Asia. He intended to emphasize that "overwhelming nuclear strength cannot stop a guerrilla war" and to end with " . . . direct United States intervention would cost us several times as much as our entire foreign aid program, and might cost us heavily in American lives as well." This was Kennedy's considered opinion on October 11, 1963, when he approved NSAM #263, and this remained his opinion until the day he died. There is no sign of any plan by Kennedy for the series of policy alterations that began with the draft of NSAM #273 on November 21, 1963, that, with significant revisions, Johnson signed five days later.

It is important to note that Kennedy did not include any statement such as "the President expects that all senior officers of the government will take energetic steps to insure that they and their subordinates go out of their way to maintain and defend the unity of the United States government both here and in the field." You will recall those words from the draft NSAM #273 that was written on November 21, 1963. Kennedy planned to make the above speech in Dallas on November 22, 1963.

Kennedy's prepared message for delivery at the Dallas Trade Mart had been planned to be the theme of a most important series of speeches to follow. Coming, as it did, not long after the publication of his National Security Action Memorandum #263 of October 11, 1963, it takes on additional significance in retrospect. He had already announced that one thousand American military advisers would be home from Indochina by Christmas and that American personnel would be out of Vietnam by the end of 1965. This subject, and the enormous pressures it evoked, were paramount in his mind on that memorable day in Dallas. Had he lived, and had he been reelected in 1964, this was to be the course he had charted for his administration and for his country.

Kennedy had learned much from experiences in Indochina since the beginning of our military/OSS involvement there in September 1945. He had seen that the billions of dollars of military aid provided to the

French had been ineffectual in preventing their humiliating defeat by the Vietminh at Dien Bien Phu in 1954.

He knew that, during the Eisenhower administration, three U.S. Air Force fighter aircraft armed with tactical-size nuclear weapons had been deployed to an air base in Thailand, just across the river from Laos, for potential use against North Vietnamese forces that had been observed marching into eastern Laos. He knew that these aircraft had been recalled because wiser heads had prevailed and had persuaded Eisenhower that the use of such massive weapons against guerrilla forces could not have altered the course of that insurrection and might have ignited superpower retaliation and the conflagration of Earth.

Kennedy had learned much from his experiences in October 1962, when aerial reconnaissance revealed the possibility that the Soviets had begun to place tactical, short-range nuclear missiles in Cuba. At that time he was presented with the stark dilemma of whether to deploy the large conventional military force that had been hastily assembled in Florida for an invasion of Cuba while realizing that if he ordered such an invasion, the Soviets who were based in Cuba may have had the option to respond by firing those missiles at targets in the United States.

This created a unique problem. No actual missiles had been observed or photographed in Cuba, despite the fact that certain "crates" covered by tarpaulin could have been missiles and that certain site-grading work observed could have been done in preparation for missiles; this led to the possibility that there might be missiles there. But if the United States did attack Cuba in full force, Cuban missiles or not, this attack itself could have led to a superpower nuclear exchange. JFK chose the wiser course—not to attack Cuba.

By 1963 Kennedy saw that prosecution of the CIA-directed covert warfare in Indochina would lead to a similar hard dilemma. By the summer of 1963, he and his closest associates had reached the conclusion that the future of South Vietnam must be placed in the hands of the South Vietnamese. He had made up his mind to Vietnamize that conflict, with American financial and material assistance, and to withdraw U.S. personnel as quickly as possible.

This was the basis for NSAM #263 of October 11, 1963, and having made that pivotal decision, Kennedy knew all too well that he would have to go before the American people to gain their understanding and approval. He knew equally well that with that decision to get out of Indochina, he faced strenuous opposition from the all-powerful military-industry combine that Eisenhower had warned him about in December 1960, just after his close election victory over Richard Nixon. He knew that his decision would be violently opposed by the innermost, dominant elements of the OSS/CIA hierarchy that had been forcing events in Indochina since the end of WWII.

They had urged Ho Chi Minh to create an independent Vietnam and had provided Ho and his military chieftain, Col. Vo Nguyen Giap, with an enormous supply of arms so they could round up remaining Japanese military elements. At the same time, this stockpile of arms, obtained from U.S. Army sources on Okinawa, provided the basis for their own national sovereignty. In this context, this OSS/CIA power structure, fortified by its worldwide allies, had been at the forefront in directing the Cold War since that time.

The CIA knew all too well that Kennedy's new Vietnamization policy was but the first step of his pledge to break the agency into a thousand pieces and limit its role to intelligence functions, a profession it did not practice seriously.

With these major burdens in mind, Kennedy had begun a series of trips around the country, during which time he planned to deliver several major speeches, all orchestrated to underscore his new direction and to plant the seeds for his reelection in 1964. This is why he had planned to open his speech in Dallas with: "I want to discuss with you today the status of our strength and our security, because this question clearly calls for the most responsible qualities of leadership and the most enlightened products of scholarship."

At the same time he opened this carefully planned course of action, his powerful opposition fully realized that the popular young President would be able to convince the American public that he was right and that he would be reelected to another four years in office. This his foes could not permit. Their course of action became clear to them: Kennedy must die!

That decision made, the rest followed like a row of dominos. A knowledgeable go-between was notified, and he arranged for the President's murder by skilled "mechanics" on the streets of Dallas—almost on the front steps of the sheriff's office. These "mechanics" are members of a select group of specialists, referred to by Lyndon Johnson as "a damned Murder Inc." and trained and supported by the CIA for use at U.S. government order. Their deeply anonymous system gets them to the target area and into safe positions and assures them of a guaranteed quick exit. Since the "mechanics" are certain to be on the side of the power elite, they never have been and never will be identified and prosecuted.

This preparatory work is charged with another important detail. An assassination, especially of the chief of state, can always be made easier and much more predictable if his routine security forces and their standard policies are removed and canceled. The application of this step in Dallas was most effective. A few examples serve to underscore this phase of the concept:

1. The President was in an open, unarmored car.
2. The route chosen was along busy streets with many overlooking high buildings on each side.
3. Windows in these buildings had not been closed, sealed, and put under surveillance.
4. Secret Service units and trained military units that were required by regulations to be there were not in place. As a result there was limited ground and building surveillance.
5. Sewer covers along the way had not been welded shut.
6. The route was particularly hazardous, with sharp turns requiring slow speeds, in violation of protection regulations.

The list is long and ominous. Such a lack of protection is almost a guarantee of assassination in any country. It is difficult, if not more difficult, to convince trained and ready units not to be there than to let them go ahead and do their job; yet someone on the inner cabal staff was able to make official sounding calls that nullified all of these ordinary acts of presidential protection on November 22, 1963.

At the same time the killers were contacted, another element of the plot—the greatest and most important element—was put in motion. Even before the murder took place, "cover story" experts (their profession is part of a secret world known as "deception" or "special plans") had already created an entire scenario with a "patsy" gunman and a whole cast of lesser luminaries, such as those concealed within the Mongoose anti-Castro project, who can be exposed and identified as the story paints a fictitious national fable through what is called the *Warren Commission Report* and other contrived releases over the years. Perhaps the strongest element of the cover-story side of the operation is the power that its perpetrators possess to prohibit normal pursuit and investigation by the media.

There is but one way all of this could have been managed, both before and after this elaborate coup d'état. That is with absolute control from the highest echelons of the superpower structure of this country and the world. When there is a complete and carefully planned assassination plot that is designed and put into operation to cover, at least all of the items touched upon above, then it becomes evident that there was a conspiracy. In most cases of this type the cabal is not concerned with this discovery, because with the death of the leader they have taken over the power position they sought, and none of them or their inner circle will be captured, identified, and prosecuted.

After JFK was shot, an unusually large force of police and FBI men charged into Dallas's Texas Theater at 231 West Jefferson Street at 2:00 P.M. and captured an unknown young man who had been sitting near the back of the house watching the movie *War Is Hell*. At 7:05 P.M. that evening, Lee Harvey Oswald was formally charged with the murder of Dallas police officer J. D. Tippit. It was 2:05 P.M. of the twenty-third in New Zealand, where I heard the awful news.

Not until more than four hours later, at 11:26 P.M., did Homicide captain Will Fritz formally charge Oswald with "the murder of the President," and it was not until the early hours of the morning, on Saturday, November 23, that Justice of the Peace David Johnston told Oswald he had been formally charged with the murder of the President and that he would be held without bond.

These were the facts that reporters on the scene in Dallas needed to know, and had to wait for, before they could rush to their own files and begin the laborious task of putting together their own "Lee Harvey Oswald" stories, if indeed there were even any facts on file to base them on.

Before being returned to his cell that evening, Oswald faced more than one hundred newsmen from throughout the nation, from international publications, and from radio and television stations. He told them, "I didn't know I was a suspect. I didn't even know the President was killed until newsmen told me in the hall." These words may have been absolutely the truth. To turn them around, how did the police first get the idea that Oswald was their man? Could the Dallas police have gone into a courtroom, had there been a trial, and explained reasonably how they got the idea that a certain twenty-four-year-old man was the suspect, when they themselves had no clues?

Oswald was formally charged at 11:26 P.M. Dallas time, on November 22, 1963. That was 6:26, P.M. New Zealand time, November 23, 1963. By that time New Zealanders had known, for hours, what the Dallas police did not know until later—that Lee Harvey Oswald had been designated as the killer of President Kennedy. These New Zealanders had read preprepared news that had been disseminated by the cover-story apparatus.

This shows clearly how the scenario of President Kennedy's death had been prepared well before the actual event and strongly suggests that Lee Harvey Oswald had been chosen to be the "murderer" of the President before Dallas police made it official and despite evidence to the contrary. There can be no question whatsoever that the cabal that arranged to have President Kennedy murdered had arranged and staged all the other terrible events of that day. They had also been able to control the dissemination of news that day, and they have been able to control the cover-up—including the report of the Warren Commission—since that date.

The evidence of that part of the plot and of the continuing cover-up becomes quite clear when one goes back through the record. It becomes easier to see why the commission permitted the publication of twenty-six volumes to conceal the bits of information it did discover. Other facets of the work of the cabal have not been as easy to see. But the findings that do exist make it clear that there had to be important reasons for the murder of the President.

Kennedy had stated his position on Vietnam on October 11, 1963. With the new South Vietnamese leader, Gen. Duong Van Minh, in charge as of November 4, 1963, the program to Vietnamize the war—which included an agreement to provide the general with necessary funds and military matériel—appeared to be headed in the right direction.

Then a trickle of reports suggested a reversal of the situation in Vietnam. With a quick, and unexplained, jump from what had been a rather optimistic view of progress in Vietnam, the Pentagon Papers add:

> These topics [the military situation and the Strategic Hamlet program] dominated the discussions at the Honolulu conference in November 20 when Lodge and the country team met with Rusk, McNamara, Taylor, Bell, and Bundy. But the meeting ended inconclusively. After Lodge had conferred with the President a few days later in Washington, the White House tried to pull together some conclusions and offer some guidance for our continuing and now deeper involvement in Vietnam.

The above paragraph, with its quotes directly from the Defense Department–prepared Pentagon Papers, is truly staggering in light of what actually took place. First of all, it does not seem to concur with what Kennedy was planning; just consider the words of the Kennedy Trade Mart speech planned for November 22 in Dallas. Let's analyze this bit of propaganda from the Pentagon Papers with care.

Kennedy, his military advisers, and his administration had concluded that things were getting better in Vietnam and that the United States would be able to turn the countersubversion activity over to the Vietnamese and get out of Indochina. Kennedy had not changed his course on Vietnam and never intended to change it.

Who called the strange Honolulu conference of the Kennedy cabinet? Who had tabled the agenda on the "deterioration of the military situation and the Strategic Hamlet program"? Not only that, but what unusual event had caused the decision that the cabinet members, or at least a majority of them, should travel on to Tokyo for other meetings—on what subjects? Keep in mind that even the secretary of agriculture and the secretary of commerce had been involved in that excursion to Tokyo via Honolulu.

In considering these strange events, which are cataloged in an official Defense Department summary of the war record, think carefully about this quote fragment: "After Lodge had conferred with the President a few days later in Washington..."

What a strange way five years later (1968) for the study task force to make the transition from the Kennedy administration to the Johnson era. Lodge had left Honolulu on November 22, the same day JFK was killed. An entry in the Pentagon Papers states: "22 Nov. 1963 Lodge confers with the President. Having flown to Washington the day after the conference, Lodge meets with the President and presumably continues the kind of report given in Honolulu."

In all the reports of this period that appear in the voluminous Pentagon Papers material, there is almost nothing at all about the assassination of President Kennedy. For example, it states, quite simply, that Lodge flew to Washington to meet with the President. It does not even make the point that when Lodge left Saigon, Kennedy was President and that when he arrived in Washington, Johnson was President—and Kennedy was dead.

The "Study of the History of United States Involvement in Vietnam From World War II to the Present" (aka Pentagon Papers) had been initiated on June 17, 1967, by Secretary of Defense Robert S. McNamara. It is inconceivable that McNamara, Leslie M. Gelb (director of the Study Task Force), and all the others involved intended to scrub that sordid event out of the pages of history; but on the other hand, what they did produce is hard to explain. Along with the rest of the cover-up, including the work of the Warren Commission, the Pentagon Papers material provides the reader with almost nothing at all about one of the most historic events of the entire era, if not the century—the murder of President Kennedy. Is that just an inexcusable omission, or is it a part of the superplanning of the cover-up?

At the very least, this means that as students and historians plunge into the record of this thirty-year period, much of it covered in elaborate detail by the McNamara-Gelb study, they are not going to find anything about the death of President Kennedy. As that tragic event drops further into history, it may be all but forgotten, thanks to this type of omission— willful or otherwise. It isn't difficult to see it as a form of negative propaganda.

It may be that this is all part of a pattern. Within a few days after Kennedy's death, most of those cabinet members who had attended the Honolulu conference with Ambassador Lodge met with President Johnson in Washington. During that meeting, they discussed the agenda of the Honolulu conference. That agenda gave lip service to the Kennedy plan—but it also laid the groundwork for the change in course that followed as soon as Kennedy was dead.

Following that meeting of November 26, 1963, the President issued NSAM #273. For the most part, its content paralleled Kennedy's NASM #263 of October 11, 1963, but it also underscored renewed efforts to improve the counterinsurgency campaign in the Mekong Delta. It may be said that this was the "toe in the door." Alas, the restraint of the policy set forth in NSAM #273 was, at best, short-lived.

It is worth a word here to emphasize the military significance of President Johnson's NSAM #273 when it states "we should persuade the government of South Vietnam to concentrate its efforts on the critical situation in the Mekong Delta." This is in the far south of South Vietnam. It is farthest away from Hanoi and the "enemy," the North Vietnamese. Yet it was then, and had been for years, the scene of much of the "insurgency" and "Vietcong activity" found in Vietnam.

This is like saying that the Canadians were an enemy of the United States and were causing violent insurgency in this country and that this outbreak was most prevalent in Florida. Because we know the geography here, we would recognize immediately that something was wrong with such a scenario.

Why was it, in Vietnam, that the most violent outbreaks of Vietcong insurgency were almost always in the Mekong Delta? It was because that is where most of the one-million-plus North Vietnamese settlers, who had been moved by the U.S. Navy and the CIA's CAT (Civil Air Transport) Airline, had been placed, the port of Saigon in the Mekong Delta being the only available port in those days. (Cam Ranh Bay was an artificial harbor dredged, and made useful, at great cost many years later.)

This refugee movement, as we have seen, had a profound impact on the southernmost part of South Vietnam. These homeless people, stranded in a strange land, moved in on the settled villages and caused great unrest—which the Diem government, and its American advisers, called "insurgency." Actually, these northern refugees were simply landless, homeless, and foodless—all conditions that the Diem government was not prepared to improve. As a result, riots and banditry broke out.

This was the framework of what was called "the warfare in Vietnam." It may not be the entire story, but it is basic to it. When President Johnson was informed by the drafters of NSAM #273 that the counterinsurgency campaign in the Mekong Delta needed to be increased, he knew precisely what they meant. That is where the trouble was, and where it had always been—since the one-million-plus refugees had been abandoned there.

At the same time, plans were requested by the White House for a series of clandestine operations against the North Vietnamese by government forces under the direction of the U.S. military. This was a new departure in a war that had been waged since 1945 under the OSS and the CIA.

For some time, various leaders in the Pentagon, and some from the Kennedy staff in the White House, had recommended that Haiphong Harbor, the main port for Hanoi, should be mined. Others had suggested "hit and run" attacks, to be operated covertly and with a cover story so that the United States could plausibly disclaim responsibility in the event of exposure or capture during a mission. This seemed to be the right time to bring these proposals up again, and Johnson agreed to consider them, provided they had the approval of the commander in chief of the Pacific (CINCPAC) and of the Joint Chiefs of Staff.

Planning for covert action against North Vietnam had begun in May 1963, when the JCS directed CINCPAC to prepare for operations that would be under the direction of the South Vietnamese. All through the summer, various "Special Operations" experts came up with all kinds of lists of "things to do." Walt Rostow, head of the Policy Planning Staff in the Department of State, had been plugging away at this idea ever since he had made a speech at the Special Forces Center in Fort Bragg in April 1961. The plan, drawn up by CINCPAC staff and known as OPLAN 34A, was approved by the JCS on September 9, 1963.

This was made a part of the agenda for the Honolulu conference of

November 20 and was discussed with President Johnson on November 26. He was quick to agree with anything that would put direct pressure on the North Vietnamese. On December 21, 1963, the President directed an interdepartmental committee to study OPLAN 34A further and appointed Maj. Gen. Victor H. Krulak to head the study. General Krulak had been one of those actively engaged in this planning from the start, and it did not take him long to come up with a proposal.

He submitted this for review on January 2, 1964. His plan was to be applied in three phases, each one raising the level of pressure on North Vietnam. Phase I, planned for February–May 1964, called for U-2 intelligence flights, COMINT [communications intelligence] missions, psychological missions and leaflet drops, propaganda kit deliveries, and radio broadcasts. It also provided for "twenty destructive undertakings designed to result in destruction, economic loss and general harassment" against North Vietnam.

While this planning had been secretly under way, a total exchange of top leadership in Saigon was taking place. Ambassador Lodge had arrived there in late August 1963, at the peak of the Diem "coup" discussions. Early in December, the CIA assigned a new station chief to Saigon, an experienced old pro—Peer de Silva—in place of John Richardson, who had been there since the winter of 1961–62. This was a most significant personnel change, because in December 1963 the CIA still retained "operational control" over all U.S. forces in Indochina. At that time both the CIA station chief and the senior U.S. military commander, Gen. Paul Harkins, were under the direct command of the ambassador.

At that time the director of central intelligence was John McCone, who had been appointed to that office by President Kennedy after Allen Dulles and his deputy, Gen. Charles P. Cabell, were sacked following the disastrous Bay of Pigs operation. In other words, McCone was not a Johnson man, and he held the new President in awe.

This was made quite apparent by McCone's words when he took de Silva under his wing in order to introduce him to the President in the White House, as related by de Silva himself:[1]

"For God's sake, remember what's been happening here recently—President Kennedy has been assassinated, President Johnson is new in the White House, and the Vietnam problem is getting worse every day. Lodge is becoming more and more obstreperous and Johnson wants no more problems out there as there were between Lodge and John Richardson;[2] remember all of these things when we go to the President's office tomorrow."

In this brief extract, we have another clue to the fact that the Kennedy concept of "things going well in Vietnam" was being eroded almost daily by the change of course being instigated by those who came into power after his death. Here was McCone, the man as responsible for events in Vietnam as McNamara, saying, in early December 1963, "The Vietnam problem is getting worse every day."

In order to underscore the significance of this change of the CIA station chief, on the same day that John McCone arrived in Saigon to preside at de Silva's introduction to Ambassador Lodge, Secretary McNamara and a large party, flying in an Air Force One White House jet from a meeting in Paris, arrived at almost the same time. De Silva's first full military briefing in Saigon was therefore held, about thirty minutes after his arrival, in an atmosphere dominated not by McCone but by the secretary of defense.

As each of these carefully orchestrated events unfolded, it was not too difficult to see that the "Vietnam phasedown" of Kennedy's plan was in the process of being completely turned around. During that same month, December 1963, the Vietnamese Civilian Irregular Defense Groups (CIDGs) were transferred from CIA control to the U.S. Army Special Forces, the Green Berets. This was the initial move of the U.S. military glacier into combat action in Southeast Asia under the operational control of its own military commanders.

At the time Peer de Silva arrived, the United States had acquired a fleet of small high-speed boats for use with OPLAN 34A–type operations against the North Vietnamese.

John Kennedy had been a PT boat commander in the southwest Pacific during WWII. In a move designed to win his sentimental approval, the CIA, with the cooperation of the U.S. Navy, had arranged to procure a fleet of fast boats from a Norwegian manufacturer. These boats were as close as anyone could come, in the sixties, to the famous PT boats of the forties.

These patrol boats were divided into two categories. The fastest, and those most like the original PT boats, were called "Swifts," and the slower but more heavily armed ones were called "Nasties." Both of them were employed in "hit and run" operations.

To augment this capability, under OPLAN 34A tactics, the CIA made use of an unusual cargo aircraft called the C-123.

The C-123 was an outgrowth of the original C-122 that had been designed and built by the Chase Aircraft Company. The success of that earlier model led to a merger of Chase and the Fairchild Aircraft Company and the production of the C-123. Some of these aircraft were later modified for spraying Agent Orange over much of Vietnam.

The use of C-123s reveals another characteristic of clandestine operations. These aircraft had belonged to the U.S. Air Force "Air Commando" units, in which many of the same people who have been involved in the Iranian "arms for hostages" swap and in Central American covert activities got their start in the "Fun and Games" business of covert activities. Because such men as Gen. Richard Secord, among others, were familiar with the venerable C-123, they selected it for use in these latter-day activities.

Behind the scenes, the PT-style boats and C-123s were used in late 1963 and 1964. The PT boats landed over-the-beach invasion parties on sabotage missions, and the C-123s were used in clandestine flights over North Vietnam to drop smaller groups of agents.

A line in the usually circumspect Pentagon Papers tells us a little more than it actually intended to: "Covert operations [as outlined in OPLAN 34A] were carried out by South Vietnamese or hired personnel and supported by U.S. training and logistics efforts." This brief statement reveals a bit more about how covert operations are mounted.

Such U.S. personnel as Special Forces troops were used to train and equip the teams to be dropped, or put "over the beach." In general, these teams were believed to have been made up of South Vietnamese natives. However, as the Pentagon Papers item reveals, these teams included "hired personnel"—and therefore, special plans were made to retrieve them and to get them safely back out of hostile territory.

These "hired personnel," as a category of clandestine operators, still exist. They are stateless people who are highly trained and equipped for special operations. They are far too valuable to expend on minor missions, and they must be kept available for such duties all over the world. They and their families are maintained in special safe areas, and their talents are called upon for covert operations of the greatest importance. The very fact that such key people were used in OPLAN 34A operations underscores how important the highest authorities considered these activities. They were seen as the leverage essential to the gradual but certain escalation of military activities in Indochina after the death of President Kennedy and during the early, and more pliable, days of the Johnson era.

These covert operations against North Vietnam were called, in the words of presidential adviser Walt Rostow, "tit for tat" activities; but with a difference. Usually in a "tit for tat" game, one party hits the other and the second party responds. In the Rostow context, the first party— the United States or South Vietnam—would strike covertly. Then, when the second party hit back, the United States would announce that it had been hit first and that it was legitimate to strike back. Such an action took place in the Gulf of Tonkin and led to the famous "Gulf of Tonkin Resolution" that gave the President the authority to "strike back" and to utilize U.S. forces against the North Vietnamese. This was all part of the very clever sequence of events that had been planned as far back as May 1963 and was then implemented in after the death of Kennedy.

On July 30, 1964, "South Vietnamese" PT boats made a midnight attack, including an amphibious commando raid on the Hon Me and Hon Nieu islands just off the coast of North Vietnam above the 19th parallel, north latitude. The North Vietnamese responded by sending their high-speed KOMAR boats after the raiders. The "Swift" PT boats escaped; but the KOMARS spotted the U.S.S. *Maddox* in the vicinity. The *Maddox* claimed that the KOMARS fired torpedoes and that "a bullet fragment was recovered from the destroyer's superstructure."

On the night of August 3, 1964, more commando raids were made on the coast of North Vietnam, and the Vinh Sonh radar installation was hit. Because of its importance, this raid was most certainly made by CIA mercenaries. Following it, a claim was made of an intercepted radio transmission saying, "North Vietnamese naval forces had been ordered to attack the patrol" consisting of the *Maddox* and the *Turner Joy*. It was this incident that triggered the action that led to the passage of the Gulf of Tonkin Resolution of August 1964. Plans laid in May 1963 and other related actions had been leading up to this event since November 22, 1963, and the guns of Dallas, and the preparatory steps had been under way since at least March 1964.

In March 1964 the familiar team of McNamara and Taylor made another fact-finding trip to South Vietnam. They returned and made their report to the President and the NSC on March 16. As a result of this report the President approved and signed NSAM #288 on March 17, 1964. By this time, of course, the Kennedy plan for Vietnam had been altered considerably. In their report, McNamara and Taylor said that "the situation in Vietnam was considerably worse than had been realized at the time of the adoption of NSAM #273" on November 26,

1963—not to mention at the time of NSAM #263, which was signed by Kennedy on October 11, 1963.

NSAM #288 said, "We seek an independent non-Communist South Vietnam....Unless we can achieve this objective in South Vietnam, almost all of Southeast Asia will probably fall under Communist dominance....Thus, purely in terms of foreign policy, the stakes are high."

This was a far cry from the Kennedy plans of late 1963. The stage was now set for military escalation in Southeast Asia. The level of activity was raised as OPLAN 34A strikes were leveraged in severity and with the response of the KOMARS against the attacks by the PT boats and their mercenary crewmen.

In mid-1964 Ambassador Lodge had resigned to run for the presidency that fall, and he had been replaced in Saigon by none other than the chairman of the Joint Chiefs of Staff, Gen. Maxwell Taylor. Taylor's staff was augmented by an old-line State Department veteran, U. Alexis Johnson, and by William Sullivan, who was made executive officer for the diplomatic mission.

At about the same time, Gen. Paul Harkins left his command in Saigon and was replaced by his deputy, Gen. William C. Westmoreland. In Peer de Silva's well-chosen words, "Thus, these three [McNamara, Taylor, and Westmoreland], as heavenly stars, were to be perfectly aligned to dominate the American government's policy and strategy in Vietnam in the crucial decision-making years of 1964–1965, a power alignment which I believe proved most unfortunate. Individually courageous, strong, and forceful, in 1964 they came to the wrong war."

It would be hard to set the stage for that crucial period better than CIA Station Chief Peer de Silva has done it:

> Prior to leaving Washington, Westmoreland had been given his orders by Taylor, then Chairman, JCS:
> "Westy, you get out there and take charge. Get the military command and the ARVN [South Vietnamese Army] organized and then fight the war right, the way we did in France. It's a big war and we'll fight it like one. We must bring enough firepower and bombs down on the Vietcong to make them realize they're finished; only then will they toss in the sponge."

De Silva added, "The principle of fighting the big war, the big action in Vietnam, had thus been established. This doctrine, and the decisions later issuing from it, led inescapably to April 1975 and American defeat."

The important thing to realize from de Silva's words is that General Taylor gave these orders to Westmoreland in December 1963—only one month after Kennedy's death, less than one month after Johnson had signed the rather tentative document NSAM #273, and more than seven months before President Johnson was to ask Congress for the authority to use the armed forces of the United States in a war in Southeast Asia.

What did Gen. Maxwell Taylor know, in December 1963, about "the big war" that caused him to make such a statement? At that time, the United States had 15,914 military personnel in South Vietnam, of whom fewer than 2,000 were "military advisers." The others were helicopter maintenance crewmen, supply personnel, and the like. Did Maxwell Taylor actually visualize the action in Vietnam as being similar to that which had confronted the Allied forces under General Eisenhower in Europe in 1944? Did General Taylor actually equate the black-pajama-clad "Vietcong" with the battle-trained armed forces of Nazi Germany? What kind of orders was he giving General Westmoreland? What did he expect the warfare in Indochina to become? More important, Taylor's orders to Westmoreland came at a time when not one single American soldier was serving in Southeast Asia under the operational command and control of a U.S. military officer. How, then, could he have seen it as "a big war"?

These are questions that trail behind the train of events that led both to the death of Pres. John F. Kennedy and to the subsequent escalation of the American military intervention in Indochina. There can be no question that there were those who wanted the fighting to develop and to become the war that General Taylor, chairman of the Joint Chiefs of Staff, described to Westmoreland in December 1963 as "big." After all, [3] they had done so much to assure it would be.

In his monumental book *Law and the Indo-China War*, John Norton Moore, professor of law and director of the graduate program at the University of Virginia School of Law, discusses several of the variables of the quality of the general community's minimum public order decisions as they pertain to the conflict in Southeast Asia and to warfare in general.

He cites, as the first of the several facts of interdependence that establish common interests in every global interaction, "the accelerating rate of population growth, along with the pluralization of both functional and territorial groups...."

Any study of the armed conflicts that have taken place during this century reveals that for whatever stated reason or excuse a particular war may have been waged, one of its most glaring results has been the wholesale murder of millions of noncombatants, such as occurred in Vietnam, Laos, and Cambodia between 1945 and 1980. Another inevitable finding would be that in addition to these genocidal murders, there have been numerous examples of the forced movement and relocation of additional millions of natives from their traditional homelands and communities to other, generally inhospitable locations. Such movements inevitably lead to the destruction of their ancient way of life and its irreplaceable social values.

The result of these actions—which have been carried out during this century both by "the West" and by "the Communists"—has often been the devastation of ancient homelands that had never been touched by warfare—at least not modern warfare, with its vast means of destruction.

The terrible 1968 massacre of more than three hundred women and children at Song My (My Lai) in Vietnam serves as no more than a minor example of the type of warfare that has overwhelmed such rural communities. As a result of the "mere gook" syndrome that prevailed in Vietnam, the enemy was frequently declared to be "anyone who ran," "anyone of either sex," "anyone of any age," or "anyone armed or unarmed."

Gen. Edward G. Lansdale, who had so much to do with the early years in Indochina, frequently regaled his associates in the Pentagon with stories of "enemy agents" who had been placed in helicopters to be flown to headquarters for interrogation. En route, "to let them know we meant business," one or two who had refused to talk would be thrown out of the helicopter, "to teach the others a lesson." Such murders were of little consequence to those warriors, as My Lai and the movie *Platoon* confirm.

These accounts from the earlier days of the war would be far surpassed by the record of the CIA's Phoenix program, which was designed to destroy and wipe out the Vietnamese rural structure, on the assumption that it was the mainstay of the "Vietcong." In open congressional testimony, William Colby, the CIA's top man in the Phoenix program, claimed, with some pride, that they had eliminated about sixty thousand "authentic Vietcong agents." These Vietnamese were "neutralized" without benefit of trial or of the rules of warfare governing the treatment of prisoners. They were simply "eliminated."

In a war where "body count" seemed to be the primary objective of the fighting forces, one must not lose sight of the great significance of underlying factors that establish a climate of legitimacy for murder, or "neutralization." In fact, these underlying beliefs serve to promote genocide. For example, there are many people in this world who believe it is not only "all right" but essential to reduce the total human population, and to reduce it by any means. This conviction, which stems from the work of the British East India Company's chief economist at the turn of the nineteenth century, Thomas Malthus, pervades certain elements of our global society. Malthusianism is a deeper motivational factor than the more popularly recognized ideological confrontations.

When it is "their turn," the Soviets have performed these common genocidal functions as well as "the West" has. Witness the slaughter of millions of noncombatants in Afghanistan and the forced movement of no fewer than 6 million Afghan natives from their ancient homeland over the great passes to Pakistan.

The U.S. Department of State's Office of Population Affairs has stated:

> There is a single theme behind our work: We must reduce population levels. Either the governments will do it our way, through nice, clean methods, or they will get the kind of mess that we have in El Salvador, or in Iran, or in Beirut. We look at resources and environmental constraints, we look at our strategic needs, and we say that this country must lower its population, or else we will have trouble. The government of El Salvador failed to use our programs to lower population. Now they get a civil war because of it. There will be dislocation and food shortages. They still have too many people there.

The above conditions merge together into a demand for war—any kind of war, anywhere. This is the root concept, and the overall excuse, for an entire series of wars in Third World countries since 1945. Because of the Malthusian belief in the need for population control, the murder, by warfare, of countless millions of noncombatants is "lawfully" justified. This has been true quite recently, and it is why such wars are certain to break out before long in the heavily populated continents of Africa and Latin America.

Of course, national leaders wish to justify their actions and to cloak them in legality. President Lyndon B. Johnson felt the need for such support as he attempted to escalate the long, warlike action in Indochina from its emergent underground stages to an all-out overt military confrontation.

With the statement that U.S. Navy vessels had been fired upon ringing in his ears, President Lyndon Johnson addressed Congress on August 5, 1964, to request a Southeast Asia Resolution, broad enough "to assist nations covered by the SEATO treaty." Congress responded quickly and affirmatively.

The Constitution provides that "the President shall be Commander-in-Chief of the Army and Navy of the United States." However, congressional authorization is necessary before the President can use the armed forces without a declaration of war.

In response to Johnson's request, Congress passed the Southeast Asia Resolution, providing:

[Sec.1] Congress approves and supports the determination of the President, as Commander-in-Chief, to take all necessary measures to repel any armed attack against the forces of the United States and to prevent further aggression....

[Sec.2]...the United States is, therefore, prepared, as the President determines, to take all necessary steps, including the use of armed force, to assist any member or protocol state of the Southeast Asia Collective Defense Treaty requesting assistance in defense of its freedom.

This resolution was passed in August 1964, nineteen years after the United States became actively involved in the affairs in Indochina. The time of preparation and development had been long. At times it seemed as though things were at a standstill, and at other times the tip of a covert-action iceberg would reveal another step along the way.

After the passage of the Gulf of Tonkin Resolution, a series of air strikes, called "Flaming Dart," was carried out against North Vietnam. On February 22, 1965, General Westmoreland recommended that American troops be landed on the east coast of Vietnam, at Da Nang. After considerable internecine hassling, it was decided that the marines would make the first landing, and two U.S. Marine Corps Battalion Landing Teams were selected. They landed at Da Nang on March 8, 1965.

This was the first time in almost twenty years of American involvement that members of the armed forces of the United States had entered combat zones under the command control of their own officers. For the first time, the CIA's role as the operational command in Vietnam was being shared with the military. Despite this development, the "War in Vietnam" was still a strange and unprecedented creation and a clear example of the CIA's master role as Cold War catalyst.

According to the science of war, as defined by Carl von Clausewitz, when diplomacy and all else fails, the army takes over. Despite nearly a century and a half of this doctrine, the management of the "War in Vietnam" broke all of the rules.

For one thing, the ambassador in Saigon was the senior, and highest-ranking, American official there, and the military and CIA officials ranked below him. This was a novel way to wage war, that is, with an ambassador over and senior to the general in command. And it did not stop there.

While testifying before the Senate Foreign Relations Committee during the latter part of the sixties, Sen. Stuart Symington revealed that the U.S. ambassador in Vientiane, Laos, had the authority to order bombings and to specify where the bombs were to be dropped. This led the senator to declare that the diplomat was virtually a "military proconsul." In these terms, the ambassador in Saigon had been given "military proconsul" powers for more than a decade.

Any consideration of leadership in time of war must inevitably lead to the question of the objective. Why was the United States involved in military action in faraway Southeast Asia?

Professor Moore addresses this question in *Law and the Indo-China War*, stating: "... the principal United States objective in the Indo-China War was to assist Vietnam and Laos (and subsequently Cambodia) to defend themselves against North Vietnamese military intervention."

This is as reliable a statement of the U.S. national objective as any other; but it fails to state a military objective. In an all-out attempt to do this, after the enactment of the Gulf of Tonkin Resolution, President Johnson built up the strength of the U.S. Army in Vietnam to 550,000 men, brought the air force to enormous strength in terms of bombing capacity [more tonnage was dropped than during all of WWII], and made the Navy Seventh Fleet the most powerful force afloat. Yet this did not get the job done. Despite all this, to put it simply, the United States lost the war; it failed to achieve its goal.

In actual practice, the tactical objective of the war had been the "body count." In Asia, that is not a good indicator of success, and it played right into the hands of General Giap. Guerrilla style, he spread the action out as much as he could, all over the landmass of Indochina. This made the tremendous U.S. military force impotent, diluted as it now was over wide areas.

One of the best examples of this was the battle for Anloa Valley. The "pacification" of Anloa Valley was part of Operations Masher and White Wing, in which about 12,000 men of the U.S. Army First Cavalry Division, Vietnamese airborne units, and South Korean marines took part. They succeeded in capturing the valley and heralded it in Saigon as "a breakthrough in winning the Vietcong-controlled people to our side."

In announcing this "victory" officially, Saigon officials would say only that the Anloa operation was successful because it killed a lot of "Vietcong." In fact, Anloa Valley was captured, lost, recaptured, etc., at least eight times—for no purpose other than to "kill lots of Vietcong." That does not win wars.

Recall General Taylor's order to Westmoreland: "... fight the war right, the way we did in France." Gen. George S. Patton, the hero of the Third Army's march across France in the face of an experienced German military machine, must have spun in his grave over those instructions for that type of guerrilla war.

It does little good to review the history of a war by basing it on the one time strategic objectives of the victor and the vanquished. What counts is the achievement: What was accomplished by winning that war?

Before WWII, Stalin had purged the Ukraine and wiped out millions of his own people. During WWII Stalin diverted his armies, with Hitler's in hot pursuit, away from Moscow and across this same "heartland of Mother Russia," the Ukraine. By the time the war was over, more than 20 million Russians had been killed, and the once vital Ukraine had been reduced to rubble.[4]

Although the Soviets have claimed victory over Hitler in that war, it would be hard to say that the Russian people won, on any count. Clearly, it had been someone's strategic objective to wipe out the natives of the Ukraine and to destroy their homeland, in the process completing Stalin's work and ending Hitler's dream.

How, then, can one assess the accomplishments of the thirty-year war in Vietnam? It is clear that the United States did not achieve its limited objective of helping the South Vietnamese establish a free democratic nation. What about the yardstick of "accomplishment"? On that score, millions of people in Indochina were killed and removed from the overhang of the Malthusian equation of world population density. Certainly no ideological, "Communist vs. anti-Communist" issues had been settled, and the domino theory and "bloodbath" projections (except in the special case of Cambodia) have not occurred, and the United States initiated that with its massive B-29 bombardment.

This leaves one more enormous accomplishment of the warfare in Indochina to be considered. As R. Buckminster Fuller has stated, "Jointly the two political camps have spent $6.5 trillion in the last thirty-three years to buy the capability to kill all humanity in one hour."

The American share of this enormous sum expended on the Cold War was spent under the leadership of the CIA, "Capitalism's Invisible Army," and no less than $220 billion went to the CIA's war in Indochina. That has been its accomplishment. Because of the success of that type of "money-making" war, it is not too difficult to be persuaded that a similar and more costly excursion lies not too far in the future.

TWENTY-ONE

Game Plan of the High Cabal

THE ASSASSINATION of President John F. Kennedy was one of the truly cataclysmic events of this century. The murder of a President was traumatic enough; but the course of events that followed and that have affected the welfare of this country and the world since that time has, in many ways, been tragic.

That assassination has demonstrated that most of the major events of world significance are masterfully planned and orchestrated by an elite coterie of enormously powerful people who are not of one nation, one ethnic grouping, or one overridingly important business group. They are a power unto themselves for whom these others work. Neither is this power elite of recent origin. Its roots go deep into the past.

Kennedy's assassination has been used as an example of their methodology. Most thinking people of this country, and of the world believe that he was not killed by a lone gunman. Despite that view, the cover story created and thrust upon us by the spokesmen of this High Cabal has existed for three decades. It has come from the lips of every subsequent President and from the top media representatives and their spokesmen. They are experienced, intelligent people who are aware of the facts. Consider the pressure it must take to require all of them, without exception, to quote the words of that contrived cover story over and over again for nearly three decades.

This is the evidence we have of the significance of the Kennedy assassination. But it is only one example. Other major events, such as the development and escalation of the Vietnam War, have been manipulated in a similar manner. In bringing this work to a close I shall provide, briefly, a look at a few of the other events during the Cold War that have taken place because the power elite planned things that way.

As a result, I am aware I may be attacked in the same fashion as Oliver Stone even before his movie *JFK* appeared in the theaters. The attack consists of words like *conspiracy* and *paranoia* similar to the verbal accusations during the Inquisition. To attack someone as conspiracy prone because he does not believe the cover story that one lone gunman killed the President is ridiculous. By now it has become clear that there was a plan to murder Kennedy in order to escalate the Vietnam war and decimate most of the less-developed countries through a form of banker-managed, predatory economic warfare. *Conspiracy* is far from the operative word. This is planning at its best or worst, depending on your point of view. Furthermore, *paranoia* cannot properly be used to define someone who studies economics and history and reveals certain facts. As a matter of proper definition, such findings are the result of the opposite of "paranoia." Having said this, let's take a look at a few recent examples of how the game plan of the High Cabal, Winston Churchill's phrase for the power elite, operates.

Ever since the murder of the President we have been told by the highest authorities that JFK was killed by one man, who fired three shots from a mail-order Italian-made rifle. Quite naturally most Americans have wanted, at first, to believe the word of their government, especially when it involved such an important matter.

Many of the most earnest of these researchers who do not believe that one man killed the President with three shots from a rifle have mistakenly spent almost three decades researching and studying the cover story and not the facts. More than six hundred books have been written on this subject. In them you can find a myriad of obscure trivia dug up by these tireless researchers. But to no avail. That is not the path to the answer to the main question, "Why was Kennedy killed?" No one will ever know who killed the President. In that business, the "mechanics" are faceless and have chameleon identities that are skillfully shielded by the system.

It is easy for anyone to learn that President Kennedy was murdered in a burst of gunfire, as reported by able and on-the-spot newsmen, that hit him at least twice, struck Governor Connally at least once and more likely two times, and that a fragment created by a stray shot hit a man named Tague who was standing on the curb of a street about a block away from where Kennedy was shot. Those are more than the "three shots" on which the Warren Commission builds its case. "More than three shots" is all the evidence needed to prove that the accounts of the crime given by the Secret Service, the FBI, and the Warren Commission are wrong.

What does it take to convince able, intelligent people that the contrived cover story published by our government is nothing more than that? If nothing else a recent episode from the pages of the *Journal of the American Medical Association* should alert the public to the seriousness of the cause underlying the decision to assassinate JFK almost thirty years ago.

This powerful, wealthy association, one of the most influential in the country, has required its spokesmen to proclaim, once again, that a bullet entered the back of the neck of the President and exited through his throat and then traveled on to seriously injure Governor Connally. "How utterly absurd," we might say; and of course it is. But that is not the point. Here is this prestigious organization being forced by a higher power, under some form of duress, to play a distasteful role before the American public by repeating a story that is untenable.

Consider the implausibility of just one of their "facts." Their spokesmen have said, using contrived diagrams, that one bullet entered Kennedy's neck from the back and exited the throat. On the other hand, anyone can look at the suit coat and the shirt that were worn by Kennedy at the time he was shot and see clearly that the bullet that entered his body from the back made a hole in the coat and a matching one in the shirt at a point well below the neck. Such a bullet would have had to have changed course immediately, inside Kennedy's body, to have advanced upward and emerge from his throat. Moreover, this bullet was allegedly fired on a downward trajectory form six floors above the President's car. Physically impossible!

The contrived story of this entire AMA presentation went beyond medical facts. Because some authors have written that a "general" was in Bethesda Naval Hospital autopsy room at the time and that the general gave orders to the autopsy doctors, it has been made to appear that the doctors had been ordered not to perform an adequate examination. Naturally the doctors concerned have rejected such a suggestion. The doctors stated in their AMA story that there were no generals in the autopsy room, there were just the "President's military aides." This was another fabrication, and an unnecessary one. One of the President's military aides was Godfrey McHugh. I have been acquainted with McHugh since the fifties, and I know that in 1963 Godfrey McHugh was an air force general. The President's military aides were at Bethesda, as the AMA spokesmen say. He was a presidential military aide, and he was a general. He was there. He was also a friend of Jackie Kennedy and had known her since before she met Kennedy. McHugh was present at Bethesda doing his duty. The AMA spokesmen erred in stating, among other things, "there were no generals in the room."

The reason I mention these things now is to underscore that the course of events in our time is planned carefully by agents of the power elite. This American Medical Association episode in the spring of 1992 is a classic example proving that the power behind the Kennedy assassination plot lives on.

Chronologically, I have brought this review of the historical record through the years from 1943 to 1971 with some discussion of the Pentagon Papers and their unusual role in the revision of the history of past events. It is clear to anyone close to the scene, and to those who have studied them with care that this massive set of documents, "37 studies and 15 collections of documents in 43 volumes" accompanied by their very contrived editorial comments on that period of history is not the true and complete story. Can anyone imagine that a review of that period of history "from World War II to the present [1969]" could have been written without more than a few relevant words about the assassination of President John F. Kennedy? In fact, you will recall, on the very date that Kennedy died the Pentagon Papers completely ignored his death, saying quite simply that Ambassador Lodge had flown to Washington to speak with the President. This was followed by the statement that on the next day, Ambassador Lodge met with the President. Not a word was said of the fact that President Kennedy had died on November 22 and that the man Lodge met with on the twenty-third was Johnson. Is that true and reliable history?

Let's tie the assassination of Kennedy and the role of the power elite to some other notable events.

It was the spring of a memorable year, 1972. On February 7, President Nixon's secretary of commerce, Maurice Stans, opened a remarkable "White House Conference on the Industrial World Ahead, a Look at Business in 1990." This three-day meeting of fifteen hundred of this country's leading businessmen, scholars, and the like concluded with a memorable and prophetic statement by Roy L. Ash, president of Litton Industries, and incidentally one of the original "Whiz Kids" from Harvard with Bob McNamara:

... state capitalism may well be a form for world business in the world ahead; that the western countries are trending toward a more unified and controlled economy, having a greater effect on all business; and the communist nation are moving more and more toward a free market system. The question posed [during the conference] on which a number of divergent opinions arose, was whether "East and West would meet some place toward the middle about 1990."

That was an astounding forecast before such an eminent group considering that it was made in 1972 and that it was actually "about 1990" when the Soviet Union did weaken and the Cold War came to an end, in much the way he had visualized. These ideas have had a major impact on all of us. The predictions of this conference proved to be another long step on the way to a New World Order.

Such ideas are not limited to a few leaders or to a few countries. During a speech made in 1991, Giovanni Agnelli, chief executive officer of the Italian Fiat Company, recalled: "In 1946 Winston Churchill spoke in Zurich of the need to build a United States of Europe." That was another long-range forecast that is being proved quite accurate. Then Agnelli updated that comment with another statement that confirms the fact that the power of ideas, of course he means the ideas of the power elite, is greater than guns: "The fall of the Soviet Union is one of the very few instances in history in which a world power has been defeated on the battlefield of ideas."

Agnelli calls this the "battlefield of ideas." Others may find evidence of "conspiracy," while still others see things as they are and speak of "planning." And if there is planning, and we have plenty of evidence there is, there must be "planners." In that sense, this becomes an accurate definition of the existence and activity of the power elite. These events are not the result of a throw of the dice. They are planned.

Turning back to the White House Conference in 1972, before February had ended Secretary Stans had resigned to become chairman of the Committee to Reelect the President. That was the spring of the year 1972, the year when the "dirty tricks" business went public, with the birth of CREEP and the days of "Watergate."

In that same year, under President Nixon, an unusual and most effective international business organization was formed by the business interests of the Dartmouth Conference, whose meetings were regularly scheduled by the Rockefellers. It was called US-TEC, for the United States-USSR Trade and Economic Council. Backed by the Nixon administration and the international banker David Rockefeller, the

Council that listed most of the Fortune 500 corporate leaders among its membership, along with hundreds of their counterparts in the Soviet Union, opened offices in New York and in Moscow for regular activities. Meetings of the membership were scheduled every six months alternately in each location. Usually these meetings were augmented by major trade fair exhibitions from each country. This organization publishes a fine magazine that is not classified. But you can not get a copy of it unless you are a member.

US-TEC has done much to make Roy Ash's forecast at the "Look at Business in 1990" conference come true. Business, in 1972, took aim at the Evil Empire, as President Reagan called the Soviet Union a decade later.

Not much has been published openly about either of these organizations, the United States membership and the Soviet membership, as they have worked busily to create the New World Order. Their work has included the promotion of the military-industrial complex and of the massive international agricultural combines in their voracious search for new business in new fields. In this connection, the CIA is one of the primary activists and promoters for these combines, especially since its more recent emphasis upon the business of economic intelligence.

Not all wars are fought with guns. Economic warfare can be just as powerful and just as deadly.

In March 1973, the White House arranged for a meeting of representatives of the largest petroleum-consuming organizations in the country. These companies included the airlines, railroads, trucking firms, utilities, and government agencies such as the Government Services Agency and the Department of Defense. This meeting took place in the Washington offices of the National Defense Transportation Association (NDTA). I attended that meeting as a railroad representative.

At that time, as I recall, gasoline was selling at the service station pumps for under forty cents per gallon, and the railroads were buying fuel on long-term contracts for about eleven cents per gallon.

The White House spokesman informed this group that a recent study had warned that petroleum use was far ahead of new discovery and that reserves of the world's oil supply might be depleted in the not too distant future, perhaps even before the year 2000. He stated that the meeting had been called to alert all major consumers that before the end of the year it would be all but impossible to make a long-term contract for petroleum and that prices would be up by a factor of two or three. I was sitting between representatives of the airlines and the General Services

Administration. You could have heard a pin drop. By the end of the year those predictions concerning price had proved to have been conservative.

At the same time the Federal Power Commission had begun a natural gas survey because "the shortage of natural gas had been a source of surprise, shock, and disbelief to many of those affected, but not to serious students of long-term United States resource development."

Then, as if right on schedule, an Arab-Israeli war broke out in late 1973. Before long it was announced that the Arabs had instituted an oil embargo and that available supplies of automobile gasoline would drop around the world. Soon thereafter we were all parked in long lines leading to the gas pumps waiting for the little gasoline available and at any price.

In early 1974 the prestigious Center for Strategic and International Studies in Washington, D.C. invited several hundred mid-level officials from all parts of the government, from congressional offices, and from local offices of major corporations to a new federal staff energy seminar. These were more or less monthly meetings where these invitees could listen to world leaders in the field of energy, particularly petroleum.

Again, I was invited as a railroad representative and was pleasantly surprised at the high caliber of the subjects and the speakers, such as Henry Kissinger and James Schlesinger, and by the fact that these sessions continued for about four years. It is clear that an objective of those meetings was to have all of us marching to the same drum. We all began to believe that the fast-rising price of petroleum was fully justified, that a "world price" was inevitable and that the "last barrel" would be drawn from some well not too long after the year 2000.

As we now know, much of this "energy crisis" was a massive production designed and orchestrated to raise the price of petroleum from its long-time base of approximately $1.70 per barrel to a high, at times, of $40.00. Except for the international drug trade, no other production in the fields of economic warfare had ever made so much money...and continues to do so.

It takes little imagination to discover that this is another product of the High Cabal elite and that while the energy and drug projects are operating most profitably the international food business cannot be far behind. As conventional battlefield warfare diminishes in value to the world planners, economic warfare is moving boldly to the front of the stage.

William J. Casey had served as a member of the President's Foreign Intelligence Advisory Board, former under secretary of state, and later the director of central intelligence under President Reagan. On December 11, 1979, during a "Law, Intelligence and National Security Workshop" sponsored by the American Bar Association, Casey said:

> I think that we are being swamped and we have an ample supply of economic information. What we are deficient in is sufficient analysis, understanding of the long-term implications where the economic facts that scream out at us from the financial pages every day are carrying us and the problems that they are creating for us in the future, and what we can do about them. It's a shocking thing to me that we have close to a complete absence of any real machinery or any place in the United States government to systematically look at the economic opportunities and threats in long-term perspective, or any fixed responsibility for recommending or acting on the use of economic leverage, either offensively or defensively for strategic security purposes.

Does that sound like big guns and real warfare to you? A little more than one year after that speech Bill Casey became the director of central intelligence, and economic intelligence became the biggest game in town for the CIA and the National Security Agency. The meanings behind these events reveal themselves to us once we see our way through the maze of the Warren Commission Report and the continuing obfuscation of the facts concerning John F. Kennedy's death.

This CIA connection in the business of making war, and more recently of making big-business bigger, has introduced another pattern of events that this country has experienced, though not as frequently as some other nations. To oversimplify, this may be seen as the agency's ability to "rekindle the fire" whenever some new occurrence is needed to raise the level of concern throughout the nation, particularly whenever another big military budget has been prepared for a vote.

By the end of direct United States participation in the warfare in Indochina, it had become clear to the long-range war planners in the government that further attempts to support an ever-increasing military budget for the type of conventional warfare practiced in Korea and Vietnam would no longer be possible. With the advent of the Reagan administration and its pro-business leaning toward a strong and ever-increasing Defense Department budget, something had to be done to raise the level of public anxiety and anger toward the only superpower available, the Soviet Union. This created a problem and a demand for a solution.

Clear evidence indicates that the old Hegelian doctrine that nations require conflict still prevails. But you may be sure that the scenario of the conflict itself must change. Here we need to look at an important example of the Reagan era that is being used repeatedly to demonstrate how the power elite and their warmakers utilize all manner of plots to achieve their ambitious goal of establishing the highest level of costly military preparedness under all kinds of political conditions. This method of international gamesmanship is called "Terrorism."

On September 1, 1983, the *New York Times*, and most other newspapers around the world, displayed the headline "Korean Jetliner With 269 Aboard Missing Near Soviet Pacific Island." Meanwhile, the same front-page article reported: "Korean Foreign Ministry officials cited the United States Central Intelligence Agency as their source for the report that the plane had been forced down on Sakhalin." The *Times* continued "All 240 passengers and 29 crew members were believed to be safe."

That front-page story related that, based upon this same CIA message that had been sent to Korea and Japan, an official of the U.S. Department of State had phoned the family of Georgia representative Larry P. McDonald, a passenger on that flight, late in the evening of August 31, 1983. The purpose of that call was to inform them that the plane, its passengers, and crew were safe on the ground at Sakhalin Island. This, of course, was untrue. The CIA message had been fabricated for other purposes, among them to cause the Japanese to recall the Air-Sea Rescue Fleet.

It is difficult to believe that officials of the Department of State would have made that humanitarian call if they did not believe in the validity of the CIA message. Why did the CIA send such a message?

The airliner never landed on Sakhalin Island, the passengers and crew have never been found and the aircraft had disappeared.

That issue of the *New York Times* had been printed late in the evening of August 31, 1983, and was accurate at that time. But a series of stunning events followed.

At ten A.M., September 1, 1983, in Washington, Secretary of State George Shultz appeared on nationwide TV to announce the Soviet Union had shot down that Korean airliner in cold blood. The plane and its occupants had vanished. Immediately out of Washington arose the ogre of the Evil Empire. The Cold War had reached its zenith. Within days, the largest Defense Department budget ever passed in peacetime whizzed through Congress and was eagerly signed by President Reagan. Thus began the most costly peacetime decade in the history of civilization.

So why was that most timely CIA message reported by the *New York Times*? During the evening of August 31, all that the *Times* knew was that the CIA message had been sent, what it said, and that the news media around the world knew about it. The same issue of the *Times* also reported that the plane had been on Japanese radar for six minutes before it disappeared. That positive radar trail led to a crash site southeast of Hokkaido, far from Sakhalin. The Japanese had sent twelve air-sea rescue vessels toward that location. While they were at sea, the CIA message arrived in Seoul and Tokyo and at the Department of State. As was predictable, as soon as the Japanese received that message, they recalled their rescue boats, and the chance to locate the wreckage, save survivors, and confirm its identity was lost.

With that essential diversion safely accomplished the government could announce any scenario it wanted for the loss of the Korean airliner and get away with it. No one was ever going to be able to locate the wreckage of the plane deep in the Kurile Trench of the Pacific Ocean.

This was the scene during the first weeks of September 1983. In the midst of this international uproar we discover the steady hand of the unruffled High Cabal. The world's largest trade fair had been scheduled by US-TEC to be held in Moscow on October 17–25, 1983. This was the month after the mysterious loss of the Korean airliner, yet representatives of 109 of the largest American companies traveled to Moscow, home of the Evil Empire, to carry out their business as usual at the "Agribusiness USA" trade show.

As we look back at this trade show, at the Evil Empire days and at the existence of this most important US-TEC organization, we discover more elements of that power elite structure that we have been describing. Furthermore, this record confirms that what Roy Ash said during the 1971 conference about "East and West would meet some place toward the middle about 1990" was not a prediction but a master plan.

Such plans are comparable to the work of Allen Dulles as the OSS chief in Geneva during World War II with selected Germans, and to the activities of T. V. Soong in China during the same period. These are examples of how these higher echelons are above warfare, both hot and cold, as they continue their own games on a more exalted level on both sides at the same time.

An item in a US-TEC journal of 1977 was written by David Rockefeller, chairman of the Chase Manhattan Bank. He has been one of the world's most important international bankers as head of one of its most important banks. His letter made reference to "an unbroken relationship with Russian financial institutions that straddles well over fifty years."

Think back fifty years, from 1977 to 1927, and recall all of the enormous ideological, military, economic, and political problems that existed between the East and the West. Yet Rockefeller and Chase Manhattan took pride in the fact that they had been in Moscow during that time doing business in the center of the maelstrom. I have mentioned earlier the statement of the American chargé in the Saigon embassy to the effect "that in case of bankruptcy [of the country] which we now confront, bankers have [the] right to organize a receivership."

That is an international banker's way of putting it. He expected, as only natural, that bankers would arrange the policy for what took place in Vietnam, and they have done just that.

All of these things come together. While the President of the United States harangued the world about the Evil Empire, his good friends, our senior businessmen, were packing their briefcases for another big meeting for business as usual in Moscow. Rockefeller had reminded everyone that he and his banking interests had been working there since 1927, and then as a small aside, related in that same letter in the US-TEC journal how "the seventh session of the Dartmouth Conference in Hanover in 1972 had led to the idea of forming a joint high-level Trade and Economic Council."

With these examples I believe we have taken a good look at the plot to assassinate President John F. Kennedy and the atmosphere in which such planning took place. You can easily visualize a businessman's club in downtown Washington, New York, London, Frankfurt, Tokyo, or Toronto. A group of senior members have gathered after lunch for a third martini. One of them mentions that a director of his company had called that morning to say that Kennedy's denial of the TFX procurement contract to the Boeing Company had hit his company, a major subcontractor, very hard. This struck a nerve of one of the other members, who reported that Roz Gilpatric, who works with that "goddamn" McNamara, had been telling the bankers things were going to change. They could no longer count on the practices that had feathered their nests for so many years.

Another member took a quick sip of his martini and said, "I had a call from one of our bankers in the City early this morning. He wanted to know how we were doing and was it true that Kennedy was going to take all Americans out of Vietnam. By God, we can't have that. We've just sold McNamara on that electronic battlefield. It will be worth about one and one-half billion to us. That'll go down the drain."

An elderly member, who used to visit the Dulles family in their summer home on Henderson Bay, leaned over toward the center of that small group and almost in a whisper said that his boys had just completed a study of how many helicopters were going to be needed for a ten-year war in Vietnam. The total was in the thousands, and the cost ran into the billions of dollars. Then he looked around the group of old cronies and snarled, "That goddamn Kennedy bastard has been working all summer with some of Old Joe's Irish Mafia and his favorite generals and they are planning every which way to get us out of Vietnam. This can't happen. He's got to go. Right now he's a sure thing for reelection and then there is Bobby and after him Teddy. I tell you that Kennedy has got to go."

On the perimeter of that intense group sat a younger man quietly attentive to every word and watching every move. Just then, as the speaker finished his words, he saw a wink in the eye of a senior member. He rose quietly and walked to a position behind his chair. That member turned and whispered a few words. They were all that he needed to hear, "In the fall, somewhere in the south. Find a way to get as many key people out of the city as possible. It's all up to you."

There was the decision. It had been the result of a consensus of not that one meeting, but of many. This meeting was the climax. This man was a skilled professional. He know the codes, how to use them and who to call. He knew exactly how to set the train of events into operation. He knew then that his biggest job would be to put a small cadre of the best men in the world at work right away on the cover story and on the deception plan.

He would handle the call to the agent for the "mechanics" who operated from a foreign country, and he would begin the moves that would result in the ever-normal selection of the site. He would have to speak to no more than three others, and they would not know him except by an exquisite code. It was his job to handle the Secret Service, the FBI, and the Pentagon. As required, he would be assisted at every step by the CIA. He would not report back to the "members." Should there be a change of plan, they could reach him. From that day until November 22, 1963, the plan ran smoothly. The game plan of the High Cabal never fails, because they are at the top. Even if it should fail, no one would ever be able to prosecute them or their allies.

I said in the beginning that this was not intended to be simply a history. It is an analysis of the secret history of the United States since World War II.

More importantly, I emphasized that I believe that God does not throw the dice. The affairs of man and of nature are not determined at random or by mere chance. You have had the opportunity to travel back through those years with me and will recall that 1963 marked a major turning point in this century because the power elite moved that year to remove John F. Kennedy from the White House and to take the course of the Ship of State into their own hands.

Furthermore, the year 1972 stands out as another one of those signal turning points. Recall the Nixon-era White House "Conference on the Industrial World Ahead" and the fact that those highly selected attendees had devoted three days to a discussion of the subject, "A Look at Business in 1990." That was February 1972, and as those sessions came to a close, Roy Ash, president of Litton Industries made his momentous closing statement that described events that would occur twenty and thirty years hence.

His words have now become fact and cannot be changed. This is the way of the world as it approaches the year 2000. There are major plans, as David Rockerfeller notes, and when a Vietnam War, the assassination of John F. Kennedy, or the destruction of a Korean airliner are necessary, they will be caused to happen. They will not be left to chance or the bad aim of a lone gunman in a sixth-floor window in Dallas. This is the way things are. Successful men plan ahead. Brave men, such as Oliver Stone, make films such as *JFK*. The rest of us are the victims or the beneficiaries of all the rest.

Stone's *JFK* and the Conspiracy

FEW MOTION PICTURES of the past several decades have had the impact upon the general public as did Oliver Stone's film *JFK*. The fact of the existence of a conspiracy to kill the President of the United States is shocking; yet many Americans try to brush it aside.

Although the great majority of Americans do not believe the Warren Commission's conclusion that Lee Harvey Oswald by himself killed Kennedy, they find it all but impossible to believe the alternative. This homespun psychological safety net was shattered by Stone's film. From the time they saw that film they have been unable to accept the creative falseness of the cover story. That film made conspiracy the only true conclusion.

Of particular note was the film's effect upon the professional community of assassination buffs. To begin with, these writers and researchers are not a homogeneous society. There are some who support the government line, with its Warren Commission, magic bullet, Lee Harvey Oswald, Jack Ruby, and all the rest of that massive, highly contrived fiction. Then there are the dedicated researchers who know that the Warren Commission Report was a smoke screen and that all of its mythology is a masterful cover story designed and nourished at the highest level by those who have spent a lifetime concealing the facts of the case. It was this latter group of buffs who found encouragement in Stone's masterful film, as well as renewed strength in its message.

To these more or less well organized groupings, we must add the new and rapidly growing hordes of assassination investigators who encountered reality and encouragement in the film and who have become interested in its challenging message. For them Stone's film presented a comprehensive coverage of the assassination and all of its ramifications, public and private, that provided everyone with material they may not have heard before.

And, then there are the pure professionals. Many of the more prominent of this group viciously attacked Oliver Stone and his movie. Now why would they, of all people, so violently denigrate the film that supported the fact of the conspiracy? Don't they see the truth? Have they made public their own personal beliefs? Quite frankly, I doubt it. These hard-liners comprise the most ardent sector of the assassination buff mélange because they are professional writers and journalists who work for some of the most important media outlets in the country.

One of them, Leslie Gelb, is the man Robert McNamara placed in charge of the task force that produced the "Defense Department History of United States Decisionmaking on Vietnam," aka the Pentagon Papers. His task force is the one that came up with the following "historical fact":

22 Nov 1963 Lodge confers with the President.
Having flown to Washington the day after the conference, Lodge meets with the President and presumably continues the kind of report given in Honolulu.

Gelb had all but concealed Kennedy's NSAM #263 in the Pentagon Papers, by dividing it into meaningless sections, and continued his assault on that Kennedy policy as he berated Stone for his film.

Another of these prominent writers was Tom Wicker of the *New York Times*. He also attacked Stone's use of Kennedy's Vietnam policy statement, NSAM #263, with the comment, "I know of no reputable historian who has documented Kennedy's intentions." NSAM #263 is the official and complete documentation of Kennedy's intentions. It was derived from a series of White House conferences and from the McNamara-Taylor Vietnam Trip Report, and it stated the views of the President and of his closest advisers as is made clear in the U.S. government publication *Foreign Relations of the United States, 1961–1963*, vol. IV, "Vietnam: August–December 1963." That source is reliable history. Wicker's December 22, 1991, *Times* article was a lengthy and unnecessarily demeaning diatribe against Stone and his movie.

So many of these professional writers attacked the film, even well before it was on the screens of the nation, that Oliver Stone took the unusual step of publishing *The Book of the Film* in 1992. In this important work, Stone does what few others have done. He presents the full *JFK* debate by publishing the demeaning articles of his detractors and the responses of his supporters side by side in the text. This even-handed approach is rare in such public debates.

For the record, these reactions and commentaries came from the following people (number of articles in parentheses):

David Ansen, (2); Robert Sam Anson, (1); David W. Belin, (3); Jimmy Breslin, (1); Joseph A. Califano, Jr., (1); Alexander Cockburn, (4); Alan M. Dershowitz, (1); Roger Ebert, (2); Gerald R. Ford, (1); Leslie H. Gelb, (1); Tom Hayden, (1); Robert Hennelly, (2); George Lardner, Jr. (4); Anthony Lewis, (1); Norman Mailer, (1); William Manchester, (1); Richard M. Mosk, (1); Daniel Patrick Moynihan, (1); John Newman, (1); Andrew O'Hehir, (1); L. Fletcher Prouty, (2); Ron Rosenbaum, (1); Arthur Schlesinger, Jr., (1); Katherine Seelye, (1); Brent Staples, (1); Oliver Stone, (12); Garry Trudeau, (1); and Tom Wicker, (1); and others.

This latter group, among them Robert Sam Anson, Leslie Gelb, George Lardner, Anthony Lewis, William Manchester, Arthur Schlesinger, and Tom Wicker came out of nowhere to attack Oliver Stone, Jim Garrison and myself for what the movie offered the public: much of their work was done before the film had been produced and shown to the public. This is a rare form of movie review and was almost universally adversarial, even though, in most cases, they, the writers, were in error and not the film itself. What is it that bonds these major writers together? The truth?

What is most interesting about this latter group of professional writers, most of whom work for major media bosses, is that they all wrote negatively about the film and all wrote in support of the anticonspiracy, lone-gunman, Warren Commission theory. They are a highly motived clan...for money.

Here is where this remarkable film of Stone's hits the hardest among all of these "experts." It strengthens the arguments of those who believe that there was a massive conspiracy, and it does battle, as did David

versus Goliath, against the power of the throne. To all of this, the film—
for both sides—enlivened the game and created new flocks of believers.

One of the film's major achievements was that it aroused the United
States Congress to "mandate a comprehensive review of all federal
government records related to the assassination of President John F.
Kennedy, including the records of the Warren Commission, the House
Assassinations Committee, the Church Committee, and all Executive
branch agencies, including the C.I.A. and the F.B.I." This was well
intentioned; but in reality it is a sham. The answers to the source of the
decision to murder John F. Kennedy are not in government files.

This action alone aroused the profession of the assassination buff to its
highest level, as evidenced by the activities of the Coalition On Political
Assassinations and others like it.

These achievements serve to make the film exceptional; but this was
not the end. It was the goal of Oliver Stone and of those of us who
worked with him that the truth about the murder of John F. Kennedy be
brought to as many viewers as possible, not only in the United States of
America but also around the world. This has been done, and the impact
upon the ordinary layman who has not made a special study of this
subject has, in many instances, been far greater, proportionately, than
upon the professionals.

As the reader will have noted, this has been a primary objective of
this autobiographical book of mine. This is one reason why Stone used
parts of it in his script.

I have tried to put the Kennedy assassination in proper prospective
with a chronological time-line as a guiding star. I recall well the first
acts of the Cold War that began in 1944, even before the end of the hot
war known as World War II. I have underscored the beginning of the
warfare in Indochina that actually began on the same day as the
surrender of the Japanese on September 2, 1945, and of the Korean War
that the "Big Four" at the Teheran Conference so amply provided for in
November 1943.

With this time-line, it became imperative that I fit the assassination of
the President into the most crucial of periods: the twenty years from
1955 to 1975 that the military-industrial complex had set for the
superescalation of the warfare in Vietnam. It was then, in late 1963, that
President Kennedy, in full coordination with his closest team of top-
level advisers in the White House and in the Pentagon, signed his
National Security Action Memorandum #263 of October 11, 1963. This
directive, among many other things, ordered that 1,000 U.S military

personnel be brought home by the end of 1963, and that the bulk of U.S. personnel be withdrawn by the end of 1965. NSAM #263 and its accompanying policy became the "straw that broke the camel's back." That carefully crafted and determined policy in the impending climate of Kennedy's assured reelection in 1964 led directly to the consensual decision at the highest levels that the President must be killed and that control of the U.S. government must be put in other hands. In other words, Kennedy's Vietnam policy announcements made a coup d'état necessary.

This was the burden of the Stone film. The inclusion of this little-known NSAM #263 in the film became the principal point of attack of the big guns that were leveled at Stone, Garrison, and myself. It really is amazing that the most vitriolic attacks were those that attempted to inform the public that there was no such directive. The furor over that one item, NSAM #263, was evidence that Stone had hit his target. This alone uncovered the "Why?" of the assassination.

In the film's closing scenes between "Garrison" and "Man X," who was a representation of this author, one could feel the tension build in every audience in every theater. When "Man X" says "Why? Why was Kennedy killed? Who benefited? Who has the power to cover it up?" the audience is forced to look at the real cause of the assassination and not at some prearranged fabrication of that terrible event. Stone had succeeded in carrying the theme from the comprehensive, widespread scope of the early and disorganized misapprehensions of the assassination lore, as typified by the Warren Commission's report, through the specific tensions of the Garrison trial in New Orleans to the summit of activity in Washington, and then attacked the real issue, "Why was John F. Kennedy killed?"

It was altogether fitting, it was purely masterful, that Stone had those last scenes filmed on the mall in Washington, D.C., between the Lincoln Memorial and the Washington Monument with the rising dome of the Capitol building looming over Costner (Garrison) and Sutherland (Prouty) in the distance. Only a few steps farther down the road from there, the Kennedy Center itself is overlooked by the old faded yellow brick building that was CIA headquarters and the long-time office of Director of Central Intelligence Allen W. Dulles until Kennedy fired him. The setting itself was classic. This scene tells its own story. This is the heart of the District of Columbia. It is the place where so much of that fatal decision, for the U.S. government and for all of us, was made by the cabal.

And with those words about the film and its terrific impact on all assassination buffs of all kinds and all beliefs, I wish to close with a few words that have become more meaningful with the passage of the decades since November 22, 1963. During my nine years in the Pentagon, I can recall no month that was more hectic, more confused and more explosive than January 1961, the last month of the eight-year Eisenhower administration and the month during which Kennedy was inaugurated. There was something about that period that bore some special message of its own—for the future. What was happening, especially there in the Pentagon, was not simply the routine changing of the guard. That month carried its own message, a premonition of sinister things to follow.

The closely knit Eisenhower team was so confident that Nixon would be elected that they had arranged such things as the annual budget, procurement schedules and other long-range objectives, including the Vietnam War, the anti-Castro activities, and the space program, for the Nixon administration to carry out. These plans included big-ticket items such as the Air Force's scheduled procurement of the new TFX swing-wing fighter aircraft at $6.5 billion, among others. The Kennedy election, assuring a drastic change in key positions up and down the line, put all of those plans in jeopardy. No one stood more to lose than our friends in the highly dedicated industrial sector of the nation, particularly in the military-industrial group.

Then, on January 17, 1961, President Eisenhower delivered his Farewell Address to the American public. Oliver Stone chose to open his film *JFK* with a few selected lines from that memorable speech:

> ...The conjunction of an immense military establishment and a large arms industry is new in the American experience. The total influence—economic, political, even spiritual—is felt in every city, every statehouse, every office of the Federal Government... In the councils of government we must guard against the acquisition of unwarranted influence, whether sought or unsought, by the military industrial complex. The potential for the disastrous rise of misplaced power exists and will persist... We must never let the weight of this combination endanger our liberties or democratic processes. We should take nothing for granted....

Two days after Eisenhower's address, I walked into the office of Secretary of Defense Thomas Gates at the close of the business day, as had been my custom for months, prepared to give him a few brief words on what was taking place in the business of "providing the military support of the clandestine operations of the CIA"—more specifically, an update on the status of the Cuban Exile operations—later to be known as the Bay of Pigs operation. On that late afternoon, a blizzard was raging outside. From the Pentagon we could barely see the buildings of Washington across the Potomac. And, on that late hour, as I approached Mr. Gates's office, I saw that the hallway, the anteroom, and his office were jammed with well-wishers. This was to be his last day as secretary of defense. As I look back at those nine years, I have always believed that he was the best and most qualified man ever to hold that office. As Mr. Gates was in no position for a briefing at that curtain-lowering time, his secretary ushered me into the office of Deputy Secretary of Defense James Douglas, another able gentleman. He greeted me with his characteristic smile, strolled across his office, and leaned against the window sill. As I looked over his shoulder, I saw nothing but raging snow. I said, "Mr. Douglas, I have briefed you from time to time over the past six years. I regret that this will be our last briefing." Then I went on to give him a report on the status of the Cuban Exile program that the Eisenhower administration had started, as a formal C.I.A. activity, back in March 1960.

When I finished the brief report, I asked an essential question, "Each time I have come in here, or into Mr. Gates's office, I have known that you gentlemen were well aware of the subject of these briefings over the years, and of their background; but tomorrow, when I come in here, there will be some new men to be briefed. Can you tell me, do I have to go back to B.C. or early A.D. with that briefing, or may I assume that they have been informed of the subjects I shall be covering?"

Mr. Douglas turned away and looked out at the snow and the dim outline of the city. Finally he turned back, and said, "Prouty, I'll be damned if I know what to say. I haven't met the bastards and I haven't the slightest idea what they know and what they do not know. They have never asked us for such information." Of course he was referring to Robert McNamara, the new secretary of defense, and to Roswell Gilpatric, the new deputy, a totally new team in both person and political ideology, let alone "military strategy in the days of the hydrogen bomb." This was the best characterization, that I can recall, of the climate that existed in Washington between the two administrations since that unexpected election of John F. Kennedy.

Few people have realized the true atmosphere of the Eisenhower-Kennedy transition, and nowhere else in the government was that transition more acrimonious than in the Pentagon. As a military officer I worked with the Gates team and without a break continued along with the McNamara team.

I cite this fact, at the close of my book, because as I look back over those years it has become clear to me that the Kennedy victory at the polls, in 1960, was perhaps as much a cause of his eventual assassination, in 1963, as anything else. There was no way he could win against the in-place power centers, including that of the military-industrial complex, as President Eisenhower himself had warned.

As you can see, such things have nothing to do with a "lone gunman" (Oswald), with Fidel Castro and the Cubans, with the Mafia, and all the rest of the lore that has blossomed since November 22, 1963. They are a part of the true story, and the others are parts of the essential "cover story" that has lived and been made to flourish since mid-November 1963.

Stone asked me to become a technical advisor as he developed the script for his film back in July 1990. He came to my home a few days after I had triple bypass coronary surgery in October 1990 and gave me a copy of the initial version of the script. I noticed as I studied it that he was arranging things so that the general public would have "a level playing field." He wanted those who knew little about the details of the assassination and its aftermath to get a good comprehensive view of the entire situation.

Then, as Stone himself learned more about the assassination, he chose the work of two highly regarded researchers and writers: Jim Garrison and Jim Marrs, along with the experienced photography expert, Bob Groden. Garrison was an excellent selection because he was the first and only official member of any court jurisdiction in the country to do what ought to have been done in Texas, where the crime had taken place, i.e., take it into a court for trial. With this endeavor Jim had put many of the actual facts of the assassination into the record and had advanced public knowledge of the crime and of its raging cover story, including the Warren Commission ruse. With Jim Marrs, Stone had one of the finest and most honest technicians in the investigation business.

It has been my endeavor, since 1985 when I first sat down at my computer, to write the story of the Cold War as few have seen it, to explain what took place at the close of World War II that led to the Korean and Vietnamese wars, and to describe the events that led to the assassination of John F. Kennedy on November 22, 1963, and answer the question *why* that terrible event was planned and executed. In this endeavor I had the invaluable assistance of Oliver Stone, Jim Garrison, and so many others dating from the eventful days of my own military career.

As Ralph Waldo Emerson wrote: "There is properly no history; only biography." With this work, I have added a bit of autobiography.

ACKNOWLEDGMENTS

To Victor H. Krulak, lieutenant general, USMC (Ret'd), my boss and friend in the Pentagon during the Kennedy years.

To Oliver Stone, for discovering in my ideas and experience the ingredient that made the theme of his great movie a challenge to America.

To my son, David, his wife, Bonnie, and my daughters, Jane and Lauren, all computer experts, without whose encouragement and assistance I could never have accomplished the burden of this work.

To Lauren Michele Prouty, again because she did all the computer chores essential to the technical quality of the final product.

To my editor, Hillel Black, for his understanding a complex manuscript and an intricate subject and for his inspiration.

To Thomas Whittle, editor of *Freedom* magazine, for recognizing the value of this work and publishing some of these earlier articles.

To Michael Baybak, my literary agent, for steering me through the intricate pathways of publishing with good sense and good humor.

NOTES

General note: *This work is based on a nineteen-part magazine series first developed by the author with and published by* Freedom *magazine, the investigative journal of the Church of Scientology.*

Chapter 1: The Role of the Intelligence Services in the Cold War

1. *Report From Iron Mountain,* Leonard C. Lewin (New York: Dial, 1967).
2. Read chapter 13, "A Conflict of Strategies" in Gen. Victor H. Krulak's *First to Fight* (Naval Institute Press, 1984).
3. It is significant to note that much of this important legislation was written by Clark Clifford at the time he was a naval officer assigned for duty in the Truman White House.
4. See Henry Pelling, *Winston Churchill* (London: Macmillan, 1974).
5. The case of Gen. Reinhard Gehlen will be discussed below. Gehlen, head of Hitler's Eastern European Intelligence Division, surrendered to American army officers before the fall of Nazi power and later was made a general in the U.S. Army for intelligence purposes by an act of Congress.
6. "The U.S. Government and the Vietnam War," GPO, April 1984.
7. *The Diaries of Edward R. Stettinius, Jr.,* by Campbell and Herring, 1975.
8. "The U.S. Government and the Vietnam War," GPO, April 1984.

Chapter 2: The CIA in the World of the H-Bomb

1. Office of Strategic Services, "Problems and Objectives of United States Policy," April 2, 1945.
2. *Dulles* by Leonard Moseley, Dial Press, 1978.
3. "Clandestine Operations Manual for Central America" Desert Publications, 1985.

Chapter 3: The Invisible Third World War

1. Leonard C. Lewin, *Report From Iron Mountain* (New York: Dial, 1967).
2. We note that President Marcos of the Philippines had been in trouble and that the public had been rising against his harsh regime...especially since the murder of his principal opponent, Sen. Benigno Aquino, in August 1983. During a visit to Manila, the director of central intelligence, then William Casey, made a modest suggestion that President Marcos ought to hold an election. At the same time we noted the rise of a new Communist-inspired insurgency there. The same Robin Hood tactic used again. At that point, the director of central intelligence knew and held the winning hand.

357

3. This was a pivotal meeting in developments leading to the steady escalation of the conflict in Vietnam. Gen. Graves B. Erskine was serving as the special assistant to the secretary of defense for special operations. As such he was responsible for all military contacts with the CIA, for the National Security Agency, and for certain contacts with the Department of State and the White House.

With the "Magsaysay Scenario" in mind, it is interesting to note that Allen Dulles had with him at this meeting both Edward G. Lansdale, whom he was sending to Saigon from Manila to head the Saigon Military Mission (SMM), and the station chief for the CIA in Manila, George Aurell. Others present were: Adm. Arthur Radford; Mr. Roger M. Kyes, assistant secretary of defense; Adm. Arthur C. Davis; Mr. Charles H. Bonesteel; Colonel Alden; and Gen. Charles P. Cabell, deputy director of central intelligence. NOTE: The author was assigned to the Erskine office, 1960–62, during a nine-year period in the Pentagon. He served as the senior air force officer for the duties of the Office of Special Operations.

4. This officer was the same Edward G. Lansdale who had skillfully and successfully brought about the election of President Magsaysay in the Philippines. He was being moved to Vietnam to see if he could work the same magic with Ngo Dinh Diem, the Vietnamese exile who was being transported from the United States to Saigon to become the president of the nation-to-be: South Vietnam.

5. The CIA's Saigon Military Mission was introduced into Indochina in June 1954. For the United States this marked the actual beginning of what we call the Vietnam War. The CIA had operational control over all forces of that war from 1954 to 1965, when the U.S. Marines, under U.S. military command, hit the beaches of Vietnam. The CIA's role was dominant during those years in this phase of WW III, which cost $220 billion, millions of noncombatant lives, and the lives of 55,000 American servicemen.

Chapter 4: Vietnam: The Opening Wedge

1. Concerning the power elite, R. Buckminster Fuller wrote of the "vastly ambitious individuals who [have] become so effectively powerful because of their ability to remain invisible while operating behind the national scenery." Fuller noted also, "Always their victories [are] in the name of some powerful sovereign-ruled country. The real power structures [are] always the invisible ones behind the visible sovereign powers." See Fuller's *Critical Path*, (New York: St. Martin's Press, 1981).

2. Potsdam Conference, held in Potsdam, a suburb of Berlin, in July 1945. This conference was attended by Truman, Churchill, and Stalin. Churchill was defeated in British parliamentary elections during the conference, and he was replaced by the newly chosen prime minister, Clement Attlee. (General Source: *Foreign Relations of the United States, 1952–54*, Volume XIII, "Indochina" [two parts], Government Printing Office, 1982.)

Chapter 5: The CIA's Saigon Military Mission

1. *Foreign Relations of the United States: 1952–54*. Department of State, Washington, D.C.

2. "Twenty-six Disastrous Years" Hugh B. Hester, Brig. Gen., U.S. Army (Retd).

3. Leonard Moseley, *Dulles* (New York: Dial Press, 1978).

4. A State Department euphemism for the various indistinct governments of Indochina at that time.

5. This special committee on Indochina consisted of the DCI, Allen W. Dulles; the under secretary of state and former DCI, Gen. Walter Bedell Smith; the deputy

secretary of defense and former vice president of the General Motors Corp., Roger M. Kyes; and the chairman of the Joint Chiefs of Staff, Adm. Arthur S. Radford.

6. There are many truly amazing documents in U.S. military records, as well as in White House files, on this subject. Those that have been used, above, are:
   a. "Civil Affairs Planning in the Cold War Era", U.S. Army Civil Affairs School, Fort Gordon, Ga., December 1959.
   b. Lecture, "Southeast Asia, Army War College, by Edward G. Lansdale, December 1958.
   c. "Training Under the Mutual Security Program" by R. G. Stilwell and Edward G. Lansdale of the President's Committee, May 1959.

Chapter 6: Genocide by Transfer—in South Vietnam

1. Interestingly, Daniel Ellsberg, who leaked the much-publicized Pentagon Papers to the press in 1971, had worked with Lansdale and others who had been on the SMM team in Vietnam.

2. *Vietnam Crisis*, edited by Allan W. Cameron (Ithaca, N.Y.: Cornell University Press, 1971).

3. Liberal extracts above are from Ralph Smith, *Vietnam and the West* (Ithaca, N.Y.: Cornell University Press, 1971).

4. *Foreign Relations of the United States, 1952–54*, vol. 13, "Indochina." (Washington, D.C.: Government Printing Office, 1982).

Chapter 7: Why Vietnam? The Selection and Preparation of the Battlefield

1. I have heard firsthand accounts wherein the CIA agents, on their way back by helicopter, tossed these natives ("mere gooks") out of the helicopter, alive, "just for the fun of it" and as a lesson to those who remained on board.

2. In terms of the act and national policy, there is a distinct difference between the meaning and the use of the words "direction of" and "approval." The National Security Act of 1947 used the word "direction" to mean that the idea for the plan originates with the NSC and, then, that the NSC directs its accomplishment by whatever department or agency, or combination thereof, it may choose. During the Eisenhower days, and with the ease with which the Dulles brothers carried out these things, it was not uncommon for Allen Dulles, the director of central intelligence, to arrive at a meeting with some scheme. He would present this idea to the NSC and then seek its "approval." This practice generally worked and was deemed permissible in that environment, but that is not how the NSC was intended to work. President Kennedy found it quite difficult to reverse this practice in later years, because the CIA had been able to have its way in these covert matters over the Department or State and the Department of Defense for so many years.

3. As a result of a presidential directive, a board of inquiry on the subject of the Bay of Pigs failure, and on what should be done in the future in such cases, met in the Pentagon in May 1961. This most unusual "Special Group" consisted of Gen. Maxwell Taylor, Allen Dulles, Adm. Arleigh Burke, and Robert F. Kennedy. A "Letter to the President" was prepared, written by General Taylor. The existence of this letter has been denied for years by various administrations and by the board members. However, it does exist. I have had a copy of this rare and most important "letter" for years, and it now appears verbatim in a book called *Zapata*.

4. As will be seen, this approval included the purchase of new helicopters.

5. Allen Dulles's favorite expression for military-type operations by the CIA, or a joint CIA/Defense Department effort, was "peacetime operations"—an Orwellian twist typical of the Dulles turn of mind.

6. A slang expression within the intelligence community for the practice of establishing one or more parallel identities, or covers, for someone engaged in intelligence work.

7. Dulles's statement may be found on page 287 of the *Report of the Executive Sessions of the Senate Foreign Relations Committee*, volume 12, which was not made public until November 1982. Printed by the U.S. Government Printing Office.

8. I was there at the time these Cuban exile leaders were in Senator Kennedy's office. After that meeting, these Cubans traveled to the Pentagon from Capitol Hill, in a military vehicle with me, to meetings that were held in the Office of Special Operations.

Chapter 8: The Battlefield and the Tactics, Courtesy CIA

1. "Pre-Brief" is the name given to the everyday, worldwide news summary that is prepared by the CIA and presented to the President early each morning. It is given to a highly select, small group of Pentagon officials just prior to the White House session.

2. During this period the Diem regime invented the term *Vietcong*, intending it to mean "Vietnamese Communist." The National Liberation Front condemned the term as meaningless. Diem and his administration applied the term loosely within South Vietnam to mean "the enemy," most of whom had no idea what communism was, and most of whom had been Cochin Chinese, or southern, natives. Thus, the intelligence "count" of Vietcong enemy included many natives who certainly were not Communist.

3. In what was broadly known as the "domino theory," it was held that if one country fell to communism, neighboring nations would follow. Countries were likened to a row of dominos set on end; the row would fall if the first domino was knocked down.

4. *U.S. News and World Report*, June 26, 1967.

5. This is an intelligence term for a secret operation supported by a unit that has a fictitious designation.

6. The director of the Joint Staffs was the senior, permanently assigned officer in the then 400-man office which supported the Joint Chiefs of Staff. General Wheeler went on to become chairman of the Joint Chiefs of Staff, a position he held for some six years.

7. The study was done by the Okanagan Helicopter Service of Canada, one of the largest commercial helicopter operators in the world.

8. It must be kept in mind that despite reference to U.S. military personnel, the CIA had operational control of all U.S. activities in Indochina until the U.S. Marines landed in Vietnam on March 8, 1965. Therefore, these helicopter tactics and tactical operations were developed by the CIA.

Chapter 9: The CIA in the Days of Camelot

1. Shortly after World War II, Nixon answered a want ad from a Los Angeles newspaper which sought a man who would run for political office. Nixon ran for Congress with the help of these anonymous backers and was elected. These people continued to support him through the ups and downs of his political career. Nixon has acknowledged that he had these backers; exactly who they were is another question.

2. Nixon was in Dallas with a top executive of the Pepsi-Cola Company, Mr. Harvey Russell, the general counsel. Nixon was a legal counsel to that corporation. That top executive's son has told of Nixon's presence in Dallas at the time of the

assassination, and Russell has confirmed the accuracy of his son's account. Later, sometime after the shooting, Nixon was driven to the Dallas airport by a Mr. DeLuca, also an official of the Pepsi-Cola Company. In addition, the son of another Pepsi-Cola executive was in Dallas at that time and had dinner with Jack Ruby, Oswald's killer, the night before JFK was murdered.

3. Most references to this CIA proposal are taken from the post–Bay of Pigs Study Group Report, which was actually Gen. Maxwell Taylor's "Letter to the President" of June 13, 1961, plus my own personal files.

4. This was known as the "5412/2 Committee" established by National Security Council directive 5412, March 15, 1954.

5. This very modest proposal was submitted to the National Security Council by DCI Allen Dulles. It was a plan for the recruitment of Cubans into a military-type organization for training purposes. At that point, the CIA had plans for very little, if any, operational activities in Cuba. From this simple beginning, the agency, spurred on by certain former senior Cuban officials, began to formulate plans for airdrops and over-the-beach landings of small groups of Cuban exiles, as well as airdrops of arms and ammunition for anti-Castro groups on the island.

6. This is taken from a U.S. Army Civil Affairs School lesson guide for U.S. and foreign military personnel. It or a similar guide was used for the training and indoctrination of the cadre of Cuban exile leaders. It is important to note what the U.S. Army teaches on this subject and to consider its applicability in this and other countries. This same document was used widely to train and indoctrinate the U.S. Special Forces Green Berets in Vietnam.

7. I was the chief of that office, which was concealed in the Plans directorate and known simply as "Team B." Its official duty was "to provide Air Force support of the clandestine operations of the CIA." This was accomplished secretly, on a worldwide basis. I had been directed, in 1955, to establish that office under the provisions of NSC 5412 and was its chief from 1955 to 1960, when I was transferred to the Office of the Secretary of Defense. In this capacity as head of the Military Support Office, in 1960, I went to Fort Gulick with CIA agents.

8. See particularly chapters 5 through 8.

9. Air America was a major CIA air transport proprietary company, with Far East headquarters in Taiwan and operations all over the world. It was a Delaware-chartered corporation and had about one hundred cover names under which it could do business, in order to conceal its identity and its connection with the CIA. At that time Air America was one of the largest airlines in the world, and one of the best.

10. The block system, an old form of control, "pacification," and surveillance made infamous during the Hungarian revolt of 1956, divides an area into blocks. Each block is under the absolute control of a leader, who knows where everyone is on that block. He uses children and schoolteachers, wives, shop foremen, and all other sources to gain total, twenty-four-hour-a-day, seven-day-a-week surveillance. No one could penetrate the Cuban system either from airdrop entry or by beach landing, and no one could evade it from the inside. The effectiveness of this system neutralized the exile group's ability to penetrate into, or to support, political guerrillas.

11. See chapter 8.

12. As described by R. Buckminster Fuller in *The Critical Path*, these are "vastly ambitious individuals who [have] become so effectively powerful because of their ability to remain invisible while operating behind the national scenery." Winston Churchill used the term High Cabal in recognition of this group's existence and supremacy.

13. Flechettes are small, rocket-powered missiles or darts that can be individually

fired from a tube much like a drinking straw. Being rockets, they have no recoil, make little or no noise, have a high terminal velocity, and are hard to detect by autopsy after they have entered a person's body. (One such weapon, fired from a specially modified umbrella, may have been used to poison President Kennedy in Dallas on November 22, 1963.)

14. Even this scheme had its uncertainties. Many CIA old-timers hated Nixon. When the CIA-directed rebellion against Sukarno in Indonesia in 1958 failed so miserably, it was Nixon who demanded, and got, the immediate dismissal of that World War II–era OSS hero Frank Wisner and the dispersal of Wisner's Far East staff. Wisner had been chief of that operation working out of Singapore. The "old boy" network never got over that move by Nixon. Wisner committed suicide some years later. This action by Nixon may have planted the seeds of Watergate.

15. See "Operation Zapata," University Publications of America.

16. I had an unusual insider's view of these developments. I knew of Kennedy's approval early Sunday afternoon, April 16. I knew the ships had been at sea and that forces would hit the beach at dawn on Monday, April 17. I had heard that three T-33s had not been destroyed in the April 15 air strike, when all of the other combat aircraft had been hit. I knew that the U-2 flight on Saturday had located the T-33 jets at Santiago, and I knew that the CIA operator at Puerto Cabezas, Nicaragua, had prepared four B-26s for the dawn air strike "coming in from the East with the sun at their backs and in the eyes of the defenders, if any."

17. Bobby Kennedy later named a son Maxwell Taylor Kennedy.

18. Ordinarily, following a disaster such as the Bay of Pigs, there would have been an official inquiry, with a full detailed report issued. The President, however, did not want a public inquiry, and he did not want a formal report. The Taylor letter was prepared by a committee that met secretly, calling itself "a paramilitary study group." About ten years later, I called Admiral Burke, whom I had worked with over the years, and asked him to lunch with a friend. During that luncheon, I asked the admiral, whom I have always believed to have been the finest chief of naval operations the U.S. Navy ever had, about that report. He still denied there had ever been a report. He did not fib; he simply toyed with words. It was not technically a "report." It was a "Letter to the President."

19. Wyden cites interviews with McGeorge Bundy as material for nearly every chapter in his book.

20. These are the exact words from paragraph 43 of the Taylor Report. Here is how Wyden distorts them to cover Bundy: "Cabell had every reason to be disturbed. He had just had a call from Mac Bundy. Bundy said no air strikes could be launched until after the brigade had secured the Giron airstrip, and strikes would ostensibly be launched from there. This was an order 'from the President.'" This is a most important bit of revisionism. The Taylor committee, with Bobby Kennedy as a member and one who closely read the report, says nothing about "an order from the President." Wyden and Bundy added that "order from the President," after the deaths of JFK and RFK, to cover Bundy's actions.

Chapter 10: JFK and the Thousand Days to Dallas

1. McCarthy and Smith, *Protecting the President* (New York: Morrow, 1985). Morrow, 1985

2. From *The Warren Report*, by the Associated Press.

3. The speaker was Mrs. William Bundy, daughter of former Secretary of State Dean Acheson, wife of Assistant Secretary of Defense William Bundy, and sister-in-law of McGeorge Bundy, whom Acheson had wanted Kennedy to make secretary of

state. Actually, Kennedy had listened to his old Harvard mentor, William Yandell Elliott, rather than Acheson, and had chosen Dean Rusk in place of Bundy, whom he brought into the White House as his national security assistant. For this service, Rusk provided Elliott with an office in the Department of State not far from his own; on the otherwise bare walls of that office hung a framed, one-page letter on White House stationery saying, "Thank you for introducing me to Dean Rusk." It was signed by John Fitzgerald Kennedy.

4. This sensational trial was known as the Medina trial, taking its name from the judge Harold S. Medina. It was held in federal court in 1948 and lasted more than nine months.

5. McNamara had little experience with service distinctions and tried to take army money as well as navy funds for this procurement. The army persuaded him to leave them out of this matter.

6. Such work neither began nor ended with the Kennedy administration. An article in the *Washington Post* on February 18, 1986, reported that U.S. representative Mike Synar had gone to see the top-secret Northrup Stealth aircraft. At the hangar, Congressman Synar noted, "They had put up this big chart which showed all the states where Stealth work was being done." That was the Goldberg/McNamara concept dressed in Reagan garb.

7. Before the Monday following this decision, the entire suite of offices that had developed the maps and data for the Goldberg study had been totally vacated and the staff transferred—moved completely out of the Pentagon building.

8. Leonard Lewin, *Report From Iron Mountain* (New York: Dial Press, 1967).

Chapter 11: The Battle for Power: Kennedy Versus the CIA

1. James D. Barber, *The Presidential Character* (Englewood Cliffs, N.J.: Prentice-Hall, 1972).

2. Theodore Sorensen, *Kennedy* (New York: Bantam Books, 1965).

3. The absence of Dulles and the ineffectiveness of his deputies, Gen. Charles P. Cabell and Richard Bissell, are described in this book as "a breakdown of leadership." One must keep in mind, however, that this apparent "breakdown" may well have been intentional. Our so-called national policy on "anticommunism" has gotten quite a bit of mileage out of Castro and his "Communist threat," just as it has continued to do in Central America, South America, Africa, and the Middle East.

4. My office was only a short distance from the rooms in the Pentagon used by the Cuban Study Group. I had worked with the CIA on anti-Castro activities since January 1, 1959. I knew almost all the men who had been called to meet with the study group. Many of them would wait in my office until they were called; many came back following their testimony and interrogation. One comment was general among them all. Their words were, in effect: "That group is highly charged with the presence of strong individuals. But the most intense man there is the one who sits in a straight-backed chair, separate from the others, and never says a word." That man was Bobby Kennedy. It was well known that he returned to the White House each day to discuss developments with the President and his inner circle; but nothing on the record gives any indication that he ever broke the stranglehold the CIA had on that investigation or that he ever became aware of being in the grip of its velvet gloves.

5. As noted in an earlier chapter, following the President's formal approval at midday of the landing plan, which included an air strike by four B-26 aircraft to destroy Castro's remaining three T-33 jet trainers on the ground, the air strike had been canceled.

6. The entire anti-Castro campaign was fraught with intrigue. De Varona was one of the four Cuban exiles who, after flying from the American Legion convention in Detroit, where Nixon had spoken in August 1960, to Washington, had gone directly to the offices of then senator John F. Kennedy in the Senate Office Building on Capitol Hill. From Kennedy's office they all went to the Office of the Secretary of Defense in the Pentagon. Kennedy had been in personal touch with de Varona and the others all through this period. This adds another element to the value of de Varona's testimony before the Taylor group.

7. Those three aircraft, Castro's last combat-capable aircraft, were the T-33 jet trainers that had been spotted by a U-2 reconnaissance aircraft, parked wingtip to wingtip on an airfield near Santiago and were the target of the four B-26 aircraft that were to have been launched from the CIA airbase at Puerto Cabezas, Nicaragua. Had that strike been flown as approved by the President, the jets would have been destroyed and the invasion would have been successful. Castro would have had no air force. The Brigade on the beach could have countered Castro's attacks along the narrow approach causeways while its own substantial air force of hard-hitting B-26 aircraft operated from the airstrip the Brigade had already captured on the beach.

8. It was Allen Dulles himself who revealed that the U-2 had not been shot down as the Soviets and the rest of the world had believed. Although Dulles revealed this information in sworn testimony before the Senate Foreign Relations Committee on Tuesday, May 31, 1960, the same month in which the crash landing occurred, his testimony was not released until 1982 and generally has been ignored by the American press.

His revelation was staggering; however, no one has ever fully investigated the possibility that this flight, launched in direct violation of President Eisenhower's order that there be no overflights before the summit conference, might have been ordered covertly by a small but powerful cabal that intended for it to fail and thereby to cause the disruption of the summit conference. Based upon a number of other strange events related to this particular flight, there is a strong possibility that this could be the case.

9. I worked in the same office with General Lansdale at that time. Those in the Office of Special Operations and the Office of the Secretary of Defense were certain, from what they had heard firsthand, that Lansdale would be named the next ambassador to Saigon.

10. The director of the Joint Staff was the senior permanently assigned officer in the then four-hundred-man office that supported the Joint Chiefs of Staff. General Wheeler went on to become chairman of the Joint Chiefs of Staff, a position he held for some six years.

11. I was the first chief of the Office of Special Operations and continued in that office until 1964, while Gen. Lyman Lemnitzer and, later, Gen. Maxwell Taylor were the chairmen of the Joint Chiefs of Staff.

12. One of the reasons Eglin Air Force Base was selected for this program was that a major CIA air facility had been established there a few years earlier and had become the worldwide center for CIA air-operation activities, excluding the U-2 program and those within the Air America proprietary airline infrastructure.

13. This program was said to have been developed under the leadership of George Ball in the Department of State.

Chapter 12: Building to the Final Confrontation

1. In addition to this memorandum, there was NSAM #56, "Evaluation of Paramilitary Requirements," and NSAM #57, "Responsibility for Paramilitary

Operations." Each of these was signed and distributed in the normal manner by McGeorge Bundy for the President.

2. Carl von Clausewitz, 1780–1831. Prussian officer and military strategist.

3. The Joint Staff is the unit that supports the Joint Chiefs of Staff. At the time of which I am writing (1961) there were some four hundred people in this unit.

4. I was the pilot of a VIP aircraft used during these conferences by the British and Americans, and as pilot of this plane I carried the Chinese delegation from Cairo to Tehran for that meeting. Actually, Chiang Kai-shek and May Ling, who had been in Cairo, went to Tehran, and I believe they traveled on Roosevelt's plane. I flew their staff of delegates only.

5. Although no relation to the previously mentioned Gen. Joseph W. Stilwell, Gen. Richard G. Stilwell was a friend and close associate of Vinegar Joe's son, Gen. Joseph W. Stilwell, Jr., and a close associate of Lansdale.

6. It may be difficult, or at least unusual, for the inexperienced reader to see in such a structured report its real and far-reaching significance. I shall provide an important example:

Just before the election of John F. Kennedy, on November 8, 1960, Gen. Edward G. Lansdale and I flew to Fort Gordon, Ga., to pick up elements of the Civil Affairs and Military Government curriculum, which was then used as the basis for drafting the new curriculum for the Army Special Warfare Center at Fort Bragg.

At that time, we were both assigned to the Office of the Secretary of Defense. By late 1960, this Mutual Security Program report had filtered down from the Eisenhower White House, without comment but with the weight of apparent approval. As a top-level document of great potential, it then became fundamental to the development of the new Special Warfare curriculum as it was rewritten and merged with the material from Fort Gordon.

Because the Fort Bragg curriculum had the blessing of the Office of the Secretary of Defense, contained elements of a White House report, and was supported by the CIA, this whole layer of apparent authority became the Special Warfare and Special Air Warfare doctrine for dealing with Third World nations--particularly with Vietnam.

There were no specific approvals of all of the above. The author has no evidence or recollection that any of this was ever discussed with the Congress or with the Department of State. Yet, on the basis of these policy statements, evolved from the writings of Mao, among others, the U.S. Army had more or less defined a new Cold War role for military forces.

With this presentation the reader is getting a rare and unusual view of the inner workings of our government as it pertains to the development and utilization of the military in Cold War operations. This is exactly what is being done today in Central America, the Middle East, and Africa.

(Note for researchers: I have been able to acquire a copy of this report, "Training Under the Mutual Security Program," May 15, 1959. It appears, complete, as Appendix 3 of my earlier book, *The Secret Team*.

Chapter 13: The Magic Box, Trigger of the Expanded War in Vietnam

1. This was run by the CIA-sponsored Saigon Military Mission, described in detail in earlier chapters. It was part of "Operation Brotherhood," an organization managed by CIA-run Filipino leaders under the aegis of the International Junior Chamber of Commerce.

2. Intelligence gleaned from paid native informers always reported massive buildups everywhere. These native sources in intelligence never saw starvation-

crazed refugees; they always saw what they were being paid to see. Every refugee area was another regiment of Vietcong. General Hunger was General Giap, and Communists were abroad in the land. After all, even the "intelligence source" was a shrewd businessman. He was a creation of the American CIA, and the CIA was running the war, with a checkbook, in 1960–61, as it had been since 1945.

Chapter 14: JFK Makes His Move to Control the CIA

1. Ike's hopes for détente were crushed by the CIA's U-2 spy-plane incident of May 1, 1960, as described earlier.

2. The reader should note the similarity of this stage of the process to that which the Reagan administration promoted on behalf of the Contras in Central America during the eighties.

3. For full details on the Bay of Pigs fiasco, see earlier chapters.

4. *New York Times*, April 25, 1966.

5. One of Robert F. Kennedy's sons is named Maxwell Taylor Kennedy.

6. OSS, the forerunner of the CIA .

7. This is a secret and secure means of direct communication. The chief agent in a country would have a direct line to CIA headquarters, bypassing every other channel of the U.S. government.

Chapter 15: The Erosion of National Sovereignty

1. Leonard C. Lewin, *Report From Iron Mountain* (New York: Dial Press, 1967). This book is not to be misunderstood. It is a novel; but its content is so close to the reality of those years that many readers insist that the "report" must be true. I have discussed this fully with the author. He assures me that the book is a novel and that he intended it to read that way in order to emphasize its serious content.

2. A recent euphemism for guerrilla warfare or counter insurgency operations.

3. Walter B. Wriston, *Risk and Other Four-Letter Words* (New York: Harper & Row, 1986).

4. Philip P. Weiner, *The Dictionary of the History of Ideas* (New York: Charles Scribner's Sons, New York, 1973).

5. As defined in my 1973 book *The Secret Team*, Secret Intelligence Operations are "clandestine operations carried out to get deep-secret intelligence data."

6. Sen. Leverett Saltonstall (R-Massa.).

Chapter 16: Government by Coup d'État

1. In what was a very accurate on-the-scene account of the murder of the President, an experienced Reuters correspondent wrote, "Three bursts of gunfire, apparently from automatic weapons, were heard." This first news report by a seasoned combat journalist shows that those in and around Dealey Plaza heard numerous shots -- more than the three bullets reported by the Secret Service, the FBI, and the Warren Commission.

2. Permitting the vice president to ride in the same procession with the President violated one hundred years of Secret Service policy. Why did this occur on that momentous day? Who directed these changes in standard procedures, and why?

3. As described in earlier chapters, this normally entails a series of orchestrated events that elevate a person, such as those mentioned, to a position where he is regarded as an extremely popular hero.

4. Less developed countries, or LDCs, is a term much used for these small, underdeveloped nations in the banking community.

5. This novel was published in 1967. Today it might have included the Strategic Defense Initiative "Star Wars" project as another boondoggle.

6. R. Buckminster Fuller, *Critical Path* (New York: St. Martin's Press, 1981).

7. A military term referring to the number of years of effective use of an item of military hardware before it is replaced by a newer or updated model. The life of type of most items normally averages between ten and twenty years.

8. On several occasions in 1964, I spent a few hours alone with President Fernando Belaunde Terry of Peru discussing the subject of border patrol. Peru controls the entry and exit of almost 100 percent of its goods through the port of Callao, adjacent to Lima, and a special "free port" in the remote region east of the Andes, at Iquitos on the upper Amazon River.

Belaunde wanted to establish a network of border surveillance by the use of small, capable aircraft, the Helio Aircraft Corporation's "Courier," which had been designed by members of the MIT aeronautical engineering staff and purchased by the hundred by the CIA. This small plane could land, STOL (short takeoff and landing) fashion, on unprepared airstrips and even on mountainsides.

Belaunde told me that in conjunction with that type of modern border patrol he had repeatedly refused foreign aid projects for road-building because "all they would accomplish would be to facilitate the movement of the indigenous natives from their ancient communities to the jammed barriadas of Lima."

With entry into Peru limited, for the most part, to these two ports and their airfields, it was possible for the government to control all import and export business to benefit the Belaunde governmental team, which included certain old and rich families with traditional and banking power.

9. Fuller, *Critical Path*.

Chapter 17: JFK's Plan to End the Vietnam Warfare

1. Theodore Shanin, "Peasants and Peasant Societies," in John Berger, "Historical Afterword," *Pig Earth* (New York: Pantheon Books, 1979).

Chapter 18: Setting the Stage for the Death of JFK

1. Senator Gravel wrote these words in August 1971 for the introduction to *The Pentagon Papers* (Boston: Beacon Press Books, 1971). They were timely and applicable then. The reader cannot help but note that they are equally timely and applicable to the more recent Iranian "hostages for arms" controversy and even to Desert Storm.

Chapter 19: Visions of a Kennedy Dynasty

1. "New Frontier" was the domestic and foreign policy program of President Kennedy's administration. It is taken from a slogan used by Kennedy in his acceptance speech in 1960. Edward C. Smith and Arnold C. Zurcher, *Dictionary of American Politics* (New York: Barnes & Noble, 1968).

2. Special Judge Advocate John A. Bingham, *The Trial of the Conspirators* (Washington, D.C., 1865), cited in *The Pope and the New Apocalypse* (S. D. Mumford, 1986).

Chapter 20: LBJ Takes the Helm as the Course Is Reversed

1. From his excellent book *Sub Rosa: The CIA and the Uses of Intelligence* (New York: Times Books, 1978). This is a good source of "inside the family" information

about certain aspects of the intervention in Vietnam and of the role played by the various participants.

2. Previous CIA station chief, Saigon.

3. At the time General Taylor issued these instructions to General Westmoreland, I was serving with the Joint Staff as chief of the Office of Special Operations in SACSA. I attended meetings at which General Taylor presided and was well aware of his brilliance and experience. His remarks to General Westmoreland cannot be taken lightly. For my work with the Joint Staff, I was awarded, by General Taylor, one of the first Joint Chiefs of Staff Commendation Medals ever issued.

4. During the summer of 1944, I had been ordered to fly from Cairo via Tehran over the Caspian Sea and then across southern Russian into the Ukraine to a point just west of Poltava. I saw firsthand the indescribable destruction of such cities as Rostov, and how the once-fertile Ukraine had been laid bare. Only the firebombed Tokyo had suffered more damage.

Index